OH

British Feminis

Hilary Tovey.

For Tessa, and for Howell as well. And for the team of teachers and the group of adult students on the Open Studies Certificate course in Women's Studies at Warwick University which ran from 1987 to 1989.

British Feminist Thought

A Reader

Edited by

TERRY LOVELL

Basil Blackwell

'The Introduction' by Juliet Mitchell is reprinted from *Feminine Sexuality: Jacques Lacan and the Ecole Freudienne*, edited by Juliet Mitchell and Jacqueline Rose. Translated by Jacqueline Rose. Used with the permission of Juliet Mitchell.

First published 1990

Basil Blackwell Ltd
108 Cowley Road, Oxford, OX4 1JF, UK

Basil Blackwell, Inc.
3 Cambridge Center
Cambridge, Massachusetts 02142, USA

British Library Cataloguing in Publication Data

A CIP catalogue record for this book is available from the British Library.

Library of Congress Cataloging in Publication Data

British feminist thought: a reader / edited by Terry Lovell.
p. cm.
ISBN 0–631–16914–8 ISBN 0–631–16915–6 (pbk.)
1. Feminism–Great Britain–History. 2. Feminism–Philosophy.
3. Psychoanalysis and feminism. 4. Feminist criticism. I. Lovell, Terry.
HQ1597.B79 1990
305.42'0941–dc20
89-18115
CIP

Typeset in 10 on 11 pt Plantin
by Graphicraft Typesetters Ltd., Hong Kong
Printed in Great Britain by
Billings & Son Ltd, Worcester

Contents

PART IV PSYCHOANALYSIS AND FEMINISM

PART V FEMINIST CRITICISM AND CULTURAL STUDIES

Acknowledgements

The sources of the readings in this book are as follows, in order of appearance:

Germaine Greer, *The Female Eunuch*, Grafton Books, a division of William Collins Sons and Co Ltd. US and Canadian rights by permission of McGraw-Hill Publishing Co.

Sally Alexander, 'Women, Class and Sexual Differences in the 1830s and 1840s: Some Reflections on the Writing of a Feminist History', *History Workshop Journal*, 17, 1984, pp. 125–49 (edited version), by permission of *History Workshop Journal*, World Copyright © History Workshop Journal.

Catherine Hall, 'Private Persons versus Public Someones: Class, Gender and Politics in England, 1780–1850', in C. Steedman, C. Urwin and V. Walkerdine, eds, *Language, Gender, Childhood*, Routledge & Kegan Paul, 1985.

Ann Oakley, 'What is a Housewife?', Ch. I of *Housewife*, Allen Lane, 1974. Copyright © Ann Oakley, 1974. Reproduced by permission of Penguin Books Ltd.

Cynthia Cockburn, 'The Material of Male Power', *Feminist Review*, 9, 1981.

Floya Anthias and Nira Yuval-Davis, 'Contextualizing Feminism – Gender, Ethnic and Class Divisions', *Feminist Review*, 15, 1983.

Ann Phoenix, 'Theories of Gender and Black Families', in G. Weiner and M. Arnot, eds, *Gender Under Scrutiny*, Unwin Hyman Ltd, 1987.

Michèle Barrett and Mary McIntosh, 'The "Family Wage": Some Problems for Socialists and Feminists', *Capital and Class*, 11, 1980 (edited version).

Johanna Brenner and Maria Ramas, 'Rethinking Women's Oppression', *New Left Review*, 144, 1984, pp. 33–71 (edited version).

Christina Loughran, 'Armagh and Feminist Strategy', *Feminist Review*, 23, 1986 (edited version).

Juliet Mitchell, 'Introduction – 1', J. Mitchell and J. Rose, eds, *Feminine Sexuality: Jacques Lacan and the Ecole Freudienne*, Macmillan, 1983, (edited version), permission of Macmillan, London and Basingstoke and Liveright Publishing Corporation (US and Canadian rights).

Elizabeth Wilson, 'Psychoanalysis: Psychic Law and Order?', *Feminist Review*, 8, 1981, reprinted in E. Wilson, with Angela Weir, *Hidden Agendas*, Tavistock, 1986.

Jacqueline Rose, 'Femininity and its Discontents', *Feminist Review*, 14, 1983. Reprinted in J. Rose, *Sexuality in the Field of Vision*, Verso, 1986.

Joanna Ryan, 'Psychoanalysis and Women Loving Women', in J. Ryan and S. Cartledge, eds, *Sex and Love*, Women's Press, 1983.

Parveen Adams, 'Family Affairs', *m/f*, 7, 1982. Back numbers of *m/f* are available from 24, Ellerdale Rd., London NW3 6BB.

Carolyn Steedman, 'Stories', pp. 5–24, *Landscape for a Good Woman*, Virago, 1986. Copyright © Carolyn Steedman, 1986. Reproduced by permission of Virago Press.

Jenny Bourne Taylor, 'Raymond Williams: Gender and Generation'. Based on a previously unpublished lecture.

Rosalind Coward, 'Naughty but Nice: Food Pornography', in *Female Desire*, Paladin, 1984, Grafton Books, a division of William Collins and Sons.

Felly Nkweto Simmonds, 'SHE'S GOTTA HAVE IT: The Representation of Black Female Sexuality on Film', *Feminist Review*, 29, 1988.

Alison Light, 'Returning to Manderley' – Romance Fiction, Female Sexuality and Class', *Feminist Review*, 16, 1984.

Cora Kaplan, 'Pandora's Box: Subjectivity, Class and Sexuality in Socialist-Feminist Criticism', in Gayle Green and Coppelia Kahn, eds, *Making a Difference*, Methuen & Co., 1985.

Toril Moi, 'Feminism and Postmodernism: Recent Feminist Criticism in the United States'. (Abridged and edited version of T. Moi 'Feminism, Postmodernism and Style', *Cultural Critique*, 9, Spring 1988, pp. 3–22.)

The short extract from *Three Guineas* by Virginia Woolf is reproduced by permission of the Executors of the Virginia Woolf Estate and The Hogarth Press.

I would like to thank Juliet Mitchell, Toril Moi, Anne Phillips, Carol Smart and Carolyn Steedman for helpful comments on my introductions to this work.

PART I

British Feminist Thought in the Second Wave

Introduction

NATIONAL FEMINISMS

> As a woman, I have no country. As a woman I want no country. As a woman my country is the whole world.
>
> *Virginia Woolf,* Three Guineas

What are we doing, then, in constructing 'national feminisms'? The problem presents itself with particular force when it is British feminism which is in question. The term 'British' carries such a heavy weight of accumulated meaning, generated over the long history of internal and external imperialisms, that it inevitably serves as a negative reference point in left thought. Black feminists, already smarting under the affront of a white middle-class movement which has systematically disregarded the situation and circumstances of black women might well feel that the national label merely compounds the injury. Feminists in the north of Ireland have additional and equally compelling reasons for rejecting it. 'English' on the other hand is too exclusive, unless we use it to refer to language users, in which case it encompasses too much. National labels being so problematic, then, why not discard them, in favour of alternative lines of intellectual demarcation within Woolf's international community of women?

The denial of national differences carries difficulties of its own. International movements such as feminism and socialism develop along significantly differentiated lines which can be related to specific historical, political and intellectual contexts. Black feminist thought in Britain arises from and addresses a different history and a different situation than does black feminist thought in America. Moreover there is a danger of slipping into patronizing postures: 'we' (first-world, white, middle-class feminists) may create for ourselves an 'imaginary' international community that knows no territorial boundaries;[1] 'you' (third-world, black feminists) may be conceded your more parochial national imaginings, only provided that they are of a progressive nature...Moreover, the very tone and terms of Woolf's discourse undermine her internationalist claims. They are instantly recognizable in terms of class, place, and historical time.

We are all shaped more than we know by identities formed in childhood within family interactions; by the 'knowable communities'[2] to which these families belonged; by the specific cultural and political formations in which we were educated and within which we came to take our bearings as feminists. This collection does not pretend to fix and reify a frozen and discrete 'British feminism', but rather it attempts to characterize what is distinctive in British feminist thought: to locate its sources in intellectual and political life, in full awareness of the deeply problematic nature of national labels.

SOCIALIST AND OTHER FEMINISMS

The collection does not purport to be representative of the whole spectrum of British feminism either. There have been a number of important developments within the women's movement and feminism in Britain which are not represented here, most notably perhaps the women's peace movement. The story of Greenham Common is widely known.[3] In 1981, a women's peace camp was set up to protest the siting of Cruise missiles at the US airbase at Greenham, and it has been occupied ever since, serving, in Lynne Segal's words, as 'the model and inspiration for an international movement of women against the threat of nuclear war'.[4] 'Radical feminism' has also been a decisive presence within British feminism.[5] Indeed it could be argued that in Britain, as elsewhere, it is radical feminism which has given the women's movement its greatest charge of energy. However, while it was American feminism which, historically, provided the major point of reference for radical-feminist thought, thereby acting as a powerful detonator of the British movement, socialist feminism conversely owes its greatest debt to British feminism.

Marxist theory had seen a widespread revival across the whole spectrum of left intellectual and political life in the decades which witnessed the emergence of the second wave of feminism. The relationship between Marxism and feminism in British socialist-feminist thought was never less than problematic, and many British feminist thinkers have moved a considerable distance from this starting point. Nevertheless a critical engagement with socialist theory and practice has been the most significant criterion of selection in this volume.

Even within these limits it has proved impossible to be comprehensive. There are whole areas of distinguished work which have been given no space, for example, feminist socio-legal studies and the sociology of health and illness,[6] and feminist film studies;[7] and there are many writers whose work would have to be included in any comprehensive collection, even one which included only the most seminal texts: Sheila Rowbotham's historical writings;[8] Veronica Beechey's theorizings of patriarchy and of women's paid work;[9] the enormously influential pamphlet *Beyond the Fragments* by Sheila

Rowbotham, Lynne Segal and Hilary Wainwright;[10] Beatrix Campbell's varied writings,[11] and many others. The collection is intended to whet the appetite of those interested in British socialist-feminist thought, and to encourage further exploration, not to present that tradition encapsulated, complete and frozen in some twenty essays.

THE SECOND WAVE: THE CASE OF GERMAINE GREER

The upsurge of feminist writings which helped to launch the contemporary women's movement in Britain brought two very different figures to prominence in the early days: Juliet Mitchell and Germaine Greer.[12] The significance of Mitchell's work for British socialist feminism cannot be overestimated. As early as 1964, long before the advent of the 'second wave' in Britain, she wrote a short piece on women's education in *New Left Review*.[13] Two years later in 1966, the same journal published 'Women: the Longest Revolution'[14] which feminists in the emerging women's movement in Europe and America appropriated – it circulated widely in numerous samizdat translations. Her impact on British feminist thought is highly visible throughout this collection.

That of Germaine Greer is less obvious. She is a household name outside the women's movement, probably the only feminist in Britain of whom this is true. But she never identified herself with the women's movement, and it is striking how seldom her work is referred to within British feminist writing. She has a space to herself here because on the one hand she cannot be left out, and on the other, she doesn't fit very neatly under any of the categories which organize this collection of writings. She is closer in many respects to the first generation of American feminists such as Kate Millett and Shulamith Firestone, with whom her work is often linked. Her case highlights the problems of demarcation in 'British' feminist thought. Australian by birth, cosmopolitan in her career, she might have found herself in any one of a number of places in the late 1960s other than where she was – in the Department of English at Warwick University. *The Female Eunuch* was a founding text of the second wave;[15] yet the distance at which she placed herself from 'the movement' may be gauged from the following quotation from an article she wrote for the underground paper, *Oz*, in 1970:

> So far the self-appointed leaders of female revolution have remained the dupes of their middle-class education, and their demands are circumscribed by cautious notions of equality with men... What women must do is invent a genuine alternative... The cunt must take the steel out of the cock and make it flesh again... There are signs that this is happening, but slowly, and so far without prophetesses and not in the workshops and chapters of the spasm called the Movement.[16]

THE FEMALE EUNUCH VERSUS THE SELF-REALIZING PERSONALITY

The Female Eunuch takes as its chief target neither masculinity, nor the institutions and practices of male domination, but the feminine woman.

Unease or hostility in the face of femininity is not of course uncommon among feminists. Mary Wollstonecraft, whom Greer quotes extensively in *The Female Eunuch*, loathed it. But while her illustrious predecessor looked to a revolution in education to free women from the thralls of feminine inferiority,[17] Greer sought a transformation of sexual relations which would also liberate men. However, unlike the sexual revolution envisaged by many radical feminists in the United States, Greer's was determinedly heterosexual in its orientation. She was sharply critical of feminists such as Anna Koedt, who appropriated Masters and Johnson to proselytize an independent, woman related, female sexuality based on clitoris rather than vagina, in which the male organ was made less flesh than redundant.[18] Her stance was, implicitly at least, anti-lesbian, and in her early writings she is distinctly cool towards homosexuality. She was formed in the earlier, pre-feminist movement of the 1960s whose heroes included Eric Fromm, Wilhelm Reich and Herbert Marcuse, and whose route to revolution lay less through the transformation of the social relations of production than in the lifting of sexual repression and the transformation of sexual relations.

In spite of Greer's anarchic determination to plough her own furrow, the trajectory of her thought over a twenty-year period shares a good deal in common with one which may be traced in the women's movement generally, in Britain and in the United States. Her early writings shared in the widespread consensus of the early days of the women's movement which attributed all or most of the differences between the sexes to sex-role learning rather than to nature. But where many radical feminists had peopled the feminist future with unisex individuals distinguished from each other by temperament, talent and interests, rather than by biological sex, in the manner of the inhabitants of Marge Piercy's fictional utopia, Mattapoissett,[19] Greer's brave new world retained a central place for sexual difference, confined it is true to its proper place, the bedroom, and to joyful and free heterosexual exchange.

The early consensus that sexual difference was the result of social learning has given way in recent years to new forms of essentialism in which both nature and fundamental sexual differences are reinstated, and again we find Greer treading a parallel path. Her co-authored *Kissing the Rod* has been identified as a species of 'gynocriticism',[20] and her anthropologically informed *Sex and Destiny*[21] links her likewise to the contemporary feminist cult of mothering.[22] However elements of this latter, more essentialist view of the differences between the sexes are present in embryo in *The Female Eunuch*. They are rooted in the formative experience of the three months in 1967 which Greer spent in an isolated and impoverished peasant community in Calabria. Greer returns again and again to this moment in her writings. The experience generated another ideal which lies alongside that of the human being ungendered save in relation to sexuality itself.

This more explicitly formulated ideal in *The Female Eunuch* figures the American psychologist A.H. Maslow's 'self-realizing personality',[23] who may be of either sex but is, in our society, more likely to be male. Greer argued that our culture of masculinity, deforming though it is, yet leaves space for the development of this type of personality to a greater extent than does the culture of femininity, even though it is only a small minority of men who are able to achieve it. In the extract from *The Female Eunuch* reprinted here, this ideal is spelt out as an ideal of love. The model for a proper, fully social form of love is one between equals, based on the attraction of like to like, not on an artificially heightened sense of difference.

THE FEMALE IDEAL IN *SEX AND DESTINY*

In *Sex and Destiny* this unisex 'self-realizing personality' has been superseded by the alternative Calabrian ideal, fleshed out after some fourteen years and time spent in a number of very different peasant communities. The artifice of femininity is still identified as a poor, despised product of modern capitalism, but the female ideal is now more firmly located in the remnants of pre-capitalist social formations on the margins of, and deeply corroded by, the developed capitalist world. Unlike the ideal of the unisex self-realizing personality, the now preferred pre-capitalist gender dispensation in all its rich variety emphasizes sexual difference, and generates spheres for men and women as rigidly separate as those of nineteenth-century British capitalism.

There are a good many U-turns traversed in the journey from *The Female Eunuch* to *Sex and Destiny*, but there are also common and recurring motifs. In both books, femininity figures as artifice, and as a fall from grace attendant on the development of capitalism. The place of feminism is less easy to see. Logically it would have to be the product of female discontent generated by the fall into capitalist femininity. But the Greer of *Sex and Destiny* has turned back to earlier social forms in her search for models of more woman- and above all, child-friendly forms of life. She takes on board, indeed, makes a virtue of, the terrible hardship endured by women in subsistence economies, and views with surprising equanimity practices not usually looked upon so sympathetically by feminists: female infanticide, clitoridectomy, polygamy, prolonged sexual abstinence for women – just so long as the outcome is 'adaptive' from the point of view of biological survival, and provided it generates a culture in which children and mothering are highly prized.

Feminist and socialist longings for a better world are both products of the experience of capitalist exploitation and oppression. Just as Marx and Engels identified forms of 'primitive communism' in pre-capitalist communities living at subsistence level, so Greer might claim that the same societies evidenced 'primitive feminism'. But where Marx and Engels made a clear distinction between 'primitive' and 'advanced' communism, Greer appears to conflate the two where feminism is concerned. She can only rail against the wanton destruction of earlier gender orders and the societies which supported them by a capitalist order which no longer promises any golden future, but only at best, its own demise in the face of the relentless logic of natural selection, and at worst to bring the whole world down with it in its final death throes.

Sex and Destiny created a stir in the media when it was published in 1984. Journalists dwelt with considerable glee on her 'betrayal' of feminism and of her earlier self. The book fell like a lead balloon among feminists. I did not come across a single reference to it in my research for this collection. This lack of engagement is a pity. *Sex and Destiny* is a deeply problematic book for feminism, but it does not deserve this censorious silence. It has certain very real strengths. It is evident that Greer listened carefully to what many women in the peasant communities she visited had to say, and that she took their words and their lives very seriously. Secondly, she pays equally serious attention to the biological exigencies of social life as they affect women. Both of these things are rare enough in feminist thought. We have, for good reason, a horror of biological reductionism which often leads us to deny such exigencies altogether. But refuse to acknowledge them, and the repressed returns with a vengeance, as witness contemporary 'cultural feminism' and the cult of mothering. Greer does not avoid these pitfalls, but she places biological constraints on the feminist agenda in a manner which should not be ignored.

Fairly early in her career as a writer, Greer became a media personality. She is a superb performer. But when all the hype is discounted, and when all the criticisms have been given due weight, her work remains a great plus for the women's movement. She is a *very* good read. She is funny, yet can be very serious to good effect. Her value is nicely captured by Carolyn Steedman in a review of *The Madwoman's Underclothes*:

> She has terrified a lot of rather dreadful men, and this can only have been for their good. She has paid serious attention to the question that no one bothers about very much: of how the girls might get to have a good time; of how, out of hard-working and difficult lives, women might snatch some kind of satisfaction before they go down into the dark. She is that rare woman: one who simply does not care – the Proper Lady has never held her in thrall.[24]

It is appropriate that a collection of British feminist writings should open with an extract from her work.

NOTES

1 Benedict Anderson uses the term 'imagined communities' in his book of that title, to refer to national identifications. Benedict Anderson, *Imagined Communities*, Verso, 1983.

2 The concept of 'knowable communities' pervades the writings of Raymond Williams. The term 'community', used to such effect by both Anderson and Williams, stands at the positive pole in left thought, against the negative connotations of 'nationalism'. It was a stroke of genius on Anderson's part to bring these two terms together in an attempt to force a rethinking of nationalism within Marxism. But he leaves the warm, positive connotations of 'family'

and 'community' within much socialist thought intact, ignoring critical feminist analyses which have located them as major sites of women's oppression, so that his analysis remains problematic for feminism.

3 For accounts of Greenham, see for example, Barbara Harford and Sarah Hopkins, eds, *Greenham Common: Women at the Wire*, The Women's Press, 1984, and Alice Cook and Gwynne Kirk, *Greenham Women Everywhere*, Pluto Press, 1983.

4 Lynne Segal, *Is the Future Female*?, Virago, 1987, p. 163.

5 Radical feminist thought in Britain, as elsewhere, has focused around such issues as sexuality, male violence against women, and reproductive technology, but also on methodological questions concerning feminist research. See for example Sheila Jeffries, *The Spinster and her Enemies: Feminism and Sexuality, 1880–1930*, Pandora, 1985; Christian McKewen and Sue O'Sullivan, eds, *Out the Other Side*, Virago, 1988; Dale Spender, *Man-Made Language*, Routledge and Kegan Paul, 1980; Liz Stanley and Sue Wise, *Breaking Out: Feminist Consciousness and Feminist Research*, Routledge and Kegan Paul, 1983; Lal Coveney, ed., *The Sexuality Papers*, Hutchinson, 1985; Deborah Cameron and Elizabeth Frazer, *Lust to Kill*, Polity, 1987; Jalna Hanmer and Sheila Saunders, *A Well-Founded Fear*, Hutchinson, 1984; Liz Kelly, *Surviving Sexual Violence*, Polity, 1988; Rita Arditti, Renate Duelli Klein and Shelley Minden, eds, *Test-Tube Babies*, Pandora, 1984.

6 See for example, Carol Smart, *The Ties that Bind*, Routledge and Kegan Paul, 1984; Carol Smart, *Feminism and the Power of Law*, Routledge and Kegan Paul, 1989; Susan Edwards, *Female Sexuality and the Law*, Martin Robertson, 1981. For the sociology of health and illness, see Lesley Doyal, *The Political Economy of Health*, Pluto, 1979; and Margaret Stacey, *The Sociology of Health and Healing*, Unwin Hyman, 1988.

7 See for example, Annette Kuhn, *Women's Pictures*, Routledge and Kegan Paul 1982; Charlotte Brunsdon, *Films for Women*, British Film Institute Publications, 1986; and a number of essays by Laura Mulvey, including 'Feminism, Film and the Avant-Garde', *Framework*, 10, Spring 1979, and 'Visual Pleasure and Narrative Cinema', *Screen*, 16, 3, 1975.

8 Sheila Rowbotham, *Hidden From History*, Pluto, 1973.

9 Veronica Beechey, 'On Patriarchy', *Feminist Review*, 3, 1979; 'Some Notes on Female Wage Labour in Capitalist Production', *Capital and Class*, 3, 1977; 'Women and Production: a Critical Analysis of Some Sociological Theories of Women's Work', in A. Kuhn and A. Wolpe, eds, *Feminism and Materialism*, Routledge and Kegan Paul, 1978.

10 Sheila Rowbotham, Lynne Segal and Hilary Wainwright, *Beyond the Fragments: Feminism and the Making of Socialism*, Merlin, 1980.

11 Beatrix Campbell, *Wigan Pier Revisited*, Virago, 1984; and *The Iron Ladies: Why Do Women Vote Tory*?, Virago, 1987.

12 Eva Figes's *Patriarchal Attitudes*, Macmillan, 1970, predated *The Female Eunuch* by a few months. Like Greer and Mitchell, she was trained in English literature; like Greer, she identified Freud as one of 'the main enemies', and like Greer also, she explained women's subordination in terms of sex-role learning, a sociological explanation which nevertheless likewise teetered precariously on the brink of an underlying and unexplained essentialism. Figes went on to write novels and literary criticism.

13 Juliet Mitchell, 'Women's Education', *New Left Review*, 28, 1964.

14 Juliet Mitchell, 'Women: the Longest Revolution', *New Left Review*, 40, 1966,

reprinted in J. Mitchell, *Women: the Longest Revolution: Essays in Feminism, Literature and Psychoanalysis*, Virago, 1984.
15 Germaine Greer, *The Female Eunuch*, Paladin, 1971.
16 Germaine Greer, 'The Slag-Heap Erupts', *Oz*, Feb 1970, reprinted in Germaine Greer, *The Madwoman's Underclothes*, Pan Books, 1986.
17 Mary Wollstonecraft, *A Vindication of the Rights of Woman* (1792), Penguin, 1982.
18 Anna Koedt, 'The Myth of the Vaginal Orgasm', in L. Tanned, ed., *Voices from Women's Liberation*, Mentor, 1970, and in A. Koedt, E. Levine and A. Rapone, eds, *Radical Feminism*, Quadrangle, 1973.
19 Marge Piercy, *Woman on the Edge of Time*, Women's Press, 1979.
20 Germaine Greer et al., eds, *Kissing the Rod*, Virago, 1988.
21 Germaine Greer, *Sex and Destiny*, Secker and Warburg, 1984.
22 See for example, Nancy Chodorow, *The Reproduction of Mothering*, University of California Press, 1978; Dorothy Dinnerstein, *The Mermaid and the Minotaur*, Harper and Row, 1976; Adrienne Rich, *Of Woman Born*, Virago, 1977. For a recent critical evaluation, see Lynne Segal, *Is the Future Female?*, Virago, 1987.
23 A.H. Maslow, *Motivation and Personality*, Harper and Row, 1954.
24 Carolyn Steedman, in *London Review of Books*, 4 December 1986.

FURTHER READING

Hannah Cantor et al., *Sweeping Statements*, The Women's Press, 1984.
Anna Coote and Beatrix Campbell, *Sweet Freedom*, Pan Books, 1982.
Juliet Mitchell and Ann Oakley, *The Rights and Wrongs of Women*, Allen Lane, 1976.
Juliet Mitchell and Ann Oakley, eds, *What is Feminism?*, Blackwell, 1986.
Sheila Rowbotham, *The Past that is Before Us: Feminism in Action Since the 1960s*, Pandora, 1989.
Lynne Segal, *Is the Future Female?*, Virago, 1987.
Angela Weir and Elizabeth Wilson, 'The British Women's Movement', *New Left Review*, 148, 1984, and the reply by Michèle Barrett, *New Left Review*, 150, 1985.

1

Germaine Greer

The Ideal

If the God who is said to be love exists in the imagination of men it is because they have created Him. Certainly they have had a vision of a love that was divine although it would be impossible to point out a paradigm in actuality. The proposition has been repeated like a mantra in hate-filled situations, because it seemed a law of life. 'God is love.' Without love there could have been no world. If all were Thanatos and no Eros, nothing could have come into being. Desire is the cause of all movement, and movement is the character of all being. The universe is a process and its method is change. Whether we call it a Heraclitean dance or the music of the spheres or the unending galliard of protons and neutrons we share an idea in all cultures of a creative movement to and from, moved by desire, repressed by death and the second law of thermodynamics. Various methods of formulation approximate knowledge of it at any time because the laws which seek to control and formalize such dynamics for the reasoning mind must be reformulated endlessly. Energy, creation, movement and harmony, development, all happen under the aegis of love, in the domain of Eros. Thanatos trudges behind, setting the house in order, drawing boundaries and contriving to rule. Human beings love despite their compulsions to limit it and exploit it, chaotically. Their love persuades them to make vows, build houses and turn their passion ultimately to duty.

When mystics say that God is love, or when Aleister Crowley says 'Love is the law', they are not referring to the love that is woman's destiny. Indeed, many Platonists believed that women were not capable of love at all, because they were men's inferiors physically, socially, intellectually and even in terms of physical beauty. Love is not possible between inferior and superior, because the base cannot free their love from selfish interest, either

This extract is taken from *The Female Eunuch*, Grafton books, a division of William Collins Sons & Co. Ltd. US and Canadian rights by permission of McGraw-Hill.

as the desire for security, or social advantage, and, being lesser, they themselves cannot comprehend the faculties in the superior which are worthy of love. The superior being on the other hand cannot demean himself by love for an inferior; his feeling must be tinged with condescension or else partake of perversion and a deliberate self-abasement. The proper subject for love is one's equal, seeing as the essence of love is to be mutual, and the lesser cannot produce anything greater than itself. Seeing the image of himself, man recognizes it and loves it, out of fitting and justifiable *amour propre*; such a love is based upon understanding, trust, and commonalty. It is the love that forms communities, from the smallest groups to the highest.[1] It is the only foundation for viable social structures, because it is the manifestation of common good. Society is founded on love, but the state is not because the state is a collection of minorities with different, even irreconcilable common goods. Like a father controlling siblings of different ages and sexes, the state must bring harmony among the warring groups, not through love, but external discipline. What man feels for the very different from himself is fascination and interest, which fade when the novelty fades, and the incompatibility makes its presence felt. Feminine women chained to men in our society are in this situation. They are formed to be artificially different and fascinating to men and end by being merely different, isolated in the house of a bored and antagonistic being.

From the earliest moments of life, human love is a function of narcissism. The infant who perceives his own self and the external world as the same thing loves everything until he learns to fear harm.[2] So if you pitch him into the sea he will swim, as he floated in his mother's womb before it grew too confining. The baby accepts reality, because he has no ego.

> The Angel that presided o'er my birth
> Said 'Little creature, form'd of joy and mirth,
> Go love without the help of anything on Earth.'[3]

Even when his ego is forming he must learn to understand himself in terms of his relationships to other people and other people in terms of himself. The more his self-esteem is eroded, the lower the opinion that he has of his fellows; the more inflated his self-esteem the more he expects of his friends. This interaction has always been understood, but not always given its proper importance. When Adam saw Eve in the Garden of Eden he loved her because she was of himself, bone of his bone, and more like him than any of the other animals created for his delectation. His movement of desire towards her was an act of love for his own kind. This kind of diffuse narcissism has always been accepted as a basis for love, except in the male–female relationship where it has been assumed that man is inflamed by what is different in women, and therefore the differences have been magnified until men have more in common with other men of different races, creeds and colours than they have with the women of their own environment. The principle of the brotherhood of man is that narcissistic one, for the grounds for that love have always been the assumption that we ought to realize that we are the same the whole world over.

The brotherhood of man will only become a reality when the consciousness of alien beings corrects man's myopia, and he realizes that he has more in common with Eskimoes and Bengali beggars and black faggots than he has with the form of intelligent life on Solar system X. Nevertheless, we are discouraged from giving the name of love to relationships between people of common interests, like footballers and musicians, expecially if they are of the same sex. In denying such a description we ignore the testimony of bodies and behaviour. If Denis Law hugs Nobby Stiles on the pitch we tolerate it because it is *not* love. If Kenny Burell blows a kiss to Albert King on stage we congratulate ourselves on knowing how to take it. The housewife whose husband goes to the local every night does not tell herself that he loves his friends more than he loves her, although she resents it despite herself as an infidelity.

The arguments about the compatibility of marriageable people stem from a working understanding of the principle of parity in love, but it is very rarely seen that compatible interests at the level of hobbies and books and cinema do not make up for the enormous gulf which is kept open between the sexes in all other fields. We might note with horror those counsels which advise girls to take up their boyfriends' hobbies in order to seduce them by a feigned interest in something they like. In any event, the man's real love remains centred in his male peers, although his sex may be his woman's prerogative. Male bonding can be explained by this simple principle of harmony between *similes inter pares*, that is, love. On the other hand, female castration results in concentration of her feelings upon her male companion, and her impotence in confrontations with her own kind. Because all her love is guided by the search for security, if not for her offspring then for her crippled and fearful self, she cannot expect to find it in her own kind, whom she knows to be weak and unsuitable. Women cannot love because, owing to a defect in narcissism, they do not rejoice in seeing their own kind. In fact the operation of female insecurity in undermining natural and proper narcissism is best summed up by their use of make-up and disguise, ruses of which women are infallibly aware. Those women who boast most fulsomely of their love for their own sex (apart from lesbians, who must invent their own ideal of love) usually have curious relations with it, intimate to the most extraordinary degree but disloyal, unreliable and tension-ridden, however close and long-standing they may be.

We can say the brotherhood of man, and pretend that we include the sisterhood of women, but we know that we don't. Folklore has it that women only congregate to bitch an absent member of their group, and continue to do so because they are too well aware of the consequences if they stay away. It's meant to be a joke, but like jokes about mothers-in-law it is founded in bitter truth. Women don't nip down to the local: they don't invent, as men do, pretexts like coin-collecting or old-schoolism or half-hearted sporting activities so that they can be together; on ladies' nights they watch frozen-faced while their men embrace and fool about commenting to each other that they are all overgrown boys. Of the love of fellows they know nothing. They cannot love each other in this easy, innocent, spontaneous way because they cannot love themselves. What we actually see, sitting at the tables by the wall, is a collection of masked menials, dressed up to avoid scrutiny in the trappings of the status symbol, aprons off, scent on, feigning leisure and relaxation where they feel only fatigue. All that can happen to make the evening for one of them is that she might disrupt the love-affair around her by making her husband lavish attention on her or seeing that somebody else does. Supposing the men do not abandon their women to their own society the conversation is still between man and man with a feminine descant. The jokes are the men's jokes; the activity and the anecdotes about it belong to the men. If the sex that has been extracted from the homosexual relationship were not exclusively concentrated on her, a woman would consider that she had cause for complaint. Nobody complains that she has sex without love and he has love without sex. It is right that way, appalling any other way.

Hope is not the only thing that springs eternal in the human breast. Love makes its appearance there unbidden from time to time. Feelings of spontaneous benevolence towards one's own kind still transfigure us now and then – not in relationships with the stakes of security and flattery involved, but in odd incidents of confidence and cooperation in situations where duty and compulsion are not considerations. This extraordinary case of free love appeared in the correspondence of the *People*:

> Eighteen years ago my husband and I moved into our first house. Two weeks later our neighbours arrived next door. We thought they were rather standoffish, and they, in return, were not too keen on us.
>
> But over the years we have blessed the day they came to live next door. We have shared happy times. They were godparents to our daughter. And when trouble was at its worst they were always at hand with help.
>
> Now they have paid us the biggest compliment ever. My husband recently changed his job and we had to move 200 miles. The parting was just too much. Rather than say goodbye, my neighbour's husband has changed his job, and they have moved with us.
>
> Although we are not neighbours, we are only five minutes away from each other. This is a friendship that really has stood the test of time.[4]

This remarkable situation is rare indeed, for it is the tendency of family relationships to work against this kind of extra-familial affection. Every time a man unburdens his heart to a stranger he reaffirms the love that unites humanity. To be sure, he is unpacking his heart with words but at the same time he is encouraged to expect interest and sympathy, and he usually gets it. His interlocutor feels unable to impose his own standards on his confidant's behaviour; for once he feels how another man feels. It is not always sorrow and squalor that is passed on in this way but sometimes joy and pride. I remember a truck driver telling me once about his wife, how sexy and clever and loving she was, and how beautiful. He showed me a photograph of her and I blushed for guilt because I had expected something plastic and I saw a woman by trendy standards plain, fat and ill-clad. Half the point in reading novels and seeing plays and films is to exercise the faculty of sympathy with our own kind, so often obliterated in the multifarious controls and compulsions of actual social existence. For once we are not contemptuous of Camille or jealous of Juliet we might even understand the regicide or the motherfucker. That is love.

The love of fellows is based upon understanding and therefore upon communication. It was love that taught us to speak, and death that laid its fingers on our lips. All literature, however vituperative, is an act of love, and all forms of electronic communication attest the possibility of understanding. Their actual power in girdling the global village has not been properly understood yet. Beyond the arguments of statisticians and politicians and other professional cynics and death makers, the eyes of a Biafran child have an unmistakable message. But while electronic media feed our love for our own kind, the circumstances of our lives substitute propinquity for passion.

If we could present an attainable ideal of love it would resemble the relationship described by Maslow as existing between self-realizing personalities. It is probably a fairly perilous equilibrium: certainly the forces of order and civilization react fairly directly to limit the possibilities of self-realization. Maslow describes his ideal personalities as having a better perception of reality – what Herbert Read called an innocent eye, like the eye of the child who does not seek to reject reality. Their relationship to the world of phenomena is not governed by their personal necessity to exploit it or be exploited by it, but a desire to observe it and to understand it. They have no disgust; the unknown does not frighten them. They are without defensiveness or affectation. The only causes of regret are laziness, outbursts of temper, hurting others, prejudice, jealousy and envy. Their behaviour is spontaneous but it corresponds to an autonomous moral code. Their thinking is problem-centred, not ego-centred, and therefore they most often have a sense of commitment to a cause beyond their daily concerns. Their responses are geared to the present and not to nostalgia or anticipation. Although they do not serve a religion out of guilt or fear or any other sort of compulsion, the religious experience, in Freud's term, the *oceanic feeling*, is easier for them to attain than for the conventionally religious. The essential factor in self-realization is independence, resistance to enculturation; the danger inherent in this is that of excessive independence or downright eccentricity; nevertheless, such people are more capable of giving love, if what Rogers said of love is to be believed, that 'we can love a person only to the extent we are not threatened by him.' Our self-realizing person might claim to be capable of loving everybody because he cannot be

> His word pronounced 'selfishness' blessed, the wholesome healthy selfishness that wells from a powerful soul – from a powerful soul to which belongs the high body, beautiful, triumphant, refreshing, around which everything becomes a mirror – the supple, persuasive body, the dancer whose parable and epitome is the self-enjoying soul.
>
> Nietzsche, 'Thus spoke Zarathustra'

threatened by anybody. Of course circumstances will limit the possibility of his loving everybody, but it would certainly be a fluke if such a character were to remain completely monogamous. For those people who wanted to be dominated or exploited or to establish any other sort of compulsive symbiosis, he would be an unsatisfactory mate; as there are many fewer self-realizing personalities than there are other kinds, the self-realizer is usually ill-mated. Maslow has a rather un-looked for comment on the sexual behaviour of the self-realizer:

> Another characteristic I found of love in healthy people is that they have made no really sharp differentiation between the roles and personalities of the two sexes. That is, they did not assume that the female was passive and the male active, whether in sex or love or anything else. These people were so certain of their maleness or femaleness they did not mind taking on some of the aspects of the opposite sex role. It was especially noteworthy that they could be both passive and active lovers. . . an instance of the way in which common dichotomies are so often resolved in self-actualization, appearing to be valid dichotomies only because people are not healthy enough.[5]

What Maslow expresses may be little more than a prejudice in favour of a certain kind of personality structure, merely another way of compromising between Eros and civilization, nevertheless we are all involved in some such operative compromise. At least Maslow's terms indicate a direction in which we could travel and not merely a theoretical account of what personality might be like if psychoanalysis accomplished the aim which it has so far not even clearly declared itself or justified to the waiting world, 'to return our souls to our bodies, to return ourselves to ourselves, and thus to overcome the human state of self-alienation'.[6]

It is surprising but nevertheless it is true that Maslow included some women in his sample of self-realizing personalities. But after all it is foreseeable, even if my arguments about the enculturation of woman are correct. In some ways the operation of the feminine stereotype is so obvious and for many women entirely unattainable, that it can be easily reacted against. It takes a great deal of courage and independence to decide to design your own image instead of the one that society rewards, but it gets easier as you go along. Of course, a woman who decides to go her own way will find that her conditioning is ineradicable, but at least she can recognize its operation and choose to counteract it, whereas a man might find that he was being more subtly deluded. A woman who decided to become a lover without conditions might discover that her relationships broke up relatively easily because of her degree of resistance to efforts to 'tame' her, and the opinion of her friends will usually be on the side of the man who was prepared to do the decent thing, who was in love with her, etcetera. Her promiscuity, resulting from her constant sexual desire, tenderness and interest in people, will not usually be differentiated from compulsive promiscuity or inability to say no, although it is fundamentally different. Her love may often be devalued by the people for whom she feels most tenderness, and her self-esteem might have much direct attack. Such pressures can never be utterly without effect.

Even if a woman does not inhibit her behaviour because of them, she will find herself reacting in some other way, being outrageous when she only meant to be spontaneous, and so forth. She may limit herself to writing defences of promiscuity, or even books about women. (Hm.)

For love's sake women must reject the roles that are offered to them in our society. As impotent, insecure, inferior beings they can never love in a generous way. The ideal of Platonic love, of Eros as a stabilizing, creative, harmonizing force in the universe, was most fully expressed in English in Shakespeare's abstract poem, 'The Phoenix and the Turtle', who

> Loved, as love in twain
> Had the essence but in one
> Two distincts, division none:
> Number there in love was slain.
>
> Hearts remote, yet not asunder;
> Distance and no space was seen
> 'Twixt the turtle and his queen:
> But in them it were a wonder.

The poem is not a plea for suttee, although it describes the mutual obsequies of the phoenix and the turtle. It states and celebrates the concept of harmony, of fusion, melting together, neither sacrificed nor obliterated, that non-destructive knowledge which Whitehead learned to value from the writings of Lao-Tse.

> Property was thus appall'd
> That the self was not the same;
> Single nature's double name
> Neither two nor one was called.
>
> Reason in itself confounded,
> Saw division grow together;
> To themselves get either neither
> Simple were so well compounded.[7]

The love of peers is the spirit of commonalty, the unity of beauty and truth. The phoenix and the turtle do not necessarily cohabit, for they are the principle of sympathy which is not dependent upon familiarity. The phoenix renews itself constantly in its own ashes, as a figure of protean existence. The love of the phoenix and the turtle is not the lifelong coherence of a mutually bound couple, but the principle of love that is reaffirmed in the relationship of the narcissistic self to the world of which it is a part. It is not the fantasy of annihilation of the self in another's identity by sexual domination, for it is a spiritual state of comprehension.

> Spirituality, by which I mean the purity of a strong and noble nature, with all the new and untried powers that must grow out of it – has not yet appeared on our horizon; and its absence is a natural consequence of a diversity of interests between man and woman, who are for the most part brought together through the attraction of passion; and who, but for that, would be as far asunder as the poles.[8]

In fact, men and women love differently, and much of the behaviour that we describe by the term is so far from benevolence, and so anti-social, that it must be understood to be inimical to the essential nature of love. Our life-style contains more *thanatos* than *eros*, for egotism, exploitation, deception, obsession and addiction have more place in us than eroticism, joy, generosity and spontaneity.

NOTES

1 In the Renaissance simple statements of the Platonic concept of love were disseminated as commonplaces. To the basic arguments drawn from the *Convivium* and other dialogues were added the eulogies of Cicero and Plutarch and the theories of Heraclitus and Aristotle. The essence of this mixture can be found in many places, from the courtesy books like the *Cortigiano* and de la Primaudaye's *Academie* to the commonplace books and moral tracts for the consumption of the newly literate, e.g. Sir Thomas Elyot's *The Boke of the Governour* (1531), section 31, *The Booke of Friendship of Marcus Tullius Cicero* (1550), John Charlton's *The Casket of Iewels* (1571), Baldwin's *Treatise of Moral Philosiphy* (1550), Bodenham's *Politeuphuia* (1597) and Robert Allott's *Wits Theater of the little World* (1599). Possibly the most accessible and the most elegant formulation, is Bacon's *Essay of Friendship*.

2 Paul Schilder, *The Image and Appearance of the Human Body* (London, 1935), p. 120, cf. Norman O. Brown, *Life Against Death* (London, 1968), pp. 50–1.

3 William Blake, Poems from MSS, *c.*1810 (*Nonesuch*, p. 124), *cf.* Ian Suttee, *The Origins of Love and Hate* (London, 1935), pp. 30–1.

4 *The People*, 12.10.1969.

5 A.H. Maslow, *Motivation and Personality* (New York, 1954), pp. 208–46; quotation from pp. 245–6.

6 Brown, *Life Against Death*, p. 144.

7 William Shakespeare, 'The Phoenix and the Turtle'.

8 S.E. Gay, *Womanhood in its Eternal Aspect* (London, 1879), p. 4.

PART II

Feminism and the Historians

Introduction

A collection such as this cannot hope to do full justice to its object for a number of reasons. One thing must be placed before another. Yet there is no obviously compelling reason to begin with history and end with cultural studies, and perhaps good reason to avoid placing 'culture' last once again. Our story opens with a socialist historiography rejecting economistic forms of Marxism, and, in an attempt to give due place to 'culture', turning to such texts as Raymond Williams's *Culture and Society* and *The Long Revolution*.[1] But it might equally well have begun with socialist literary critics like Williams, rejecting both the reductionism of simplistic base-superstructure models and the idealism of Leavisite literary critical practice, and turning to the work of the socialist historians. The title of Juliet Mitchell's seminal essay, 'Women: the Longest Revolution'[2] acknowledges Williams, and the essay itself founded British feminism in the space opened up by this engagement of socialist history and cultural studies.

The danger of reducing culture to its material base is not, however, a present threat. We live at a time in which socialist politics as well as Marxist theory are distinctly unfashionable; when a widespread and popular move to the right has coincided with a shift on the left into forms of theorizing which are closer to the idealism which lives and breathes in the shadow of reductionism. The project on the left in the early 1960s was to found a historiography and a cultural studies which gave full and proper space to 'culture' without turning history into something approximating the history of ideas. It is this latter danger which is the more threatening today.

Contemporary feminist writing in Britain and elsewhere has followed a trajectory whose route is visible throughout this collection. The journey begins with Marxist- or socialist-feminist writings (in history, social science *and* cultural studies), seeking to uncover the material conditions of women's oppression under capitalism; it advances with the recognition that certain aspects of that oppression do not yield very readily to Marxist categories and that a more adequate account of feminine subjectivity is required for an understanding of the ways in which that oppression is *lived*, which might be sought in psychoanalysis rather than Marxism. Then, via Lacan and modern theories of language, the journey continues into the 'poststructuralism' and 'deconstructionism' whose luminaries include Foucault, Derrida and Kristeva. Some travellers continue beyond feminism itself, into a 'post-feminism' and 'postmodernism' which understand both Lacanian psychoanalysis and Marxism to have been mere staging-posts along the way.[3]

The organization of this volume recognizes that these latter tendencies, evident throughout, are most fully developed in feminist cultural studies, while the earlier stages are more in evidence in historical and sociological writings. But I would also want to argue that it is those feminists, in history, social science and cultural studies, who have attempted to construct some kind of synthesis of contemporary theories of subjectivity and Marxist materialism, that have most to offer to contemporary feminist thought today.

PUTTING WOMEN INTO THE FRAME

The project of recovering the 'hidden history' of women has been common to all contemporary feminisms. But history is not an incomplete jigsaw puzzle. Rival schools of historiography construct differing historical landscapes within which women are both visible and obscured. Putting the women back in may cause much upheaval and a good deal of resistance. Equally the history of women may be ignored or patronised rather than opposed. It may be traced, to lie alongside dominant histories, providing no more than a decorative border to the canvas. Or it may flesh out the landscape with additional figures without changing its topography.

Eileen Power's *Medieval Women* for example was until recently one of the few available accounts of the lives of women in feudal Europe.[4] The debate on the transition from feudalism to capitalism inaugurated by Maurice Dodd and Paul Sweezy predates Power's work.[5] But later contributors to that debate are as innocent of any reference to her work, or to gender divisions, as were the originators. Whether women had, as Power argued, a 'rough and ready equality' with men under feudalism, or whether as Christopher Middleton was to argue,[6] there is evidence of a complex sexual division of labour which in some respects anticipated that of capitalism, was simply not relevant to the terms in which the transition debate was conducted. Middleton's formulation rationalised the ommission. He argued that the prevalent sexual division of labour by and large removed women from the arena in which history was made, that of the expropriation of a surplus, in labour dues or other forms of feudal extraction. Women were 'hidden from history' because they did not make it. Unless the history of women which feminists uncover is made to bear on those aspects of the social world which are identified as 'prime movers' of historical change, or unless the location of those prime movers is successfully challenged, then it will continue to be ignored or patronized.

The domestic labour debate which took place in the pages of *New Left Review* and elsewhere in the early 1970s was one attempt by feminists to make the history of the sexual division of labour impinge on Marxist theory at a critical point – the labour theory of value.[7] An alternative strategy is to redefine what counts as significant historical change, and on the whole this has been preferred by more radical elements within the women's movement. In so far as Marxist historians identify the same temporalities in their causal stories of transition from one mode of production to another, motored by the class struggle, and in those other stories of changes in the social relations of gender, then the likelihood is that the second story will always be subordinate to the first: a subplot within the dominant tale which adds intrigue, but whose resolution turns on what is happening to the main characters. The story told by Engels of the subordination of women was just such a one-sided affair.[8] This subordination of women's history is in part the reason why some feminists otherwise sympathetic to Marxism, have argued that the 'marriage' of Marxism and feminism is at present an unhappy one resting as it does on a deeply unequal relationship.[9]

The radical-feminist alternative has obvious attractions since it has no truck with the subordination of the history of women's oppression to the history of the class struggle. Radical feminists argue that the oppression of women by men is primary fundamental and irreducible: the earliest oppression which provides the model for all subsequent forms, including those of class and race.[10]

THE HISTORY WORKSHOP MOVEMENT

Each of the various intellectual contexts within which the second wave of feminism emerged had its own distinctive historiographical landscape, and the feminist project of recovering women's history inevitably began by taking its bearings within that landscape. In Britain, feminist historiography found a niche within the school of socialist working-class history. A group of feminist historians emerged as part of the History Workshop movement. Their object, women's history, was defined as much in terms of class as of gender.

The institutional base for the History Workshop movement was provided by the adult education movement in its working-class constituency. Ruskin College Oxford was founded in 1899 as a residential college for working-class adults, and it was Ruskin which hosted the History Workshop Conference from the mid 1960s, which in turn led to the founding of the History Workshop Journal in 1976. The editorials in the first issue defined the aim of the Journal: that of wresting history from the monopolistic grasp of professional historians writing primarily for each other. The Journal was committed to the generation of an alternative history with a new subject which was also its object: a 'people's history' which would uncover the 'lost' histories of working-class struggle, returning them to the working-class reader in an open, two-way exchange. The adult education context was vital, since the adult working-class learner was the preferred reader addressed by the Journal.[11] Many of the labour historians, including some of the feminists who wrote for the Journal, had been adult students themselves, and had taught in adult education colleges. In the Journal women's history was produced as the history of working-class women, and women were defined primarily as workers, paid or unpaid, industrial or domestic.

The History Workshop movement hosted the first national Women's Liberation Conference at Ruskin in 1970. It is not surprising then that feminism was high on the agenda of the Journal from its inception in 1976, even though this concern was not given recognition in its subtitle until vol 13, 1982, when it became 'a journal of socialist and feminist history'. Pride of place in the first issue was given to an editorial statement written by Anna Davin and Sally Alexander on feminist history. A second, by Gareth Stedman Jones and Raphael Samuel entitled 'Sociology and History' identified another recurrent source of anxiety within the socialist history movement, the relationship to theory. This second editorial took a critical stance towards borrowings from sociology. A promised engagement within the Journal with sociology would, it was hoped, 'move historians to think more critically about the theoretical resources they are drawing upon and... encourage them to engage in theoretical work for themselves'.[12] Times were changing, and when the engagement with theory took place, sociology had long since been upstaged by Althusserian 'structuralism'. An article by Richard Johnson set the breakers rolling, and a regular storm brewed up, the more turbulent because Johnson chose to establish his critique of socialist historiography through an analysis of the theoretical shortcomings of the writings of E.P. Thompson and Eugene Genovese, giants within the socialist history movement.[13] He identified a tendency towards what he termed 'cultural Marxism', which he understood in terms of the reaction against an earlier Marxist economism dominated by the Communist Party. In turning away from this economism the cultural historians had, claimed Johnson, shot clean over into a 'culturalism' which effectively neglected the economic base altogether, and in so doing, had also turned its back on the strengths as well as the limitations of writers such as Maurice Dobb. Marxist *theory*, argued Johnson, was jettisoned in favour of an empiricism which restricted itself to the discovery and presentation of lived working-class experience of class struggle. The remedy proposed by Johnson was a (critical) engagement with the Marxism of Louis Althusser.

THEORY, FEMINISTS, AND HISTORIANS

The response to Johnson was immediate and forthright.[14] I am not here concerned with the merits of the argument which ensued, but with the notable silence in this engagement over theory on the part of the feminist historians associated with the Journal. This silence was eloquent not of empiricist hostility to theory, but of a dissatisfaction with *Marxist* theory. For there was nothing critically at stake in the debate for the project of women's history. Each rival formulation offered some space within which a feminist historiography might be and was developed,[15] but the history of women was not insistently required to be there as a central condition of the theory. Sally Alexander gave expression to these reservations in a later article in the Journal, reprinted in this collection:

> 'A history of our own', 'a language of our own', 'the right to determine our own sexuality', these were the distinctive themes of rebellion for the Women's Liberation Movement in the early 1970s. We were asking the impossible perhaps. As a feminist I was (and still am) under the spell of those wishes, while as a historian writing and thinking in the shadow of a labour history which silences them. How can women speak and think creatively within Marxism when they can neither enter the narrative flow as fully as they wish, nor imagine that there might be other subjectivities present in history than those of class (for to imagine that is to transgress the laws of historical materialism)?

'Histories of feminity and feminism', she went on to argue, 'have temporalities of their own – apart from those of class and of men.'[16]

Increasingly feminist historians associated with the Journal were turning to other, or additional, sources to meet their needs for theory, and especially towards psychoanalysis. Marxism permits feminist history, but without necessarily permitting it to *make a difference*. While psychoanalysis is every bit as male centred as Marxism, because it theorizes sexual difference and sexed subjectivity, then feminist intervention here *must* make a difference. Sex and gender are quite crucially at stake in a way in which they need not be in Marxism.

The ways in which psychoanalysis might be used as a resource in feminist and socialist historiography remain to be fully explored.[17] While many of the feminist historians associated with the Journal have been influenced by psychoanalysis, this influence cannot always be detected very clearly in their historical writings.[18]

CLASS AND WOMEN'S HISTORY

The importance of the adult education movement to the History Workshop project, and to socialist historiography generally has already been stressed. In recovering women's history as part of 'people's history' some hard choices had sometimes to be made, nowhere more so than in the history of this very movement. Sheila Rowbotham wrote a moving piece for the Journal on working men's experience of the middle-class sponsored and dominated University Extension Movement which was founded in 1873.[19] Priorities of class rather than sex prevailed in this account. For the Extension Movement had been preceded some six years earlier by a movement for the provision of adult education for women. The Northern Council for the Promotion of Higher Education for Women was formed in 1867 and had been responsible for persuading Cambridge University to supply peripatetic lecturers who toured a circuit of northern towns offering lectures to women on a variety of topics from astronomy to literature.[20] It was the phenomenal success of these lectures which led to the foundation of the Extension movement and which in turn played a crucial role in the history of the development of provincial universities.

This episode has attracted little attention. It does not form part of the stock of knowledge of women's history among feminists. In fact it has been argued that we know as little about the history of 'ordinary' middle-class women as we do about their working-class sisters. Patricia Branca made this point in her *Silent Sisterhood*.[21] The Victorian 'lady', she argued, had been more stereotyped than studied. Yet if we accept that there is a specific sex-oppression which is not reducible to class relations or to the exigencies of capitalism, and further, that it may have different temporalities, then the rationale for a specifically working-class feminist history diminishes. Thanks to Leonore Davidoff and Catherine Hall's major study, *Family Fortunes*, our knowledge of the lives of provincial middle-class women in the nineteenth century has been greatly extended.[22] Their case is that middle-class identity was in important part constituted by class-differentiated gender-conceptions, and relations between the sexes. The making of the English middle class was also the making of the Proper Lady; the making of middle-class masculinity.

It was not possible to include an extract from *Family Fortunes* in this collection, because editing a chapter to the required length diminished the richness of the study to an unacceptable degree, as its wealth of examples drawn from the lives of those families which it enters so intimately were axed for want of space. Instead, included here is an earlier piece by Catherine Hall, published while the research was in progress. I would strongly urge readers to treat themselves to the complete study.

NOTES

1 Raymond Williams, *Culture and Society*, Hogarth, 1958; *The Long Revolution*, Hogarth, 1961.
2 Juliet Mitchell, *Women: the Longest Revolution*, Virago, 1984.
3 Denise Riley's *'Am I That Name?'*, Macmillan, 1988, pulls up short of post-feminism, but is a good example of the logic of poststructuralism in feminist historiography.
4 Eileen Power, *Medieval Women*, Cambridge University Press, 1975.
5 Maurice Dobb, *Studies in the Development of Capitalism*, Routledge and Kegan Paul, 1946; Paul Sweezey initiated the transition debate in his rejoinder to Dobb. The debate is reprinted with additional contributions and an introduction by Rodney Hilton in Paul Sweezey et al., *The Transition from Feudalism to Capitalism*, Verso, 1978.
6 Chris Middleton, 'Peasants, Patriarchy, and the Feudal Mode of Production in England: a Marxist Appraisal', parts 1 and 2, *Sociological Review*, 29,1,1981; and 'Sexual Divisions in Feudalism', *New Left Review*, 113/4, 1975.
7 See Part III p. 72 below, for a discussion of the domestic labour debate.

8 F. Engels, *Origins of the Family, Private Property and the State* (1884), Allen Lane, 1972.

9 Lydia Sargeant, ed., *Women and Revolution: a Discussion of the Unhappy Marriage of Marxism and Feminism*, Pluto, 1981.

10 For an example, see Barbara Burris, 'The Fourth World Manifesto', in A. Koedt, E. Levine and A. Rapone, eds, *Radical Feminism*, Quadrangle, 1973. For criticism of this type of comparison, see Bell Hooks, *Ain't I a Woman? Black Women and Feminism*, and Angela Davis, *Women, Race and Class*, Random House, 1981.

11 This point of reference was tremendously important for a number of left intellectuals in the post-war period. Writing of the journal, *Politics and Letters*, Raymond Williams commented, 'increasingly what for me became the decisive world was adult education. Virtually every WEA tutor was a Socialist of one colour or another. We were all doing adult education ourselves. So we saw the journal as linked to this very hopeful formation with a national network of connections to the working-class movement. If there was a group to which *Politics and Letters* referred, it was the adult education tutors and their students.' Raymond Williams, *Politics and Letters*, NLB, 1979, p. 69.

12 Raphael Samuel and Gareth Stedman Jones, 'Editorial: Sociology and History', *History Workshop Journal*, 1, 1976, p. 8.

13 Richard Johnson, 'Edward Thompson, Eugene Genovese, and Socialist-Humanist History', *History Workshop Journal*, 6, 1978.

14 See replies to Johnson by Keith McClelland, Gavin Williams, Simon Clarke, and Gregor McLennan, in *History Workshop Journal*, 7 and 8, 1979.

15 The Althusserian influence was pervasive. The position adopted by Clarke informed the work of many of the feminists associated with the Conference of Socialist Economists (CSE) and writing in the CSE journal, *Capital and Class*.

16 Sally Alexander, 'Women, Class and Sexual Differences in the 1830s and 1840s: Some Reflections on the Writing of a Feminist History', *History Workshop Journal*, 18, 1984, p. 27.

17 In spite of the special issue of *History Workshop Journal* on Psychoanalysis and History (no. 26, 1988), Alexander's essay remains exceptional.

18 See for example, Barbara Taylor, *Eve and the New Jerusalem*, Virago, 1983.

19 Sheila Rowbotham, 'Travellers in a strange country: responses of working-class students to the University Extension Movement, 1873–1910', *History Workshop Journal*, 12, 1981.

20 Sheila C. Lemoine, *The North of England Council for Promoting the Higher Education of Women*, unpublished M.Ed. thesis, University of Manchester, 1968.

21 Patricia Branca, *Silent Sisterhood*, Croom Helm, 1975.

22 Leonore Davidoff and Catherine Hall, *Family Fortunes*, Hutchinson, 1987.

2

Sally Alexander

Women, Class and Sexual Differences in the 1830s and 1840s: Some Reflections on the Writing of a Feminist History

...

If the meaning of femininity, the political implications of Womanhood have at moments in the past 300 years been contested, then it must be that what they represent is not some eternal and universal essence of woman, but the difficulty of the sexual relation itself between women and men; which is always a social ordering, and one where the unconscious and its conflicting drives and desires presses most urgently on conscious behaviour, where political thought, though most capable of producing principles of equality and justice in its delineations of the proper relations between the sexes, nevertheless cannot always anticipate or circumscribe the urgency of those conflicts as they are lived...By suggesting that what both feminism and femininity stand for is not Woman – who like Man is no more nor less than human – but the social organization of sexual difference and division, I am refusing to abandon femininity to an enigma/mystery beyond history. But then the problem becomes how to write a history of women and feminism which engages with those issues...

...

INTELLECTUAL FEMINISM

In the early 1970s socialist feminists struggled to transform those dichotomies into political and theoretical relationships through campaigns and study groups. We diligently appraised and attempted to secure for our own purposes some of the traditions of Marxist thought, appropriating the concepts of political economy, historical and dialectical materialism and assessing their revolutionary practices through a feminist lens. If I ask what was/is the relationship between class struggle and the sexual division of labour, then historical materialism's focus on the mode of production is illuminating and suggestive. It imaginatively speculates on labour both as a form of activity which involves a relationship between Man and Nature, and as a system of social relations between women and men. But if the categories of political economy can sometimes reveal the operations of the labour market convincingly, the political traditions of Marxism have had little to say about feminism or the needs and aspirations of women; while historical materialism, by identifying class struggle as the motor of history pushes the questions of sexual divisions and difference to the periphery of the historical process. Whether posited as objects of analysis, or included as part of the narrative, they can be present in Marxist – and most labour – history, only as digressions from the real subject of history – class struggle; and their theoretical status is subservient to the study of modes of production.

If feminism has been only one of the detonators of 'crisis' in Marxist thought and practice it has been the most insistently subversive because it will not give up its wish to speak in the name of women; of women's experience, subjectivity and sexuality. 'A history of our own', 'a language of our own', 'the right to determine our own sexuality', these were the distinctive themes of rebellion for the Women's Liberation Movement in the early 1970s. We were asking the impossible perhaps. As a feminist I was (and still am) under the spell of those wishes, while as a historian writing and thinking in the shadow of a labour history which silences them. How can women speak and think creatively within Marxism when they can neither enter the narrative flow as fully as they wish, nor imagine that there might be other subjectivities present in history than those of class (for to imagine that is to transgress the laws of historical materialism)?...

Other intellectual traditions and ways of thinking about women, sexual divisions and feminism pushed the categories Woman and Labour, Sex and Class, Feminism and Socialism apart in my mind, refusing any analogy between them, or any mutual set of determinations and effects. The discovery of histories of women written by earlier generations of feminists showed how women's experience has to be remembered anew with each resurgence of feminist consciousness; between times it leaves scarcely a trace. Why this recurring amnesia, and why the attenuated feminist voice?

...

Radical feminism...offered a breathtakingly audacious understanding of relations between the sexes in history. Sexual divisions prefigure those of class was the message that Shulamith Firestone and Kate Millett flung at a male dominated intellectual world, patriarchy the concept which they restored to the centre of debates around social formations and social relations between the sexes.[1]

Since the seventeenth century feminists have rallied against the tyranny of men, male power, male domination and, in the idiom of the 1970s, sexism. But those categories, while retaining a polemical conviction, I believe, have to be transcended too in any full history of women or feminism. Ironically radical feminism writes women's subjectivity and active agency out of history as effectively as any Marxism. Little girls become women because of what male dominated institutions tell and compel them to do. History is simply one long death knell of women's independent activity and consciousness. There were witches, but men killed them; women were sensual, erotic and adventurous but men used and abused them; women loved each other, but men forbade that love to be spoken; women were wives and mothers, but only because men wanted them to be; women were workers, but men seized their skills, etc., etc. Men have much to answer for, but the envy and fears and desires of one sex can't carry all the determinations of history. If they can, then we are again in a world where women's identity, action, speech and desires are all explained in terms of something else, in this case, the male psyche. Women are subordinated and silenced because they live in a world shaped in the interests of and dominated by men. Only a political revolution of women could ever destroy male power if it is conceived as so absolute in its effects.

But the writings and campaigns of previous feminisms exhibit contradictions and difficulties internal to the thoughts of both individual feminists, and the movements for which they claimed to speak, that cannot be reduced to the tyranny of men. As the vindicator of women's rights, Mary Wollstonecraft, for instance, did not absolve women from culpability in their own history: she castigated the coquetry of women of the leisured classes, condemned their feeble development of reason and virtue, their excess of sensibility, their false modesty. All this she attributed to an education which fitted women exclusively for marriage and the pleasures of men. But reading her letters and novels brings the irresistible recognition that she could diatribe so thoroughly against the thrall of men's authority and desires over women's lives, because she herself fell so violently and seemingly arbitrarily a prey to them herself. Do we reject the authenticity of those conflicting desires because men have placed them there for us? And then, how do we explain divisions within the women's movement itself?

. . .

Every moment of dissonance and disagreement within feminism, as well as between women and men, demands recovering and disentangling – demands a historical reading. Neither Marxism nor radical feminism yet offer a history which can grasp the issues that feminism both stands for and raises. If Marxism persistently avoids sexual anatagonism by relegating sexual difference to a natural world, then radical feminism conceives of women as shaped literally by men's desires. Histories of femininity and feminism have temporalities of their own – apart from those of class or men.

The political narratives of feminism are as diverse and fractured as the vocabulary of individual rights and egalitarian aspiration itself is, when it surfaces now among the ascendent bourgeoisie in eighteenth-century Britain, now among the English jacobins in the 1790s, among the Owenites and Unitarians in the 1820s and 1840s, and in Victorian Britain, accumulating an intensity of grievance and yearning among women from very different social and political milieux.

The emergence of a mass feminist politics is most often attributed to the effects of the industrial revolution and the ideological hegemony of the bourgeoisie.[2] The former, by separating work and home, the latter by instilling ideas of domesticity among the working classes, allocated women and men to the private and public domains respectively. But we come closer to the terrain of feminist grievance and capture a decisive moment in its political temporality if we examine the forms of working-class politics themselves in the 1830s and 1840s, and their language of demand and aspiration. If the working class emerged as a political category in those years (remembering its long history of gestation) then Woman emerged as a social problem. The emergence was simultaneous, the roots of grievance and their political representation different.

FEMINIST CONSCIOUSNESS AND CLASS STRUGGLE

Feminism, as a self-conscious political movement appears when women, or some women in the name of their sex, distinguish themselves and their needs, from those of their male kin within families, communities and class. Feminism's protest is always posed in terms of women's perceptions of themselves and their status in relation to men. From a litany of their discontents feminism gathers an identity of women, and formulates the demands and aspirations that will transform the social relations/conditions in which women and men will live. Whatever the starting point of its dissatisfactions – lack of education, men's property over women in marriage, 'domestic drudgery', the prohibitions on female labour, the double standard of sexual morality, exclusion from the franchise – feminists from the seventeenth century have refused to concede that relationships between the sexes belong outside history in any conception of the natural world, which is where philosophers, poets or Marxist historians, until provoked, have been content to abandon or place them. Feminism looks outward at the social forms of sexual division and the uneven destinies that claim the two sexes, but the critical look becomes an enquiry into the self and sexual difference and asks 'what am I a woman, and how am I different from a man?' No social relationship is left unturned, if only by implication, in this endeavour.

Feminism's return to the individual subject in its attempt to distinguish woman as a social category from man is one clue to some of its moments of emergence. There must be available a language of the individual political subject – a language which articulates the dissemination of a political order through the individual's identification with (and subjection to) its law. Some seventeenth-century protestant sects which proposed the unmediated communion between the Soul and God and dissolved the family in the community of all believers enabled women to claim an equal right with men to 'preach and prophesy', for the 'soul knows no distinction of sex';[3] and in the eighteenth and nineteenth centuries feminism seized on the language of democratic rights within both liberal and utopian political discourse. But for the individual voice of a 'Sophia' or Mary Wollstonecraft to become a movement there had to be not only feminine discontent but also a widespread yearning for another way of life. Before a language of rebellion can pass into general speech it must appeal to the imagination of a wide social group. Thus feminism appears at moments of industrial and political dislocation when disparate social groups are struggling to 'find a voice' in the new emerging order, when seemingly stable forms of social organization are tumbling down, as in the English and French revolutions and in the 1830s and 1840s.[4]

In speaking of the self and sexual difference feminism is at its most disturbing. Sexuality, intimacy, divergent conceptions of need are evoked and haunt the Marxist historian with the spectres of bourgeois individualism, gossip, and the crumbling of working class unity. Ten years of women's history has calmed immediate fears. Few labour historians now hesitate to write of women's work, to mention the family or note the absence of women from some forms of political life. Working class 'experience' has been stretched – though the political significance of those worlds beyond the workplace, ale-house, clubroom, union branch meeting are still argued about.[5] But if we are to pursue the history of women's experience and of feminism there can be no retreat from a closer enquiry into subjectivity and sexual identity. For if feminism insists on the political significance of the female subject and on the urgent need to reorganize sexual difference and division, it is to convey a more generous conception of human consciousness and its effects at the levels of popular resistance, collective identifications, and forms of political address and organization.

SOCIAL BEING: CONSCIOUSNESS OR SUBJECTIVITY?

The focus on the self and sexual difference throws into disarray the smooth elision assumed within Marxist thought between social being, consciousness and politics. Two distinctions are drawn: between material and mental life and true and false consciousness. Mental life flows from material conditions. Social being is determined above all by class position – location within the relations of production. Consciousness and politics, all mental conceptions spring from the material forces and relations of production and so reflect those class origins.[6] Collective class consciousness is the recognition of the shared experience of exploitation, and working-class politics its expression, which in its most advanced form is revolutionary socialism. Thus there are graduated levels of consciousness (from spontaneous to political) before the historic destiny of the working class can be realized.[7] When historical materialism is compressed in this way into a series of laws, they are abandoned only at the risk of jettisoning the dynamics of history.

Let a more skilled philosopher unravel the polarities: material/mental; true/false; cause/effect. Here I only want to point to the absence of the individual sexually differentiated subject in Marxism. The question marks hover over social being, and how it is experienced – by women and by men.

'Experience' of class, even if shared and fully recognized, does not, as Edward Thompson and others have suggested, produce a shared and even consciousness.[8] Class is not only a diverse (geographically, from industry to industry, etc.) and divisive (skilled/unskilled; male/female labour, etc.) 'experience', but that experience itself is given different meaning. For Marxists, meaning is produced through ideologies. The bourgeoisie as the dominant class has control over the relations and the forces of production and therefore the production of ideologies, which mask the reality of social being to the working class. Thus ideologies serve the interests of antagonistic classes.

Debates within Marxism which attempt to release ideology from its economic/material base are inexhaustible. Engels and Lenin have been perhaps the sternest advocates of the grip of the base on the superstructure; Gramsci and Mao Tse-Tung elaborating on the continuum and flux of ideas among the people, the tenacity of traditions, and the irrepressible capacity of human consciousness to produce forms of communal order and ways of thinking independent of the sway of hegemonic ideologies. But if we step aside from these debates to ask not how are ideologies produced, but how, in Juliet Mitchell's phrase, do 'we live as ideas', then we enter the realm of social being and experience along another path – the path of subjectivity and sexual identity.[9] Against Marxism's claims that the determining social relationship is between wage labour and capital, exploiter and exploited, proletarian and capitalist, feminism insists on the recognition that subjective identity is also constructed as masculine or feminine, placing the individual as husband or wife, mother or father, son or daughter, and so on. And these subjectivities travel both into political language and forms of political action, where they may be severed from class or class interests, indeed may be at odds with them.

In order to place subjectivity and sexual difference firmly at the centre of my research and historical writing I draw on the psychonanalytic account of the unconscious and sexuality. Psychoanalysis offers a reading of sexual difference rooted not in the sexual division of labour (which nevertheless organizes that difference), nor within nature, but through the unconscious and language. This poses the issue of psychic reality – a reality which like Marx's concepts of commodity fetishism and exploitation, will not be encountered through empirical observation. Psychoanalysis allows for a rich elaboration of subjectivity, identification and desire – essentially psychic processes which give a political movement its emotional power.

The French psychoanalyst Jacques Lacan's re-emphasis on the part played by language – the symbolic order – in the production of meaning, and unconscious phantasy in the construction of subjectivity has been taken up by some feminists because it retrieves sexual difference from the seemingly obvious 'anatomy is destiny'.

. . .

SUBJECTIVITY, SEXUAL DIFFERENCE AND LANGUAGE

For Lacan the acquisition of subjectivity and sexual identity are a simultaneous and always precarious process which occurs as the human infant enters language; that is, as s/he is spoken to and about and as s/he learns to speak. The human animal is born into language and comes into being through its terms.[10] Or, to put it another way, language, which pre-exists the infant, identifies us first as boy/girl, daughter/son. Language orders masculinity and femininity, they are positions which shift between and within discourses. The infant takes up these positions and moves between them as s/he journeys through the oedipal trauma, which marks the entry into human culture for every infant. The infant is compelled to acknowledge the significance of sexual difference through the presence or absence of the phallus – the primary and privileged sign of sexual difference. Neither little boys nor little girls possess the phallus; they are placed in a different relationship to it through the threat of castration and prohibition, which have different implications for femininity (lack) and masculinity (loss). The relationship to the phallus is mediated through phantasy; recognition of loss/lack, absence/presence is prefigured from birth as the infant differentiates itself from others – the absence/presence of the desired object (breast/mother); the look and speech of others. Phantasy fills the void left by the absent object. Castration and prohibition represent human law, within which every infant has to take up a place, initially as masculine or feminine, and never without a struggle. A struggle, because it is around these moments – absence/loss, pleasure/unpleasure – that the libidinal organization of need, demand and desire is shaped.

Subjectivity, and with it sexual identity, is constructed through a process of differentiation, division and splitting, and is best understood as a process which is always in the making, is never finished or complete. In this sense, the unified coherent subject presented in language is always a fiction, and so susceptible to disruption by the unconscious (or in collision with an alternative concept of the self in language). Everyday speech with its discontinuities, hesitations, contradictions, indicates on the one hand the process itself, and on the other, the difficulty the individual subject has in aligning her or himself within the linguistic order, since there are as many different orders as there are discourses to structure them and always the possibility of more. A difficulty which is underlined for the little girl/woman by the impossibility for her of taking up a positive or powerful place in a culture which privileges masculinity and therefore men. Subjectivity and sexual identity are always achieved with difficulty, and the achievement is always precarious. The unpredictable effects of that achievement remain inaccessible to conscious thought in the repressed wishes to be one with the other, to belong to the other sex, as well as envy of and desire for the other sex. Both subjectivity and sexual identity are therefore unstable and involve antagonism and conflict in their very construction. Antagonism and instability are lived out not only within the individual psyche and its history, they mediate all social relations between women and men; they prefigure and cohabit with class antagonisms, and, as the history of feminism demonstrates, may well disrupt class solidarities.

Post-Saussurian linguistics' non-referential theory of language and insistence on the arbitrary nature of the sign, marks these instabilities. Meaning is produced through the chain of signifiers – the way words are strung together and organized into narratives, analysis, systems of thought – and may be gleaned from the study of those, rather than from reference to the objects and phenomena which they only designate, leaving them always open to dispute and redefinition.[11]

. . .

It is partly because feminism enquires into the self in its concern to distinguish woman from man as a social category, and because one of the points of that return has been a dissatisfaction with historical materialism's privileging of class (narrowly defined) as the determining social experience, economic relation and agency of political change, that the limits of Marxist history's notions of social being, consciousness and politics, and the articulations between them are so clearly revealed. Feminist history has to emancipate itself from class as the organizing principle of history, the privileged signifier of social relations and their political representations.

. . .

The subjectivity of psychoanalysis does not imply a universal human nature, it suggests that some forms of mental functioning – the unconscious, phantasy, memory, etc. – seem to be so. Subjectivity in this account is neither universal nor ahistorical. First structured through relations of absence and loss, pleasure and unpleasure, difference and division, these are simultaneous with the social naming and placing among kin, community, school, class which are always historically specific.

. . .

It is not my intention to reconstruct the individual unconscious, or individual subjectivity (which maybe glimpsed nevertheless by the historian through autobiography, memory or speech). But merely to emphasize that the symbolic sets the terms within which any social group must position itself and conceive of a new social order and that the symbolic has a life of its own. And secondly, that human subjectivity shapes, as it is itself shaped by, political practice and language – it leaves its imprint there.

. . .

Both feminism and psychoanalysis suggest (in different ways), and history appears to confirm their findings, that antagonism between the sexes is an unavoidable aspect of the acquisition of sexual identity, and one that can be explained neither by anatomy nor environment alone. If antagonism is always latent, it is possible that history offers no final resolution, only the constant reshaping, reorganizing of the symbolization of difference, and the sexual division of labour. The questions for the historian of feminism are why at some moments does sexual difference and division take on a political significance – which elements in the organization are politicized, what are the terms of negotiation, and between whom?

RADICALISM AND WOMEN

. . .

If we turn to the 1830s and 1840s with these reflections in mind and ask the question why were some women able to speak of their rights to sexual and economic independence and to deliberate on the formation of the new morality and social order within Owenism and not within contemporary movements of similar class composition undergoing similar experiences of industrial dislocation, then the focus on subjectivity and language is suggestive.

The Short-time Committees from the 1820s, Anti-Poor Law struggles, Owenism and Chartism in the 1830s and 1840s involved women; speaking for the poor, the working classes, the unenfranchised, the dispossessed, they included both sexes and all generations. But if we listen more closely to the common elements in their analysis of discontent and language of aspiration we discover firstly that women could only speak as active subjects at selective moments, and within the community. Men spoke in the first person for the community as a whole when appealing to public opinion; while political demand, communal rights, distribution and dispensation of the law was a dialogue of negotiation between the men of the communities and the ruling class – 'capitalists and lawgivers'. And secondly, the place in the vision of the new social order that these movements afforded women was founded on conceptions of the sexual division of labour, property, laws of inheritance and the relative 'capacities' and status of women and men within marriage prevalent among rural and urban industrial communities from the eighteenth century which had never scrupulously observed the principle of equality between the sexes. Sexual difference was intimately bound up in notions of labour, property and kin in popular radical thought, and through their respective organization women's access to knowledge, skill and independent political subjectivity depended.

When whole communities rebelled against punitive legislation, or the depredation of customary rights, against unemployment or starvation – as they did in different parts of the country through the Factory Movement, Anti-Poor Law campaigns and Chartism – then women rioted, attended public assemblies and processions, formed committees, though women and men were often segregated. In active resistance against proletarianization the political subject was the community and radical rhetoric addressed wives as well as husbands, mothers as well as fathers, female and child labour as well as male. Nevertheless, whenever community resistance was formally organized into democratically elected committees with powers to negotiate with employers, justices of the peace, government representatives, then men were in the forefront and the spokesmen of those committees. Women were excluded from these forms of public speech not through the separation of workshop and home (though their increasing distance did underlie the 'separate spheres' emphasis of nineteenth-century feminist thought, and the different forms of political and industrial organization of women and men in the second half of the nineteenth century) they had been excluded from formal political organization and conceptions of the individual legal, political and economic subject since the end of the seventeenth century.[12]

The legal, political and economic subject in radical popular speech reaching back to the seventeenth-century Levellers, was the propertied individual, and the propertied individual was always masculine – whether head of household, skilled tradesman or artisan whose property was his labour, or the evocation of the Freeborn Briton. Early nineteenth-century radicalism did not so much refer to the 'experience' of the dispossessed communities as draw on the rules of association, the idiom and rhetoric of the leaders of their struggles: the small master craftsmen, the displaced domestic worker, the artisan and mechanic, the skilled factory operatives. Men with a long history of trade association, for whom custom and status as well as skill determined the level of wages, length of the working day, entry to a trade, etc.; for whom the collective wisdom and knowledge of their skill was lodged in the custom and practice of the workshop, and whose authority and control extended through apprenticeship rules to their children and other kin. Skilled men outlining the grievances that fuelled the factory reform movements in the textile districts from the 1820s to the 1840s, the several attempts at general unions, spoke of being 'robbed' or 'disinherited' of the right to practice their trade; of the 'slavery' of the mills; of their resistance to becoming the 'hired servants' of the 'new breed of employers'. The vocabulary of grievance is similar among the tailors, shoe-makers and cabinet makers in London resisting the 'sweating and puffing' system; and it stretches back to the small master clothiers in the North and West of

England who gave evidence to the 1806 Royal Commission on the Woollen Industry, Britain's first and major capitalized industry, and one which employed a majority of women and children through the seventeenth and eighteenth centuries. In the minds of these different groups of male workers their status as fathers and heads of families was indelibly associated with their independence through 'honourable' labour and property in skill, which identification with a trade gave them.[13]

It was as fathers and heads of household that the radical artisan spoke of the loss of parental control and authority over kin, the predatory sexual freedom of the mills, the destruction of 'habits and morals'. Despair and anger still reverberates through the speeches, petitions and addresses to the public, the employers, the people, or Parliament, at the destruction of a whole way of life wrought by the 'despots of capital', the factory, the workhouse or 'class legislation'. But it was the anger of men threatened in their whole being with loss of skill, sexual and economic authority. John Doherty, mule-spinner, radical, factory reformer, trade unionist, commenting on the manufacturer who advertised in a Glasgow newspaper for women to work in his mills:

> If he could not find in his heart to employ, and pay men for doing his work, he should look out for women whose morals are already corrupted, instead of those whose lives are yet pure and spotless. For everyone will admit, that to place persons of both sexes, of fifteen or sixteen years, indiscriminately together, and put them in receipt of 12s and 16s a week, which is entirely at their own disposal, without education and before their habits are fixed, and their reason sufficiently mature to controul (sic) their passions and restrain their appetites...such persons will (not) grow up as chaste, moral and obedient to their parents, as if they had still not remained under the salutary restraint of parental controul (sic). If the practice were to become general, of employing girls and boys instead of men, it could place the son and daughter of fifteen, at the head of the family, to whose whims and caprices the father must bend and succomb, or in many cases starve.[14]

POPULAR POLITICAL ECONOMY

John Doherty and his contemporaries resisted 'capitalists and lawmakers' as deeply because they usurped 'parental controul' as for any change in the work process. Underlying this resistance were the two themes which spanned all visions of a new social order, whether for a General Union of the trades, social regeneration, co-operative communities, or the Charter: labour, as the producer of wealth and knowledge, should receive its just reward; and kinship was the natural and proper relation of morality, authority and law.

The labour theory of value expounded in radical political economy assigned neither labour nor responsible parenthood exclusively to men. Thomas Hodgskin, philosophical anarchist, stated only that labour's share of wealth should provide the

> necessaries and conveniences required for the support of the labourer and his family; or that quantity which is necessary to enable the labourers one with another, to subsist and to perpetuate their race without either increase or diminution.

Skilled labour is the labourer's knowledge, and 'the time necessary to acquire a knowledge of any species of skilled labour. . . is, in many cases, several years.' Hodgskin describes the 'most important operation' in the accumulation and transmission of knowledge and skill – the parent's work in rearing and educating the children:

> The labor (sic) of the parents produces and purchases, with what they receive as wages, all the food and the clothing which the rising generation of labourers use, while they are learning those arts by means of which they will hereafter produce all the wealth of society. For the rearing and educating of all future labourers (of course I do not mean *book* education, which is the smallest and least useful part of all which they have to learn) their parents have no stock stored up beyond their own practical skill. Under the strong influence of natural affections and parental love, they prepare by their toils, continually day after day, and year after year, through all the long period of the infancy and childhood of their offspring, those future labourers who are to succeed to their toils and their hard fare, but who will inherit their productive power, and be what they now are, the main pillars of the social edifice.[15]

Food, clothing, knowledge, love and labour are equally the possessions and gifts of both parents, and theirs equally to pass on to their children. But this was the world as it should be. Utopian thinkers expunged from their vocabulary any privileged relation between men and either skill, or inheritance. But if there was in small rural manufacturing communities or urban crafts and trades, a community of skill and knowledge within families, it was not transmitted in public speech – whether the discourse of bargain and polemic with employers and government, or popular propaganda – as it wasn't in formal organization of the trades and communities. Masculine privilege was embedded in popular conceptions of both skilled labour and authority, and inheritance was through male and not female kin.

Women simply could not speak within these terms. From the mid-eighteenth century, though women were drawn into the informal and intermittent trade associations, they received full authority to practice their craft only through male kin: father, husband, or if a widow, through her eldest son or principal journeyman. Skilled men's unions throughout the nineteenth century excluded women, and the wage 'sufficient to support a wife and children' was the father's and not the mother's. There was reciprocity between the respective 'capacities' of women and men when considered as husbands and wives within a domestic system of industry. But somehow there slips into the discourse of men as they defend or expound that system, an estimation of women as wives, workers and mothers which belies full equality of status. Wives of wool-combers, weavers, cobblers, tailors and all skilled men or small masters 'assisted' their husbands in their trades, besides fulfilling their household duties; with their husbands they 'brought up the children to a trade', until the age of thirteen or fourteen when the child came under the proper supervision of his father or male relative (which girls seldom did). If women's work was mentioned it was described as an 'inferior' sort of work, always with the implication that it required less skill and strength, or even that such a task as picking or burling was done by 'inferior people, women and children', as one witness explained to the 1806 Royal Commission on the Woollen Industry.[16] A woman's skill resided in the household and her property in the virtue of her person. Separated from the home, her family and domestic occupations, or outside the bonds of matrimony, a woman was assured of neither skill nor virtue.

. . .

'The reign of the wife over the husband as inevitably brought about by the factory system' – the 'condition which unsexes the man' – underlined all the polemic and rhetoric deployed by working class movements against the 'new breed of employers', the 'capitalist lords and despots'.[17] Those who have studied the literature of grievance in the history of the industrial revolution are familiar with the lament of skilled men threatened with loss of skill and knowledge by the factory or sweatshop, and made anxious about the destruction of the family and the home by the competition of the wives and children.[18] The motivation was not in any simple sense class-war, nor the pursuit of economic self-interest, nor even (at least not in every case?) the conscious desire to dominate their women – but to posit a vision of the social organization of labour centred around kin and the household which permitted natural affections and love as well as skill to flow simultaneously from domestic and working life; which allowed for a continuing dialogue between 'masters and men'; and which enabled the 'natural differences and capacities' of the sexes to determine the division of labour between wife and husband, male and female labourer. This was a language of grievance which embraced moral and sexual orders as well as economic discontents – social preoccupations which became severed in political demands within the labour movement (but not the feminist) in the later nineteenth century.[19] In the early nineteenth century this vision was posed again and again by representatives of the working classes as a mode of industrial organization which had once been there, that was natural and that was being wantonly destroyed by capital and the government.

We come closer to grasping the reasons for the emergence of a feminist voice within Owenism and not within other working class movements (or not in a sustained form) if we consider briefly their political diagnosis and strategy, and secondly their different social visions and the implications of these for the nature and place of women and men.

THE PEOPLE'S CHARTER

'Fellow Country Women', the Female Political Union of Newcastle upon Tyne declared in 1843,

> we entreat you to join us to help the cause of freedom, justice, honesty and truth, to drive poverty and ignorance from our land, and establish happy homes, true religion, righteous government, and good laws.[20]

The plea could have been made by Parson Bull, belligerent enemy of the new Poor Law and its implementation in the North of England at the end of the 1830s, Richard Oastler, Tory Radical and 'King' of the factory operative and starving hand-loom weaver (whose motto was 'The Altar, the Throne and the Hearth'), or any one of the many radical men active in those campaigns. Chartism was a mass movement of women as well as men which united all those movements against 'bad laws and unjust legislators'. Richard Pilling's defence speech at his trial in Lancaster in 1843 on a charge of seditious conspiracy, reveals the overlapping of grievance and aspirations in those struggles.

> Suppose, gentlemen of the jury, you were obliged to subsist on the paltry pittance given to us in the shape of wages, and had a wife and six helpless children...to support, how would you feel? Though you were to confine me to a dungeon I should not submit to it. I have a nervous wife – a good wife – a dear wife – a wife that I love and cherish, and I have done everything that I could in the way of resisting reductions in wages that I might keep her and my children from the workhouse, for I detest parish relief. It is wages I want. I want to be independent of every man and that is the principle of every man in this court...it has been a wage question with me. And I do say that if Mr. O'Connor has made it a chartist question he has done wonders to make it extend through England, Ireland, and Scotland. But it was always a wage question, and ten hours bill with me.[21]

The women of Newcastle did not demand independence; their interests were those of their 'fathers, husbands and brothers', and their place was in the home, from which they had been torn by poverty and the 'scorn of the rich' who, 'not content with despising our feelings...demand the control of our thoughts and wants'. The People's Charter mobilized the whole of the labouring population behind its demand for universal suffrage, and, at moments, shopkeepers and tradesmen, as well as humanitarian philanthropists, though it deleted women from that universality,

> lest the false estimate man entertains of this half of the human family may cause his ignorance and prejudice to be enlisted to retard the progress of his own freedom.

Those women who acquiesced in their exclusion did so because they shared the social visions of their men. 'Love of God, and hatred of wrong' compelled the women of Newcastle to 'assist' their men to have the 'Charter (made) into a law and emancipate the white slaves of England'.[22] Dorothy Thompson has documented women's participation in Chartism (as well as its ambivalence on the question of women's suffrage):

> (women) joined in protests and action against the police, the established Church, the exploitation of employers and the encroachments of the state. They articulated their grievances sometimes in general political terms, basing their case on appeals to former laws and to natural rights, sometimes in ethical or religious terms, appealing to the Bible for the legitimation of protest.[23]

It was these last – natural rights and Biblical Law – which together with the evocation of a golden age always prove insecure foundations for equality between the sexes.

THE GOLDEN AGE: THE LAW OF NATURE AND THE LAW OF GOD

Chartism appealed for a return to a golden age, or at least to an imagined Eden before 1832 'invaded' the civil liberties of the people (in Disraeli's and Oastler's phrase), introducing 'class legislation', and before the factory system reduced the working classes to slavery and impoverishment. For Chartists the association of the working classes was one which clung to a hope of industrial organization rooted in the household and kinship, and based on the land. The appeal to the land always evokes, when it recurs in popular ideologies, a lost and more egalitarian past, one closer to natural sources of affection, feeling and community. The place of women in that evocation seldom escapes submission. The tendency is – and I'm oversimplifying – to place women closer to nature and the animal world, distancing them from human law and knowledge. Somehow women are placed under a different law from men because of their natural function and capacity. Men become the natural protectors and defenders of women, whose place is in the home, with their children, providing those comforts which – to quote the Newcastle women again – 'our hearts told us should greet our husbands after their fatiguing labours'. Women's exclusion from independent political subjectivity is then a consequence of their different capacity and place. Valued for their household skills and domestic virtue as part of the family under the protection of men, independence is almost inconceivable.

. . .

Such a highlighting of sexual difference cannot help but undermine the demand for political equality between women and men, especially when that difference is given a divine authorization. Christian humanitarianism – of all denominations – distinguished the emotional fervour of much popular oratory and polemic. The law of the Bible was employed to defend the rights and liberties of the working man against the 'Church, the Throne and the Aristocracy', who would 'rob the poor man' not only of his liberty but also 'of his wife and of his children'.[24] The social vision of the Chartists met the political and economic critique of Whiggery and Utilitarianism expounded by the Tory democrats. The meeting point was women: the protection of the rights of the 'weakest and most defenceless, the widow and the fatherless'; a social order in which each person had her or his special place, and the appeal to a benevolent Constitution whose executive exercised political power with responsibility, always with care for the freedoms and liberties and rights of the people – a people for whom only men could speak publicly.

A NEW MORAL WORLD

Owenism differed from radicalism in the possibilities it offered women. Determinedly secular, Owenism envisaged a new science of human nature and promised to revolutionize emotions and feelings as well as labour and law. Since environment not God or nature made character, environment could be changed. There was nothing natural in the sexual division of labour, nor in the 'despotic' rule of wives by their husbands. The confinement of women to 'domestic drudgery' was an unjust usurpation of human freedom and female capacity (the difference between the radicals and the Owenites echoes the quarrel between Rousseau and Mary Wollstonecraft). The only natural aspect of the relation between the sexes was the flow of sensuality, the 'sacred pleasures of the flesh', about which, as Barbara Taylor drily points out, female Owenites were more circumspect on the whole (except those fleeing tyrannical husbands or living the life of the 'liberated libido') than men. The Owenites imagined a whole New Moral World. Theirs was a vocabulary of transcendence not negotiation; there was neither a longing to return to a golden past, nor any submission to the natural laws of the market. Owenism reached out for new social forms which would displace industrial competitive society with co-operative modes of work, egalitarian communities, a reformed marriage and a new religion of reason and universal love. As Barbara Taylor has so ably and eloquently argued, utopian socialism promised the liberation of all humanity at once, of all human relations and social institutions.[25] Egalitarian and democratic in spirit if not always in practice, some women found a voice for their discontents and desires as women there. It was a vision of progress and a renewed humanity; a language of community and co-operation which only sometimes foundered on the democratic rights of the individual.

A new science of human nature, a new moral world, these were more fertile soil for feminism – the independent voice of women demanding equality with men and their full inclusion in humanity – than natural order and natural difference. And Owenism's vision of transcendence (anticipating the millenarianism of the late nineteenth-century women's suffrage movement) invited some women to imagine a full emancipation, for it was partly through negotiation with existing law and government that equality or reciprocity between women and men within working class movements – or their public political discourses collapsed.

Natural differences between the sexes could easily slip into a relation of inequality between women and men as the possibility of a domestic system of industry, with a family of labourers and household economy, faded, and with that fading the dialogue between masters and men, who sometimes addressed each other as 'men, as husbands, as fathers, as friends and Christians', hardened into the confrontations between capital and labour. Symptomatic of the changing class relations is the changing value and status of 'female labour' as it moved in and out of the home, and in and out of those modes of address. The equivocation of political discourse of working class movements on the questions of 'female labour' is illustrated by John Doherty's prevarications. Imprisoned for obstructing the use of female 'knobsticks' to break a strike of spinners in Glasgow in 1818, a leader of the mule spinners through the 1820s and early 1830s, he opposed the 'cotton lords' use of female labour to undercut the men. Men's resistance to women spinners – justified on grounds of their lesser strength and skill – was part of the struggle against machinery and an attempt to retain a notion of apprenticeship, which, as Doherty conceded to the Select Committee into the Combinations of Workmen in 1838, did not 'exist formally, but it does frightfully to the workmen'. And Doherty suggests to the same Committee that men's monopoly in mule spinning (except in Glasgow where there had been strikes for equal pay) should be extended to the wheel (prevalent in Manchester). He agreed that women's employment in the mills had a 'bad effect on morals and domestic habits', and that the greater strength required on wheels in Manchester would 'shortly put women out'. On the other hand, Doherty, a humanitarian and Owenite, as well as a trades unionist, addressing the London tailors in an article in May 1834, both condemned the 'dastardly strategem' of hiring female labour to replace the men, and urged on the tailors that this undercutting would not be possible if they themselves acknowledge 'the natural equality of women; include them in all your schemes of improvement, and raise them as high in the sense of scale and independence as yourselves'.[26] But natural difference fitted ill with 'natural equality'.

MALE FEARS AND FEMALE LABOUR

The spectacle of female labour aroused the deepest fears among many different sectors of public opinion in the mid nineteenth century – alerted as they were by a prolific and diverse literature to the 'condition of England' question. The disintegration and demoralization of the working class family in the midst of economic growth and imperial power haunted social consciences among both Whigs and Tories as they pondered the possibility of social revolution. This fusion of anxiety is less surprising when we remember that what women stood for was not simply domestic virtue and household skills, but sexual ordering itself. If men represented – to such different groups as radical artisans, Tory democrats, utilitarian legislators – labour, then what woman represented first of all was sexuality – which, if not harnessed to reproduction threatened sexual anarchy and chaos (epithets applied to both the prostitute and the militant feminist in Victorian England). Men's desire to confine women to their proper place must be understood – at least in part – as a desire to (legally) control and (morally) order sexuality. Women's capacity to bear children – if infused with divine sanction – makes her one with God in creating life. 'It is bad enough if you corrupt the man', Lord Shaftesbury declared to a silent House of Commons as he introduced the bill banning women's underground work in the mines, 'but if you corrupt the woman, you poison the waters of life at the very fountain.'[27] It was the power of this thought that eventually persuaded even such die-hard opponents of the Ten-Hour Day as Peel to, if not relent, at least adhere to the principle of the protection of women. *The Northern Star* put their case on female labour in the mines rather more bluntly:

> Keep them at home to look after their families; decrease the pressure on the labour market and there is then some chance of a higher rate of wages being enforced.[28]

Through the history of wage labour female labour has meant cheap labour to working-class men, and the threat of cheap labour sets sexual antagonism, always latent between women and men, into livid activity at the workplace and in the unions. Reorganization of the labour process produced continual shifts in the sexual division of labour, provoking anxiety about the destruction of the home and family which were imprinted in the language of popular resistance since the late eighteenth century. There is a sense in which the vocabulary and rhetoric of the radical artisan evoked a memory of a past that was never there – except in aspiration. It nevertheless retains still a powerful hold over the political imagination of the labour movement, bequeathing a vocabulary of loss and nostalgia to working-class struggle. The appeal to the family, home and hearth and women's place beside it is its conservative edge – though the yearning for harmony and for sources of emotional satisfaction for which they stand are more tenacious. The labour theory of value remains alive in the labour movement, too, lending weight to men's demands for a family wage. But except when held within egalitarian principles of community and equal rights of women and men in marriage, the notion of the family wrapped up in that theory was (and is) inimical to the 'full and complete' emancipation of women. For whereas for men the threat of cheap labour means *loss* of employment, status and skill, to women workers their cheapness represents *lack* of independence, status and skill. Feminism's demand for work, training, and economic independence has always unnerved the male dominated labour movement, while 'lack' of those things permeates the idiom of nineteenth-century feminism. Ironically what women lacked became one of the defining features of femininity, and on the shop-floor, in the unions and working-class political parties this lack could become politically divisive. In fact, women's special needs received short shrift in the labour movement, whether femininity was defined positively as motherhood, or negatively as lack. The former produced demands for birth control, family endowment, easier divorce – which never received more than a luke-warm reception in the labour movement as a whole until the late 1930s; and the latter produced the demands for equal pay, equal right to skill and training, to which men's response was always the reassertion of their status as breadwinners for the family.

I am not suggesting that the public speech of skilled men as they addressed their employers, the public or the government, was the only form of popular discourse. That communities imposed their own moral laws, as well as conceptions of the value of women's and men's different social skills and responsibilities is certain. And women themselves often spoke a different reality. But we capture only fragments of those customs. Many of them were conveyed through oral traditions destroyed (if not altogether lost or forgotten) by the swell in population, movements into the towns, destruction of crafts and dismantlement of apprenticeship rules, wage controls, etc. What we are witnessing from a distance is the uneven erosion of local cultures and the submergence of political communities into a political order which through representative government gradually (and unwillingly) drew the individual into a contract with national government. The process was uneven and did not immediately replace other forms of communal relations of power and law, but increasingly came to dominate all public political discourse as the Parliamentary legislature became more intrusive and claimed to be the seat of representative democracy.

Whatever their intentions, the Chartists by deleting women, the factory reformers by submitting to the principle of the protection of women and every working class custom, insofar as it refused an equal status to women within the class, placed women in a different relationship to the state than men.[29] Women fell under the protection of their fathers, husbands or Parliament and were denied an independent political subjectivity. When feminism emerged as a self-conscious and sometimes mass political movement of women in the nineteenth century it was to demand economic independence and the full rights and duties of citizenship – to combat the exclusion of women from a 'common humanity' and women's lack of masculine privilege. Women's protest gathered force until nothing less than the 'whole world of labour' and nothing short of Womanhood suffrage would satisfy the most radical feminists. Both women and the working class emerged in the 1840s, two universal social and political categories which demanded universal rights and liberties in, as Ethel Snowden, feminist and socialist, carefully phrased it – 'all those matters of their common humanity where sex does not enter and impose an impassible barrier'.[30] But if there is nothing 'impassible' about the social ordering of sexual difference, representing difference as a relation of equality in language through political culture was – and remains – elusive.

ACKNOWLEDGEMENTS

Raphael Samuel's provocative criticism and enthusiasm helped me in the writing of this essay. Gareth Stedman Jones and Barbara Taylor have been both critical and encouraging. Special thanks to Tony Wailey and Kate Shuckburgh.

NOTES

1 Shulamith Firestone, *The Dialectics of Sex*, London 1971. Kate Millett, *Sexual Politics*, New York 1970. For a survey of feminist theories of patriarchy, see Veronica Beechey, 'On Patriarchy', *Feminist Review*, no. 3, 1979, pp. 66–83.

For a disagreement among feminist historians, see Sheila Rowbotham, Sally Alexander, Barbara Taylor, 'Debate on Patriarchy', ed. Raphael Samuel, *People's History and Socialist Theory*, London 1983.

2 Histories of the suffrage movement pursue a fairly straightforward narrative of the achievement of women's suffrage. The more comprehensive histories focus on the intellectual components of feminist thought, and the class composition of the feminists. There is a general consensus: the former derives from Protestant individualism, Enlightenment thought and philanthropy; and the feminists were overwhelmingly middle class (e.g. Richard Evans, *The Feminists*, London 1977; Olive Banks, *Faces of Feminism*, Oxford 1981). Feminism's middle-class character has led to its neglect by socialist historians. A valuable exception is Juliet Mitchell, 'Women and Equality', in eds J. Mitchell and A. Oakley, *The Rights and Wrongs of Women*, Pelican 1976, pp. 379–99. No recent histories of British feminism have surpassed two classic studies: Ray Strachey's *The Cause*, 1928, and Sylivia Pankhurst's *The Suffragette Movement*, 1931, both reprinted by Virago. Written by protagonists in the Cause, both view the struggle as a study in human progress. Ray Strachey, a liberal/socialist, gives a brief but comprehensive survey of the Women's Movement from the mid nineteenth to the 1920s. Despite Sylvia Pankhurst's tendency to shape her narrative around the achievements of her family (beginning with her father), *The Suffragette Movement* is nevertheless a mine of information on the early radical, socialist and labour movements, is full of fascinating thumb-nail portraits and packed with analysis. The reader is swept along by the messianic vision of the author, the elements of idealism, sacrifice and martyrdom that characterized the 'Cause'.

3 Keith Thomas, 'Women and the Civil War Sects', *Past and Present*, no. 13, 1958, pp. 42–57. Christopher Hill, *The World Turned Upside Down*, London 1972, chapter 15.

4 For a feminist reading of the GNCTU, Barbara Taylor, *Eve and the New Jerusalem*, London 1983, chapter 4.

5 For a recent example of that 'stretching', Ellen Ross, 'Survival Networks: Women's Neighbourhood Sharing in London before World War One', *HWJ*, Spring 1983, issue 15, pp. 4–28.

6 Karl Marx, 'Preface to a Contribution to the Critique of Political Economy', Marx and Engels, *Selected Works*, London 1970, pp. 180–5, is the most succinct statement.

7 V.I. Lenin, *What is to be Done*? Moscow 1969.

8 E.P. Thompson, *The Making of the English Working Class*, Pelican, 1968. The Preface.

9 Juliet Mitchell, *Psychoanalysis and Feminism*, London 1974, Introduction p. XV.

10 Juliet Mitchell's Introduction in, eds J. Mitchell and J. Rose, *Feminine Sexuality, Jacques Lacan and the École Freudienne*, London 1983, p. 5.

11 The use I make to Lacan's Freud, and the significance of language in the production of meaning and the construction of the subject are my own responsibility. Useful essays are Jacques Lacan, 'The Function and Field of Speech and Language in Psychoanalysis', and 'The Agency of the Letter in the Unconscious or Reason Since Freud', *Ecrits*, London 1980, pp. 30–113, 146–78. E. Benveniste, *Problems in General Linguistics*, Miami 1971, chs. 19, 20 and 22. Ferdinand de Saussure. *Course on General Linguistics*, London 1981.

12 I am only speaking of the *public* political speech of these movements. While these do not and cannot convey less accessible forms of popular consciousness,

many of which transmitted through oral traditions, myth, ritual, etc. have been lost or forgotten, public political discourse nevertheless indicates some incidents of popular identification. Dorothy Thompson's essay, 'Women in Nineteenth-Century Radical Politics', in eds J. Mitchell and A. Oakley, *The Rights and wrongs of Women*, Pelican 1976, pp. 112–38, has shaped discussion around women's participation in working class movements in the first half of the nineteenth century. Lin Shaw, 'Women in Working Class Politics in Norwich', paper given to the Feminist History Group, London, December 1979, covered forms and content of working class politics in detail and related their decline to the changing local political and industrial structure of Norwich in the second half of the nineteenth century.

13 See for example the many reports on The Handloom Weavers and industrial populations in the 1830s and 1840s. And in particular, Report and Minutes of Evidence of the Select Committee on the State of the Woollen Manufacture in England, P.P. 1806, vol. 3, and Report from the Select Committee to examine Petitions from Hand-Loom Weavers, P.P. 1834, vol. 10.

14 R.G. Kirby, A.E. Musson, *The Voice of the People, John Doherty, 1798–1854*, Manchester 1975, p. 73. Neil J. Smelser's *Social Change in the Industrial Revolution*, London 1979 is often criticized by historians for its dense methodology, mechanistic model of change, and specific inaccuracies. The central hypothesis, however, that operatives grew restless as kinship ties were severed in the reorganization of the labour process is suggestive in the context of this essay. Jane Humphries in 'Class Struggle and the Persistence of the Working-Class Family', *Cambridge Journal of Economics*, 1977, 1, pp. 241–58, and Protective Legislation, the Capitalist State and Working Class Men: The Case of the 1842 Mines Regulation Act', *Feminist Review*, no. 19, Spring 1982, argues that the resilience of the working-class family stems in part from men's defence of 'an institution which affects their standard of living, class cohesion and ability to wage the class struggle'.

15 Thomas Hodgskin, *Labour Defended Against the Claims of Capital*, 1825, reprinted London 1922, pp. 31, 48, 50.

16 Lin Shaw describes the Norwich weaver's political economy (drawn from Hodgskin) as including the demand for a wage to support a wife and three children. Adam Smith, *The Wealth of Nations*, Chicago ed. 1976, pp. 76–7, suggests 'the husband and wife together' must earn sufficient to raise four children, on the expectation that two will die, but implies that the woman's wage will only have to support herself. Smith's political economy was approved by radical working men; it was the infusion of Malthusianism into political economy that provoked hostility. For a discussion of the 'family wage' in the transition from manufacture to modern industry see Sally Alexander, *Women's Work in Nineteenth-Century London*, London 1983, pp. 20–32. For women's exclusion from skill and workmen's organizations, Ivy Pinchbeck, *Women Workers and the Industrial Revolution, 1750–1850*, London 1969, pp. 126–7; for examples of women weaving with husbands, fathers, etc., A.P. Wadsworth and J. De Lacy Mann, *The Cotton Trade and Industrial Lancashire, 1600–1780*, Manchester 1965, pp. 332, 336. For women in the early textile unions, Wadsworth and Mann, Chapter 18; H.A. Turner, *Trade Union Growth Structure and Policy*, London 1962, Parts II, III and IV. For the masculine language and character of the early Trade Unions, A. Aspinall, *The Early English Trade Unions*, London 1949.

17 F. Engels, *The Condition of the Working Class in 1844*, in K. Marx and F. Engels, *On Britain*, Moscow 1962, pp. 177–9.

18 For example, the skilled tailor speaking to Henry Mayhew quoted in S. Alexander, *Women's Work in Nineteenth-Century London*, pp. 31–2.

19 Michael Ignatieff, 'Marxism and classical political economy' in, ed. R. Samuel, *People's History and Socialist Theory*, London 1981, pp. 344–52, describes the similar narrowing of preoccupations as political economy became an economic science in the mid-nineteenth century.

20 'Address of the Female Political Union of Newcastle upon Tyne to their Fellow Countrywomen', in ed. D. Thompson, *The Early Chartists*, London 1971, p. 130.

21 Richard Pilling's Defence, from the *Trial of Fergus O'Connor and 58 other Chartists on a Charge of Seditious Conspiracy at Lancaster*, 1843, ed. F. O'Connor. I'm grateful to Eileen Yeo for this reference.

22 Address of the Female Union, *The Early Chartists*, II, 128–9. For a fuller discussion of the political language of Chartism, Gareth Stedman Jones, 'The Language of Chartism', ed. James Epstein and D. Thompson, *The Chartist Experience*, London 1972, pp. 3–58. The wording of the 1838 Charter is worth quoting in full: 'Among the suggestions we received for improving this Charter, is one for embracing women among the possession of the franchise. Against this reasonable proposition we have no just arguments to adduce, but only to express our fears of entertaining it, lest the false estimate man entertains of this half of the human family may cause his ignorance and prejudice to be enlisted to retard the progress of his own freedom. And therefore, we deem it far better to lay down just principles, and look forward to the rational improvement of society, than to entertain propositions which may retard the measure we wish to promote.' *Address of the Working Men's Association to the Radical Reformers of Great Britain and Ireland*, London 1838, p. 9. Whether the false estimate is attributed to their fellow working men, or their representatives in Parliament is not clear.

23 D. Thompson, 'Women in Nineteenth-Century Radical Politics', p. 131.

24 Cecil Driver, *Tory Radical. The Life of Richard Oastler*, Oxford 1946, p. 434, but see whole of chapter 32 for Oastler's Tory democracy.

25 Barbara Taylor, 'Lords of Creation', *New Statesman*, 7 March 1980, pp. 361–2, and G. Stedman Jones, 'Utopian Socialism Reconsidered', unpub. MS, 1979, B. Taylor, *Eve and the New Jerusalem*, ch. 2 for a discussion of Owenite ideas on the position of women.

26 Minutes of Evidence, Select Committee on Combinations of Workmen, P.P. 1838, vol. 8, p. 263; *The Voice of the People*, p. 299, and passim.

27 Quoted in Pinchbeck, *Women Workers*, p. 267.

28 Angela John, *By the Sweat of their Brow, Women Workers at Victorian Coal Mines*, London 1981, p. 57. Those for and against the Factory Acts did not divide along party lines. By the 1840s there was universal agreement that female labour should be protected; the argument in Parliament was how best that intervention should be made. Samuel Kydd (pseud. Alfred), *The History of the Factory Movement*, London 1857, is the most interesting discussion of contemporary political opinion as it divided between those who interpreted the laws of nature and revelations with benevolence (e.g. pp. 117, 118 and 208) and those who feared the dangers of intervening in the freedom of labour, and all opinion in between (esp. ch. 15).

29 Intentions are blurred, but whereas the working men delegates from the factory districts celebrated their victory in 1847 with the following resolution: 'That we are deeply thankful to Almighty God for the success which has on all occasions attended our efforts in this sacred cause, and especially for the final result of all

our labours, by which the working classes are now put in possession of their long-sought-for-measure – The Ten Hours Bill'; their friends in parliament reaffirmed their hopes that the increased leisure won would be used for 'mental and moral improvement' and especially that the female factory operatives would promote and improve their 'domestic habits'. *The Ten Hours Advocate*, ed. Philip Grant, for the Lancashire Short-Time Committee, 1846–7, pp. 300–1.

30 Ethel Snowden, *The Feminist Movement*, London n.d. (1911), p. 258.

3

Catherine Hall

Private Persons versus Public Someones: Class, Gender and Politics in England, 1780–1850

In 1810, Martha Syms, the daughter of an Evangelical clergyman, was writing to her father from India, where she was living with her husband who was in the Indian army. 'Syms desires me to present to you his best regards', she wrote, continuing, 'and to add that he perfectly coincides with you in the political opinion contained in your last letter, I do not understand and therefore do not enter into these subjects myself.'[1] Martha's assumption, that she did not understand political matters and would not risk expressing a political opinion, was one that was shared by many middle-class women in the early nineteenth century. But the process whereby that assumption came to be shared is one that is worth examining. Dorothy Thompson has explored the ways in which working-class women became marginalized in radical politics in the 1830s and 1840s and has demonstrated the extent to which that marginalization was associated with the increasing formalization of working-class politics.[2] Barbara Taylor has analysed the problems involved with developing a socialist-feminist politics in the 1820s and 1830s and the decline of that politics as industrial capitalism established a more stable base and ideologies about masculinity and femininity became more rigidly defined.[3] But both these case studies deal with the experience of working-class women in relation to politics and as yet the experience of middle-class women has been relatively neglected. The entry of middle-class women into politics has tended to be constructed in terms of their entry into organized feminist movements in the mid-nineteenth century, with an assumption that between Mary Wollstonecraft and early Victorian forms of feminism little happened other than a few hiccups on the radical sidelines. It would be possible to construct this period rather differently and to see it as one in which a whole set of ideologies and social practices developed which saw middle-class women as essentially non-political beings, belonging to the private rather than the public sphere, having at most a supportive role to play in the rapidly expanding political world of their fathers, husbands and brothers. The ways in which such definitions were built into political institutions and related social practices ensured that the barriers against women thinking or acting politically were very extensive.

At one level the exclusion of middle-class women from the public world of politics is hardly surprising. After all, women never had been very involved in the political sphere. But neither had middle-class men. Their active involvement in the political process was a development largely associated with the late eighteenth and early nineteenth centuries. It was also an involvement of their own making, fought for and insisted upon in a society which had traditionally only legitimated the rights of the landed to be directly represented. After 1832 that legitimation was extended to all those men with sufficient property to ensure that their voices should be heard. It was in 1832 that for the first time the prefix 'male' was inserted into the act defining the right to a vote, thus making crystal clear something which had always been assumed previously, that in naming the propertied as those with the vote it was men of property who were being demarcated, not women. This process, of defining middle-class men as within the political arena and middle-class women as outside of it, did not simply happen by default. It is undoubtedly true that had a demand been made for the inclusion of women it would have been even more surprising, and certainly very much harder to achieve, than the demand on behalf of men. But many precedents were broken and assumptions challenged in the struggle by manufacturers, merchants, professional men and farmers to win the vote for themselves. The process whereby women were marginalized from that struggle needs explaining and documenting, rather than being assumed.

The late eighteenth and early nineteenth centuries marked a period of transition in English society when traditional values and beliefs were subjected to attack and criticism. Established social hierarchies were breaking down and common-sense notions being turned upside down. It was in this context that middle-class men articulated their new demand for representation. This was a demand which did not grow naturally by a process of evolution, but rather was forged out of the recognition that political influence was a necessary concomitant to their economic power. In the same way, there was nothing 'natural' about the process whereby women were not included in that demand. Certainly it coincided with custom. But middle-class men were busy challenging custom in other arenas. Customary patterns about gender divisions were reworked in this period of transition. It was in that re-working that men were firmly placed in the newly defined public world of business, commerce and politics; women were placed in the private world of home and family.

Wherever public power has been separated from private power women have tended to be excluded from that public power.[4] As Rosaldo and Lamphere show in their anthropological work, those societies in which men and women inhabit the same domain tend to exhibit more egalitarian patterns of power and authority.[5] Historically the same patterns can be illustrated. In Roman society, for example, where there was a clear concept of public power, women were expressly excluded from it. In Carolingian times, however, there was scarcely any distinction between public and private power and consequently few restrictions on the power of women in any spheres of activity. It was landed families which were central to the exercise of power, rather than the state. Sons and daughters were able to share inheritance and some women were able to exercise considerable power. As the machinery of government was gradually developed and some control wrested from the aristocracy, so the influence of women declined. It was difficult for them to become part of the new state bureaucracies in the way men did.[6]

The early nineteenth century marked a point when the division between public and private became very highly demarcated. The notion of the division between public and private was an old established one but it always has to be understood as historically specific and socially constructed.[7] In classical Greece, for example, the public or *polis* was seen as purely political; it was separated from both production and reproduction. Both production and reproduction were centred on the household, but political life was carried on by a small number of adult male citizens who depended on women and slaves to provide for their social and economic needs. The Greek household, with its many functions, was seen as the private sphere. Such a narrow definition of the public would have been mysterious to Victorian men and women who understood the public as including the world of business and commerce, the market, and the world of politics. The private, on the other hand, was the haven from the anxieties of the market, and was constituted around the home and family. This notion of public and private was itself significantly re-worked from the late eighteenth century. Adam Smith, for example, conceptualized the market, governed as it was by freely made contracts, as part of the private, different from those public elements in life which were governed by the state.[8]

This re-formulation of the public and the private was to do with making sense of a world which was changing very rapidly and in which pre-existing definitions and boundaries no longer fitted very well. Central to this was the development of the market and of wage labour and the subsequent decline of paternalism in its eighteenth-century form. The social relations of industrial capitalism were not easily contained within a pre-industrial mode of thought. Not surprisingly, however, the traditions of classical liberal theory remained very important in the struggle to establish new values and beliefs. The work of Hobbes and Locke, resting squarely as it did on the notion of theoretical individualism, at least in the public sphere, had marked the initial course. They were both concerned to critique and undermine the case made by Filmer for the divine right of kings – which rested on a notion of patriarchal power as natural and given by God. The line of command for Filmer passed from God to the king and then to the father in the household. He insisted on an analogy between kingly civil authority and husbandly familial power. There was no split between the public and the private – the family was politicized and the state familiarized. Hobbes and Locke both rejected familial authority as the paradigm for political authority and rejected divine sanction in favour of rationality. Locke saw the development of rationality as going together with a split between public and private. Reason was for him separate from passion. Reason existed in the public world, where individuals were free and equal and made contracts. Passion or desire survived in the private world, a world in which contracts and rationality had no place. In arguing against Filmer's case for patriarchy Locke had presented women almost as men's equals for he claimed that both male and female parents had power over children. He claimed that the fifth commandment called for the child to honour his father and his mother and that the father should do nothing to discourage respect for the mother. But although he used parental equality to combat absolutism in the political realm he concluded elsewhere that there was a natural foundation to the customary and legal subjection of wives to their husbands. He assumed that fathers would represent the interests of their families in the wider society. For both Hobbes and Locke the fundamental subject matter of political philosophy was not the adult human individual but the male-headed family.[9]

Locke's argument that women by consenting to marriage gave up their civil rights to their male protectors was mirrored by Rousseau's views on the distinctiveness of male and female characteristics.[10] And Rousseau was another powerful influence on late eighteenth- and early nineteenth-century thinking. Rousseau understood women as being defined by their natural procreative functions. He categorized man in terms of his limitless potential for rationality and for abstract thought. Women were seen as physical and sensual, deficient in rationality and incapable of rational thought. The nuclear family and patriarchy were both seen by Rousseau as natural. The sexes were complementary and man was free to become whatever he could or would whilst women were defined in terms of their capacity to bear children. Men were to do, whilst women were to be, as Charlotte Brontë put it.[11] Rousseau had no notion of citizenship for women; their influence should be exercised through their husbands.

The assumption that women should be represented politically by their husbands or fathers, whether it descended from the classical English philosophical tradition or through the French, continued to govern thinking about the political position of women in the late eighteenth and early nineteenth centuries. Fox, the great Radical, when asked why it was that women should not have the vote, replied that nature and convention had made women dependent on men and, therefore, 'their voices would be governed by the relations in which they stand to society'.[12] This view, enunciated in 1797, was little different from that of Hannah More, whose conservative thinking was central to the emergence of Evangelicalism in the 1780s and 1790s as a powerful social and political force.[13] It was reiterated in 1824 by James Mill in his *Essay on Government*:

> One thing is pretty clear, that all those individuals whose interests are indisputably included in those of other individuals, may be struck off without inconvenience. In this light may be viewed all children up to a certain age, whose interests are involved in those of their parents. In this light also, women may be regarded, the interest of almost all of whom is involved either in that of their fathers or in that of their husbands.[14]

Mill's formulation caused considerable offence at the time but the position he enunciated was widely accepted. As the *Edinburgh Review* was to put it, women should be represented politically *in* their families.[15] The commonsensical character of the view that women should be represented by men is even reflected in Harriet Martineau's novel *Deerbrook* where the two sisters Hester and Margaret accept unquestioningly the political wisdom and principles of Hester's husband Edward, who by voting against the interests of the landlord in a county election finds himself ostracized and his practice as a doctor almost destroyed. They are proud to see Edward representing their principles for them.[16] As Harriet Martineau herself commented, 'I want to be doing something with the pen, since no other means of action in politics are in a woman's power.'[17] Such a view co-existed comfortably with the definition of women as exercising power through a beneficial moral influence over men – a view which was again held by both conservative and feminist thinkers. Hannah More, Mary Wollstonecraft and Harriet Martineau could all have agreed on the central importance of women's influence.

The issue of the vote for women was not a central political issue in this period; indeed it hardly surfaced until mid-century when the suffrage societies began to be organised. One explanation for the lateness of the emergence of this issue lies in the existing assumptions which have been mapped out here. Another important explanation, however, focuses on the activities of middle-class men and the ways in which they moved towards the struggle for the vote. Merchants, professionals and the 'middling sort' had, in the late seventeenth and the eighteenth centuries, tended to rely on influence and pressure on their MPs to get their views represented in Parliament. The City of London had its own representatives, as did the established boroughs. But in the rapidly expanding industrial provincial towns such as Birmingham, Manchester and Sheffield the commercial interests had to rely on the county members to make their voice heard. As the 'middling sort' became increasingly important, and as the old established client economy gradually began to break down in the face of the broadening of the market and the growth of liquid forms of capital, so these commercial men began to seek more independence from the patronage and power of the aristocracy. 'Traders and merchants saw independence not as freedom conferred by landed property but as. . . freedom from the economic political control of the patricians', as John Brewer has put it.[18] Joseph Priestley, the Unitarian scientist and theologian, was one of the most influential voices articulating the new demands of the 'middling sort'. 'A sense of political and civil liberty', he wrote,

> though there should be no great occasion to exert it in course of a man's life, gives him a constant feeling of his own power and importance, and is the foundation of his indulging a free, bold and manly turn of thinking, unrestrained by the most distant idea of control.[19]

The connections made here between political rights, power, control and manliness were to become part of the rhetoric of middle-class men's politics in the early nineteenth century.

The 'middling sort', who probably constituted roughly one-seventh of the English population, began during the eighteenth century to separate themselves both socially and politically from those above them and those below them. Crucial to this process of the establishment of an independent social and political identity were the clubs. There were clubs of every kind, from masonic lodges to clubs for drinking, for singing or for organising the raising of capital. The economic and social functions of such clubs were always closely intermixed, since in a period before the development of a commercial and financial infrastructure arrangements for credit and other forms of economic support relied on family first, but second on friends. The existence of such clubs and voluntary societies gave their members a sense of collective identity such as they had not previously enjoyed. The power of this collective sense was well illustrated by the support for Wilkes, which relied heavily for its orchestration on the clubs. In less troubled times many of the societies 'boasted of the way in which they united Anglicans and dissenters, men from different trades, merchants and gentlemen, whigs and tories, in a common association, promoting unanimity and harmony where only conflict had previously existed.'[20] The atmosphere of these clubs is well evoked by a painting of 'Freeth's Circle', a group of Birmingham men who met regularly in the pub run by Freeth for a pint, a pipe and a chat. The twelve men are represented as sitting around the table with their drinks and tobacco, ready for any discussion. Such convivial evenings were characterized by being exclusively male; these were not the kinds of occasions at which women were welcome. James Bisset, a Birmingham japanner and member of Freeth's circle, recalled in his memoirs his membership of a whole range of groups of this kind:

> [We] used often to meet at 'The Poet Freeth's, as also at Joe Warden's and at 'The Fountains', where I very frequently attended, but my general evenings were spent at 'The Union', 'Shakespeare', or 'Hen and Chickens Tavern', then kept by Mrs Lloyd. I was president for many years of a debating society, and president also of Saint Andrew's Club, and in the Masonic Order, I was Provincial Grand Master for the County of Warwick.[21]

Bisset loved convivial evenings of this kind and being of a cheerful disposition, and always good for a song, he was greatly in demand. It was only in retrospect that he was sorry for leaving his wife alone so many evenings, after she put the children to bed, whilst he enjoyed himself with his friends. In later life he decided to give up this social round and devote himself more to the pleasures of domestic life, and this decision reflected a growing interest in domesticity amongst men of his class.

The fact that the location of so many of these clubs was in the tavern clarifies one reason for women's exclusion from them. Pubs were increasingly being defined as inappropriate settings for women who wished to maintain their gentility in the late eighteenth and early nineteenth centuries. At one time they had provided an easy and informal social space for both men and women.[22] But the attack on drinking habits associated with the rise of temperance, together with the general attempt which was spearheaded by the Evangelicals in the late eighteenth century to improve the manners and morals of the nation in an attempt to raise the moral tone of English society and fend off a social upheaval such as that which had afflicted France, made the pub increasingly a place where respectable women should probably not be seen, except perhaps behind the bar. But the pub remained vital to middle-class men, a central meeting place, though sometimes it was transformed into the more genteel 'hotel'. Eliezer Edwards in his recollections of Birmingham in the early nineteenth century stressed the importance of tavern life: 'As in the West End of London, every man has his club, so in Birmingham, about the commencement of the present century, almost every man had his tavern, where he regularly spent a portion of each day.'[23] The tavern was 'the exchange and news-room of the period'. Often the taverns were divided into separate rooms, with facilities for different classes. 'Commercial rooms', 'smoking rooms' and 'snuggeries' abounded, with the landlady often making herself responsible for preventing any breach of decorum.

'The Union', another Birmingham hostelry, had two special rooms for their most favoured clubs.[24] One was for the Bucks Society, or 'The Order of Bucks', which was devoted to the promotion of 'good fellowship, freedom of conversation and innocent mirth';[25] the other was for the Staffordshire Ironmasters who had been meeting regularly since the late eighteenth century to defend their interests and promote their trade.[26] Initially the ironmasters at their quarterly meetings had dealt with questions about prices and conditions of sale but very soon became involved with political issues too. Samuel Garbett, a prominent Birmingham ironmaster, having failed to persuade Burke 'to take the lead in considering our commerce as a subject of politics', decided that he would have to lead the way himself and played a significant part in the opposition to Pitt's excise scheme in 1784.[27] The iron trade was not an arena in which women could easily engage and the ironmasters' meetings were certainly no place for women. Richard Reynolds, a Quaker ironmaster, thought of the quarterly meetings as 'times of peculiar trial' and warned his son about the temptations he would encounter there. 'I will not say', he wrote,

> that the consideration of the dangers to which I was about to be exposed, and the desire that sometimes accompanied it for preservation from them, was always attended with that degree of watchfulness and circumspection which would have ensured the plaudits of my own conscience after it was over. For though I may say, with humble thankfulness, I hope my conduct did not bring any reproach on my religious profession...yet, when I reflected upon the levity of the conversation (to speak of it in the mildest terms) and how far

> I had contributed to it, or at least, countenanced it by sitting longer among them than was absolutely necessary, it has brought sorrow and condemnation on my part.[28]

The ironmasters' meetings were clearly times of excess and intemperance and by the early nineteenth century these meetings were taking place weekly at 'The Union' with a grand dinner after the main part of the business was concluded. 'Money was easily made, and freely spent in those days,' recollected Edwards, and the share of the dinner bill 'was often a heavy sum, such as even such potentates as ironmasters would not care for their wives to know of.'[29]

Groups such as the Staffordshire Ironmasters, which started off with a commercial rationale but gradually became involved in more directly political matters as these impinged on their business, were responsible for much of the political education of men of the 'middling sort'. It was an education which women were excluded from. It was sufficient for family businesses to be represented by their male head at such gatherings, even when wives and daughters were actively involved in the running of the enterprise. When large public meetings were held the patterns of male conviviality tended to be maintained, with drinking and toasts. The General Chamber of Manufacturers, the first nationally organised expression of manufacturing opinion, was established in this sort of context. It relied on the activities of a group of men who were both friends and business associates. Its immediate trigger was the threatened lowering of the tariffs between Britain and Ireland but as its founding document pointed out it was high time that the manufacturers as a group should have their interests represented. 'It seems hitherto to have escaped the notice of the manufacturers', proclaimed their manifesto:

> That whilst the *landed* and the *funded interests*, the *East India* and other *commercial bodies*, have their respective advocates in the great council of the nation, *they* alone are destitute of that advantage; and it is probable from this source that many of their grievances have arisen – that they have repeatedly and perhaps inadvertently been oppressed by ministers unacquainted with their real interests, and misled by the designs of interested individuals.[30]

This Chamber of Manufacturers, which provided the basis for the Chamber of Commerce in Birmingham, played an important part in defining and articulating the interests of manufacturers and merchants. No women were ever listed in the press reports of those attending the meetings, nor were there any women subscribers. Yet it had been resolved at the founding meeting of the Chamber of Commerce, at Birmingham's Royal Hotel in 1813, that 'All persons interested in the manufactures and commerce of this town and neighbourhood, subscribing a sum of not less than one guinea, be considered members of the society'.[31] 'Persons', from the point of view of the Chamber of Commerce, were clearly men. Similarly when the voice of the town of Birmingham was to be heard, it was the principal male inhabitants who collectively spoke.

The formation of the Chamber had been immediately preceded by the struggle nationally amongst manufacturers and the commercial interest to get the Orders in Council revoked which were having such disastrous consequences on trade. Birmingham, led by Thomas Attwood the banker, had been very prominent in this agitation which was widely understood as a triumph for the middle classes. As Castlereagh wrote gloomily to Wilberforce, 'One does not like to own that we are forced to give way to our manufacturers.'[32] Those manufacturers were increasingly finding it necessary to instruct the governing classes on trading matters and to insist that their voices should be heard. It was this experience which fed directly into the demand for the reform of Parliament and for the vote for middle-class men. It was Attwood who led the Birmingham Political Union to their great victory in 1832, and it was he and his like who were extolled in the liberal poet Horton's poem about the town,

> The noblest men that dignify our age,
> The brightest names that live on history's pages.[33]

Middle-class men made their claim for direct representation on the grounds of the contribution which they were making to national wealth and prestige; it was their industriousness and their competence which meant that they had earned political recognition. It was clear that men and women were not in the same place and would not expect to be treated in the same way. Thomas Wright Hill and his sons, who were running their school for boys at Hazelwood in Birmingham, and whose venture had gained fame through the publication of *Public Education* and the recognition of Bentham, were so committed to the fight for reform that it was decided that Frederick, one of the sons, should devote himself fully to activity in the Birmingham Political Union. This was a decision for the men of the family and was made at one of the Family Councils, which it appears that neither Mrs Hill nor her daughter Sarah attended, even though they were both fully involved in the running of the school as a family enterprise.[34] Women attended the great political rallies organized by the Birmingham Political Union and were encouraged to wear blue garters inscribed with 'Attwood forever' but they played no part in the political discussions or decision making.[35] They were *spectators* and *supporters* rather than being active in their own right and on their own behalf.

The Political Union was revived in Birmingham in 1837. There was a serious economic depression and Attwood revived his plans for currency reform in response. He had always been very enthusiastic about the reforming potential of currency policies but it was the vote, not currency, which had made him popular. This time the Union had little middle-class support, since the middle classes had fundamentally got what they wanted in the Reform Act, and the platform soon became universal male suffrage. Faced with an urgent need for support and a less genteel membership, a Female Political Union was formed. Part of the strategy for reform was that all taxed or excisable articles should be abstained from until the demands were won. Since tea was one of these it was thought by Titus Salt, one of the leaders, that the support of women was essential. He called upon the women of Birmingham to break their normal patterns and 'meddle with politics'; the 'whole family of the people' must unite.[36] The Female Political Union was established and its meetings were regularly reported in the *Birmingham Journal*, the paper of the reformers. The purpose of the Union was seen as to provide support for the men. Women should not be indifferent to politics but should be active on behalf of their men. Needless to say this was in itself a progressive position and would certainly not have been supported by conservative thinkers. The radical/liberal position was that women should participate in politics through men, using their moral agency. As the Whig *Edinburgh Review* trumpeted:

> we assume that it is never contemplated that the right of voting should be claimed for married women during their husbands' lives; or for unmarried women living under the protection of their parents. The divisions which would thereby be created in the heart of families, and the extensive injury consequent therefrom to domestic peace, are objections too obvious to require discussion.[37]

The male leaders of the Birmingham Political Union had no illusions about the supportive functions of their female counterpart. At a large tea-party held at the Town Hall, at which Attwood was the main speaker, all of the public speaking was done by men. Even the address from the Female Political Union which was presented to Attwood was read by a Mr Collins. As Scholefield, one of the town's first MPs, declared, 'it was gratifying to him to meet so many excellent and intelligent women, who, by their presence, showed very plainly that they took a lively interest in all that concerned the welfare of their husbands, fathers, brothers and sons', and, he quickly added, 'which also deeply affected their own interests'.[38] He went on to argue for women's involvement in politics and cited their participation in the storming of the Bastille as an historic precedent of their engagement with the struggle for liberty. Mindful of the criticisms which had been made of the Union for encouraging women to desert their proper duties, he argued that he was 'far from wishing that politics should ever supersede the important duties of social and domestic life, which constituted the chief business of the female', but he still hoped that 'the women of Birmingham would never become indifferent to politics'.[39] Still it was clear that the leadership of the Political Union had a limited view of what the women could achieve. The women themselves sometimes had to insist on the part which they were playing. A meeting was reported in February, for example, at which Mr Collins spoke. In his address to the women he assured them that 'he could not but congratulate them on the glorious victory that had been that day achieved in the Town Hall by the men of Birmingham'. A 'female' present at this called out sharply, 'And by the women, Mr Collins; for we were there.' Mr Collins, chastened, 'was willing to admit the assistance the women had rendered.'[40]

This marginalization of the contribution made by the women with its concurrent assumption that women were not really a part of the 'body politic' is nowhere better illustrated than in the ritual celebration of Birmingham's winning of borough status. This had been a long-drawn-out battle. Only the Liberals had been enthusiastic for incorporation in the wake of the Municipal Reform Act of 1835. The Whigs were neutral since their interests were well covered by the existing Street Commissioners, while the Tories were hostile. The charter was finally granted in October 1838 and in February of 1839 a dinner was held in the Town Hall to celebrate. This event was described in the *Birmingham Journal*, the wonderful decorations were enumerated, the atmosphere evoked:

> When to the effect of these very tasteful decorations, we add the attractions of the hall itself, with the blaze of light running along its extensive walls, the cheerful faces of not less than five hundred gentlemen at the tables below, and above all the blooming cheeks and bright eyes of nearly twice that number of elegantly dressed ladies in the galleries, the rich tones of the magnificent organ, and the pealing anthem swelling the note of praise. . . .[41]

The symbolic importance of this occasion was clear to all – the town was now both represented in Parliament and had its own local government. But the presence of the 'blooming cheeks' in the galleries was less straightforward than it might have seemed. Those 'bright eyes' were only in the side galleries in 'consequence of many pressing applications'. Initially it had been intended to put them in either the grand gallery, where they would have been able to hear nothing, or in the side gallery, where they would have been able to neither see or hear. As the editor of the *Journal* commented, however, their voices, usually gentle and low, became sharp when faced with this relegation and the seating arrangements had to be rethought.[42] This did not mean that the ladies were able either to dine or to drink, but they were able to enjoy a toast being drunk to them. The mayor, in his toast, made the traditional invocation to women as being above politics, and in that way morally superior to men:

> 'Gentlemen', he cried, 'we live in times of great political strife and exasperation. We sometimes forget in the animosity of our contentions, that differ as we will, we are still of the same kind and of the same country, kith and kin one of another, united by one common bond of mutual dependence and of mutual interest. We often forget this. Woman's gentle nature never forgets it. She knows no hatred, nor will let us know any, if we but appeal to her. Let us then, gentlemen, whenever we feel our hearts hardening towards each other, or towards our political opponents, let us fly for counsel to those whose province and whose dearest task it is to soften, to bless, and to purify our imperfect nature. Then, believe me, we shall ever find a store of charity, large as our deficiencies, and learn how easy a thing it is to conciliate, without the sacrifice of independence, and to contend without the bitterness of animosity.'[43]

Those 'elegantly dressed ladies' could not have been told more clearly that they did not occupy the same political sphere as men. Those 'fit and proper persons' who had voted both nationally and locally and stood as candidates in Parliamentary and council elections relied on their women to soften, bless and purify their imperfect, and political, natures.

The marginalization of women in the political world has to be understood as part of a larger process whereby women were being marginalized from, or indeed excluded from, the public world generally. The debate over what part women should play in philanthropy illustrates this very clearly. As long as they were concerned with private philanthropic work, visiting people in their homes in particular, there was no problem.[44] The difficulties arose when they attempted to step outside of that domestic arena and take on a more public role. We can find the same pattern repeated in the churches; women were, again, at least amongst 'serious Christians', encouraged to engage in visiting and tract distribution but anything more public, or indeed more official, was discouraged. The formalization of philanthropic and religious societies invariably marginalized women from the process of decision making; their role was to support privately rather than engage publicly. Nevertheless, 'serious Christians', with their belief in spiritual equality, did provide women with some basis for trust in their own individual and independent judgment and their own moral sense. It was possible, if difficult, to argue that women's special moral sense should be interpreted in political terms and indeed that argument underpinned many feminist interventions in the later nineteenth century. But the move from spirituality and morality to politics was a difficult one to make.

One arena in which women had asserted their right to a political engagement was on the issue of anti-slavery. Here the line between philanthropic work and politics was hard to draw and it was this blurring which had made it a possible area for women. The female anti-slavery societies were mainly established by Quaker women, who had benefited from their traditions of autonomous organization. This in its turn stemmed from the Quaker belief in the spiritual equality of men and women. But the female anti-slavery societies never did the same kind of work as their male counterparts. Rather than lobbying Parliament or organizing demonstrations they relied on appealing to women as wives and mothers, preferably in their own homes. The Birmingham Female Society for the Relief of British Negro Slaves was established in 1828 and initially concerned itself with producing workbags, albums and portfolios to raise money for the relief of neglected and deserted negro slaves. In a discussion in their report of 1828 as to why more women had not got involved with their activities, they concluded that few realized how useful they could be. Female 'weakness and feebleness', they argued, far from meaning that women had nothing to offer, guaranteed them a special kind of strength. For God had chosen 'the weak things of the world, and the things that are despised, and the things that are not, to bring to naught the things that are'. Women must use their special skills and gifts rather than pretending to be like men. The Birmingham Society appealed to women as consumers not to buy slave-grown sugar and to engage in house-to-house visiting in the town on this issue, saying:

> Is it for Christian females to be bribed by the greater *cheapness* of this, or the other articles of daily consumption, to lend themselves to the support of a flagrant system of blood-guiltiness and oppression, which cries to heaven for

> vengeance? – and can we think the cry will not be heard? The influence of females in the minor departments (as they are usually deemed) of household affairs is generally such, that it rests with them to determine whether the luxuries indulged in, and the conveniences enjoyed, shall come to them from *the employers of free men, or from the oppressors of British slaves*. When the preference is given to the latter, we see, therefore, with whom the responsibility must mainly rest; – we see at whose door the burden of the guilt must lie.[45]

Women should use their power as household managers to see that slave-grown sugar was not bought; this was the kind of political sphere in which they could have legitimate influence. Even this legitimacy was, however, contested. There were many men involved in the anti-slavery agitation, indeed Wilberforce himself, who were unhappy at this uncalled-for forwardness from ladies whom they preferred to think of as existing quietly in the domestic sphere.

The contestation over what were, and what were not, appropriate public arenas for women continued throughout the nineteenth century. It was not a contest which could be easily resolved since boundaries were open to change. Furthermore the debates over the nature of woman's influence and woman's mission embraced a wide number of issues. Politics, indeed, was rarely mentioned directly for it was assumed that it was not a sphere appropriate to women. What was 'political' was indeed partly defined by where the men were. Influential texts such as those by Mrs Ellis on the duties of the wives, mothers and daughters of England did not discuss the question of women's involvement in politics at all.[46] Mrs Ellis, like many others, believed that moral influence was the key. Nevertheless on occasions the support of 'the ladies' could be very useful politically though this could lead to acute disagreements.

There was of course a well-established tradition of aristocratic ladies using what influence they could in support of their candidates. In Emily Eden's novel *The Semi-Attached Couple* Lady Teviot wanted to do what she could for her husband's candidate in an election. She acquired a poll book and went through it carefully to see whether any of her tradespeople were in it so that she might be able to exert some pressure. She and her mother:

> drove into the town constantly, and seemed suddenly to have discovered that they were without any of the necessaries or luxuries of life, for the extent of their dealings with well-thinking tradespeople was prodigious, and it might have been supposed that they were covertly sullying the purity of election; but, as they justly alleged, shopping was what every woman was born for, and could not, under any circumstances, be considered illegal.[47]

Undoubtedly there were middle-class versions of this kind of pressuring. George Eliot observed in *Felix Holt* that at a time when controversies between the Church and Dissent were very sharp retailers who were Dissenters had to keep a strict hold on their tempers.[48] Tradespeople could not afford to be too sectarian. Similarly, Dr Hope's friends in *Deerbrook* assured him that no one would expect him to vote in a disputed election. 'You are quite absolved from interfering in politics', he was advised. 'Nobody expects it from a medical man. Everyone knows the disadvantage to a professional man, circumstanced like you, of taking any side in a party matter.'[49] No doubt well-to-do female customers and patients had ways of indicating their political preferences to those who provided them with services. But there was a marked difference between aristocratic and middle-class patterns when it came to the relation between women and politics. One aspect of the middle-class critique of aristocratic culture was that society hostesses neglected their families and their religious and moral responsibilities to their children in favour of more worldly pursuits.[50]

Sometimes this kind of 'behind the throne' influence was exercised more openly. The Anti-Corn Law League was quite prepared to utilize the support of middle-class women in their agitation for repeal. They were encouraged to run bazaars and fancy fairs as ways of raising money, capitalizing on the experience gained from such activities in the philanthropic world. The League was of course a Radical organization and as such took a more progressive position on the question of appropriate spheres for women than more conservative groups. They were happy to use lady collectors for the collecting of subscriptions and it was resolved by the Council of the League that 'in every town a committee must be formed, consisting of ladies and gentlemen, having a secretary and treasurer'.[51] Not surprisingly, however, these committees represented the highest echelons that ladies could reach. J.W. Croker in the *Quarterly Review* denounced the use that the League made of women as providing a clear indication of the Jacobin influences at work. 'It has been a frequent device of revolutionary agitators', he asserted, 'to bring women forward as a screen and safeguard to their own operations.' He regarded the great bazaar held by the League with its stalls organized by women as 'a practice in our opinion equally offensive to good taste and good feeling, and destructive of the most amiable and valuable qualities of the female character'. Of a tea-party held with sixty lady stewardesses he commented:

> We exceedingly wonder and regret that the members of the Association and League [the *Councils* of these two bodies organised the bazaar], and still more that anybody else, should have chosen to exhibit their wives and daughters in the character of political agitators; and we most regret that so many ladies – modest, excellent and amiable persons we have no doubt in their domestic circles – should have been persuaded to allow their names to be *placarded* on such occasions – for be it remembered, this Bazaar and these Tea-parties did not even pretend to be for any *charitable* object, but entirely for the purposes of *political agitation*.[52]

J.W. Croker was right to be worried, for many of the daughters of Radicals who were involved in the agitation over the Corn Laws later became committed feminists. One thing could indeed lead to another! Many of the same objections had, however, been made to women's involvement in philanthropic bazaars, for, amongst other things, such occasions invited easy mixing between young men and women.[53] For many people amongst the respectable middle class there was a prohibition on genteel ladies appearing in public at all, except at church or chapel. The stress on the *private* definition of women made participation in the political world exceedingly difficult. For the political world was quintessentially a public world. The kinds of public recognition that were an essential part of political involvement were not accessible to women. Hobsbawm in his *The Age of Capital* tackles the question as to what defined the bourgeoisie as a class:

> the main characteristic of the bourgeoisie as a class was that it was a body of persons of power and influence, independent of the power and influence of traditional birth and status. To belong to it a man had to be 'someone'; a person who counted *as an individual* because of his wealth, his capacity to command other men, or otherwise to influence them.[54]

Such a definition is essentially male. There was no way in which women could be 'someone' in this sense. They did not have that kind of power or influence in either the world of business or in the sphere of voluntary associations of any kind. They were *private persons*, not *public someones*. As such they did not possess the necessary prerequisites for citizenship, nor indeed did they expect to occupy the world of political ideas. It was a source of acute amazement when a woman, Harriet Martineau, published a series on political economy, a subject not often associated with the 'fair sex'. When George Dawson, the influential preacher who inspired the 'civic gospel' which was taken up by Joseph Chamberlain and the Birmingham Liberals in the 1850s, fired his initial sally it was addressed to the 'Men of the Middle classes'.[55] He would have been breaking with custom to have appealed to women as well, despite the fact that his church, with its large female congregation, provided the base for the civic gospel. He would also have been breaking with new social practices in relation to gender and politics which had been established in his own lifetime. Middle-class men had successfully established their pitch; middle-class women remained on the boundaries.

ACKNOWLEDGEMENT

This article is part of a larger study, sponsored by the Social Science Research Council, later published as *Family Fortunes* (Hutchinson, 1987), on the relation between domesticity and the development of industrial and agrarian capitalism in the late eighteenth and early nineteenth centuries. The study was jointly undertaken by Leonore Davidoff and myself at the University of Essex. All my ideas have been discussed with her.

NOTES

1 Martha Syms, 'Letters and reminiscences'. This manuscript was kindly lent to me by the late Margaret Wilson.
2 Dorothy Thompson, 'Women and nineteenth-century radical politics: a lost dimension', in J. Mitchell and A. Oakley eds, *The Rights and Wrongs of Women*.

3 Barbara Taylor, *Eve and the New Jerusalem.*
4 M. Stacey and M. Price, *Women, Power and Politics.*
5 M.Z. Rosaldo and L. Lamphere, *Women, Culture and Society.*
6 J.A. McNamara and S. Wemple, 'The power of women through the family in medieval Europe: 500–1100', in M. Hartman and L.W. Banner eds, *Clio's Consciousness Raised.*
7 J.B. Elshtain, *Public Man, Private Woman.*
8 Adam Smith, *The Theory of Moral Sentiments.*
9 S.M. Okin, *Women in Western Political Thought*; E. Fox-Genovese, 'Property and patriarchy in classical bourgeois political theory', in *Radical History Review*; R.W. Krouse, 'Patriarchal Liberalism and beyond: from John Stuart Mill to Harriet Taylor', in J.B. Elshtain ed., *The Family in Political Thought*; G. Schochet, *Patriarchalism in Political Thought.*
10 Okin, *Women in Western Political Thought.*
11 Elizabeth Cleghorn Gaskell, *The Life of Charlotte Brontë*, p. 123.
12 Quoted in R. Fulford, *Votes for Women*, p. 23.
13 C. Hall, 'The early formation of Victorian domestic ideology', in S. Burman ed., *Fit Work for Women.*
14 Quoted in Fulford, *Votes for Women*, pp. 26–7.
15 *Edinburgh Review*, vol. 73, 1841.
16 H. Martineau, *Deerbrook.*
17 Quoted in E. Moers, *Literary Women*, p. 20.
18 J. Brewer, 'Commercialization and politics', in N. McKendrick, J. Brewer and J.H. Plumb, *The Birth of a Consumer Society: The Commercialization of Eighteenth-Century England*, p. 199.
19 Quoted in R. Porter, *English Society in the Eighteenth Century*, p. 274.
20 Brewer, 'Commercialization and politics', p. 219.
21 J. Bisset, *Memoir of James Bisset*, p. 76.
22 M. Girouard, *Victorian Pubs.*
23 E. Edwards, *The Old Taverns of Birmingham*, p. 5.
24 Ibid.
25 J. Money, *Experience and Identity: Birmingham and the West Midlands, 1760–1800*, p. 138.
26 T.S. Ashton, *Iron and Steel in the Industrial Revolution.*
27 Ibid., p. 164.
28 B. Trinder, *The Industrial Revolution in Shropshire*, p. 202.
29 Edwards, *The Old Taverns of Birmingham*, p. 77.
30 Ashton, *Iron and Steel in the Industrial Revolution*, p. 169.
31 G.H. Wright, *Chronicles of the Birmingham Chamber of Commerce*, p. 54.
32 C. Emsley, *British Society and the French Wars 1793–1815*, p. 160.
33 H.H. Horton, 'Birmingham', poem, Birmingham, 1851.
34 F. Hill, *An Autobiography of Fifty Years in Reform.*
35 C. Flick, *The Birmingham Political Union.*
36 T.C. Salt, 'To the women of Birmingham', 16 August 1838.
37 *Edinburgh Review*, vol. 73, 1841, p. 203.
38 *Birmingham Journal*, 12 January 1839.
39 *Birmingham Journal*, 12 January 1839.
40 *Birmingham Journal*, 2 February 1839.
41 *Birmingham Journal*, 16 February 1839.
42 *Birmingham Journal*, 16 February 1839.
43 *Birmingham Journal*, 23 February 1839.

44 A. Summers, 'A home from home – women's philanthropic work in the nineteenth century', in S. Burman ed., *Fit Work for Women*; F.K. Prochaska, *Women and Philanthropy in Nineteenth-Century England*.
45 Female Society of Birmingham for the Relief of British Negro Slaves, Album, *c*.1828.
46 Mrs Ellis, *The Women of England, Mothers of England and The Daughters of England*.
47 Emily Eden, *The Semi-Attached Couple*, p. 215.
48 George Eliot, *Felix Holt*, p. 226.
49 Martineau, *Deerbrook*, p. 183.
50 L. Davidoff, *The Best Circles*.
51 N. McCord, *The Anti-Corn Law League*, p. 139.
52 *Quarterly Review*, vol. 71, 1842–3, p. 262.
53 J.A. James, *Female Piety*.
54 E.J. Hobsbawm, *The Age of Capital*, p. 286.
55 G. Dawson, 'A letter to the middle classes on the present crisis', Birmingham, 1848.

PART III

The Politics of Difference: Class, Race and Gender

Introduction

DUAL SYSTEMS AND THE THEORY OF PATRIARCHY

The various labels which came to be used to differentiate between feminisms made demarcations where boundaries were actually very fluid. But the choice of label could be significant. A preference for 'socialist feminist' for instance usually indicated, as we have seen in the case of the historians, a certain critical distance from Marxism and a willingness to draw on more libertarian socialist traditions. While both libertarian socialism and socialist feminism might be critical of Marxism for its economism, its work-centred politics of class and its neglect of sex and gender, having no well-developed alternative theory of capitalism and class, both have had frequent recourse to Marxism, sometimes in selective and ad hoc fashion. It is only Marxists who are obliged to strive to be *rigorous* Marxists. Except among those feminists who discounted the significance of class in their insistence that sex oppression was primary, most adopted the strategy of ceding to Marxism what it could best explain, and turning to a feminist theory of 'patriarchy' for a complementary understanding of 'sex-gender systems'.[1]

Ironically, Marxist feminists were often less indulgent towards Marxism. As Veronica Beechey remarked, dual systems approaches 'tended to leave the Marxist analysis of production uncriticized by feminist thinking.'[2] Although Marxist feminists were frequently accused, and with some justice, of reducing sex oppression to class subordination, or the needs of capitalism, or both, this very reductionism necessitated a critical engagement with Marxism on its own terms and in the very heart of its analysis. The idea that modes of production and social classes might be systematically gendered was in some ways more challenging to Marxism than the notion of two parallel systems in interaction.

Marxist feminists who rejected dualism were obliged to seek common terms for the analysis of both 'systems', and this is what happened in the notorious domestic labour debate of the 1970s.[3] Labour power in Marx's theory was a commodity, and like all such, its value was determined by the amount of 'necessary labour time' invested in its production. In the case of this particular commodity, it was measured by the value of the goods and services purchased with the wage, and used to restore human energies used up in the production process: food, clothing, shelter, and, over a longer time-span, the costs of producing the next generation of labourers. 'Surplus value' was a function of the difference between the value of labour power so calculated, and the amount of value generated *by* that labour power when put to work in the process of production. For as a commodity labour power was unique in not only *having* value, but in its capacity to *produce* it.[4]

What this formula on the labour theory of value left out of account was the very considerable amount of labour time expended in the various processes through which used up energies were restored to the labourer – shopping, cooking, cleaning etc. A regular battle broke out over whether such labour was to be classed as 'productive' or 'unproductive' within Marxist terms.[5] Some argued that as domestic labour produced no commodity and no surplus value, it could not be productive, and therefore must be unproductive.[6] Mariarosa Dalla Costa and the Wages for Housework Collective argued on the contrary that domestic labour did produce a commodity, one which was moreover absolutely central to capitalism: labour power itself.[7] Domestic labour, they argued could and should be waged. The debate was brought full circle, then closed by those who argued that domestic labour was neither 'productive' nor 'unproductive' because these terms operated within a body of theory in which they were applicable only to waged work.[8] Domestic labour was outside its terms.

This inconclusive debate consumed a degree of intellectual energy and time which even the least diligent of Ann Oakley's extraordinarily hard-working housewives would have been hard pressed to spare from their labours in the interests of theorizing its place in the reproduction of capitalist social relations (see chapter 4).[9] The domestic labour debate helped to confirm and harden WLM attitudes of hostility towards theory, and it is easy now to ridicule the whole earnest endeavour. Yet for those who became engaged it proved of lasting value in promoting a clearer understanding of Marxist theory and of the problems involved in using it to generate a comprehensive explanation of women's oppression.

The Wages for Housework Collective used a broad concept of domestic labour such that practically everything a woman did in her personal and domestic life was included, from cleaning the house to sexual intercourse. It is by now widely conceded that Marxism has little explanatory power over the specific dynamics of sex and gender and that other theories give greater purchase here. But dualism, or pluralism, necessary at the level of theory, is damaging when it is interpreted, as it often is, at the level of substantive systems of social interaction: where one 'system' is identified as that of productive relations, explicable in terms of Marxism, the other, a sex-gender system which is enacted in the family and in interpersonal relations, explicable by some other theory such as psychoanalysis. Marxist-feminist resistance to dual systems theory has lasting validity insofar as the family and personal relations belong exclusively as objects of analysis neither to psychoanalysis, nor to Marxism. They are arenas in which the dynamics of both capitalism and sexuality are in play. The same point must be made of workplace relations which are often highly sexualized and almost always gendered. Relations between bosses and secretaries are not *only* social relations of production, and social relations of production include more than workplace relations. Dual *systems* approaches as against a principled and non-eclectic pluralism at the level of theory tend to be too rigid and discrete in their ascriptions of whole areas of social life to the governance of one or another theory.

The second selection in this section, Cynthia Cockburn's analysis of the sexual politics of the British printing workers' manner of organizing in the fight for their class and sectional interests, illustrates the gains to be made from the recognition that workshop relations are not only relations of production. No dual systems approach could have generated this type of analysis – nor indeed could any theoretical monism. Work of this type will perhaps do more to break down the boundaries between 'radical' and 'socialist' feminism, to produce really fruitful use of the developed resources of both, than any general encounter between the two at more abstract levels.

THE POLITICS AND THEORY OF DIFFERENCE

The prolonged and general political shift to the right in Britain over the past decade has coincided with a fragmentation of the WLM. The concept of a sisterhood of shared and common oppression, of the interests of all women in feminist struggles, has given way to a politics of difference. White middle-class heterosexual feminists have been urged to confront the ways in which feminist politics, practice and theory have masked material differences in the position and forms of oppression suffered by women who are outside one or another of these categories. Differences grounded in 'deviant' sexualities were the first to explode. Marxist and socialist feminism as such have had little to say about lesbianism,[10] which has been theorized and politicized above all in radical-feminist thought and practice, and within the objects-relations school of feminist psychoanalysis rather than Marxism. The next section includes an example of this latter approach to lesbian sexuality.[11]

The contributions of Catherine Hall to the last section, and Cynthia Cockburn to this one indicate the alternative to dual systems theory preferred by many Marxist and socialist feminists. Classes are historically constructed, and gender-differences are central components of class identity. What has still to be fully appreciated is the extent to which this is true of social divisions based on 'race' and ethnic identity. The selection by Floya Anthias and Nira Yuval-Davis brings this out with great clarity.

White feminists in Britain still find it difficult to take on board the implications of the black feminist critiques which began to appear in the late 1970s and this has lead to recurrent, exasperated charges of racism in the WLM.[12] Such charges must be taken very seriously. There can be no doubt that feminism(s) in their politics and their theories, have suffered by the failure to recognize that women are not homogenous: that we occupy differing social spaces with interests that may, as a result, diverge. Ann Phoenix's contribution pinpoints the inadequacies of much sociological and psychological, including feminist, research on the family. Afro-Caribbean families are consciously or unconsciously excluded from research into 'normal' family life, to come under scrutiny only where 'deviant' forms are under consideration. Phoenix confronts theories of the development of gendered subjectivity in the course of family interaction with the specific conditions often found among Afro-Caribbean families in Britain and the United States: mother-parented families; working mothers; a greater degree of non-parental involvement in primary child care, etc. She is enabled to pose two questions as a result: firstly, how do the psychic processes identified for example in psychoanalysis operate in such circumstances? Secondly, what socialization strategies have been adopted in response to these differing material contingencies? Her analysis here may be related to that offered by Johanna Brenner and Maria Ramas of the constraints under which working-class families adopted the 'family-household system' with its gendered division of labour in nineteenth-century Britain, (see chapter 9). Phoenix argues that for Afro-Caribbean families this option is, for many, simply not available, and knowing this to be the case, socialization strategies based on the development of a submissive femininity would have made little sense for daughters in whom independence and marketable skills acquired through education were likely to have far greater survival-value.

THE GENDERING OF SOCIAL CLASS

Recognition that 'women' is not a unitary category, and that women have not been passive victims, but agents in the construction of gender orders and gender meanings, has profound implications which have still to be explored. The stake which bourgeois women in nineteenth-century Britain may have had in the development of a sexual division of labour based on the concept of 'separate spheres' is beginning to be acknowledged.[13] But to concede the class benefits of this gender order in the case of the bourgeoisie is no skin off the nose of socialist feminists. The gendering of the working-class in structured sex inequality raises deeper emotions. Any suggestion here of a *class* interest, shared by working-class women, in gendered inequality arouses passionate disavowal. The argument was first made by Jane Humphries in an article in the Cambridge Economic Journal in 1977.[14] She argued that there were major gains for the working class as a whole, albeit unequally distributed within class and family, in the development of the 'family-household system' in the nineteenth century, with its sex-based division of labour. This argument was contested by Michéle Barrett and Mary McIntosh in their demystification of 'the family wage' reprinted here.

The family wage never really existed, they argue: the breadwinner's wage always had to be supplemented by the earning of wives and other household members to create sufficient resources for the working-class household; it created intolerable conditions for those many women who were primary breadwinners because it kept women's earnings so low; and crucially, it weakened the working class by dividing it. The material gains, they conclude, have been small or non-existent, and the price paid for them by working-class women in any case unacceptably high.

The argument was revived and recast recently in a critical review of Michèle Barrett's *Women's Oppression Today*. The new element, which was to prove even more contentious, provoked the charge of biological determinism.[15] The argument was that 'the family-household' system, while not strictly determined by biology, was the almost inevitably preferred solution to the exigencies of biological reproduction – perpetual pregnancy and childbearing which was well-nigh unavoidable.

There is not space here to include all the relevant contributions to this debate. I have included edited versions of Barrett and McIntosh's reply to Humphries because it contains a fairly full summary of the latter, and Brenner and Ramas's critique of Barrett. Also relevant, but not included here, is the debate sparked off by Wilson and Weir's lengthy article on the British Women's Movement,[16] which, like Humphries, and Brenner and Ramas, constitutes a defence of the working class movement against what is presented as socialist feminism's drift away from class analysis and politics, and its tendency to place more blame for women's oppression at the feet of the working class and the labour movement than at those of capitalism.

The final selection here looks at the fortunes of the feminist movement in Northern Ireland, and illustrates graphically that to argue that race, ethnic and gender oppressions create divided loyalties only in the short term is to offer little comfort in the face of such pressing demands to choose between radically conflicting political priorities in the not-so-very short term.

NOTES

1 Gayle Rubin, 'The Traffic in Women', in R. Reiter, ed., *Toward an Anthropology of Women*, Monthly Review Press, 1975.

2 Veronica Beechey, 'On Patriarchy', *Feminist Review*, 3, 1979, p. 78. See also Sheila Rowbotham, 'The Trouble with Patriarchy', *New Statesman*, Dec 1979, reprinted in Feminist Anthology Collection, *No Turning Back: Writings From the Women's Liberation Movement, 1975–80*, Women's Press, 1981, and Sally Alexander and Barbara Taylor, 'In Defence of Patriarchy: a Reply', in the same volume of essays.

3 See Ellen Malos, ed., *The Politics of Housework*, Alison and Busby, 1980; and Maxine Molyneux, 'Beyond the Domestic Labour Debate', *New Left Review*, 116, 1979.

4 The *locus classicus* is Karl Marx, *Capital*, vol. 1, part 1, Lawrence and Wishart, 1970 (first published 1887). For a recent exposition see Simon Clarke, *Marx*,

Marginalism and Modern Sociology, Macmillan, 1982, ch. 4, 'Value, Class and the Theory of Society'.

5 For Marx, productive labour was labour which generated surplus value. Many types of wage labour were specifically excluded. The distinction did not depend on the type of work, but on the social relations within which it occurred. Thus the unpaid domestic labour of the housewife engaged in cleaning the home, that of a cleaner employed by a firm, a private individual, or an institution, and that of the employee of a cleaning agency, may be indistinguishable in terms of the labour process. But the first two would not come into the category of 'productive labour' while the third would. As Malos observes, 'although Marx was always careful to make clear that the distinction was a technical one which did not describe the usefulness or importance of the work that fell into either category, those who followed him...have spoken as if "productive" was the same as useful or "important to capitalism".' Ellen Malos, ed., *The Politics of Housework*, Alison and Busby, 1980, p. 25.

6 Wally Seccombe, 'The Housewife and her Labour under Capitalism', *New Left Review*, 83, 1974; M. Benston, 'The Political Economy of Women's Liberation', *Monthly Review*, 21, 4, 1969.

7 Mariarosa Dalla Costa and Selma James, *The Power of Women and the Subversion of the Community*, Falling Wall Press, Bristol, 1972.

8 I. Gernstein, 'Domestic Labour and Capitalism', *Radical America*, 7, 1973, and L. Vogel, 'The Earthly Family' in the same issue.

9 Ann Oakley, *Housewife*, Allen Lane, 1974.

10 But see for example, Elizabeth Wilson, 'Gayness and Liberalism' and 'Forbidden Love', in Wilson, *Hidden Agendas*, Tavistock, 1986.

11 See Joanna Ryan, 'Psychoanalysis and Women Loving Women'.

12 See Hazel Carby, 'White Woman Listen! Black Feminism and the Boundaries of Sisterhood', in Centre for Contemporary Cultural Studies, *The Empire Strikes Back*, Hutchinson, 1982; also the special issue of *Feminist Review* on black feminism, 17, 1984.

13 See Leonore Davidoff and Catherine Hall, *Family Fortunes*, Hutchinson 1987, and in another context, Patsy Stoneman, *Elizabeth Gaskell*, Harvester, 1987.

14 Jane Humphries, 'Class Struggle and the Persistence of the Working-Class Family', *Cambridge Journal of Economics*, 1, 3, 1977.

15 Michèle Barrett, 'Rethinking Women's Oppression: a Reply to Brenner and Ramas', *New Left Review*, 146, 1984; and Jane Lewis, 'The Debate on Sex and Class', *New Left Review*, 149, 1985.

16 Angela Weir and Elizabeth Wilson, 'The British Women's Movement', *New Left Review*, 148, 1984. See also the reply by Michèle Barrett in issue 150.

4

Ann Oakley

What is a Housewife?

A housewife is a woman: a housewife does housework. In the social structure of industrialized societies, these two statements offer an interesting and important contradiction. The synthesis of 'house' and 'wife' in a single term establishes the connections between womanhood, marriage, and the dwelling place of family groups. The role of housewife is a family role: it is a feminine role. Yet it is also a work role. A housewife is 'the person, other than a domestic servant, who is responsible for most of the household duties (or for supervising a domestic servant who carries out these duties).'[1] A housewife is 'a woman who manages or directs the affairs of her household; the mistress of a family; the wife of a householder.'[2]

The characteristic features of the housewife role in modern industrialized society are (1) its *exclusive allocation to women*, rather than to adults of both sexes; (2) its association with *economic dependence*, i.e. with the dependent role of the woman in modern marriage; (3) its *status as non-work* – or its opposition to 'real', i.e. economically productive work, and (4) its *primacy* to women, that is, its priority over other roles.

A man cannot be a housewife. A man who says he is a housewife is an anomaly. On the level of fact his statement may be true: he may indeed do housework and assume the responsibility for it. But on another level his claim rings of absurdity, or deviation. It runs counter to the social customs of our culture.

In 1970, Albert Mills of Coventry claimed to be a housewife. His wife, Vera, who was employed, wished to claim the dependent wife's benefit for her husband under the National Insurance Act of 1965. Albert had kept house for five years, while Vera brought home the money: Albert was the housewife. But the Mills lost their battle. As the lawyer representing the Department of Health and Social Security interpreted the relevant section of the Act: 'When the Act refers to a person as a wife, the word is used with the meaning given to it in English law – a matrimonial partnership of a monogamous character. In law it is a man and a woman who make a natural pair.'[3] Within this 'natural' partnership, it is the woman 'naturally' who takes the role of housewife.

A woman's performance of the housewife role is thus not a random event. It is possible, of course, to be a housewife and to be unmarried, but the majority of housewives are married women, and the allocation of the housewife role to the woman in marriage is socially structured. Marriage is not simply a personal relationship: rather it is 'an institution composed of a socially accepted union of individuals in husband and wife roles'.[4] A biological male cannot legally take the social role of wife-housewife, and a biological female cannot legally take the role of husband:

> Detectives today prepared a report for the Director of Public Prosecutions on the couple who went through a form of marriage at Southend register office knowing they were both women...The couple are Terry Floyd, 24, and blonde 23-year-old Carole Mary Lloyd...Floyd said, 'I am technically female. But I feel and I always have felt like a man.' Carole said, 'I have known all along that my husband is a woman...but it does not make the slightest difference to us.'[5]

To society, however, biological sex is the all-important criterion.

Through the location of the housewife role in marriage, housewifery is an economically dependent occupation. As the Registrar General neatly and condescendingly puts it, married women 'engaged in unpaid home duties are not regarded as retired, but treated as "others economically inactive"'.[6]

Within this definition lie three aspects of the economics of housework. Firstly, the housewife does not herself produce commodities of direct value to the economy. Her primary economic function is vicarious: by servicing others, she enables them to engage in productive economic activity. Secondly, instead of a productive role, the housewife acts as the main consumer in the family. The tools of her trade are mostly bought by her outside the home – the food with which meals are made, the furniture with which the home is filled, the clothes with which the family are dressed, the appliances with which housework is done. 'Shopping' is one of the housewife's main work activities. The reality of the equation 'woman = housewife = consumer' is clearly illustrated by the role the housewife is allocated in the anti-inflationary campaigns of governments. The government 'appeals' to the housewife to report rising prices, to buy 'wisely' and so on and so forth. In the 1972 British Government price-freeze, the onus was put entirely on 'the housewife' to report illicit price rises: 'The suggestion is that they [housewives] should first challenge the shopkeeper if they think a price is being unfairly raised', explained Prime Minister Heath: 'The housewife is quite capable of doing this.'[7]

The third aspect of the Registrar General's definition is that the housewife's work is not regarded as work because she receives no wage or salary for it. Not only is the housewife not paid for her work, but in almost all industrialized countries the housewife as a houseworker has no right to the financial benefits – sickness benefit, unemployment benefit, and so on – which accrue to other workers through state insurance systems.[8] Any benefits for which she qualifies come to her indirectly, through marriage, and because, in marriage, she acknowledges her condition of economic dependence. As a worker, she does not exist. The situation once established is self-perpetuating. The housewife is not paid, is not insured, cannot claim sickness benefit, etc.: therefore the housewife does not work. The alternative logic is: the housewife does not work and *therefore* she has no right to any financial benefit or reward. In either case, the modern concept of work, as the expenditure of energy for financial gain, defines housework as the most inferior and marginal work of all.

This central contradiction – housework is work, housework is not work – appears as a constant theme in the analysis of the housewife's situation. On the one hand, she is a privileged person: she is exempt from the need, binding on other adult members of society, to prove her worth in economic terms. 'Both my husband and I', said one reader of a newspaper article on housewives and their work, 'think the housewife is one of the privileged classes.' Or as another reader expressed it:

> To my mind she [the housewife] is a queen and her husband and children are her adoring subjects. Tradespeople are her courtiers whom she can dispense with at will if they displease her. Her home gives her scope to try out her artistic ability, the culinary arts, her sociability. She is free to work eighteen hours a day...or just take things easy...At least she is not a slave to an employer.[9]

But while the assertion, 'I am a housewife,' acts as a validation of the right to withdraw from economic activity, the admission, 'I am just a housewife', disclaims any right to feel pride in this status. From privilege stems deprivation.

Housework is low-status work. 'Menial', a term used to describe low-status work generally, should properly be used to describe only housework. As the dictionary says: 'Menial (1) adjective of service, servile (of servant, usually derogatory), domestic (2) noun, servant. From old French *mesnie*, household.'

Some of housework's low status is due to the low status of the people who do it – women. A phonetic reduction of the term 'housewife' produces the appellation 'hussy'. 'Hussy' means 'worthless woman'. This equation of linguistic meaning reflects the equation of social meaning. A housewife and a woman are one and the same: one and the same, they are subject to deprivation and oppression in relation to the position of the dominant group in society. Neither housewives in their work roles nor women in their social and economic roles generally, are incorporated into the image and ideology of this group: if they were they would not have 'a situation'. They would not be set apart, different, unequal.

The status of housework is interwoven specifically with the status of married women. As a member of the British Government explained in 1970: 'The role of housewife is an extremely honourable profession, but the normal responsibility for looking after her welfare falls to her husband.'[10] In other words, however honourable the housewife's role, hers is, and must be, a situation of economic dependence, which marriage, by definition, involves. Feminists might well ask what kind of honour this is, and what other profession places its (unpaid) workers in the precarious situation of depending for economic survival on the beneficence of those with whom they share their beds.

The primacy of the housewife role in women's lives today is perhaps less obvious than its associations with femininity, economic dependence, and low-status work. Yet a growing mass of evidence points to the conclusion that progress towards sex equality is hampered by women's domestic responsibilities, even when legal or other institutional barriers have been removed.... A major problem is the failure to appreciate that housework *is* work in terms of the time and energy it involves, a fact which is nicely epitomized in the following anonymous rhyme, entitled 'On a Tired Housewife':

> Here lies a poor woman who was always tired,
> She lived in a house where help wasn't hired.
> Her last words on earth were: 'Dear friends, I am going
> To where there's no cooking, or washing, or sewing.
> For everything there is exact to my wishes,
> For where they don't eat there's no washing of dishes.
> I'll be where loud anthems will always be ringing
> But having no voice, I'll be quit of the singing.
> Don't mourn me for now, don't mourn me for never,
> I am going to do nothing for ever and ever.'[11]

No precise figures are available for the number of women who are housewives, but a British survey found that 85 per cent of all women aged between sixteen and sixty-four in a random sample of over 7,000 women were housewives – they carried the responsibility for running the household in which they lived. While nine out of ten women who were not employed were housewives, so were seven out of ten of those with a job outside the home. Housework is clearly the major occupational role of women today. Employment does not itself alter the status (or reduce the work) of being a housewife.

With the virtual disappearance of the 'underclass' of private domestic servants, housewife and houseworker roles have merged. The average housewife spends between 3,000 and 4,000 hours a year on housework.[12] Housewives in the urban British sample studied by the author in 1971 reported an average of 77 hours weekly housework.[13] The amount of time housework takes shows no tendency to decrease with the increasing availability of domestic appliances, or with the expansion of women's opportunities outside the home. A comparison of data available from different countries over the last four decades (shown in table 1) demonstrates a remarkable consistency in housework hours.

The social trivialization of housework (and of women) is in part responsible for the tendency to underestimate or ignore the amount of time women spend doing it. But other features of the housewife role also conspire to

Table 1 A comparison of data on housework hours

Study	*Date*	*Average weekly hours of housework*
1 Rural Studies		
United States	1929	62
United States	1929	64
United States	1956	61
France	1959	67
2 Urban Studies		
United States	1929	51
United States	1945	
Small city		78
Large city		81
France	1948	82
Britain	1950	70
Britain	1951	72
France	1958	67
Britain	1971	77

conceal it. Housework differs from most other work in three significant ways: it is private, it is self-defined and its outlines are blurred by its integration in a whole complex of domestic, family-based roles which define the situation of women as well as the situation of the housewife. Housework is an activity performed by housewives within their own homes. The home is the workplace, and its boundaries are also the boundaries of family life.

In modern society, the family and the home are private places, refuges from an increasingly impersonal public world. There are no laws which oblige the housewife to make the home a safe place for her family, although, by contrast, industrial employers are subject to a mass of controls. There are regulations governing the safety of domestic appliances, but the housewife as the manager of the domestic environment is not bound to see that their safety is maintained (or, indeed, to buy them in the first place). Accidents are now the prime cause of death for people under forty-five in most Western countries, and domestic accidents make up the bulk of all accidents. What people do in their own homes is their affair. Physical violence or dangerous neglect subject the lives of six children in every thousand to the risk of mortality.[14]

The physical isolation of housework – each housewife in her own home – ensures that it is totally self-defined. There are no public rules dictating what the housewife should do, or how and when she should do it. Beyond basic specifications – the provision of meals, the laundering of clothes, the care of the interior of the home – the housewife, in theory at least, defines the job as she likes. Meals can be cooked or cold; clothes can be washed when they have been worn for a few hours or a few weeks; the home can be cleaned once a month or twice a day. Who is to establish the rules, who is to set the limits of normality, if it is not the housewife herself?

Housewives belong to no trade unions; they have no professional associations to define criteria of performance, establish standards of excellence, and develop sanctions for those whose performance is inadequate or inefficient in some way. No single organization exists to defend their interests and represent them on issues and in areas which affect the performance of their role.[15] These facts confirm the diagnosis of self-definition in housework behaviour.

The housewife's isolation emphasizes her differences from other workers. She lacks the sociability of a work-group: informal associations of workers engaged on the same job are an important source of standards of performance in employment work. The housewife lacks the opportunity to associate with her co-workers and to reach agreement with them on the shape and substance of work activity. Although other people – friends, neighbours, relatives – may be an important source of housework standards and routines, the work itself has to be done in the individual home. (Shopping as a work activity is an exception to this rule.)

So infinitely variable and personal a role as the housewife's might well seem to contravene accepted definitions of what a 'role' is. (A role is 'a set of rights and obligations, that is, an abstraction to which the behaviour of people will conform in varying degree'.)[16] In the social image of a woman, the roles of wife and mother are not distinct from the role of housewife. Reflections of this image in advertising, and in the media generally, portray women as some kind of statistical mean of all three roles combined. A particularly clear presentation of this image appears in women's magazines, which show women 'how to dress, eat, housekeep, have their babies and even make love' all at the same time. 'In psychological terms they [women's magazines] enable the harassed mother, the overburdened housewife, to make contact with her ideal self: that self which aspires to be a good wife, a good mother, and an efficient home-maker.'[17] 'Housewife' can be an umbrella term for 'wife' and 'mother'. Women's expected role in society is to strive after perfection in all three roles.

A study of housework is consequently a study of women's situation. How did the present position of women as housewives come about? Has housewifery always been a feminine role? Housewives are neither endemic to the structure of the family, nor endemic to the organization of human society. Societies and family systems differ: human beings have no species-specific environment and no species-specific form of behaviour: 'It is an ethnological commonplace that the ways of becoming and being human are as numerous as man's [woman's] cultures.'[18] Other people in different cultures may live in families, but they do not necessarily have housewives.

NOTES

1 Hunt, *A Survey of Women's Employment*, vol. 1, p. 5.
2 *Oxford English Dictionary*.
3 *Guardian*, 20 August 1970.
4 Adapted from Wells, *Social Institutions*, p. 168.
5 *Evening Standard*, 24 August 1970.
6 General Register Office, *Sample Census 1966*, summary tables, p. xv.
7 Quoted in *The Times*, 7 November 1972.
8 An exception is Sweden where taxation and national insurance systems aim to treat people as individuals, not on the basis of sex or marital status. See Wynn, *Family Policy*, pp. 217–18.
9 *Guardian*, 2 November 1970.
10 Ibid., 10 March 1970.
11 Quoted in *Shrew*, July 1971, p. 2.
12 This average – 3,796 hours a year of housework time – is calculated from five studies: Girard 1958, Girard 1959, Mass Observation 1951, Moser 1950 and Stoetzel 1948.
13 Ann Oakley, *The Sociology of Housework*.
14 This is the estimate of Professor Henry Kempe, the American paediatrician who invented the phrase 'the battered baby', cited in *Guardian*, 26 June 1970.
15 Organizations like the Housewives' Register meet certain needs, especially the need for social contact, but they are neither professional organizations nor trade unions.
16 Banton, *Roles*, p. 21.
17 Quoted in White, *Women's Magazines*, p. 276.
18 Berger and Luckmann, *The Social Construction of Reality*, pp. 66–7.

5

Cynthia Cockburn

The Material of Male Power

A skilled craftsman may be no more than a worker in relation to capital, but seen from within the working class he has been a king among men and lord of his household. As a high earner he preferred to see himself as the sole breadwinner, supporter of wife and children. As artisan he defined the unskilled workman as someone of inferior status, and would 'scarcely count him a brother and certainly not an equal' (Berg, 1979:121). For any socialist movement concerned with unity in the working class, the skilled craftsman is therefore a problem. For anyone concerned with the relationship of class and gender, and with the foundations of male power, skilled men provide a fertile field for study.

Compositors in the printing trade are an artisan group that have long defeated the attempts of capital to weaken the tight grip on the labour process from which their strength derives. Now their occupation is undergoing a dramatic technological change initiated by employers. Introduction of the new computerized technology of photocomposition represents an attack on what remains of their control over their occupation and wipes out many of the aspects of the work which have served as criteria by which 'hot metal' composition for printing has been defined as a manual skill and a man's craft.[1]

In this paper I look in some detail at the compositors' crisis, what has given rise to it and what it may lead to in future. Trying to understand it has led me to ask questions in the context of socialist-feminist theory. These I discuss first, as preface to an account of key moments in the compositors' craft history. I then isolate the themes of *skill* and *technology* for further analysis, and conclude with the suggestion that there may be more to male power than 'patriarchal' relations.

PRODUCING CLASS AND GENDER

The first difficulty I have encountered in socialist-feminist theory is one that is widely recognized: the problem of bringing into a single focus our experience of both class and gender. Our attempts to ally the Marxist theory of capitalism with the feminist theory of 'patriarchy' have till now been unsatisfactory to us (Hartmann, 1979a).

One of the impediments I believe lies in our tendency to try to mesh together two static structures, two hierarchical systems. In studying compositors I found I was paying attention instead to *processes*, the detail of historical events and changes, and in this way it was easier to detect the connexions between the power systems of class and gender. What we are seeing is *struggle that contributes to the formation of people within both their class and gender simultaneously*.

One class can only exist in relation to another, E.P. Thompson wrote 'we cannot have two distinct classes each with an independent being and then bring them into relationship with each other. We cannot have love without lovers, nor deference without squires and labourers.' Likewise, it is clear we cannot have masculinity without feminity: genders presuppose each other, they are relative. Again, classes are made in historical processes. 'The working class did not rise like the sun at an appointed time. It was present at its own making. . .Class is defined by men [sic] as they live their own history' (Thompson, 1963). The mutual production of gender should be seen as a historical process too.

So in this paper I set out to explore aspects of the process of mutual definition in which men and women are locked, and those (equally processes of mutual creation) in which the working class and the capitalist class are historically engaged. Capital and labour, through a struggle over the design and manipulation of technology that the one owns and the other sets in motion, contribute to forming each other in their class characters. Powerfully-organized workers forge their class identity vis-a-vis both capital and the less organized and less skilled in part through this same process. And men and women too are to some extent mutually defined as genders through their relation to the same technology and labour process. In neither case is it a balanced process. By owning the means of production the capitalist class has the initiative. By securing privileged access to capability and technology the man has the initiative. Each gains the power to define 'another' as inferior.[2] I will try to draw these occurrences out of the story of the compositors as I tell it.

COMPONENTS OF POWER

The second theoretical need which an examination of skilled workers has led me to feel is the need for a fuller conception of the material basis of male power, one which does not lose sight of its physical and socio-political ramifications in concentrating upon the economic.

As feminism developed its account of women's subordination one problem that we met was that of shifting out of a predominantly ideological mode and narrating also the concrete practices through which women are disadvantaged. Early literature relied on 'sexist attitudes' and 'male chauvinism' to account for women's position. Socialist feminists, seeking a more material explanation for women's disadvantage, used the implement of Marxist theory, unfortunately not purpose-designed for the job but the best that was to hand. The result was an account of the economic advantages to capital of women as a distinct category of labour and their uses as an industrial reserve army. The processes of capitalism seemed to be producing an economic advantage to men which could be seen uniting with their control over women's domestic labour to form the basis of their power.[3]

Many feminists, however, were dissatisfied with what seemed a narrow 'economism' arising from Marx (or through mis-interpretation of Marx according to the point of view). The ideological vein has been more recently worked with far more sophistication than before, in different ways, by Juliet Mitchell on the one hand and Rosalind Coward on the other (Mitchell, 1975; Coward, 1978). But, as Michèle Barrett has pointed out, while 'ideology is an extremely important site for the construction and reproduction of women's oppression...this ideological level cannot be dissociated from economic relations' (Barrett, 1980).

There is thus a kind of to-ing and fro-ing between 'the ideological' and 'the economic', neither of which gives an adequate account of male supremacy or female subordination. The difficulty lies, I believe, in a confusion of terms. The proper complement of *ideology* is not the *economic*, it is the *material*.[4] And there is more to the material than the economic. It comprises also the *socio-political* and the *physical*, and these are often neglected in Marxist-feminist work.

An instance of the problems that arise through this oversight is Christine Delphy's work, where a search for a 'materialist' account of women's subordination leads her to see marriage in purely economic terms and domestic life as a mode of production, an interpretation which cannot deal with a large area of women's circumstances (Delphy, 1977).

It is only by thinking with the additional concepts of the socio-political and the physical that we can begin to look for material instances of male domination beyond men's greater earning power and property advantage. The socio-political opens up questions about male organization and solidarity, the part played by institutions such as church, societies, unions and clubs for instance.[5] And the physical opens up questions of bodily physique and its extension in technology, of buildings and clothes, space and movement. It allows things that are part of our practice ('reclaiming the night', teaching each other manual skills) a fuller place in our theory.

In this account I want to allow 'the economic' to retire into the background, not to deny its significance but in order to spotlight these other material instances of male power. The socio-political will emerge in the shape of the printing trade unions and their interests and strategies. The physical will also receive special attention because it is that which I have found most difficult to understand in the existing framework of Marxist-feminist thought. It finds expression in the compositor's capability, his dexterity and strength and in his tools and technology.

PHYSICAL EFFECTIVITY IS ACQUIRED

One further prefatory note is needed. In 1970, when Kate Millett and Shulamith Firestone, in their different ways, pinned down and analysed the system of male domination they spoke to the anger that many women felt (Millett, 1971; Firestone 1971). But many feminists were uneasy with the essentialism inherent in their view, and especially the biological determinism of Firestone and its disastrous practical implications.

Marxist-feminist theory has consequently tended to set on one side the concept of the superior physical effectivity of men, to adopt a kind of agnosticism to the idea, on account of a very reasonable fear of that biologism and essentialism which would nullify our struggle. I suggest however that we cannot do without a politics of physical power and that it need not immobilize us. In this article I use the term physical power to mean both corporal effectivity (relative bodily strength and capability) and technical effectivity (relative familiarity with and control over machinery and tools).

To say that most men can undertake feats of physical strength that most women cannot is to tell only the truth. Likewise it is true to say that the majority of men are more in their element with machinery than the majority of women. These statements are neither biologistic nor essentialist. Physical efficiency and technical capability do not belong to men primarily by birth, though DNA may offer the first step on the ladder. In the main they are appropriated by males through childhood, youth and maturity. Men's socio-political and economic power enables them to do this. In turn, their physical presence reinforces their authority and their physical skills enhance their earning power.

Ann Oakley, among others, has made the fruitful distinction between biologically-given sex (and that not always unambiguous) and culturally constituted gender, which need have little correlation with sex but in our society takes the form of a dramatic and hierarchical separation (Oakley, 1972). The part of education and that of child-rearing in constituting us as masculine and feminine *in ideology* is the subject of an extensive literature (e.g. Wolpe, 1978; Belotti, 1975). But there is evidence to show that *bodily difference* is also largely a social product. With time and work women athletes can acquire a physique which eclipses the innate differences between males and females (Ferris, 1978). Height and weight are correlated with class, produced by different standards of living, as well as with gender.[6] Boys are conditioned from childhood in numberless ways to be more physically effective than girls. They are trained in activities that develop muscle, they are taught to place their weight firmly on both feet, to move freely, to use their bodies with authority. With regard to females they are socialized to seize or shelter them and led to expect them in turn to yield or submit.

While so much of the imbalance of bodily effectiveness between males and females is produced through social practices it is misguided to prioritize that component of the difference that may prove in the last resort to be inborn.[7] More important is to study the way in which a small physical *difference* in size, strength and reproductive function is developed into an increasing relative physical *advantage* to men and vastly multiplied by differential access to technology. The process, as I will show, involves several converging practices: accumulation of bodily capabilities, the definition of tasks to match them and the selective design of tools and machines. The male physical advantage of course interacts with male economic and socio-political advantage in mutual enhancement.

The appropriation of muscle, capability, tools and machinery by men is an important source of women's subordination, indeed it is part of the process by which females are constituted as women. It is a process that is in some ways an analogue of the appropriation of the means of production by a capitalist class, which thereby constituted its complementary working class. In certain situations and instances, as in the history of printers, the process of physical appropriation (along with its ideological practices) has a part in constituting people within their class and gender simultaneously.

THE HAND COMPOSITOR: APPROPRIATION OF TECHNIQUE

Letterpress printing comprises two distinct technological processes, composing and printing. Before the mechanization of typesetting in the last decade of the nineteenth century compositors set the type by hand, organizing metal pieces in a 'stick', and proceeded to assemble it into a unified printing surface, the 'forme', ready for the printer to position on the press, coat with ink and impress upon paper.

The hand compositor, then, had to be literate, to be able to read type upside down and back to front, with a sharp eye for detail. He had to possess manual dexterity and have an easy familiarity with the position of letters in the 'case'. He had to calculate with the printers' 'point' system of measurement. Furthermore he had to have a sense of design and spacing to enable him to create a graphic whole of the printed page, which he secured through the manipulation of the assembled type, illustrative blocks and lead spacing pieces. The whole he then locked up in a forme weighing 50lbs or more. This he would lift and move to the proofing press or bring back to the stone for the distribution of used type. He thus required a degree of strength and stamina, a strong wrist, and, for standing long hours at the case, a sturdy spine and good legs.

The compositor used his craft to secure for himself a well-paid living, with sometimes greater and sometimes less success depending on conditions of trade. Through their trade societies (later unions) compositors energetically sought to limit the right of access to the composing process and its equipment to members of the society in a given town or region, blacking 'unfair houses' that employed non-society men.

Comps deployed all the material and ideological tactics they could muster in resistance to the initiatives of capital in a context of the gradual, though late, industrialization of printing. Capitalists continually aimed for lower labour costs, more productive labour processes, the 'real subordination' of labour. Their two weapons were the mobilization of cheap labour and the introduction of machinery. They repeatedly assaulted the defences of the comps' trade societies. The organized, skilled men saw their best protection against capital to lie in sharply differentiating themselves from the all-but-limitless population of potential rivals for their jobs, the remainder of the working class. They sought to control the numbers entering the trade and so to elevate their wage-bargaining position by a system of formal apprenticeship. They tried to limit the number of apprentices through an agreed ratio of boys to journeymen and to keep the period of apprenticeship as long as possible. The introduction of unapprenticed lads, 'the many-headed monster', the 'demon of cheap boy labour' was always a source of fear to compositors. Comps' jobs were kept within the class fraction by the custom of limiting openings wherever possible to members of existing printer families. Thus the struggles over physical and mental capability and the right of access to composing equipment was one of the processes in which fractions of classes were formed in relation to each other.

How did women enter this story? The answer is, with difficulty. Women and children were drawn into industrial production in many industries in the first half of the nineteenth century but in printing their entry was almost entirely limited to the bookbinding and other low-paid finishing operations held to require no skill. Girls were not considered suitable for apprenticeship. Physical and moral factors (girls were not strong enough, lead was harmful to pregnancy, the social environment might be corrupting) were deployed ideologically in such a way that few girls would see themselves as suitable candidates for apprenticeship. A second line of defence against an influx of women was of course the same socio-political controls used to keep large numbers of boys of the unskilled working class from flooding the trade.

Women who, in spite of these barriers, obtained work as non-society compositors were bitterly resisted and their product 'blacked' by the society men, i.e. work typeset by women could not be printed. Their number remained few therefore (Child, 1967). After 1859 a few small print shops were organized by philanthropic feminists to provide openings for women. It is worth noting that these enterprises did prove that women were in fact physically capable, given training and practice, of typesetting and composition, though they did not work night shifts and male assistants were engaged to do the heavy lifting and carrying. These projects were dismissed by the men as 'wild schemes of social reformers and cranks'.[8]

The process of appropriation of the physical and mental properties and technical hardware required for composing by a group of men, therefore, was not only a capitalist process of class formation, as noted above, but also a significant influence in the process of gender construction in which men took the initiative in constituting themselves and women in a relation of complementarity and hierarchy.

THE MECHANIZATION OF TYPESETTING: APPROPRIATION OF THE MACHINE

The compositors' employers had for years sought to invent a machine that could bypass the labour-intensive process of hand typesetting. They hoped in so doing not only to speed up the process but to evade the trade societies' grip on the craft, introduce women and boys and thus bring down the adult male wage. The design of such a machine proved an intractable problem. Though various prototypes and one or two production models were essayed in the years following 1840, none were commercially successful. It was only when highspeed rotary press technology developed in the 1880s that typesetting became an intolerable bottleneck to printing and more serious technological experiment was undertaken. Among the various typesetting machines that then developed, the overwhelmingly successful model was the Linotype. It continued in use almost unchanged for sixty or seventy years.

The Linotype was not allowed to replace the hand typesetter without a struggle.[9] The men believed the Iron Comp would mean mass unemployment of society members. They did not (as an organized group) reject the machine out of hand, however. Their demand was the absolute, exclusive right of hand comps to the machine and to improved earnings. Their weapons were disruption, blacking and deliberate restriction of keyboard speeds. The outcome of the struggle was seen finally by both print employers and compositors as a moderate victory for both sides. There was unemployment of hand compositors for a few years in the mid-nineties, but with the upturn of business at the end of the Great Depression the demand for print grew fast and the demand for typesetters with it. Indeed, the first agreement between the London Society of Compositors (LSC) and the employers on the adaptation of the London Scale of Prices to Linotype production was a disastrous error for the capitalists, who had underestimated the productive capacity of their new force of production and over-estimated the strength of the organized comps. The bosses only began to share fully in the profits from their invention when the agreement was revised in 1896. A lasting cost to the comps was an increasing division of labour between the two halves of their occupation: typesetting and the subsequent composing process. They did succeed however in continuing to encompass both jobs within the unitary craft and its apprenticeship as defined by their societies.

Those who really lost in the battle scarcely even engaged in it. They were the mass of labour, men and women who had no indentured occupation and who, if organized at all, were grouped in the new general unions of the unskilled. Jonathan Zeitlin firmly ascribes the success of the compositors (in contrast to engineers) in routing the employers' attempt to break their control of their craft in the technological thrust of the late nineteenth century to the former's success in ensuring that during the 'preceding decades no unskilled or semi-skilled categories of worker had been allowed to enter the composing room to fill subordinate roles (Zeitlin, 1981). And the incipient threat from women had been largely averted by the time the Linotype was invented. An exception was a pocket of female compositors in Edinburgh who had entered the trade at the time of a strike by the men in 1872 and had proved impossible to uproot.

A more sustained attempt was made by employers ten years later to introduce women to work on another typesetting process that was widely applied in the book trade: the Monotype. The Monotype Corporation, designers of the machine, in contrast to the Linotype Company Ltd., opened the way to a possible outflanking of the skilled men by splitting the tasks of keyboarding and casting into two different machines. Men retained unshaken control of the caster, but an attempt was made by employers to introduce women onto the keyboards, which had the normal typewriter lay.

In 1909–10 the compositors' societies organized a campaign, focusing on Edinburgh, to eliminate women from the trade once and for all. They succeeded in achieving a ban on female apprentices and an agreement for natural wastage of women comps and operators. This male victory was partly due to an alliance between the craft compositors and the newly organized unions of the unskilled men in the printing industry (Zeitlin, 1981).

That there were large numbers of women, literate, in need of work and eminently capable of machine typesetting at this time is evidenced by the rapid feminization of clerical work that accompanied the introduction of the office typewriter, in a situation where the male incumbent of the office was less well organized to defend himself than was the compositor (Davies, 1979). Men's socio-political power, however, enabled them to extend their physical capabilities in manual typesetting to control of the machine that replaced it. (The gender-bias of typesetting technology is discussed further below.) The effect has been that women's participation in composing work, the prestigious and better-paid aspect of printing, was kept to a minimum until the present day, not excluding the period of the two World Wars. The composing room was, and in most cases still is, an all-male preserve with a sense of camaraderie, pin-ups on the wall and a pleasure taken in the manly licence to use 'bad' (i.e. woman-objectifying) language.

ELECTRONIC COMPOSITION: THE DISRUPTION OF CLASS AND GENDER PATTERNS

In the half-century between 1910 and 1960 the printing industry saw relatively little technical change. Then, in the 1960s two big new possibilities opened up for capital in the printing industry as, emerging from post-war restrictions, it looked optimistically to expanding print markets. The first was web offset printing, with its potential flexibility and quality combined with high running speeds. The logical corollary was to abandon the machine-setting of metal type and to take up the second component of 'the new technology': letter assembly on film or photographic paper by the techniques of computer-aided photocomposition. The new process began to make inroads in to the British printing industry in the late sixties and swept through the provincial press and general printing in the seventies. The last serious redoubt of hot metal typesetting and letterpress printing was the national press in Fleet Street.

Photocomposition itself has gone through several phases of development. At first, the operation comprised a keyboarding process whereby the operator tapped a typewriter-style keyboard producing a punched paper tape. The operator worked 'blind', that is to say he saw no hard copy of his work as he produced it. The 'idiot tape' was fed into a computer which read it, made the subtle line-end decisions formerly the responsibility of the operator and output clean tape. This second tape drove a photosetter, each impulse producing a timed flash of light through a photographic image on a master disc or drum. The result was a succession of characters laid down on film or bromide paper. The columns of text were taken by the compositor, cut up, sorted and pasted in position on a prepared card, later to be photographed as a whole and reproduced on a printing plate.

In the latest electronic composing technology there is no such photomatrix of characters. The computer itself holds instructions that enable it to generate characters, in an almost limitless range of type faces and sizes and at enormously rapid speeds, on the face of a cathode ray tube. The inputting operation is performed with a keyboard associated with a video display unit on which the operator can assist computer decisions and 'massage' the copy into a desired order before committing it to the computer memory. The matter is transmitted direct from computer to photosetter and may now be produced in complete sections as large as a full newspaper page, making paste-up unnecessary.

The process is clearly seen by capital as a means of smashing the costly craft control of the compositor. The system is greatly more productive and requires less manpower. It would require less still if operated in the manner for which it is designed, i.e. avoiding two keyboarding processes by having typists, journalists, editors and authors key matter direct onto the computer disc for editing on screen and thence to direct output.

The work is much lighter, more sedentary. The abilities called upon are less esoteric, more generally available in the working population outside print. Inputting requires little more than good typing ability on the QWERTY board, something possessed by many more women than men. The implications for compositors of this twist in their craft history are dramatic. Combined with a recession it is causing unemployment in the trade, something unknown since the thirties. The individual tasks in the overall process have become trivialized and the men feel the danger of increased sub-division, routinization and substitution of unskilled workers.

The union response has not been to reject the new technology. Instead it has fought an energetic battle to retain the right to the new equipment as it did to the old. It resists 'direct input' by outsiders, asserts exclusive right to the photosetting keystroke (if necessary to a redundant second typing), to paste-up and the control of the photosetters, and where possible the computers. It is demanding increased pay and reduced hours in exchange for agreement to operate the new technology. And it is insisting (in principle at least) that all composing personnel get the chance to retrain for all aspects of the *whole* photocomposing job...an uphill struggle for reintegration of the now transformed craft.

SKILL AND ITS USES

An extensive literature has demonstrated the effect of craft organization on the structure of the working class. 'The artisan creed with regard to the labourers is that the latter are an inferior class and that they should be made to know and kept in their place' (Hobsbawm, 1964). The loss of demands on manual skill brought about by electronic photocomposition does not necessarily mean the job has become more 'mental'. On the contrary, present-day compositors feel their new work could be done by relatively unskilled workers. Many members feel they have lost status and some resent the strategic necessity to seek amalgamation of the National Graphical Association (NGA) with the unions representing the less skilled.

Our account shows however, that the purposeful differentiation between skilled and unskilled workers was also a step in the construction of *gender*. This is a more recent conception. Heidi Hartmann has suggested that 'the roots of women's present social status' lie in job segregation by sex and demonstrates the role of men and their unions in maintaining women's inferiority in the labour market by deployment of skill (Hartmann, 1979b). The fact that females in the closed-shop NGA (which embodies a large proportion of the better paid workers in the printing industry) until recently amounted to no more than 2 per cent of its membership is directly connected with the fact that women's average earnings have always been lower relative to men's in printing than in manufacturing occupations as a whole. Through the mechanisms of craft definition women have been constructed as relatively lacking in competence, and relatively low in earning power. Women's work came to be seen as inferior. Now that the new composing process resembles 'women's work' stereotypes it is felt as emasculating. The skill crisis is a crisis of both gender and class for comps.

Anne Phillips and Barbara Taylor propose that skill is a direct correlate of sexual power. 'Skill has increasingly been defined against women...far from being an objective economic fact, skill is often an ideological category imposed on certain types of work by virtue of the sex and power of the workers who perform it' (Phillips and Taylor, 1980). It is important to recognize this ideological factor. It has become increasingly important in printing with the advance of technology. The compositor sitting at a keyboard setting type is represented as doing skilled work. A girl typist at a desk typing a letter is not – though the practical difference today is slight. Nonetheless, the formulation here again, posing the ideological as foil to the economic, leads to an under-emphasis on the material realities (albeit socially acquired) of physical power and with them the tangible factors in skill which it is my purpose to reassert.

Phillips and Taylor cite several instances of job definition where the distinction between male and female jobs as skilled and unskilled is clearly no more than ideological. But in printing, and perhaps in many other occupations too, unless we recognize what measure of reality lies behind the male customary over-estimate of his skill we have no way of evaluating the impact of electronic photocomposition, the leeching out of the tangible factors of skill from some tasks and their relocation in others, out of the compositor's reach. What was the hot metal compositor's skill? He would say: I can read and calculate in a specialized manner; I can understand the process and make decisions about the job; I have aesthetic sense; I know what the tools are for and how to use them; I know the sequence of tasks in the labour process; how to operate, clean and maintain the machinery; I am dexterous and can work fast and accurately under pressure, can lift heavy weights and stand for hours without tiring. No-one but an apprenticed compositor can do ALL these things.

There are thus what we might call tangible factors in skill – things that cannot be acquired overnight. They are both intellectual and physical and among the physical are knack, strength and intimacy with a technology. They are all in large measure learned or acquired through practice, though some apprentices will never make good craftsmen. The relative importance of the factors shifts over time with changing technology. Skill is a changing constellation of practical abilities of which no single one is either necessary or sufficient. Cut away the need for one or two of them and the skill may still be capable of adaptation to remain intact, marketable and capable of defence by socio-political organization.

The tangible factors in skill may be over-stated for purposes of self-defence and are variably deployed in socio-political struggle. Thus, against the unskilled male, defined as corporally superior to the skilled, hot metal comps have defended their crafts in terms of (a) its intellectual and (b) its dexterity requirements. Against women, with their supposed superior dexterity, the skilled men on the contrary used to invoke (a) the heavy bodily demands of the work and (b) the intellectual standards it was supposed to require.[10] (Among comps today it is sometimes done to keep a list of the 'howlers' they detect in the typescripts coming to them from the 'illiterate' typists upstairs.)

The bodily strength component of the compositor's craft may be isolated to illustrate the politics involved. Men, having been reared to a bodily advantage, are able to make political and economic use of it by defining into their occupation certain tasks that require the muscle they alone possess, thereby barricading it against women who might be used against them as low-cost alternative workers (and whom for other reasons they may prefer to remain in the home). In composing, the lifting and carrying of the forme is a case in point. Nonetheless, many compositors found this aspect of the work heavy and it was felt to be beyond the strength of older men. They were always torn between wishing for unskilled muscular assistants and fearing that these, once ensconced in part of the job might lay claim to the whole.

The size and weight of the forme is arbitrary. Printing presses and the printed sheet too could have been smaller. And heavy as it is, the mechanization exists which could ease the task. It is, in printing, purely a question of custom at what weight the use of hoists and trolleys to transport the forme is introduced.

Units of work (hay bales, cement sacks) are political in their design. Capitalists with work-study in mind and men with an interest in the male right to the job both have a live concern in the bargain struck over a standard weight or size. But the political power to design work processes would be useless to men without a significant average superiority in strength or other bodily capability. Thus the appropriation of bodily effectivity on the one hand and the design of machinery and processes on the other have often converged in such a way as to constitute men as capable and women as inadequate. Like other physical differences, gender difference in average bodily strength is not illusory, it is real. It does not necessarily matter, but it can be made to matter. Its manipulation is socio-political power play.

Above everything, a skill embodies the idea of wholeness in the job and in the person's abilities, and what this 'whole' comprises is the subject of a three-way struggle between capital, craftsman and the unskilled. The struggle is over the division of labour, the building of some capabilities into machines (the computer, the robot), the hiving off of some less taxing parts of the job to cheaper workmen, or to women. Craft organization responds to capitalist development by continually redefining its area of competence, taking in and teaching its members new abilities. Wholeness has become of key significance to the compositors' union as electronic technology has trivialized and shifted the pattern of the individual tasks. Socio-political organization and power has become of paramount importance as the old tangible physical and intellectual factors have been scrapped along with the old hardware.

CONTROL OF TECHNOLOGY

Capitalists as capitalists and men as men both take initiatives over technology. The capitalist class designs new technology, in the sense that it commissions and finances machinery and sets it to work to reduce the capitalist's dependency on certain categories of labour, to divide, disorganize and cheapen labour. Sometimes machinery displaces knack and know-how, sometimes strength. Yet it is often the knowledge of the workers gained on an earlier phase of technology that produces the improvements and innovations that eventually supersede it. For instance, in a radical working men's paper in 1833, claiming rights over the bosses' machines, the men say: '*Question:* Who are the inventors of machinery? *Answer:* Almost universally the working man' (Berg, 1979:90).

In either case, it is overwhelmingly males who design technological processes and productive machinery. Many women have observed that mechanical equipment is manufactured and assembled in ways that make it just too big or too heavy for the 'average' woman to use. This need not be conspiracy, it is merely the outcome of a pre-existing pattern of power. It is a complex point. Women vary in bodily strength and size; they also vary in orientation, some having learned more confidence and more capability than others. Many processes could be carried out with machines designed to suit smaller or less muscular operators or reorganized so as to come within reach of the 'average' woman.

There are many mechanized production processes in which women are employed. But there is a sense in which women who operate machinery, from the nineteenth-century cotton spindles to the modern typewriter, are only 'lent' it by men, as men are only 'lent' it by capital. Working-class men are threatened by the machines with which capital seeks to replace them. But as and when the machines prevail it is men's hands that control them. Comps now have twice adopted new technology, albeit with bad grace, on the strict condition that it remain under their own control. They necessarily engage in a class gamble (how many jobs will be lost? will wages fall?) but their sexual standing is not jeopardized.

The history of mechanized typesetting offers as an instance of clear sex-bias within the design of equipment. The Linotype manufacturing company has twice now, in contrast to its competitors, adopted a policy that is curiously beneficial to men. A nineteenth-century rival to the Linotype was the Hattersley typesetter. It had a separate mechanism for distributing type, designed for use by girls. The separation of the setting (skilled) from dissing (unskilled) was devised as a means of reducing overall labour costs. A representative of the Hattersley company wrote 'it would be a prostitution of the object for which the machine was invented and a proceeding against which we would protest at all times' to employ *men* on the disser (Typographical Association, 1893).

The Linotype machine on the other hand did not represent the destruction but merely the mechanization of the comp's setting skills as a *whole*. In fact, the LSC congratulated the Linotype Company Ltd. 'The Linotype answers to one of the essential conditions of trade unionism, in that it does not depend for its success on the employment of boy or girl labour; but on the contrary, appears to offer the opportunity for establishing an arrangement whereby it may be fairly and honestly worked to the advantage of employer, inventor and workman' (Typographical Association, 1893). While Linotype were not above using male scab trainees when driven to it by the comps' ca'canny, they never tried to put women on the machines and indeed curried favour with the LSC by encouraging employers who purchased the machine to shed female typesetters and replace them with union men.

Ninety years on, Linotype (now Linotype-Paul) are leading designers and marketers of electronic composing systems. Most present day manufacturers, with an eye to the hundreds of thousands of low-paid female typists their clients may profit from installing at the new keyboards, have designed them with the typewriter QWERTY lay, thus reducing Lino operators at a single blow to fumbling incompetence. Linotype Paul is one of the few firms offering an optional alternative keyboard, the 90-key lay familiar to union comps. Once more, they seem to be wooing the organized comp as man and in doing so are playing, perhaps, an ambivalent part in the class struggle being acted out between print employers, craftsmen and unskilled labour (since employers would profit more by the complete abolition of the 90-key board).

Now, electronic photocomposition is an almost motionless labour process. The greatest physical exertion is the press of a key. The equipment is more or less a 'black box'. The intelligence lies between the designers, maintenance engineers and programmers and the computer and its peripherals. Only the simplest routine processes and minimal decisions are left to the operator.

Two factors emerge. It is significant that the great majority of the electronic technical stratum are male (as history would lead us to expect). Male power deriving from prestigious jobs has shifted up-process leaving the compositor somewhat high and dry, vulnerable to the unskilled and particularly to women. In so far as he operates this machinery he has a 'female' relationship to it: he is 'lent' it by men who know more about its technicalities than he does.

The NGA, faced with a severe threat to composing as a craft, has been forced into innovatory manoeuvres in order to survive as a union. It is widening its scope, radically re-designing and generalizing its apprenticeship requirements, turning a blind eye to the fact that some of the new style comps it recruits 'on the job' come in without apprenticeships (and a handful of these are now women who have graduated from typing to simple composers). It is seeking to recruit office workers, a proportion of whom will be female typists who are seen as a weapon employers may try to use against comps. They are to be organized in separate division within the union and thus will be under supervision by the union but not permitted to invade the area of existing comps' work.

CONCLUSION: MEN'S POWER AND PATRIARCHY

This study has been of the workplace. Marxist theory proposed the workplace as the primary locus of capitalist exploitation, while women's disadvantage was seen as having its site in the property relations of the family. The corollary of this view was the belief (disproved by the passing of time) that women would evade their subordination to men when they came out into waged work (Engels, 1972). Feminists have shown on the contrary that the family, as the throne of 'patriarchy', has its own malevolent effectivity within capitalism and capitalist relations, it pursues women out into waged work (Kuhn, 1978; Bland, 1978).

Many women, however, are relatively detached from conjugal or paternal relationships. Many are single, childless, widowed, live independently, collectively, without husbands, free from fathers. Can 'the family' satisfactorily account today for the fact that they hesitate to go to the cinema alone, have to call on a man to change a car wheel, or feel put out of countenance by walking into a pub or across a composing room floor? Our theories of sexual division of labour at work have tended to be an immaculate conception unsullied by these physical intrusions. They read: women fill certain inferior places provided by capitalism, but do so in a way for which they are destined by the shackles of family life. The free-standing woman, the physical reality of men, their muscle or initiative, the way they wield a spanner or the spanner they wield, these things have been diminished in our account.

The story of compositors, for me, throws doubt on the adequacy of the explanation that the sexual relations of work can be fully accounted for as a shadow cast by the sex-relations of the family. It seems to me that the construction of gender difference and hierarchy is created at work as well as at home – and that the effect on women (less physical and technical capability, lack of confidence, lower pay) may well cast a shadow on the sex-relations of domestic life.

In socialist-feminist thought there has been a clear divide between production (privileged site of class domination) and the family (privileged site of sexual domination). The patriarchal family is recognized as adapted to the interests of capital and the capitalist division of labour as being imprinted with the patterns of domestic life. They are conceded to be mutually effective, but are nonetheless still largely conceived as two separate spheres, capitalism holding sway in one, patriarchy in the other.

Yet the compositors' story reveals a definable area of sex-gender relations that cannot be fully subsumed into 'the family', an area which has tended to be a blindspot for socialist-feminist theory. It is the same as that spot within the class relations of wage labour and capitalist production, invisible to Marxist theory, in which male power is deployed in the interests of men – capital apart. In our analysis we can accommodate men as 'patriarchs', as fathers or husbands, and we can accommodate capitalists and workers who are frequently men. But where is the man as male, the man who fills those spaces in capitalist production that he has defined as not ours, who designs the machines and thereby decides who will use them? Where is the man who decorates the walls of his workplace with pin-ups of naked women and whose presence on the street is a factor in a woman's decision whether to work the night shift?

It was an incalculable breakthrough in the late sixties when the sexual relations of private life came to be more generally recognized as political. But somehow those sexual relations have remained ghettoized within the family. Only slowly are we demolishing the second wall, to reveal in theory what we know in practice, that the gender relations of work and public life, of the factory and the street, are sexual politics too.[11]

It is in this sense that the prevailing use of the concept of 'patriarchy' seems to me a problem. Some feminists have argued, I think rightly, that it is too specific an expression to describe the very diffuse and changing forms of male domination that we experience, and that it should be reserved for specific situations where society is organized through the authority of fathers and husbands over wives and offspring and of older men over younger men (Young and Harris, 1976). Such a 'patriarchy' would usefully enable us, for instance, to characterize certain historical relations in the printing industry: the archaic paternalism of journeyman-apprentice relations, the handing of job from father to son, the role of the 'father' of chapel in the union etc. But these practices are changing in printing – just as Jane Barker and Hazel Downing have shown that patriarchal relations of control in the office are being rendered obsolete by the new capitalist office technology (Barker and Downing, 1980).

Do we then assume that male supremacy is on the wane in the workplace? I think not. The gap between women's earnings and men's in printing has widened in the last few years. What we are seeing in the struggle over the electronic office and printing technology is a series of transformations within gender relations and their articulation with class relations. The class relations are those of capitalism. The gender relations are those of a wider, more pervasive and more long-lived male dominance system than patriarchy. They are those of a sex-gender system[12] in which men dominate women inside and outside family relations, inside and outside economic production, by means which are both material and ideological, exercising their authority through both individual and organizational development. It is more nearly andrarchy[13] than patriarchy.

Finally, in what practical sense do these questions matter to women? Seeing bodily strength and capability as being socially constructed and politically deployed helps us as an organized group in that we can fight for the right to strengths and skills that we feel to be useful. On the other hand, where we do not see this kind of power as socially beneficial, our struggle can seek to devalue it by socio-political means in the interests of a gentler world (or to prevent our being disadvantaged by what may turn out to be our few remaining innate differences).

Identifying the gendered character of technology enables us to overcome our feelings of inferiority about technical matters and realise that our disqualification is the result not of our own inadequacy, nor of chance, but of power-play. Understanding technology as an implement in capital's struggle to break down workers' residual control of the labour process helps us to avoid feeling 'anti-progress' if and when we need to resist it. Understanding it as male enables us to make a critique of the exploitation of technology for purposes of power by men – both over women and over each other, in competition, aggression, militarism.

Unless we recognize what capital is taking away from some men as workers, we cannot predict the strategies by which they may seek to protect their position as men. As one technology fails them will they seek to establish a power base in another? Will they eventually abandon the deskilled manual work to women, recreating the job segregation that serves male dominance? Or will the intrinsic interdependency of keyboard and computer force a re-gendering of 'typing' so that it is no longer portrayed as female? As men's physical pre-eminence in some kinds of work is diminished will they seek to reassert it heavily in private life? Or is the importance of physical effectivity genuinely diminishing in the power relations of gender? Can the unions, so long a socio-political tool of men, be made to serve women? We need to understand all the processes that form us as workers and as women if we are to exert our will within them.

ACKNOWLEDGEMENTS

Thanks for helpful criticism of this paper in draft to Marianne Craig, Jane Foot, Nicola Murray, Anne Phillips, Eileen Phillips, Caroline Poland, Mary Slater, Judy Wajcman, Kate Young and members of the *Feminist Review* collective.

NOTES

1 The article is based on a project in progress, 'Skilled printing workers and technological change', funded by the Social Science Research Council and carried out at The City University, London. The paper was first given at the annual conference of the British Sociological Association in 1981.
2 The fact that a mode of production and a sex-gender system are two fundamental and parallel features of the organization of human societies should not lead us to expect to find any exact comparability between them, whether the duo is capitalism/'patriarchy' or any other. In the case of a sex-gender system there is a biological factor that is strongly, though not absolutely, predisposing. This is not the case in a class system. The historical timescale of modes of production appears to be shorter than that of sex-gender systems. And the socio-political and economic institutions of class seem to be more formal and visible than those of gender – though one can imagine societies where this might not be the case.
3 Michèle Barrett has reviewed in detail the progress of this endeavour (Barrett, 1980). An important contribution to the 'appropriation of patriarchy by materialism' has been Kuhn and Wolpe (1978).
4 I adopt here Michèle Barrett's useful re-assertion of the distinction between ideology and 'the material', in place of a simplistic fusion 'ideology is material'. She cites Terry Eagleton, 'there is no possible sense in which meanings and values can be said to be "material", other than in the most sloppily metaphorical use of the term...If meanings *are* material, then the term "materialism" naturally ceases to be intelligible' (Barrett, 1980:89–90).
5 Heidi Hartmann's definition of patriarchy is novel in including 'hierarchical relations between men and *solidarity among them*' (Hartmann, 1979b).
6 For instance, children whose families' low income entitles them to free school milk are shorter than the average child (demonstrated in articles in *The Lancet*, 1979). More information relating class and stature is available from Department of Health and Social Security 'Heights and Weights Survey' (1982).
7 Griffiths and Saraga (1979) have argued the same of sex difference in cognitive ability.
8 A fuller account exists in Cynthia Cockburn (1980) 'The losing battle: women's attempts to enter composing work 1850–1914', Working Note No. 11, unpublished.

9 I have traced the course of this technological development in 'The Iron Comp: the mechanization of composing', Working Note, no. 10, 1980, unpublished.
10 For an interesting discussion of 'dexterity' versus 'skill' in relation to gender see Ramsay Macdonald (1904).
11 A sign of change in this direction was Farley (1980), concerning sexual harrassment of women at work.
12 Gayle Rubin's term (Rubin, 1975)
13 Rule by *men* as opposed to rule by fathers or male heads of household or tribe, cf. androgynous, polyandry, andro-centrism.

REFERENCES

Barker, Jane and Downing, Hazel (1980) 'Word processing and the transformation of patriarchal relations of control in the office' *Capital & Class* no. 10.
Barrett, Michèle (1980) *Women's Oppression Today* London: Verso.
Belotti, Elena (1975) *Little Girls* London: Virago.
Berg, Maxine (1979) ed., *Technology and Toil in Nineteenth-Century Britain* London: CSE Books.
Bland, Lucy et al. (1978) 'Women "inside and outside" the relations of production' in Women's Studies Group, Centre for Contemporary Cultural Studies (1978).
Child, John (1967) *Industrial Relations in the British Printing Industry* London: Allen and Unwin.
Coward, Rosalind (1978) 'Rethinking Marxism' *m/f* no. 2.
Davies, Margery (1979) 'Woman's place is at the typewriter' in Eisenstein (1979).
Delphy, Christine (1977) *The Main Enemy* London: Women's Research and Resources Centre.
Eisenstein, Zillah (1979) ed., *Capitalist Patriarchy and the Case for Socialist Feminism* New York and London: Monthly Review Press.
Engels, Frederick (1972) *The Origin of the Family, Private Property and the State* London: Pathfinder Press.
Farley, Lin (1980) *Sexual Shakedown* USA: Warner Paperback.
Ferris, Elizabeth (1978) 'Sportswomen and medicine, the myths surrounding women's participation in sport and exercise' in Report of the 1st International Conference on Women and Sport, Central Council of Physical Recreation, London.
Firestone, Shulamith (1971) *The Dialectic of Sex* London: Jonathan Cape.
Griffiths, Dorothy and Saraga, Esther (1979) 'Sex differences and cognitive abilities: a sterile field of enquiry' in Hartnett (1979).
Hartmann, Heidi (1979a) 'The unhappy marriage of Marxism and feminism: towards a more progressive union' *Capital & Class* no. 8.
Hartmann, Heidi (1979b) 'Capitalism, patriarchy and job segregation' in Eisenstein (1979).
Hartnett, O. et al. (1979) *Sex-role Stereotyping* London: Tavistock Publications Ltd.
Hobsbawm, E.J. (1964) *Labouring Men* London: Weidenfeld and Nicholson.
Kraft, Philip (1979) 'Industrialization of computer programming: from programming to software production' in Zimbalist (1979).
Kuhn, Annette (1978) 'Structures of patriarchy and capital in the family' in Kuhn and Wolpe (1978).
Kuhn, Annette and Wolpe, AnnMarie (1978) editors, *Feminism and Materialism* London: Routledge and Kegan Paul.

Millett, Kate (1971) *Sexual Politics* London: Rupert Hart-Davis.
Mitchell, Juliet (1975) *Psychoanalysis and Feminism* London: Penguin.
Oakley, Ann (1972) *Sex, Gender and Society* London: Temple Smith.
Phillips, Anne and Taylor, Barbara (1980) 'Sex and skill: notes towards a feminist economics' *Feminist Review* no. 6.
Ramsay Macdonald, J. (1904) editor, *Women in the Printing Trades, a Sociological Study* London: P.S. King and Son.
Reiter, Rayna R. (1975) ed., *Toward an Anthropology of Women* New York: Monthly Review Press.
Rubin, Gayle (1975) 'The traffic in women: notes on the political economy of sex' in Reiter (1975).
Thompson, Edward P. (1963) *The Making of the English Working Class* London: Victor Gollancz.
Typographical Association, Report of the Delegate Meeting in Sheffield, December 4, 1893.
Wolpe, AnnMarie (1978) 'Education and the sexual division of labour' in Kuhn and Wolpe (1978).
Women's Studies Group, Centre for Contemporary Cultural Studies (1978) *Women Take Issue* London: Hutchinson.
Young, Kate and Harris, Olivia (1976) 'The subordination of women in cross-cultural perspective' in *Papers on Patriarchy* London: PDC and Women's Publishing Collective.
Zeitlin, Jonathan (1981) 'Craft regulation and the division of labour: engineers and compositors in Britain 1890–1914' PhD Thesis, Warwick University.
Zimbalist, A. (1979) ed., *Case Studies in the Labor Process* New York and London: Monthly Review Press.

6

Floya Anthias and Nira Yuval-Davis

Contextualizing Feminism – Gender, Ethnic and Class Divisions

INTRODUCTION

'Sisterhood is powerful.' 'Sisterhood' can also be misleading unless contextualized. Black, minority and migrant women have been on the whole invisible within the feminist movement in Britain and within the literature on women's or feminist studies. This paper attempts to explore the issue of the interrelationship of ethnic and gender divisions.[1] Not only is such an attempt long overdue theoretically but it also raises political issues which must be central to feminist struggle.

Our analysis serves to problematize the notion of 'sisterhood' and the implicit feminist assumption that there exists a commonality of interests and/or goals amongst all women. Rather we argue that *every* feminist struggle has a specific *ethnic* (as well as class) context. Although the notion of the 'ethnic' will be considered later in the paper we note here that for us it primarily relates to the exclusionary/inclusionary boundaries of collectivities formed round the notion of a common origin.[2] The 'ethnic' context of feminist struggles has been systematically ignored (except in relation to various minorities, especially 'black') and we suggest this has helped to perpetuate both political and theoretical inadequacies within feminist and socialist analyses.

The black feminist movement has grown partly as a response to the invisibility of black women and to the racism of the white feminist movement. Recently several books have appeared, mostly American, which discuss black women and feminism. Bell Hooks puts her case against white feminism clearly when she states:

> In much of the literature written by white women on the 'woman question' from the nineteenth century to the present day, authors will refer to 'white

> men' but use the word 'woman' when they really mean 'white woman'. Concurrently, the term 'blacks' is often made synonymous with black men (1981:140).

In addition she points out that there has been a constant comparison of the plight of 'women' and 'blacks' working with these racist/sexist assumptions and which has diverted attention from the specificity of the oppression of black women. We share this critique of white feminism which is found within the black feminist movement in Britain also. However we want to broaden out the frame of reference of the existing debate. Within black feminism the most dominant approach defines black women as suffering from the 'triple oppression' of race, gender and class. This approach is inadequate, however, both theoretically and politically. Race, gender and class cannot be tagged on to each other mechanically for, as concrete social relations, they are enmeshed in each other and the particular intersections involved produce specific effects. The need for the study of the intersection of these divisions has been recognized recently by black feminists.[3]

We also suggest, however, that the issue of the interrelationship of the different social divisions cannot focus only on black versus white women's position. This has the theoretical effect of singling out 'racism' as applicable only to 'black' women and focuses then on the colour rather than on the structural location of ethnic groups as determinants of their social relations. In addition an exclusive focus on 'racism' fails to address the diversity of ethnic experiences which derive from other factors like economic or political position. The notion of 'black women' as delineating the boundaries of the alternative feminist movement to white feminism leaves non-British non-black women (like us – a Greek-Cypriot and an Israeli–Jew) unaccounted for politically. Although we recognize the impetus behind the black women's movement and the need for its autonomous organization, black feminism can be too wide or too narrow a category for specific feminist struggles. On the one hand, there are struggles which concern all migrant women, like those against immigration laws, and on the other hand there are struggles which might concern only Sikh Indian women for instance.

For these reasons, our paper will use the notion of ethnic divisions rather than the black/white division as a more comprehensive conceptual category for struggling against racism. One of our tasks will be to consider the links between the concepts of racism and ethnicity as well as attempting to relate ethnic divisions to those of gender and class.

The Marxist tradition of analysis which has informed much of socialist-feminist analysis has been partly responsible for the invisibility of ethnic divisions (as well as the feminist tradition itself which assumes unitary and biological roots to 'women'). Contemporary Marxist analysis has indeed recognized the importance of relating ethnic to class divisions and gender to class divisions but there has been little attempt to link ethnic and gender divisions to each other. In addition Marxism has had difficulty in analysing ethnic or gender divisions without reducing them to some form of class division. Because of the significance of this tradition of analysis for us we shall present a critique of Marxism as a necessary preliminary to developing our own position.

We shall then present an exploratory framework for analysing the interrelationship of ethnic and gender divisions. We shall briefly examine these divisions within two central areas of feminist analysis, employment and reproduction. The paper will conclude by considering some of the implications of the analysis presented for the western/Third World feminist debate.

ETHNIC AND GENDER DIVISIONS AND MARXISM

As already noted Marxism has particular difficulties in analysing non-class social divisions. The Marxist concept of the mode of production is based on an abstract model of relations that does not signal the concrete groups of people within it. It does however establish a firm grounding for class divisions in as much as the concept of class is hierarchically incorporated within a systematic theory whose central concept is that of mode of production. But ethnic divisions and gender divisions cannot be situated within this theory for they are not essential constituents of it – the theoretical basis for them is missing.[4] The abstract level of analysis in Marx's *Capital* presents problems for the analysis of concrete social relations including those of class. In some versions of Marxism found in economistic approaches, classes as concrete groups of people are reduced to the workings of the economy or the 'needs' of capital. We do not accept the depiction of class in concrete analysis as reducible to its own dynamics as found within the sphere of the economy. Indeed much recent analysis has treated classes as concrete historical groupings whose actual practices are not reducible to mode of production effects. We would take issue with a reductionist position that sees a necessary relationship between, for example, class determination and political/class position. Particularly we reject this not only because of the usual reasons given by Marxists, i.e. the separate effectivity of the ideological and political realms, but also because we consider the intersection between class, ethnic and gender divisions as important in the development of particular forms of political consciousness and action.

Unlike the analysis of class which finds a theoretical basis in Marxism despite the difficulties encountered in concrete analysis, different problems are presented in the analysis of gender and ethnic divisions. When these categories are used by Marxists they often involve very common-sense usages since Marxism has not systematically concerned itself with them as theoretical constructs. This has led to very unclear and unspecific usages and shifts in meaning from, for example, identifying gender with a biological constituent and at other times seeing it as a social construct or race as historically produced and yet as basically organized around the ascriptive characteristic of 'blackness'.

Because of Marxism's failure to specifically deal with gender and ethnic divisions, Marxist feminists and Marxist anti-racists have attempted to ground them within economic relations, although Marxist feminists particularly have sought to do so in a non-class-reductionist way. Ethnic and gender groups have been seen as structured by the 'needs' of capital for migrant labour or cheap labour. The reserve army of labour debate is an example of this.[5] In addition there has been a tendency to reduce these groups to fundamentally class groupings. For example we have seen attempts to theorize black people in Britain as a class fraction, or an underclass and migrants in Europe as a 'class stratum' of the working class. This approach empirically fails to note the differentiation within the ethnic or migrant category, both in terms of ethnicity and gender and in terms of economic, political and ideological location. In addition this reduction to class can only present gender and ethnic identities as some form of 'false-consciousness' – as illusionary. For example some attempts to theorize ethnicity have seen it as a form of incipient class consciousness whose essential project develops into that of class.[6] (Interestingly the notion of women as a class is mostly systematically presented by Delphy (1977) from a radical-feminist position.)

The Marxist theorization of the state, ranging from the classical Marxist tradition of Engels, Lenin and Rosa Luxemburg to more recent developments (instrumental, coordinator functional and state derivation approaches) presents a different problem for the analysis of ethnic divisions.[7]

Marxist theories of the state have tended to identify the boundaries of the national collectivity with that of the relations of production. This is found in Marx's own assumption concerning the overlapping of the boundary between civil and political society. In Marx's words 'In the state the whole civil society of an epoch is epitomized.' For Marxists, on the whole, the rise of the nation-state is actively bounded by the relations of production and conditions of class conflict. For example the classical analysis of Engels of the emergence of the state depicts it as a result of society's entanglement in insoluble class antagonisms (Engels, 1972). Thus Marxist analyses have been sensitive to differential access to power of different classes but not to other forms of differential access based on gender or ethnic, national or racial divisions.[8] These assumptions are not seriously challenged by the various recent Marxist theorizations of the state.

Our view is that it is not sufficient to assert as Schermerhorn (1970) does that each nation-state in the modern world contains sub-sections or sub-systems. It is also the case that in almost all social formations there are sections of the population that are to varying degrees excluded from political participation and representation. This exclusion operates at least partially in a different manner from the exclusion of 'classes' of the dominant national or ethnic group. For example, the new Nationality Bill in Britain presents exclusion not on the basis of class (as does legislation concerning private property for example) but on the basis of ethnicity and gender.

A further problem within some Marxist literature is the suggestion that internal ethnic divisions are ideological in the sense of 'false' or non-real. The attempt to theorize a distinction between historical (i.e. real) and non-historical (i.e. non-real) nations assumed that if an ethnic minority was able to obtain a separate and independent state, then it was based on a real and historical origin and other minorities were non-historical and only 'ideological'.[9]

All three divisions have an organizational, experiential and representational form, are historically produced and therefore changeable, are affected by and affect each other and the economic, political and ideological relations in which they are inserted. Relations of power are usually found within each division and thus often the existence of dominant and subordinate partners. They are all therefore framed in relation to each other within relations of domination. They may thus involve political mobilization, exclusion from particular resources and struggles over them, claims to political representation and the formation of concrete interests and goals which may shift over time. It is not a question therefore of one being more 'real' than the others or a question of *which* is the most important. However it is clear that the three divisions prioritize different spheres of social relations and will have different effects which it may be possible to specify in concrete analysis. However we suggest that each division exists within the context of the others and that any concrete analysis has to take this into account.

Firstly, we shall briefly comment on these divisions, clarifying the sense in which we use them and noting some of the main differences amongst them. Secondly, we shall begin to situate them in relation to each other in the spheres of employment and reproduction, two central areas of feminist analyses. We shall particularly note the links between gender and ethnic divisions since this has rarely been considered.

CLASS, GENDER AND ETHNIC DIVISIONS

As socialists working within a broadly Marxist-informed analysis we see class divisions as grounded in the different relations of groups to the means of production which provides what has been called a group's class determination. However class mobilization cannot be read from class determination for class goals are constructed through a variety of different mechanisms with ideological practices having a central role in this. Concrete class groupings may be composed of both men and women, of black and white and different cultures and ethnic identities. These concrete groupings are constructed historically. At times there may be a coincidence of class and gender or ethnic position (and at other times there maybe cross cuttings). For example, some fractions of the working class may be primarily composed of women or black people. This may reflect economic, political and ideological processes but may also be structured through struggle and negotiation between the groups themselves and in relation to the state. Classes are not homogeneous ethnically, culturally or in terms of gender in most cases but class fractions may constitute some kind of homogeneity.

Gender divisions relate to the organization of sexual difference and biological reproduction and establish forms of representation around these, although their concrete contents will include notions of the appropriateness of wage-labour, education and so on to men and to women. Usually sexual difference and biological reproduction (the ontological basis of gender) are represented as having necessary social effects (from say 'sexual intercourse' to 'class position'). Gender divisions thus usually work with a notion of a 'natural' relationship between social effects and sexual differences/biological reproduction. We do not accept such a depiction nor that biological *reproduction* is an equivalent material basis for *gender* to that of *production* for *class*. Indeed the attempt to discover a feminist materialism in the social relations of reproduction fails precisely in the attempt to superimpose a materialist project onto a different object and reproduce its terms of reference.[10] Finally the end result is indeed to reduce these social relations to their material base (biology) just as within Marxist materialism the reduction is to 'mode of production'.

Rather we reject both biological reductionism and class reductionism. We are suggesting that there is an *object* of discursive reference in the sphere of gender divisions which relates to groups of subjects *defined* by their sexual/biological difference as opposed to groups of subjects defined by their economic production difference as in class. Gender divisions are 'ideological' to the extent that they do not have a basis in reproduction, but reproduction is represented as their basis. However, the ideological nature of gender divisions does not mean they do not exist nor that they do not have social origins and social effects or involve material practices.

Unlike class and gender divisions, ethnic divisions are difficult to ground in some separate sphere of relations. This makes the various Marxist and sociological attempts to try to find systematic conceptual differences between national/ethnic and racial groupings even more problematic. This attempt is never successful because it is impossible to systematically ascribe particular and different realms to them. Migration, conquest and colonization have developed a vast heterogeneous body of historical cases.

The only general basis on which we can theorize what can broadly be conceived as 'ethnic' phenomena in all their diversity are as various forms of ideological construct which divide people into different collectivities or communities. This will involve exclusionary/inclusionary boundaries which form the collectivity. In other words although the constructs are ideological, they involve real material practices and therefore origins and effects. Whether the boundaries are those of a tribe, a nation or a linguistic or cultural minority, they will tend to focus themselves around the myth of common origin (whether biological, cultural or historical). Although sometimes there will be other means of joining the collectivity than being born into it (like religious conversion or naturalization), group membership is considered as the 'natural' right of being *born* into it. The salience of the collectivity and the social relations involved can vary greatly.

Ethnicity is not only a question of ethnic identity. This latter does not exhaust the category of the 'ethnic' nor does it necessarily occur. Ethnicity may be constructed outside the group by the material conditions of the group and its social representation by other groups. However in practice ethnic identity and often solidarity may occur either as a pre-requisite for the group or as an effect of its material, political or ideological placement. In addition ethnicity involves struggle, negotiation and the use of ethnic resources for the countering of disadvantages or perpetuation of advantages. Conditions of reproduction of the ethnic group as well as its transformation are related to the divisions of gender and class. For example, class homogeneity within the ethnic group will produce a greater cohesion of interests and goals.

The concept of ethnicity has too often been identified in Britain with the Ethnic School tradition which tends to concentrate on issues of culture or identity and has come under a great deal of justified attack for ignoring racism and the structural disadvantages of minority ethnic groups.[11] However our use of the term ethnicity has as a central element exclusion/inclusion practices and the relations of power of dominance/subordination that are aspects of these. Majority groups possess an ethnicity as well as minority groups. Ethnicity and racism share both the categories of exclusion and power but racism is a specific form of exclusion. Racist discourse posits an essential biological determination to culture but its referent may be any group that has been 'socially' constructed as having a different 'origin', whether cultural, biological or historical. It can be 'Jewish', 'black', 'foreign', 'migrant', 'minority'. In other words any group that has been located in ethnic terms can be subjected to 'racism' as a form of exclusion. The 'Racist' category is more deterministic than the mere 'ethnic' category.

Concerning the difference between ethnic and national groups, it is often a question of the different goals and achievements of the collectivity. The nationalist project is more strictly political for its claims will necessarily include rights to separate political representation or to territory (as in the case of Palestinians and Jews in Israel and Turkish-Cypriots and Greek-Cypriots in Cyprus).

We consider that gender and ethnic divisions particularly are underpinned by a notion of a 'natural' relation. In gender divisions it is found in the positing of necessary social effects to sexual difference and biological reproduction and in ethnic divisions by assumptions concerning the 'natural' boundaries of collectivities or the 'naturalness' of culture. In capitalist societies like Britain very often the 'natural' ideological elements of gender and ethnic divisions are used to 'naturalize' unequal class divisions. Gender and ethnic divisions are used as legitimizors in two major ways.

In patriarchal white societies it is perceived as 'natural' that men will occupy a higher economic position in the labour market than women and white people than black people. For example notions of women's sexual difference (more 'submissive', 'feminine', 'intuitive', 'expressive', 'dextrous') and their 'essential mothering role' are used and are often manipulated for economically justifying (explaining) women's position (at times by women themselves). Racism and ethnicity also have a role in justifying the economic/class subordination of black people. For example arguments about the cultural choices of ethnic groups – and racial stereotypes about Asian men (money-seeking) and Afro-Caribbean men (work idle) – are used to account for their economic position. The second way in which the 'natural' elements of gender and ethnic divisions are used is as rallying points for political struggle against class inequality as well as gender and ethnic inequalities. This is the case in most anti-imperialist struggles where notions of national identity are used. The black power movement has often used racial-ethnic identification partly as a counter to existing racial stereotypes and oppressions (for example in black nationalism the identification with Africa and in black power the 'black is beautiful' rhetoric and more recently, culturalist and religious revivals such as Rastafarianism). As regards gender, feminists have used women's 'nature' as a rallying point, particularly with reference to the positive values of women's culture and 'nature'. However, using ethnic and gender categories in this way as rallying points for political mobilization in class-related struggles can present a problem for class unity.

As well as ethnic and gender divisions being used for class goals, class divisions can provide the material conditions for ethnic and gender groups, for these will give unequal access to economic resources. State practices may exclude class, ethnic and gender groupings in different ways, structure their relationship to each other and give differential political power to different groups. Therefore when we analyse specific historical cases these divisions often cannot be separated.

We have suggested that the 'natural' ideological aspects of ethnic and gender groupings inform class relations. In addition we would suggest that ethnic and gender divisions are more socially immutable. Whereas it is possible theoretically for subjects to change class position (although empirically it may be difficult), it is not so for gender or ethnic position (especially for the 'racial' category). Gender position is fixed (apart from transexuals) and generally one is 'born' into one's ethnic position. In particular cases, women can become 'honorary' men (when men are not available for example to do 'male' work as in war) or religious conversion can occur. But the major mechanism is ascriptive for both ethnic and gender divisions.

THE RELATIONS BETWEEN GENDER AND ETHNIC DIVISIONS

We suggested above all that three divisions are intermeshed in such a way that we cannot see them as additive or prioritize abstractly any one of them. Each division presents ideological and organizational principles within which the others operate, although in different historical contexts and different social arenas their role will differ. The fusion of gender and class and ethnicity and class will also operate in the relationship between gender and ethnic divisions.

For example if we consider the household we will find gender divisions will differ according to ethnicity. Ethnically specific definitions of women's and men's roles underlie the sexual division of labour in the family. Such aspects as mothering, housework, sexual obligations, obedience and submissiveness to male commands (and indeed to other members of the family) will differ according to ethnicity (as well as class of course). We would suggest that ethnic divisions are particularly important in the internal gender divisions within the household and family therefore, although state practices will affect them.

If we consider the sphere of employment – the more public or external sexual division of labour – this will be affected particularly by the gender divisions of the majority ethnic group. Values and institutionalized practices about women's 'nature' and 'role' present constraints to men and women from minority/subordinate ethnic groups despite their own gender ideologies.

Another link between ethnic and gender divisions is found in the way in which the *boundary* of ethnicity depends on gender. The definition of membership within the ethnic group often depends on performing gender attributes correctly. Both identity and institutional arrangements of ethnic groups incorporate gender roles and specify appropriate relations between sexes such as, for example, who can marry them. A Greek-Cypriot girl of the second generation is regarded as 'Kypraia' usually when she conforms to rules about sexually appropriate behaviour – otherwise she becomes excluded. The definition of boundaries is far from being an internal practice alone. If we consider racial stereotypes we can see the centrality of gender roles; for example stereotypes about the 'dominant' Asian father and the 'dominant' black mother, or stereotypes about black men and women as sexual 'studs'. These all indicate the reliance on gender attributes for specifying ethnic difference. We want to briefly suggest some more specific links between ethnic and gender divisions in employment and reproduction.

EMPLOYMENT

The internal gender divisions of an ethnic group will also affect the participation of men and women of the group in the labour market. Men and women of a specific ethnic group will tend to hold particular but different positions in the labour market; for example Afro-Caribbean men in the construction industry and on the buses, Afro-Caribbean women as service workers in manufacturing and as nurses, Asian men in textile firms and Asian women as outworkers in small-scale dress-making factories. A sexually differentiated labour market will structure the placement of subjects according to sex but ethnic divisions will determine their subordination within them – so, for example, black and white women may both be subordinate within a sexually differentiated labour market but black women will be subordinated to white women within this.

We would suggest that within western societies, gender divisions are more important for women than ethnic divisions in terms of labour market subordination. In employment terms, migrant or ethnic women are usually closer to the female population as a whole than to ethnic men in the type of wage-labour performed. Black and migrant women are already so disadvantaged by their gender in employment that it is difficult to show the effects of ethnic discrimination for them. When examining the position of ethnic minority men in the labour market, the effect of their ethnic position is much more visible. This may lead to a situation where for example Afro-Caribbean or Asian women have at times had greater ease in finding employment – as cheap labour in 'women's work', whether it be nursing, assembly-line or clerical work – than the men.

But the interrelationship between ethnic and gender divisions in employment goes beyond the mere differentiation in employment of ethnic subjects according to their gender. This additional dimension however is even less stressed in the literature on ethnic and race relations. The economic and social advancement of a migrant group may depend partly on the possibility of using the *household* and in particular the women within it as a labour resource. The extent to which migrant ethnic men have become incorporated into wider social production and the form this takes may also depend on the use of *migrant* women's labour *overall*. Men from different migrant/ethnic groups have been incorporated differently economically. Afro-Caribbean men for example are in the 'vanguard' of British industry in large-scale production (Hall et al., 1978:349). Asian and Cypriot men on the other hand have had a greater tendency to go into small-scale entrepreneurial concerns and into the service sector of the economy. In particular, entrepreneurial concerns both within the formal and hidden economy depend on the exploitation of female wage-labour and in particular on kinship and migrant labour. Ethnic and familial bonds serve to allow the even greater exploitation of female labour (Anthias, 1983). The different form of the family and gender ideologies may partly explain the differences between Afro-Caribbean employment patterns and those of Asians and Cypriots.

REPRODUCTION

We want now to turn to the area of reproduction and briefly consider it as a focus for the interrelation of gender, ethnic and class divisions.

The concept of reproduction itself is a problematic one. This partly derives from the inconsistent and heterogeneous treatment it has received in the literature.[12] Edholm et al. (1977:103) suggest that the notion of reproduction might be read as assuming that 'social systems exist to maintain themselves through time (to reproduce themselves) and secondly, that all levels of the system must be maintained through time in the same way'. This assumption indeed, would have all the pitfalls of the functionalist approach to social analysis. The reproduction of people and collectivities is directly shaped by the historical and social context in which it takes place. Nor is it an homogeneous process, and contradictions and conflicts are found not only in the reproduction of various entities that partially overlap each other but also in the form of the reproduction process itself.

Women not only reproduce the future human and labour power and the future citizens of the state but also ethnic and national collectivities. As in other aspects of the gender division of labour, the ethnic and class position of women will affect their role in the reproduction process. Questions concerning who can actually reproduce the collectivity and under what conditions are often important here. Such things as the legitimacy of marriage, the appropriate religious conviction and so on are often preconditions for the legitimate reproduction of the nation or collectivity. The actual degree and form of control exercised by men of ethnic collectivities over their women can vary. In the Muslim world for example and in Britain under the old nationality law, the ethnic, religious or national position of women was immaterial. In other cases, like in the Jewish case, the mother's origin is the most important one in delineating the boundaries of the collectivity, and this determined the reproduction of the Jewish 'nation' (Yuval-Davis, 1980). This clearly does not mean such women have greater freedom but only that they are subject to a different set of controls.

As in other areas, the links between gender divisions and ethnic divisions can be and often are subject to the intervention of the state. For example, in Israel even secular people have to marry with a religious ceremony and according to traditional religious rules, in order for their marriage to be recognized by law. In the most extreme cases; the way the collectivity is constituted by state legislation virtually prevents inter-marriage between collectivities. In Egypt, for instance, while a Christian man can convert to Islam, Muslim women are prevent from marrying Christian Copts – if they do, they are no longer part of the Muslim community nor are they recognized as part of the Christian community and they virtually lose their legal status. The state may treat women from dominant and subordinate ethnic collectivities differently. For example, the new nationality law in Britain has given autonomous national reproduction rights to white British women, while totally withholding them from many others, mostly black women.

This differential treatment does not relate only to ideological or legal control of reproduction. The infamous contraceptive injection Depo-Provera has been given in Britain and elsewhere virtually exclusively to black and very poor women, and a study found more birth control leaflets in family planning clinics in Asian languages than in English (see Brent Community Council, 1981). In Israel, Jewish families (under the label of being 'relatives of Israeli soldiers') receive higher child allowances than Arab ones, as part of an elaborate policy of encouraging Jewish population growth and discouraging that of Arabs. Indeed the Beveridge Report in Britain justified the establishment of child allowances in order to combat the danger of the disappearance of the British race (1942:154).

On the other hand, reproduction can become a political tool at the hand of oppressed ethnic minorities. A common Palestinian saying is that 'The Israelis beat us at the borders and we beat them at the bedrooms' – Palestinian women, like Jewish ones (and with a higher rate of success due to various material and ideological factors) are under pressure by their collectivity, although not by the state, to reproduce and enlarge it. It is a fact, for example, that no Palestinian children in Lebanon were allowed (unlike Vietnamese children under similar circumstances) to be adopted by non-Palestinians – all the children are looked on as future Palestinian liberation fighters. In other words, the control of reproduction can be used both as a subordinating strategy – by dominant groups against minority groups – as well as a 'management' strategy by ethnic collectivities themselves.

We started the section by pointing out that the process of reproduction of human subjects, as well as of collectivities is never unitary. We want to emphasize that this is the case also concerning the participation of women themselves in the control of reproduction. We can point out that virtually everywhere, the interests of the nation or the ethnic group are seen as those of its male subjects, and the interests of 'the state' are endowed with those of a male ethnic class and not just a class which is 'neutral' in terms of ethnicity and gender. However, very often women participate directly in the power struggle between their ethnic collectivity and other collectivities and the state, including by voluntarily engaging in an intensive reproductive 'demographic' race. At the same time women of dominant ethnic groups are often in a position to control the reproductive role of women of other ethnic groups by state welfare and legal policies, as well as to use them as servants and child minders in order to ease part of their own reproductive burden.

This last point leads us to consider the political implications of the above discussion concerning feminist politics and the commonality of feminist goals.

POLITICAL IMPLICATIONS

As mentioned in the introduction to this paper, our interest in the subject is far from being merely academic. It originates from our own frustration in trying to find a political milieu in which ethnic divisions will be seen as an essential consideration, rather than as non-existent or as an immovable bloc to feminist politics.

The theoretical part of this paper pointed out how misleading it is to consider gender relations without contextualizing them within ethnic and class divisions. Once we take the full implications of this into account, the mystification of the popular notion of 'sisterhood' becomes apparent. As we pointed out there can be no unitary category of 'women'. The subordination of women to men, collectivities and the state operates in many different ways in different historical contexts. Moreover, very often women themselves participate in the process of subordinating and exploiting other women.

One major form of women's oppression in history has been their invisibility, their being 'hidden from history'. The invisibility of women other than those who belong to the dominant ethnic collectivity in Britain within feminist analysis has been as oppressive. Except for black feminists who fought their own case in isolation, minority women have been virtually absent in all feminist analysis. Anthropological and historical differences in the situation of women have been explored, but only in order to highlight the social basis of gender relations in contemporary Britain. The heterogeneous ethnic character of the latter has never been fully considered.

Recently there have been some signs of a developing awareness of the need to take into account ethnic diversity. Earlier writings by socialist feminists like Michèle Barrett (1980) and Elizabeth Wilson (1977) on women in Britain had completely ignored minority, migrant, ethnic or black women. In the introduction to their latest books however (Barrett and McIntosh, 1982; Wilson, 1983) they acknowledge that they do not deal with 'ethnic' women or families. This recognition is clearly no substitute for an attempt to situate ethnic divisions when analysing 'the family' in Britain.

On the political level some concessions have been made to the black feminist movement. For example, the inclusion of black women in the Spare Rib Collective and on the Women's Committee of the Greater London Council were unprecedented and very important political achievements. However, these concessions to black feminists are not a substitute for a coherent self-critique and analysis of the white feminist movement in contextualizing its own ethnic interests.

When we talk about the need of white feminists in Britain to recognize their own ethnicity, we are relating to questions as basic as what we actually mean when we talk about 'feminist issues'. Can we automatically assume, as has been done by western feminist movements, that issues like abortion, the depiction of the family as the site of female oppression, the fight for legal equality with men and against sex discrimination and so on are *the* feminist issues? Maxine Molyneux (1983) has recently argued that what separates Third World and western women is not so much the specific cultural or historical contexts in which they are engaged but differences of a theoretical and political nature.

Different theoretical and political positions exist, of course, as Maxine claims, both in the West and in the Third World. But feminist goals cannot be the same in different historical contexts. For instance, the family may *not* be the major site for women's oppression when families are kept apart by occupying or colonizing forces (as in Lebanon or South Africa), abortion may *not* be the major issue when forced sterilizations are carried out, nor is legal equality for women the first priority in polygamic societies where there is no independent autonomous mode of existence open to women whose husbands marry other younger and more fertile women. In their paper on the South African women's movement, Judy Kimble and Elaine Unterhalter (1982) suggest that 'the analysis and objective of western feminism cannot be applied abstractly and universally'. Western feminist struggles cannot be seen as dealing with 'the feminist issues' but with culturally and historically specific issues relevant mainly to middle-class white women who have their own (invisible to them?) ethnicity. Judy and Elaine stress an essential point. However, it seems that in their search for an alternative perspective, they go to the other extreme and end up in fact with a circular argument – that feminist struggles in the context of national liberation movements are to be found in what the women in these movements do. In other words, once we stop perceiving western white feminism as providing the ultimate criteria for defining the contents of feminism, we are faced with the problem of how to politically evaluate various women's struggles.

The beginning of a possible approach might be found in an article by Gail

Omvedt (1978) in which she suggests that there is a differentiation between 'women' struggles and 'feminist' struggles, in as much as the latter are those that *challenge* rather than *use* traditional gender divisions within the context of national or ethnic struggles. We would add, however, that the challenge has to be, in our opinion, directed to both women's and men's work. All too often, in national liberation struggles, as in other periods of social crisis, women are called upon to fulfil men's jobs, as men are otherwise engaged at the front (as in war). This expansion in women's roles is seen too often as an act of women's liberation rather than as another facet of women's work. When the crisis is over, women are often assigned again to the more exclusively feminine spheres of women, to the surprise, as well as disappointment, of all those who have seen in the mere participation of women in the 'struggle' (whether in the Israeli Kibbutz, Algiers or Vietnam), a feminist achievement. We claim therefore that the challenge has to be to the actual notion of the sexual division of labour rather than only to its specific boundaries. This is far from being simple, because so many, if not all ethnic cultures, as we have noted before, have as central the construction of a specific form of gender division. It is too easy to pose the question, as many anti-imperialist and anti-racist feminists do, as if the origin and site of their oppression is only constructed from above, by white male sexism.

Ethnic and gender liberation struggles and solidarities can cut across each other and be divisive. We do not believe that there is one 'right' line to be taken in all circumstances. The focus or project of each struggle ought to decide which of the divisions we prioritize and the extent to which separate, as opposed to unified, struggle is necessary. Political struggles, however, which are formulated on an ethnic or sexual essence, we see as reactionary. Nor do we see it as a viable political option for women of subordinate collectivities to focus all their struggle against the sexism of dominant majority men.

The direct conclusion from our analysis in this paper is that any political struggle in relation to any of the divisions considered in this paper, i.e. class, ethnic and gender, has to be waged in the context of the others. Feminist struggle in Britain today cannot be perceived as an homogeneous struggle, for the participation and oppression of women, both in the family and at the work site, are not homogeneous. White middle-class feminists have to recognize the particularity of their own experiences, not only in relation to the Third World but also in relation to different ethnic and class groupings in Britain and integrate this recognition into their daily politics and struggles. Only on this basis can a valid sisterhood be constructed among women in Britain.

NOTES

1 Our analysis in this paper has benefited much from discussions with and feedback from our colleagues in the Sociology Division at Thames Polytechnic who are working with us on the Ethnic and Gender Division Project and we

would like to thank them all. We should also like to thank all those who participated in the Gender and Ethnic Divisions seminars arranged by the Sociology Division. Additionally we would like to thank the Sex and Class Group of the CSE, and the Feminist Review Collective, especially Annie Whitehead and Lesley Caldwell, for their insightful comments after reading the first draft of our paper.

2 The term 'ethnic' and 'ethnicity' have come under a great deal of attack recently for mystifying racist social relations. However, as we argue later, we do not use these concepts within a mainstream sociological tradition. For a critique of these terms see for example E. Lawrence (1982).

3 In a series of seminars organized by the Thames Polytechnic Sociology Division on Gender and Ethnic Divisions. Valerie Amos, Pratibha Parmar and Amina Mama all presented analyses that stressed the importance of studying the way in which the fusion of ethnic, gender and class divisions for black women gave a specificity to their oppression.

4 For the problems of theorizing gender divisions using a Marxist framework see H. Hartmann (1979). For problems of theorizing race in Marxism see particularly J. Gabriel and G. Ben-Tovim (1978).

5 See V. Beechey (1977) for an attempt to apply the concept to women. See S. Castles and G. Kosack (1972) for an analysis of migrants as a reserve army. For a critique of such attempts see F. Anthias (1980).

6 For critical reviews of this position see J. Kahn (1981) and J.S. Saul (1979).

7 For a review of Marxist theories of the State see Bob Jessop (1982).

8 Socialist-feminist analysis of course is an exception to this. For example see the work of E. Wilson (1977).

9 For example H.B. Davis (1973:31) states 'Engels was using the theory of "historyless peoples" according to which peoples that have never formed a state in the past cannot be expected to form a viable state in the future.'

10 This approach is found for example in Z. Eisenstein (1979).

11 For a critique see J. Bourne and A. Sivanandan (1980).

12 See M. Mackintosh (1981), F. Edholm et al. (1977) and N. Yuval-Davis (1982).

REFERENCES

Anthias, F. (1980) 'Women and the Reserve Army of Labour' *Capital & Class* no. 10.

Anthias, F. (1983) 'Sexual Divisions and Ethnic Adaptation' in Phizacklea (1983).

Barrett, M. (1980) *Women's Oppression Today* London: Verso.

Barrett, M. and McIntosh, M. (1982) *The Anti-social Family* London: Verso.

Beechey, V. (1977) 'Some Notes on Female Wage Labour in the Capitalist Mode of Production' *Capital & Class* no. 3.

Bourne, J. and Sivanandan, A. (1980) 'Cheerleaders and Ombudsmen: the Sociology of Race Relations in Britain' *Race and Class* vol. XXI, no. 4.

Brent Community Council (1981) *Black People and the Health Service*.

Castles, S. and Kosack, G. (1972) 'The Function of Labour Immigration in Western European Capitalism' *New Left Review* no. 73.

Centre for Contemporary Cultural Studies (1982) *The Empire Strikes Back* London: Hutchinson.

Davis, H.B. (1973) *Nationalism and Socialism* New York: Monthly Review Press.

Delphy, C. (1977) *The Main Enemy* London: Women's Research and Resources Centre.

Edholm, F., Harris, O. and Young, K. (1977) 'Conceptualizing Women' *Critique of Anthropology* vol. 3, nos. 9–10.

Eisenstein, Z. (1979) ed., *Capitalist Patriarchy and the Case for Socialist Feminism* New York: Monthly Review Press.

Engels, F. (1972) *The Origin of the Family, Private Property and the State* London: Lawrence and Wishart.

Gabriel, J. and Ben-Tovim, G. (1978) 'Marxism and the Concept of Racism' *Economy and Society* vol. 7, no. 2.

Hall, S. et al. (1978) *Policing the Crisis: Mugging, the State and Law and Order* London: Macmillan.

Hartmann, H. (1979) 'The Unhappy Marriage of Marxism and Feminism: Towards a More Progressive Union' *Capital & Class* no. 8.

HM Government (1942) *Social Insurance and Allied Services* (The Beveridge Report) Cmd 6404 London: HMSO.

Hooks, B. (1981) *Ain't I a Woman?* South End Press.

Jessop, B. (1982) *The Capitalist State* Oxford: Martin Robertson.

Kahn, J. (1981) 'Explaining Ethnicity' *Critique of Anthropology* vol. 4, no. 16, Spring.

Kimble, J. and Unterhalter, E. (1982) '"We opened the road for you, you must go forward" ANC Women's Struggles 1912–1982' *Feminist Review* no. 12.

Lawrence, E. (1982) 'In the abundance of water the fool is thirsty: sociology and black "pathology"' in Centre for Contemporary Cultural Studies (1982).

McIntosh, M. (1981) 'Gender and Economics' in Young, Wolkowitz and McCullogh (1981).

Molyneux, M. (1983) 'First and Third World Feminism: Solidarity and Conflict' Paper presented to Socialist Society Conference on the Family, March 1983.

Omvedt, G. (1978) 'Women and rural revolt in India' *Journal of Peasant Studies* vol. 5, no. 3.

Phizacklea, A. (1983) ed., *One Way Ticket* London: Routledge and Kegan Paul.

Saul, J.S. (1979) 'The dialectic of class and tribe' *Race and Class* vol. XX, no. 4.

Schermerhorn, R. (1970) *Comparative Ethnic Relations* New York: Random House.

Wilson, E. (1977) *Women and the Welfare State* London: Tavistock Publications.

Wilson, E. (1983) *What is to be done about violence against women?* London: Penguin.

Young, K. Wolkowitz, C. and McCullogh, R. (1981) eds, *Of Marriage and the Market* London: CSE Books.

Yuval-Davis, N. (1980) 'The bearers of the collective: Women and religious legislation in Israel' *Feminist Review* no. 4.

Yuval-Davis, N. (1982) 'National Reproduction: Sexism, Racism and the State'. Unpublished paper presented to BSA Conference, April 1982.

7

Ann Phoenix

Theories of Gender and Black Families

A great deal has already been written about gender relations and how women and men come to have gendered subjectivities. However, most of this writing, whether theoretical or empirical, has been based on the experiences of white women and men (or white girls and boys). This chapter first explores the consequence of this concentration on gender relations exclusively in white people, then considers whether existing theories of gender are relevant to black people of Afro-Caribbean origin. Black people of Asian origin are similarly omitted from theories of gender development. However, some of their gender experiences differ from black people of Afro-Caribbean origin and therefore need to be dealt with separately.

GENDER RELATIONS AND COLOUR

Work on gender is usually reported as if colour and class were not salient to gender relations (see for example the review by Henshall and McGuire, 1986). From this it might be presumed that black people and white people develop gender identities in similar ways. If that were the case colour would be irrelevant to work on gender.

However, the reality of racism means that black people have less access to sources of societal power than white people. Black children and white children therefore have different developmental experiences. There is no evidence that gender relations as described in the literature are not specific to the white people who were the subjects of the research on which the theories were founded. In order to understand why black people are omitted from most work on gender relations it is necessary to consider how black people are generally treated in research and academic literature.

When 'normal' processes are being studied, black people are usually excluded from samples for two sorts of reasons. The first set of reasons is to do with the strict control of the number of variables in studies. This is thought to be necessary if the findings of the study are to be clearly interpreted as being due to the independent variables being investigated. Phrases like 'No blacks or Hispanics were included. . . hence some degree of homogeneity was established.' (Sebald, 1986) are indicative of this set of reasons. This exclusion of black people suggests that it is white people who develop and behave in normal ways, while black people are exceptions to the norm, deviant or pathological.

The other set of reasons for the exclusion of black people from research samples are the result of what Jennifer Platt (1985) calls 'samples of opportunity'. Researchers frequently study samples that live conveniently near their university departments, or that are visiting the university for some purpose. These localities are frequently white and middle class. This means that the sampling does not ensure that the final sample is representative of the general population of a town or of the country as a whole. Platt points out that samples of opportunity are not adequate when generalizations are to be made from data. This criticism is even more pertinent when generalizations are to be made from a local study which completely omits a significant section of the population, namely black people.

Whatever the reason for the exclusion of black people from certain research projects, the effect is to underline the common-sense view that black people are different from white people. This differentiation is reinforced by studies of pathological or deviant situations which focus exclusively on black people. So for example there are a number of studies of 'teenage' mothers which include only or predominantly black women (Furstenberg, 1976; Field et al., 1980). This focus is especially significant because when 'normal' mothering and 'normal' child development are being studied black women are excluded in the ways already described. 'Teenage motherhood' is highly socially stigmatized and yet this is one of the areas in which black women are made visible. Black households are included in a similar way when 'father-absence' (another stigmatized category) is being studied.

However, this normalized absence/pathologized presence couplet is not the sole constituent of research's contribution to the maintenance of existing power relations between black people and white people. Academic work is conducted within a social context in which racism means that black people are socially devalued and white people are socially valued. Most researchers are white, and as a result are likely not to share the same perspectives as black people. Research therefore must be suspect when conducted within the value systems of a racist society. This means that when comparisons are made between groups of black people and groups of white people research continues to construct white people as the norm and black people as abnormal by comparison. This is equally true of studies which concentrate mainly on white people but include a single section on black people (see, for example, Sharpe, 1976).

The best-known examples of comparisons between black people and white people are probably black–white IQ differences, and differences in educational achievement between black children and white children. It is not that black–white comparisons are in themselves reprehensible; rather the interpretations placed on findings (particularly by those who espouse hereditarian views) are individualistic and locate pathology in black people while leaving social and political causes untheorized and unchallenged in a way that Ryan (1972) calls 'blaming the victim'. (For a more detailed discussion of how black families are pathologized in British society see Parmar, 1982 and Lawrence, 1982.)

The treatment of women in academic literature has paralleled the treatment of black people described above. Researchers on major social issues have in the past omitted women from their samples but made generalizations about the whole population from the data (see, for example, Willis, 1977). Comparisons have also been made between women's and men's abilities and behaviours in such a way that women are presented as being inferior (see Archer and Lloyd, 1982, for further discussion of this). It is therefore ironic that white feminist writings, which have had significant impact on the way that women are treated in academic (and popular) literature, should themselves also exclude black (and working-class) women and hence help maintain the power differentials between black women and white women (see Carby, 1982; the black women's issue of *Feminist Review*, 1984; Brah and Minhas, 1985; Hooks, 1982 and 1984; and Bhavnani and Coulson, 1986, for discussions of how white feminism has refused to address issues of racism, and hence colluded with racism).

THEORIES OF GENDER DEVELOPMENT AND 'THE FAMILY'

Human development does not, of course, occur in a vacuum. It occurs within specific contexts. 'The family' is implicitly given centrality in most theories of normal or optimal child development. In studies of child development parents (predominantly mothers), are usually either observed in interaction with or interviewed about their children. This emphasis on parents only occurs because parents are considered to be (and in this society undeniably are) a major influence on their children. The family therefore is a crucial site for the production of the 'normal' child, who among other things shows appropriate gender behaviour and has the gender identity appropriate to her/his sex.

The social construction of the normal family which is thought best suited to the production of the normal children described above is a highly specific one. In the 'normal' family, marriage and the having of children are inextricably linked so that marriage entails having children, and the conception of children should necessarily follow marriage (Busfield, 1974). Once children are born, provision for them is divided between the parents on gender lines.

Fathers are expected to be in a position to make economic provision for their children by having paid employment. By contrast women are expected to stay at home with their children and to be responsible not only for fulfilling their children's basic needs, but also for the ways in which their children develop. This means that mothers need to engage in high quality interactions with their children and to have some knowledge of child development (Urwin, 1985). Mother–child dyads are observed in interaction together as if their homes were isolated from the rest of society. This 'desert-island' approach (Riley, 1983) ignores considerations of how material conditions such as housing and income affect how parents are able to deal with their children. It also has a 'normalizing effect' (Henriques et al., 1984) in that it confirms that it is both right and normal for women and children to be locked up alone with each other all day.

The pervasiveness of this model of the 'normal' family within current dominant ideology means that it is the model implicitly assumed in cultural theories of gender development. (Biologically determinist explanations suggest that gender differences are naturally occurring rather than being subject to environmental influences. They therefore do not require any particular family type for gender development and will not be dealt with here.)

There are three major theories of the processes by which gender development occurs. In social-learning theories the child learns gender stereotyped roles through observation and imitation of the same sex parent. In addition parents, by using rewards and punishments, condition children into appropriate gender behaviour. In cognitive-developmental theory (Kohlberg, 1966) the child actively learns that each person throughout life belongs to one of two genders. In psychoanalytic theory it is the awareness of genital sex differences between males and females that eventually leads young children to identify with the same gender parents...

What these three theories have in common is that they assume that children live with both parents. Parents provide the child with the first experiences of what it means to be gendered. So, for example, according to social learning theory parents act as role-models for their children as well as providing them with reinforcement for their gender related behaviour. Similarly, in cognitive-developmental theory parents are an important source of information about gender related behaviours. In psychoanalytic theory children learn gender identification both by observing the behaviour of their parents towards each other, and competing with and identifying with them. This is not to suggest that parents are the only influence on children's gender development. School, other adults and other children, the media, etc. all have an acknowledged role in theories of gender development. The point is that the nuclear family is implicitly included as important in these theories.

The assumed importance of this family type has led to a great deal of research on parental influences on gender development. This research in general has searched for pathological gender development in 'father absent' households (which in reality is frequently synonymous with 'single parent' households), and for the concomitants of normal development, as well as the significance of particular parental behaviours in two parent households.

Many children in western societies do not, however, live in nuclear families. In Britain it is estimated that at any one time 9 per cent of all children under sixteen years of age live with their mothers but not with their fathers (New and David, 1985). This percentage represents over 1.25 million children. A large number of children, for some or all of their childhood, do not, therefore, live in the type of family which has been used to construct theories of gender development and which has gained acceptance as the best site for the production and reproduction of gendered subjectivity.

FAMILIES WITHOUT FATHERS

The occurrence of female-headed households is not evenly spread among the population. For a variety of socio-political and historical reasons (including the fact that there are many more black women than black men in the USA) black women of Afro-Caribbean origin in this country, and of African origin in the USA are much more likely not to live with their children's fathers (see Bryan et al., 1985, for discussion of the British situation, and Hooks, 1982; Davis, 1981; and Marable 1983 for the USA). In the USA 50 per cent of black children of African origin live in female-headed households. In Britain the comparable figures are 31 per cent for black women of Afro-Caribbean origin compared with 5 per cent for black women of Asian origin and 10 per cent for white women (Brown, 1984). Black children are thus least likely to live in the family grouping considered most suitable for gender development or development in general.

Black women of Afro-Caribbean origin are not the only mothers who are likely to live apart from their children's fathers. In 1985, 65 per cent of births to women who were under twenty years of age were to single women (OPCS, 1986). This percentage is not solely composed of women who do not live with their children's fathers because some of these women will be cohabiting. However, it is an indication that in this age group it is now not normative to follow the pattern expected in dominant reproductive ideologies.

Since different family structures are now not uncommon in British society, it is important to gain some understanding of how this diversity affects children's gender development. Research on 'father absence' has concentrated on comparing children who live alone with their mothers with children who live with both parents. The findings of these studies usually show that children who live in households without their fathers are less academically successful, and have more behaviour problems than those who live with both parents (Lamb, 1976; Biller, 1981). These findings are usually attributed to lack of paternal interaction for children of both genders and to boys' lack of a role model to provide sufficient opportunities for social learning. Boys are considered to suffer more than girls from 'father absence'.

By extension the poor educational achievement of black children of Afro-Caribbean descent is frequently blamed on 'father absence' (Scarr et al., 1983; Swann Report, 1985), which is used as a shorthand for inadequate socialization. Similarly, analyses of urban unrest in the popular media give explanations in terms of the pathology of the West Indian family (Lawrence, 1982). Recent reviews of literature in this area have pointed out the unsatisfactory nature of research in this field, and how it fails to take into account such factors as length of father absence, age of children when absence begins, reason for absence etc. as potentially significant (Henshall and McGuire, 1986; Archer and Lloyd, 1982).

Because research on gender development starts from a theoretical position which presumes that fathers are crucial to good child development it fails to give sufficient consideration to precisely how, when, and what it is that fathers actually contribute to the process of child development. Most people would agree that it is desirable that fathers should share the care of their young children. However a study which compares how much modern fathers do with their one-year-old children compared with thirty years ago suggests that, contrary to popular beliefs, fathers have not started to interact significantly more with their children than their fathers' generation (Lewis, 1984). More research is required on what interactive and non-interactive fathers contribute to their children's gender development.

For black people this lack of research, together with the popular definition of black parents as predominantly 'single parent', helps to both produce and reproduce dominant ideological assumptions about the pathology of black families. It also means that black children are not considered to have received proper gender socialization.

Interest in 'father absence' has meant a concentration on parents and the household as primarily responsible for child outcomes. This excludes social network influences and wider social and political influences on gender identity. Children are not, however, monocultural. It is rare for them to be exposed only to their parents and to stay only in one setting. Television, for example, is an external influence and in addition most children eventually go to school where they meet a variety of people. This approach is therefore not 'ecologically valid', to use Bronfenbrenner's (1977) terms.

Ecologically valid attempts to theorize the process whereby all children acquire gendered subjectivity would require developmental researchers to expand the age range they study beyond the current concentration on the very early years. It would also require that children be studied in interaction with other people as well as their parents, and in more than one setting (for instance, Dunn and Kendrick, 1982, study on siblings and mothers; Tizard and Hughes, 1984, study of young children learning at home and in the nursery school). It must also be remembered that children do not learn about gender in isolation. They learn about it as they simultaneously learn about other social facts in their world, like race and class.

So far it has been suggested that the only structural difference between black households which have children in them and similar white households that has been discussed is the greater likelihood that black mothers will be single rather than married or cohabiting. However black women are more likely to be in full-time paid employment than are white women. In 1982, 41 per cent of black women of Afro-Caribbean origin were in paid employment compared with 21 per cent of black women of Asian origin and 21 per cent of white women. If part-time employment and self-employment are included, then 59 per cent of black women of Afro-Caribbean origin were in paid employment compared with 29 per cent of black women of Asian origin and 41 per cent of white women (Brown, 1984).

These figures unfortunately do not tell us how many of these employed women have children, particularly children who are under five years of age. However, the Women and Employment Survey showed that 20 per cent of women with pre-school children in Britain work part time, while 7 per cent work full time. 56 per cent of mothers with dependent children are in some form of paid employment (Martin and Roberts, 1984). Thus a substantial proportion of young children receive some care from people other than their mothers. It seems clear that black mothers of Afro-Caribbean origin are more often in paid employment outside the home than are white mothers.

It is thus important to consider issues of ecological validity in research on the acquisition of gender identity. Many children, particularly black ones, are cared for by people other than their mothers. The fact that 'it is almost always women's work to care for and educate children, whether at home' or elsewhere (New and David, 1985) does not mean that children learn exactly the same things from the different women who look after them. Black women know that their structural circumstances mean that they have no choice but to try to be economically independent (see Bryan et al., 1985). This means that black mothers tend to explicitly teach this to their daughters (Joseph, 1981), while the mothers described by Eichenbaum and Orbach (1985) (who are presumably white), subtly encourage their daughters to be emotionally, rather than economically, independent. Moreover the process of gender development may well be different if there is lack of congruence between mother and caregiver about the way boys and girls are treated and expected to behave, than it would be if they were congruent.

There is no substantial evidence that maternal employment outside the home by itself causes children to hold less gender stereotypic views about women's roles (New and David, 1985). This adds weight to the argument that it is over-simplistic for theories of gender development to implicitly assume that the mother necessarily has a privileged position of influence on gender development. This must be particularly so in families where several individuals share the care of children. These families are currently more likely to be black than to be white. The psychic development of children who grow up in these circumstances remains unexplored in psychoanalytic literature probably because therapists are more likely to see white middle-class rather than black working-class women.

GENDER DIFFERENCES

While different processes for the acquisition of gender have been theorized, the structure that facilitates those processes (that is, the nuclear family) is, as discussed above, usually implicitly assumed. In a similar way the content that is to be processed is presumed to be obvious and commonly shared. However, societal divisions of race and class mean not only that the process of gender development is different for different groups of people, but also that gender is differently experienced by black people and white people, by working-class people and middle-class people.

Comparing differences between any two groups tends to polarize them and minimize their similarities. A secondary effect of this is that the two polarized groups appear internally homogeneous. However, there are important within-group differences between women and between men which have relevance for theories of gender development. The effects of racism and what this means for the class position of black people means that black children grow up knowing that black women and black men are in a qualitatively different position from white women and white men.

In western patriarchal societies men gain more educational qualifications than women. Even if educational qualifications are controlled, men obtain proportionally more high status jobs (Archer and Lloyd, 1982). These differences are reflected in family relationships. Governments as well as the rest of society accord men the status of 'heads of households' and provide family benefits on that basis. If there are children in a household, it is women, not men, who bear the weight of societal expectations (which they may or may not share) that they will stay at home, care for and educate those children, giving up any paid employment they have in order to do so.

Since stereotypes usually have political implications and can provide a window on how different groups are perceived in a society, it is useful to consider how women and men are commonly stereotyped. Women are stereotyped as being the complementary opposite of men. They are supposed to be nurturant, passive, weak and non-competitive while men are supposed to be aggressive, active, powerful and competitive – qualities which have frequently been used to justify male dominance of society. This is allegedly the content that girls and boys learn in the process of becoming gendered. Not surprisingly, however, these stereotypes do not fit all women or all men. In fact descriptions of male and female behaviour and dominant-subordinate positions actually relate only to the situation of those who hold most power within society, the white middle classes. This leaves gender relations between black people and working-class people untheorized and invisible.

In general black people of African origin in the USA and of Afro-Caribbean origin in Britain, gain few educational qualifications (Swann Report, 1985; Eggleston, Dunn and Anjali, 1984; and Staples, 1985). When they do gain educational qualifications it is more likely to be women rather than men who achieve these (Fuller, 1983; Hare, 1984). Black people (particularly men) are much more likely than white people to be unemployed. When they are employed it is likely to be in the most menial, least-paid jobs (Brown, 1984; Hare, 1984; Staples, 1985). The realities of racism also mean that black men are more likely to be imprisoned than are white men.

Hence, black men are frequently not in a position to support women and children economically. The choice of being supported by a man while staying at home with children is therefore not a realistic one for many black women (Hooks, 1982). This gives an indication of one reason why marriage is less common for black couples than for white couples. While western marriage is often portrayed as being solely the result of romantic love, there still are (and always have been) economic reasons for the contracting of marriage (Gittins, 1986). Where men cannot fulfil an economic role, there is less incentive for marriage.

Thus black men of Afro-Caribbean origin do not fit the stereotype of the powerful male in western societies. Instead they are stereotyped as feckless, violent, criminal, and oversexed, even to the extent that they are likely to be rapists (see Davis, 1981). It is not that black men are stereotyped as being outside the category 'male' or as emasculated, but as pathological/devalued males who have some stereotypically male characteristics to excess, and completely lack others. The gender positions that black men occupy illustrate the boundaries of stereotypic maleness. While 'normal' males have some degree of aggression and strong sexual drives, to be too aggressive and have too much sexual drive (as black men are stereotyped to have) is not to be a supermale but rather to be bestial. 'Normal' males (who are white) are measured in their maleness and their bestiality is carefully controlled.

Black women similarly are stereotyped as having some 'feminine' characteristics to excess, but also some 'male' characteristics. Thus black women are perceived as being easily available sexual objects who are prone to prostitution. King (1984) calls this the 'depreciated sex object' stereotype. The mythology of black women as having different sexuality from white women has served to permit the rape and sexual exploitation of black women (since they are stereotyped as being more bestial than white women) without public outcry being equivalent to when white women are raped (Hooks, 1982). For this reason it is not surprising (although the researcher does not make this point explicitly), that in a study of one hundred fifteen-year-old girls in three London comprehensives it is a black girl who reports the most sexist interchange with a male teacher.

> He picks me out. 'Jenny', he goes. I go 'Yeah'. 'You little f——'. . . . He's heard from another teacher that I'm cheeky so he goes 'Oh Jenny, cheeky little cunt, ain't you'. (Lees, 1986, p. 125)

Black women are also stereotyped as being matriarchs who are tough (as opposed to the weakness assumed for white women who require protection from a strong white male). Such toughness means that black women can be expected to work hard, in a way that would not be expected for white women, and to dominate their households. This stereotype was given academic credence in the United States by Moynihan (1965) who blamed black females and the black female-headed household for the emasculation of the black male, and hence all the problems of American black people. Lees (1986) gives a clear example of how this stereotype also operates in the British context in this quote from a white girl.

> They look black and somehow stronger. If you got a white girl and a black girl you say 'Oh she looks stronger *'cos she's black*'. [italics added] (Lees, 1986, p. 141)

Black children's acquisition of gender identity is therefore qualitatively different from that of white children. Contact with the media and with other societal institutions means that black children cannot help but learn that black people and white people occupy different structural positions. They learn that their parents, and hence they, are excluded from positions of power within society. Black children simultaneously learn that black people are stereotyped in different ways to those in which white people are stereotyped. From this they learn that gender differences between black males and black females are qualitatively different from white female–male differences. Hence black children learn about racism as well as about gender differentiation.

However, in contrast with what they learn from the wider society, black children learn more positive gender models from their own social networks. Black women's participation in the labour market means that black children grow up accepting that mothers can also be employed. The fact that black children are more likely than white children to live with other relatives as well as their parent(s) means that they have a wider variety of people to interact with and with whom to develop close relationships.

While there are undoubtedly gender differences between black women and black men (see Hull et al., 1982), the denial of power to black people that results from racism, and the fact that black women and black men occupy different gender positions from white women and white men, mean that the 'dominant/subordinate model' of sexual power relationships is not applicable to black people in the same way it is to white people (Lorde, 1984).

This does not mean that black people automatically reject the dominant ideological stereotypes of gender roles. Being subject to the same ideological forces as white people means that many black people accept dominant ideologies of gender (see Staples, 1985). This probably occurs for three reasons. First, because being relatively powerless makes people desire the positions, and so espouse the attitudes of those who are perceived to be more powerful (see Fanon, 1952; and Henriques, 1984). Second, because being at variance with accepted societal practice means that individuals are subject to stigmatization. Avowed acceptance of dominant ideology may well be, in Goffman's terms (1963), in compensation for the stigma that attaches to individuals who do not fit societal norms. An effort is thus made to reduce the social distance between stigmatized individuals and the rest of society, and hence to remove stigma. The third reason is because the pervasiveness of patriarchal structures means that individual subjectivity cannot help but be affected by them (Thompson, 1977).

It is important to recognize that individuals can simultaneously accept dominant gender stereotypes and actively resist racism because they disagree with the basis on which black people and white people come to occupy different societal positions. It is because black women and white women occupy different structural positions that many young black women actively resist the gender stereotypes that are constructed as 'normal' femininity. So, for example, the passivity and weakness that is meant to elicit a powerful male's protection is redundant for black women (and white working-class women) whose fathers and male peers do not occupy positions of power. It is not surprising then that black female school students and white working-class school students are reported to be more boisterous at school than their white middle-class counterparts, and should be sceptical about the benefits of marriage for them (Sharpe, 1976; Bryan et al., 1985; Lees, 1986).

RACE, CLASS AND GENDER

Because racism operates structurally to maintain black people in a state of relative powerlessness in comparison with white people, most black people are working class. Black children and white working-class children therefore have some common experiences of what it means to be gendered – in particular learning what it means to be excluded from and different from mainstream society. The impact of experiences that give working-class children insight into what it means to be a working-class woman or man is unfortunately not theorized in literature on gender, as the following example from a woman who experienced a working-class childhood makes clear.

> A sense of dislocation can provide a sharp critical faculty in a child.... Working-class autobiography frequently presents, as a moment of narrative revelation, a child's surprise at the humility of a domestic tyrant witnessed at his work-place, out in the world.... Beyond the point of initial surprise, none of the literature deals with what happens to children when they come to witness the fracture between social and domestic power. (Steedman, 1986, p. 72)

To be a black child, to be a black working-class child, or to be a white, working-class child is to occupy qualitatively different societal positions from white, middle-class children.

> Subjectivity as multiple, produced in contradictory and shifting positions, through power and desire, has specific and harmful effects upon those whose lack of fit is rendered pathological. (Walkerdine, 1985, p. 237)

Moving between home, school and other contexts provides children who are other than white and middle-class with contradictions which lead them to the understanding that they and their parents are outside the social construction of gender, and are relatively powerless. The results are that,

> Black daughters learn at an early age that their mothers are not personally responsible for not being able, through their individual efforts, to make basic changes in their lives or the lives of their children. (Joseph, 1981, p. 96)

However, racism does not only differentiate between black women and white women. It also differentiates the working class in such a way that in a public context white working-class women are advantaged over black working-class women and over black working-class men. This is graphically illustrated in the following quote from Gail Lewis's description of relationships between her black father and white mother.

> Another thing was my Mum's contempt for my Dad because of his humble demeanour in the face of white authority. Throughout their marriage it was agreed that Mum would deal with any authorities that had to be faced.... And since they both believed that by 'rights' the man should do this kind of stuff, then it only served to reinforce their shared belief in my Dad's inadequacy. Which led to him having to 'prove' himself by reasserting his dominance over her as a man. It was a situation that was fed by racism and their attempt at overcoming it. (Lewis, 1985, p. 232)

CONCLUSIONS

By ignoring issues of race and class, current theories of gender, and the research on which these are based, actually address the development of gender identity in the white middle classes. This means that black children (and white working-class children) are rendered invisible in the processes of normal gender development, but visible in pathological categories like 'father-absent' households.

It is not only that the structure of family life presumed by theories of gender development implicitly reinforces race and class divisions but that the content they presume also does so. Black children and white working-class children experience the disjunction between their parents' power over them as children, and their parents', particularly fathers', lack of social power, as contradictions that have to be reconciled as they learn about their social world in the different contexts they experience. This means that the account of their gender development must be different from that of white middle-class children who are less likely to experience such contradictions.

Theories of gender will become ecologically valid (Bronfenbrenner, 1977) if that they take account of household organizations other than the nuclear family, and the different experiences of people of different classes and colours. This must not, however, be an adding-on of an account of black gender development to an unchanged account of white middle-class development, since this would still result in black people appearing pathological by comparison with the familiar account of white gender development.

Instead, theoretical accounts of gender development must centrally include structural factors like participation in the employment market, household structure, the operation of class and of racism. Gender development is therefore much more complex than current theories recognize. To concentrate solely on race would obscure the fact that shared class means that black working-class people and white working-class people have common exclusions from sources of societal power. However the fact of racism means that there are experiences which are exclusive to black people. Structural relations and emotional relations need to be related together so that we gain insights into the psychic development of black children and white working-class children.

REFERENCES

Archer, J. and Lloyd, B., *Sex and gender*, Harmondsworth, Penguin, 1982.

Bhavnani, K. and Coulson, M., 'Transforming socialist feminism: the challenge of racism', *Feminist Review*, 23, 1986, pp. 81–92.

Biller, H., 'The father and sex-role development', in M. Lamb ed., *The role of the father in child development*, (2nd edition), New York, John Riley, 1981.

Brah, A. and Minhas, R., 'Structural racism or cultural difference: school for Asian girls', in G. Weiner ed., *Just a bunch of girls*, Milton Keynes, Open University Press, 1985.

Bronfenbrenner, U., 'Towards an experimental ecology of human development', *American psychologist*, 23, 1977, pp. 513–31.

Brown, C., *Black and white in Britain: the third PSI survey*, London, Heinemann, 1984.

Bryan, B., Dadzie, S. and Scafe, S., *The heart of the race: Black women's lives in Britain*, London, Virago, 1985.

Busfield, J., 'Ideologies and reproduction', in M. Richards ed., *The integration of a child into a social world*, Cambridge, Cambridge University Press, 1974.

Carby, H.V., 'Schooling in Babylon'. In Centre for Contemporary Cultural Studies, *The Empire Strikes Back: Race and racism in 70s Britain*. London, Hutchinson, 1982, pp. 183–211.

Davis, A., *Women, race and class*, London, The Women's Press, 1981.

Dunn, J. and Kendrick, C., *Siblings*, London, Grant McIntyre, 1982.

Eggleston, S., Dunn, D. and Anjali, M., *The educational and vocational experiences of 15–18 year old young people of minority ethnic groups*, Report to the DES, 1984.

Eichenbaum, L. and Orbach, S., *Understanding women*, Harmondsworth, Penguin, 1983.

Fanon, F., *Black skins, white masks*, London, Pluto Press, 1952.

Field, T., Widmayer, S., Stringer, S. and Ignatoff, E., 'Teenage, lower class, black mothers and their pre-term infants: An intervention and developmental follow-up', *Child Development*, 51, 1980, pp. 426–36.

Fuller, M., 'Qualified criticism, critical qualifications', in L. Barton and S. Walker eds, *Race, class and education*, Kent, Croom Helm, 1983.

Furstenberg, F., *Unplanned parenthood: The social consequences of teenage childbearing*, New York, The Free Press, 1976.

Gittens, D., *The family in question: Changing households and familiar ideologies*, London, Macmillan, 1986.

Goffman, E., *Stigma*, Harmondsworth, Penguin, 1963.

Hart, N., 'Revolution without a revolution: The psychology of sex and race', in *The best of the black scholar: the black woman* II, 1984.

Henriques, J., Hollway, W., Urwin, C., Venn, C. and Walkerdine, V., *Changing the subject*, London, Methuen, 1984.

Henshall, C. and McGuire, J., 'Gender relations', in M. Richards and P. Light eds, *Children of social worlds*, Cambridge, Polity Press, 1986.

Hooks, B., *Ain't I a women: black women and feminism*, London, Pluto Press, 1982.

Hooks, B., *Feminist theory: from margin to centre*, Boston, South End Press, 1984.

Hull, G.T., Scott, P.B. and Smith, B. eds., *All the women are white, all the blacks are men, but some of us are brave*, New York, The Feminist Press, 1982.

Joseph, G. and Lewis, J., *Common differences. Conflicts in black and white feminist perspectives*, New York, Anchor Books, 1981.

King, M., 'The politics of sexual stereotypes', in *The best of the black scholar: the black woman* II, 1984.

Kohlberg, L., 'A cognitive-developmental analysis of children's sex-role concepts and attitudes', in E. Maccoby ed., *The development of sex differences*, London, Tavistock Press, 1966.

Lamb, M. ed., *The role of the father in child development*, New York, John Wiley, 1976.

Lawrence, E., 'Just plain common sense: the roots of racism', in Centre for Contemporary Cultural Studies, *The Empire Strikes Back: Race and racism in 70s Britain*, London, Hutchinson, 1982, pp. 47–94.

Lees, S., *Losing out: Sexuality and adolescent girls*, London, Hutchinson, 1986.

Lewis, C., *Fathers of one-year-olds*, Paper presented to the Annual Conference of the Developmental Section of the British Psychological Society, Lancaster, September 1984.

Lewis, G., 'From deepest Kilburn', in L. Heron ed., *Truth, dare or promise: Girls growing up in the fifties*, London, Virago, 1985.

Lorde, A., 'Scratching the surface: some notes to barriers to women and loving', in *The best of the black scholar: the black women* II, 1984.

Marable, M., *How capitalism underdeveloped black America*, London, Pluto Press, 1983.

Martin, J. and Roberts, C., *Women and employment: A lifelong perspective*, London, HMSO, 1984.

Moynihan, D.P., *The negro family: A case for national action*, Office of Policy Planning and Research, United States Department of Labor, 1965.

New, C. and David, M., *For the children's sake*, Harmondsworth, Penguin, 1985.

Office of Population Censuses and Surveys, Fertility trends in England and Wales: 1975–1985, *OPCS Monitor. Reference FMI 86/2*, 15 July 1986.

Parmar, P., 'Gender, race and class: Asian women in resistance', in Centre for Contemporary Cultural Studies. *The Empire Strikes Back: Race and racism in 70s Britain*, pp. 236–75.

Platt, J., *What can case studies do?*, Paper presented to the ESRC Field Research seminar on case study research, March 1986.

Riley, D., *War in the nursery: Theories of the child and mother*, London, Virago, 1983.

Ryan, W., *Blaming the victim*, New York, Vintage Books, 1972.

Scarr, S., Caparulo, B., Ferdman, B., Tower, R. and Caplan, J., 'Developmental status and school achievements of minority and non-minority children from birth to 18 years in a British Midlands town', *British Journal of Developmental Psychology*, I, 1983, pp. 31–48.

Sebald, H., 'Adolescents shifting orientation towards parents and peers', *Journal of marriage and the family*, 48, 1986, p. 5–13.

Sharpe, S., *'Just like a girl': How girls learn to be women*, Harmondsworth, Penguin, 1976.

Staples, R., 'Changes in black family structure: the conflict between family ideology and structural conditions', *Journal of marriage and the family*, 47, 1985, pp. 1005–13.

Steedman, C., *Landscape for a good woman: A study of two lives*, London, Virago, 1986.

Swann Report, *Education for all*, Report to the Department of Education and Science, London, HMSO, 1985.

Thompson, E.P., 'Happy families', *New Society*, 8 September 1977, pp. 499–501.

Tizard, B. and Hughes, M., *Young children learning: Talking and thinking at home and at school*, London, Fontana, 1984.

Urwin, C., 'Constructing motherhood: the persuasion of normal development', in C. Steedman, C. Urwin and V. Walkerdine eds, *Language, gender and childhood*, London, Routledge and Kegan Paul, 1985, pp. 164–202.

Walkerdine, V., 'On the regulation of speaking and silence: subjectivity, class and gender in contemporary schooling', in C. Steedman, C. Urwin and V. Walkerdine eds, *Language, gender and childhood*, London, Routledge and Kegan Paul, 1985, pp. 203–41.

Willis, P.E., *Learning to labour: How working class kids get working class jobs*, Farnborough, Saxon House, 1977.

8

Michèle Barrett and Mary McIntosh

The 'Family Wage': Some Problems for Socialists and Feminists

INTRODUCTION

The notion of a 'family wage' has been in the past a divisive issue (Land 1980), though lately it has been less discussed. It is the idea that an adult man ought to earn enough to enable him to support a wife and children. It has often, though not always, had support in the labour movement and has often, though again not always, been opposed by feminists. In so far as the balance of the labour movement has historically been in favour of it and the tendency of the present women's movement is to oppose it, it is clearly a divisive and important political issue for both socialists and feminists today. In this paper we address some of the arguments about the history and desirability of a 'family wage' system, and also question the usefulness of this notion as a description of the means by which the reproduction of the working class has in fact been accomplished.

...

Today the idea of a family wage is so much taken for granted that it is standard trade-union practice to draw up pay claims for low-paid workers which refer to the need to maintain the level of living of a standard married man with two children. The newspapers routinely supply us with calculations of the effects of tax changes or price changes for the same man married with two children. . . The principle is articulated most clearly in a social-security system that differentiates radically between bread-winners and their dependants,[1] providing insurance benefits for a man's dependants but not for a wife's and no supplementary benefit to a wife or a 'cohabiting' woman at all.

. . .

Since equal pay legislation was introduced in 1970, the conventional wisdom on all sides has been to take for granted that discussions should be couched in terms of the wage form: 'Equal pay for work of equal value' or at least for (in the words of the Act) 'like work', 'the rate for the job' and so forth. Yet it was not always so. Although the Trades Union Congress adopted the principle of equal pay in 1888 and much of the public discussion revolved round the question of whether women's work *was* in fact worth as much as men's, nevertheless such discussions always dealt also with the question of needs and family responsibilities. Thus it was in a minority report of the 1919 War Cabinet Committee on Women in Industry (the Atkin Report) that Beatrice Webb first put forward proposals for child allowances as a way of enabling equal pay for men and women without endangering the maintenance of children. The 1946 Royal Commission on Equal Pay devoted much time to considering the dependants of employed women, and also to the argument that 'Most women . . . unlike most men, do not expect either now or in the future, to support a married partner or a family of children out of the proceeds of their labour; on the contrary most of them look forward to being themselves supported in the relatively near future' (para 362). So earlier discussions of equal pay always recognised that it would cause immense problems for the principle of the male worker as family breadwinner.

Recently, however, the trade union movement has tried to have its cake and eat it too. While day-to-day bargaining has routinely used the argument of family needs, the official pronouncements of the TUC in relation to equal pay have tended to play down this consideration and emphasise the wage as payment for work performed. Thus, as Bea Campbell and Val Charlton so lucidly put it (1979:32):

> The Labour Movement has managed to combine a commitment to equal pay with a commitment to the family wage; you can't have both.

HISTORY OF THE IDEA

. . .

The idea of the family wage is associated historically with the development of the modern relation between the family and social production and with the modern sex-structured labour market and the marginal position of women, especially in industrial production. The early period of factory production was marked by the employment of men, women and children from a very young age. During the course of the nineteenth century children became excluded almost totally from the factories and from all other full-time paid work. Women became marginalised in many fields of factory production, became located in specifically female occupations and sectors, and many women spent much or even the whole of their married lives outside of regular waged employment altogether (Gardiner 1974). Children became more dependent and in need of greater and longer care; women too became more dependent and more taken up with the tasks of caring for children and other family members.

Marxist historians have tended to see the introduction of female and child labour into factories, mines and so on, in the context of the process of deskilling set in motion by the mechanization of capitalist production. Indeed, this is the context in which Marx himself locates his discussion in Volume 1 of *Capital*. During this period surplus value was predominantly extracted in absolute form, through the extension of the working day, and many contemporary sources document the almost incredibly long hours worked by labourers in the first decades of machine production.

By the 1830s, however, it was becoming apparent that these conditions were incompatible with the reproduction of a working class fit to carry out its task: the extraction of absolute surplus value founders on the physical condition of the working class. Hence it became imperative, both from the point of view of the capitalist class as a whole and from the point of view of the working class, to protect the life and health of the industrial proletariat. There has been dispute as to whether the measures subsequently taken to asssure the adequate reproduction of the working class are to be understood as the fruit of successful class struggle on the part of the working class, or as successful collective control by capital of the instruments of production – the labourers themselves. Certainly it seems the case that there was a coincidence of interests, though not of course a formal alliance, between bourgeois philanthropists and the bourgeois state on the one hand and the emergent Chartist and trade union movement on the other. The Factory Acts of the 1840s, limiting the length of the working day, the protective legislation aimed at the reduction of female and child labour and, later in the century, the introduction of elementary education all formed part of this process.

It is worth noting, in relation to the demand for a family wage, that the relegation of women to the home cannot be explained solely with reference to the 'needs of capitalism' but was the object of struggle, and therefore choice, of the working class. It was presumably open to the working class organizations of the 1830s and 1840s to struggle for better conditions of reproduction of the class through some other means. In textile districts, for instance, the high level of women's employment and aggregate family income meant that practices like eating shop-made pies and puddings, and having the day-care of infants, the washing and basic cleaning done by women who specialized in these jobs were common among the working class. Improved standards of home life do not necessarily involve more unpaid domestic labour. It appears, however, that the organizations of the working class colluded with pressure from the bourgeoisie to structure the working population along the lines of gender.

What was most forcibly articulated in bourgeois philanthropy was the degeneration of the family caused by the conditions in which mothers undertook wage labour, the way in which working wives neglected the home and so drove their husbands to the alehouse, the moral impropriety of men and women and young people all working together in the same place, the moral danger of the influx of independent single girls to the factory towns (Hutchins and Harrison 1911, Pinchbeck 1930, Hewitt 1958, Davidoff et al. 1976:167). But a further and more important dimension to their arguments was the attempt to establish the idea of the hard-working man who was responsible for the support of his wife and children.

It has been said that the Ten-Hours movement in a sense compromised with the philanthropists, seeing the restriction of women's and children's factory hours as the only way to achieve a reduction of hours for all. As Ray Strachey (1978:53) put it, the men were 'hiding behind the petticoats of women' in pushing for the 1847 Ten Hours Act on compassionate grounds for women and young persons, knowing that it would force their own hours down to ten as well. (See also Webb and Webb 1894:296 for a similar interpretation of 1873–4.) But the factory legislation did play a part in further differentiating men's from women's work and in reinforcing patterns of job segregation in which women were found mainly in a narrow range of low-paid occupations, especially outside of the factories themselves.

The working class was itself highly diversified, and became more so during the course of the nineteenth century. And gender divisions played an important part in the development of a segmented working class. Historians have debated whether there was a distinct and identifiable 'labour aristocracy', what Hobsbawm (1964:272) described as the 'distinctive upper strata of the working class, better paid, better treated and generally more "respectable" and politically moderate than the mass of the working class' (see also Foster 1974, Stedman Jones 1975, Gray 1976, Gray 1980). Much of the discussion has been about the political outlook and role of these strata, but as Foreman (1977) points out, little attention has been paid to the conception of women and the family that was embodied in their notions of 'respectability'. An exception is Robert Gray, who has pointed to the ways in which ideas about the 'respectable artisan' involved a particular life-style which emphasized home-ownership, domesticity, the woman's place in the home...Gray sees these as ideas which although found among the bourgeois reformers and philanthropists were also a response of the would-be 'respectable' male workers to their own economic and social environment.

In the trade union movement, at that stage a movement largely of the 'skilled' male upper strata, an association between reducing competition in paid work and women as dependent homemakers was explicitly articulated. For instance, a speaker at the 1877 Trades Union Congress said that men

> had the future of their country and their children to consider and it was their duty as men and as husbands to use their utmost efforts to bring about a condition of things, where their wives could be in their proper sphere at

> home, instead of being dragged into competition for livelihood against the great and strong men of the world. (Henry Broadhurst, quoted in Ramelson 1967:103)

Housework and childcare (with the large families and primitive domestic technology of the day) were indeed heavy and time-consuming tasks and it was, in many ways, a fortunate woman whose husband earned enough to enable her to do this work in the day-time rather than after a day's paid work. It was for this reason that Hutchins and Harrison (1911), historians of the Factory Acts, castigated the 'women's rights opposition' to protective legislation for 'transferring their own grievance (against being excluded from the professions) to a class whose troubles are little known and less understood by them. . . Not exclusion but exploitation, is the trouble here' (1911:184). A position like this is consonant with Barbara Hutchins's later adherence to the 'new feminism' of the 1930s which rejected the focus on equal rights with men and concentrated on improving women's condition in the family through support for family endowment and the retention of protective legislation. It is not, of course, consonant with the feminism of the women's liberation movement today (though the debates on protective legislation itself have taken a new twist which may well lead us to defend it, as Angela Coyle (1980) has argued).

Hutchins and Harrison were wrong to accept the 'protective' rhetoric of the short-time movement (especially as they were well aware that it was a tactic designed to bring about a reduction of over-all factory hours), for the factory acts did not attempt to limit the exploitation of women in the whole range of employment, but only in specific kinds of jobs, which happened to be in the places where men also worked. As Sally Alexander has noted:

> There was not much to choose – if our criteria are risk to life or health – between work in the mines and work in the London dress-making trades. But no one suggested that sweated needle-work should be prohibited to women (1976:63)

. . .

The voices of working-class women were little heard in the debates, for they were unorganized and unrepresented. . . It seems likely that some women would have welcomed the shortening of their hours; others feared that it might bring about either a reduction in their wages or their displacement from the better jobs and that the married and young single women would think of an improvement in men's wages as some sort of compensation for the weakening of their own position and be glad that men offered to shoulder family responsibilities which they were less and less able to carry.

But whatever the response to their immediate situation may have been, the eventual outcome of this demand for a family wage and its persistence as an ideal, has placed the working class and the women of this class in a worse position than if it had continued to be assumed that husband and wife would both earn wages.

. . .

The bitter opposition of many employers to the factory legislation and, even more, to its implementation suggests that individual capitalists did not favour the exclusion of women from the factories. Yet it seems clear that the collective interests of capital as a whole, as eventually articulated in state policies, lay in establishing the principle, if not the practice, of the male breadwinner and that the state has played an important part in fostering this idea.

THE MYTH OF THE FAMILY WAGE

Attacking the family wage is a bit like an atheist attacking god the father. She wants to say that its does not exist, that the false belief that it does has evil consequences and that even if it did exist it would not be a good thing. We shall look first at the evidence that there has never in fact been a family wage system for the support of the wives, children and other non-waged relatives of working men.

Official statistics of women's labour-force participation are notoriously unrevealing of the real extent to which women engage in paid work. . . Oral history (for instance, Taylor 1977) is beginning to fill out the picture for the early decades of this century, when few married women were employed within the factories, but many seem to have made ends meet by out work, 'charring', laundry or taking in boarders (see also Tilly and Scott, 1978:25 and Davidoff 1979). It seems likely that it has never been possible for the majority of working class families to manage on one income.

. . .

Recent historical work on social policy (notably that of Hilary Land and Pat Thane) demonstrates the force of Eleanor Rathbone's arguments for family allowances. In pointing to the essential contribution of working-class women to the family income, and to the dire poverty of the many women who were financially responsible for the support of their children or other people, such work has exploded, in Hilary Land's terms, 'the myth of the male breadwinner'. For whatever arguments and political conclusions we may draw from the history of the demand for a male 'family wage', there is one point that is certain: this notion does not serve as an accurate description of the means by which the working class has been supported and reproduced.

The fact is that today, as in the past, many male wage-earners do not have dependants and many of the unwaged members of the working class do not have broadwinners. Taking the population as a whole, the household consisting of a man, woman and children is far from being the typical household. In 1976 it represented only 30 per cent of all households, with one-woman-one-man households another 30 per cent and one-person households 20 per cent (Family Expenditure Survey for 1976). Only 79 per cent of men aged twenty to sixty-five are married and only 42 per cent of those have dependent children, so that the supposed justification for the family wage – the children – in reality exists only for a third of adult men of working age. An increasing proportion of married women work for wages: the official figure for their economic activity rate (including the over-sixties) is now 50 per cent and for the age group 35–54 it rises to 68 per cent, almost as high as for unmarried women (*Department of Employment Gazette*, June 1977).

It is not surprising, then, to find that, taking households as a whole, the wages or salaries of 'heads of household' (some of whom are women anyway) contribute only 51 per cent of household income, the rest coming from other sources such as state benefits, self-employment and investments, and from the wages and salaries of wives (11.4 per cent) and other household members (10.8 per cent) (*Family Expenditure Survey* for 1976).

It is clear that many men supposedly earning a family wage do not have any dependants; it is less easy to say how many unwaged people there are who are unsupported. Among the great advances in welfare during this century has been the fact that increasingly, category by category, starting with the old age pension in 1908, unwaged individuals have become eligible for social security support, though often means-tested and set at a mean and minimal level...Nevertheless, despite child and supplementary benefits, invalid care allowances and retirement pensions, there is ample evidence of extreme poverty among those – predominantly women – who have sole care of children or of disabled people and also among old people – again often women – who are not subsidized by a wage-earner but rely entirely on their pension. For such people the family wage system provides no support or protection.

However, perhaps even more important than the inadequacy of the household structure to sharing the wage around the working class is the inadequacy of the size of the wage to supporting an entire household. This is evidenced most starkly in that modern revival of the Speenhamland system of poor relief, the Family Income Supplement – a long-term benefit available to families with children where the 'head' is in full-time low-paid work. There are almost a hundred thousand families that qualify because the 'head's' wages are simply not enough to support the family even at the exiguous levels laid down...

Wives' earnings at all income levels are an essential part of the household budget.... A study in 1974 found that there were in Britain over half a million couples where the wife was the sole or primary earner ... The importance of wives' earnings, together with the uncertainty of marriage (given the high divorce rate) and of the husband's employment, means that they cannot be expected to be dependants who work only for 'extras'.

THE CASE AGAINST THE FAMILY WAGE

The question we have to confront, then, is whether this idea of the family wage represents an ideal that we should aim to realize or a myth that we should aim to destroy. The arguments in favour of a family wage structure and indeed of 'the family' itself have recently been re-presented by a socialist feminist, Jane Humphries (1977a and b), who has set out very clearly the issues that we need to take up and the conclusions we wish to dispute.

Jane Humphries has argued that the case against the working-class family is not proven; defence of the family was, she insists, based on a correct perception of the material advantages it carried for the working class. According to Humphries the family wage system brings the following material benefits: (i) it provides a non-degrading form of support for non-labouring members of the working class; (ii) it gives the working class a lever on the supply of labour and therefore enables it to resist a fall in the value of labour power; and (iii) it has historically been crucial for the creation and transmission of a militant class consciousness, and has motivated political struggle.

We, however, have arrived at the opposite conclusions and will be arguing the following:...

(i) A family wage system would enforce the dependence and oppression of all women and subject single women, especially mothers, to severe poverty.

...

There is no shortage of evidence to support the suggestion that financial dependence carries in its train a significant degree of ideological subordination. Studies by Laura Oren (1974) and others have shown that women's levels of consumption within the family tend to be lower than those of men, and the degrading aspects of a struggle over the distribution of the wage within the family have been explored by Pauline Hunt (1978) – and there are stark examples in *Coal Is Our Life* (Dennis et al. 1956). Hilary Land has pointed out that women who return to wage labour after a period of child-bearing have lost ground and go back to lower wage rates: 'marriage and motherhood', she comments, 'effectively "deskill" women' (1978:282). Indeed the assumption of a male family wage affects all women's wages adversely, since even single women suffer from the lower rates of pay, poorer working conditions and constraints on promotion generally applied to women wage workers. Marriage and motherhood are not, in any case, a secure livelihood: for many women the consequences of divorce are a much lower standard of living and a structurally disadvantaged place in the labour market.

Even if married women were better off under a family wage system, those who were not married would be worse off. At the end of the nineteenth century only 85 per cent of women married, and often later than now (today the figure is 95 per cent, but many of these divorce).... Unmarried mothers, widows and deserted wives were in the direst straits. Even the most respectable, the widow, was subjected to the 'workhouse test' before she could obtain relief.... Deserting husbands and putative fathers were also expected to pay maintenance (for unmarried mothers from 1844 and for deserted wives from 1878), but it was unlikely that they often did so. Indeed, many thousands of these 'liable relatives' were imprisoned for failing to reimburse the poor law authorities for the maintenance of their dependants. The Finer Report on One-Parent Families has documented the fact that maintenance is still rarely and irregularly paid today and that many men, and their dependants, suffer real hardship from the fact that men are expected to maintain two consecutive families simultaneously. When poor relief in the nineteenth century and supplementary benefit today are granted to a single woman, she is subject to a cohabitation rule, on the assumption that if she shares a household with a man he should be supporting her. The expectation of dependence on a man can thus have disastrous consequences for the woman who has no man to depend upon, yet provisions for state support show a remorseless determination to enforce that expectation wherever possible.

Dispute rages about exactly what economic or sociological theory best explains women's position in the wage-labour market, their concentration in a limited range of sectors and occupations and their lower average pay (see, for instance, Beechey 1978; Breugel 1979). This is not the place to enlarge on that discussion. It is sufficient for our purposes to note that there is broad agreement that domestic responsibilities and the supposed possibility of dependence upon a husband (and in the nineteenth century on a father) must figure largely in the explanation. Furthermore, the belief that women reduce men's wages by undercutting has served to justify trade union pressure to exclude them from work, or at least from the better-paid trades.

...

Part of the ideal model of the family wage and women's peripheral place in wage-work is the idea of women's domestic responsibilities. Jane Humphries argues that the family wage frees the woman to produce use-values in the home which actually raises the 'family's' standard of living above what is necessary to reproduce the members. The need of a man for a clean cheerful home and a meal prepared on his return from work was one of the powerful arguments for restricting the hours and types of paid work that women should do. Low wages, dependence and housework for women are a trio of mutually reinforcing ideas, each justifying and producing the conditions for the others...

Many feminists have argued that the enforcement of domestic responsibilities, especially childcare and doing the man's housework, lies at the root of women's oppression. Childcare has been thought, by non-feminists, to be an inalienable task of women and to both justify and explain most of the division of labour and the differences between women and men. Yet it is interesting that childhood as a period of prolonged dependence and child-care as a separate task are relatively recent and developed hand-in-hand with dependent motherhood. However, in this century, as women have lived longer and concentrated their childbearing into a few early years of life (the youngest child usually starts school before the mother is thirty-five) the appeal to motherhood as a justification for dependence has become less plausible (even to those who think that privatized mothering is the only way to bring up children). Yet the risk of marriage and motherhood is often mobilized as a justification for not training women and not giving them better-paid and supervisory jobs.

Responsibility for caring for the old and the mentally and physically handicapped also falls most naturally to female relatives, (especially married women) who can expect support from their husbands if they have to give up paid work or reduce the number of hours they do...

In fact, housework seems to fall to women's lot whether or not they are dependent and whether or not they go out to work (Boulding, 1976:112, Hunt, 1968:176). Young and Wilmott (1973:113) found that while the men in their sample of couples aged 30 to 50 spent an average of 10 hours a week on household tasks, women in full-time jobs spent 23 hours, those in part-time jobs 35 hours and those not in paid work 45 hours...[2] This does not square with the argument put by Jane Humphries that it is women staying at home that makes available the extra use-values from domestic production. It seems that women are obliged to work a good deal at this form of production in any case.

We have argued that the demand for the family wage, and the belief that it exists, enforces the dependence and oppression of all women. If the demand were actually realized and married women no longer went into paid employment, married couples might possibly be as well off in purely financial terms; but the women would not necessarily get their share, and if they did, it would be under conditions of subordination to their husbands. And single women, especially mothers, would be at an acute economic disadvantage. Hence, if the men of the working class struggle for a family wage, they do so in opposition to one of the central demands of the women's liberation movement and against the interests of working-class women.

(ii) A family wage system would not necessarily raise the value of labour power and the acceptance of the family wage principle has historically tended to reduce the standard of living of the working class as a whole.

Jane Humphries's central thesis is that the working class had a material interest in the maintenance of family structures.

> Since it seems at least possible that a retreat of certain family members from the labour force, in conjunction with an organized attempt to secure a 'family wage' could raise their standard of living (1977b:34).

She adds that working class control over the supply of labour was limited and married women represented one of the few variable sources, and also presented one of the few opportunities for mobilization of bourgeois ideology. Although it was a tragedy that this strategy systematically reinforced sex-based relations of domination and subordination, it was not in itself disadvantageous to working-class women since they benefitted from the advances it brought to the working class as a whole.

It is important to locate this argument by Jane Humphries as an explicit critique of many of the conclusions drawn by contributors to the 'domestic labour debate'. Marxist-feminist analysis of the political economy of housework, and of its relationship to wage labour, has tended to stress the benefits to capital of a household structure in which women's unpaid domestic work lowers the costs of reproduction of the working class as a whole and hence tends to lower the value of labour power... These arguments have been subjected to a number of criticisms, of which the most pertinent for our purposes is the one suggesting that since the male wage upon which the dependent domestic labourer in this model relies must itself be met by collective capital this system represents a redistribution rather than a reduction of the costs to capital of the reproduction of the working class.

Jane Humphries, however, has raised a set of arguments which fundamentally shift the site of this debate. Instead of considering domestic labour and wage labour from the point of view of the interests of capital, she considers the relationship of the household to wage labour from the point of view of the working class... Her work therefore raises for discussion a question begged in much of the literature: whether what is beneficial for capital is necessarily disadvantageous for the working class.

Although this shift of emphasis is welcome, we want to take issue with the argument Humphries presents. In particular we want to challenge the theoretical link she establishes between the value of labour power, control over the labour supply and domestic labour... The existence of wage differentials dating from the earliest period of the transition to capitalism and apparently relating to minimum subsistence needs of men and women, suggests that the wage has never, historically, been determined as a family wage. And if it never had been a 'family wage', reflecting a family-based calculation of costs of reproduction, it is inappropriate to argue that the employment of women and children would necessarily lower the value of labour power...

Furthermore, the relationship of domestic labour to the value of labour power cannot be posed in the terms Humphries uses when she suggests that the products of housework are a bonus brought by a family wage system where the single male wage is equal to the combined wage all the family members would have got and where in addition the wife is freed for domestic labour. Leaving aside the contentious question of whether the male wage would, historically, be equal to the family's combined wages (discussed in Humphries 1977a:251–2), the evidence we have already considered suggests that wives do a good deal of housework even when they do earn a wage, so their domestic contribution is available under systems other than that of a 'family wage'. The point at issue here is whether we can specify theoretically a general relationship between domestic labour and the value of labour power. All insistence on the historical determination of the value of labour power suggests that this relationship too will be an historically rather than theoretically given one. Maxine Molyneux, in arguing for an historical approach to this question, puts forward the possibility that the input of domestic labour to the household may rise when the value of labour power is high and fall when it is low, and that a high level of domestic labour may be contingent upon a high value of labour power (1979:11). The amount of domestic labour performed in the household is clearly related to wages in complex ways...

Further difficulties are encountered with Humphries's argument that the value of labour power could be raised by working class control of the labour supply – in this case through the withdrawal of married women and children from the workforce. This, too, must be seen as historically variable...In fact, the working class did not succeed in withdrawing the labour of married women in this way and it could well be argued that this strategy merely exacerbated the tendency for them to be constituted as a reserve labour force capable of undercutting male wages and being substituted for male workers in periods of recession. Control of the labour supply obviously does constitute an important aspect of working class resistance, but its relative historical power must vary with capital's demand for labour as production expands and contracts. When demand falls in a recession, as Jane Humphries has herself convincingly demonstrated in the case of the great depression of the twenties and thirties (1976), the labour movement's stringent attempts to exclude women workers were not remarkably successful in resisting a fall in living standards. In fact it is not clear that control over the labour supply would necessarily affect the value of labour power, as opposed to the standard of living.

...

We would want to argue, then, that there is no necessary connection between the withdrawal of women from wage work and the value of labour power. Although a rise in the value of labour power, complemented by a rise in wages, might enable more families to maintain a dependent wife if they chose, this rise in the value of labour power would be the outcome of historical struggle over the standard of living and would not be achieved by the dependency of wives.

Historically, in any case, the struggle for an ideal of a 'family wage' has not tended to raise the standard of living of the working class as a whole. As an exclusionary practice it has had a limited success in reducing competition from women workers in those sections of the working class which have achieved a definition of their work as skilled, but in periods of high unemployment it presents capital with a cheaper workforce, and in periods of full employment it militates against a rise in wages by enabling more workers to be drawn in. The value of labour power is not determined unambiguously by exclusionary practices of this kind, but by the historical general strength of the working class in defining its costs of reproduction at an acceptable standard of living.

(iii) The family wage principle divides and weakens the working class.

One way of approaching this question is to consider whether the family wage principle tends to encourage militancy or not. Humphries has argued that family responsibilities may have promoted the radicalization of working men: 'the experience of watching the suffering and oppression of their families could instigate class action' (1977a:255). There is a general point to be made here, however, that suffering and poverty do not necessarily induce political consciousness and action. On the contrary, there may be more evidence to suggest that the responsibility for a hungry family may, particularly in the absence of adequate strike pay and so on, significantly reduce the likelihood of militant struggle. Many writers on wage labour in the early period of capitalist expansion cite a telling remark from Lord Shaftsbury's speech in Parliament on the Ten Hours Bill.

> Mr. E., a manufacturer...informed me that he employed females exclusively at his power-looms...gives a decided preference to married females, especially those who have families at home dependent on them for support; they are attentive, docile, more so than unmarried females, and are compelled to use their utmost exertions to procure the necessities of life. (March 15th, 1844)

It is a matter of dispute whether we interpret this docility in terms of the peculiar tenderness of the female nature (as Shaftsbury did) or in terms of the industrial consequences of the worker – in this case female – having a vulnerable and dependent family.

It is true that the friendly societies, and later the trade unions, were the organizations that fostered the working-class militancy of the nineteenth century and that these organizations were largely founded upon the principles of excluding women, relegating them to a dependent status and demanding a family wage. However, the debate among the historians of the labour aristocracy revolves around the question of whether this exclusionary formation of an upper stratum – and it involved the exclusion of many other than women – did not lead to a conservatism, a desire to sustain the differentiation of the working class and a tendency to collude with the bourgeoisie to this end. So it is at least plausible to suggest that the attempt to relegate women to domestic dependence was associated with a restraint of militancy to a lower level than it might otherwise have reached.

The question of the militancy of working-class women is a clearer one... Despite the disguised and contradictory character of the wage under capitalism, and the specific abuses to which women wage labourers have been subjected (see for example Engels's discussion of Jus Primae Noctis and women factory workers), it is clear that, from the point of view of raising political consciousness, wage labour is more desirable than the isolation and privatization of full-time domestic labour.

...

The family wage principle weakens the working class by creating divisions between men and women within it. It does this in two ways, both of which we have discussed in other contexts earlier in this paper: by creating the conditions for conflict between individual men and women in the family in the struggle over the distribution of the wage, and by creating the conditions for competition and undercutting of wages between men and women generally in the labour force. In dividing the working class into wage-earners and those dependent on the wage for support the family wage system colludes with the moralism surrounding the wage contract in capitalist production and fails to question the disguised appearance of the wage (that is, it reproduces the view that those who earn the wage are actually being paid for their labour, whereas in fact what they sell is their ability to labour, or labour power).

Furthermore, acceptance of the family wage system involves the principle that the obligation to support non-labouring members of the working class should fall on the shoulders of the labouring individuals rather than being met from capitalist surplus. In this respect the demand for support from the state is one that stimulates revolutionary class consciousness. For although Jane Humphries is right to point out that working-class organizations fiercely resisted the state provision of support as embodied in the 'new poor law' of 1834, there is no evidence that this represented a principled preference for a family system of support over a state system. Outrage against the 'workhouse test' was directed against its degrading and offensive form rather than against the principle of poor relief in general, which had been accepted as a right since the introduction of the Elizabethan poor law...

The parish system was preferred to the bureaucratic inhumanity of the nineteenth-century poor law. So too in the twentieth century the working class has struggled for state support, in the form of old-age pensions, unemployment and sickness benefit, family allowances and so on; yet it has resisted and criticised means-testing, red tape and offensive treatment in the administration of this support.

...

The demand for state support renders more visible the irrationality and inadequacy of the wage in capitalist production. This indeed formed the basis of Rathbone's campaign for family allowances, since she demonstrated that the assumed family wage in fact catered (in the early decades of the twentieth century) for approximately 3 million 'phantom' wives and 16 million 'phantom' children, the fictitious dependants of men who were in fact bachelors, and left 6¼ million children insufficiently fed and clothed (1949:15–16). The fact is that the family wage system has never been adequate to ensure the reproduction of the working class. The belief that it does, or that it could be perfected if only men's wages were raised, merely masks the fact that the capitalist wage system can never meet the needs of the working class. So the belief leads to attempts to reform it that cannot succeed and that do not improve the chances of more radical change.

. . .

NOTES

An earlier version of this paper was read at the Leeds CSE conference in July 1979 and at the CSE Sex and Class group in October 1979. We have learned a great deal from the discussions at both these meetings and also from the comments sent to us by *Capital and Class* and by the following people: Sally Alexander, Irene Bruegel, Bob Connell, Sue Himmelweit, Jane Humphries, Hilary Land, Kerry Schott, Judy Wajcman and Elizabeth Wilson.

1 Indeed at present the distinction is between men and married or cohabiting women, but it seems likely that 'man' will soon be translated euphemistically as 'breadwinner' to conform with EEC rules against sex discrimination (Rights of Women, 1979).
2 Interestingly too, a study in the United States found that men's 'help' in the home did not reduce the amount of women's work commensurately: when men helped with physical childcare, women spent even more time on it; when men put in time preparing meals, women only gained half that time (Leibowitz, 1975:223).

REFERENCES

Adamson, Olivia, Brown, Carol, Harrison, Judith, and Price, Judy, 1976 'Women's Oppression Under Capitalism' *Revolutionary Communist* no. 5.

Alexander, Sally, 1976 'Women's Work in Nineteenth-Century London, A Study of the Years 1820–50' in Mitchell and Oakley.

Atkin Report, 1919, *Report of the War Cabinet Committee on Women in Industry*, Cmd. 135, HMSO, London.

Auchmuty, Rosemary, 1975 'Spinsters and Trade Unions in Victorian Britain' in Curthoys (1975).

Beechey, Veronica, 1978 'Some Notes on Female Wage Labour in Capitalist Production' *Capital and Class* no. 3.

Blaxall, M. and Reagan, B., 1976 *Women and the Workplace* (University of Chicago Press).

Boulding, E., 1976 'Familial Constraints on Women's Work Roles' in Blaxall and Reagan, 1976.

Bruegel, Irene, 1979 'Women as a Reserve Army of Labour' *Feminist Review* no. 3.

Campbell, Beatrix and Charlton, Valerie (undated) 'Work to Rule – Wages and the Family' *Red Rag* (late 1978?).

CIS (counter information services), 1976 *Women Under Attack* Anti-Report no. 15, CIS, London.

Coyle, Angela, 1980 'The Protection Racket' *Feminist Review* no. 4.

Curthoys, Anne, Eade, Susan, and Spearitt, Peter (editors) 1975 *Women at Work* Australian Society for the Study of Labour History, Canberra.

Davidoff, Leonore, 1979 'The Separation of Home and Work?' in Burman, S., ed., *Fit Work for Women* (Croom Helm, London).

Davidoff, Leonore, et al., 1976 'Landscape with Figures' in Mitchell and Oakley.

Dennis, N., Henriques, F. and Slaughter, C., 1956 *Coal is Our Life* Eyre and Spottiswoode, London.

Department of Health and Social Security, Economic Adviser's Office, 1976 'Wives as Sole and Joint Breadwinners' (Mimeo).

Department of Health and Social Security, 1971 *Two-Parent Families: A Study of their Resources and Needs in 1968, 1969 and 1970* DHSS Statistical Report Series, no. 14 (HMSO, London).

Engels, Frederick, 1977 *The Condition of the Working Class in England* Lawrence and Wishart, London.

Finer Report, 1974 (Report of the Committee on One-Parent Families) *Cmnd 5629* (HMSO, London).

Finer, Morris and McGregor, O.R., 1974 'The History of the Obligation to Maintain' in Finer Report (1974).

Foreman, Ann, 1977 *Femininity as Alienation* (Pluto Press, London).

Foster, John, 1974 *Class Struggle and the Industrial Revolution* (Weidenfeld and Nicholson London).

Gardiner, J., 1974 'Women's Work in the Industrial Revolution' in Allen, S., Sanders, L. and Wallis, J., eds, *Conditions of Illusion* (Feminist Books, Leeds).

Gray, R.Q., 1976 *The Labour Aristocracy in Victorian Edinburgh* (Oxford University Press, London).

Gray, R.Q., 1980 *The Aristocracy of Labour in Nineteenth Century Britain c.1850–1900* (Macmillan, Studies in Economic and Social History, London).

Hartman, Mary and Banner, Lois W., 1974, eds, *Clio's Consciousness Raised* (Harper and Row, New York).

Hewitt, Margaret, 1958 *Wives and Mothers in Victorian Industry* (Rockliff, London).

Hobsbawm, E.J., 1964 *Labouring Men* (Weidenfeld and Nicholson, London).

Humphries, J., 1976 'Women: Scapegoats and Safety Valves in the Great Depression' *Review of Radical Political Economics* vol. 8, no. 1.

Humphries, Jane, 1977a 'Class Struggle and the Persistence of the Working Class Family' *Cambridge Journal of Economics* vol. 1, no. 3.

Humphries, Jane, 1977b 'The Working Class Family, Women's Liberation and Class Struggle: The Case of Nineteenth-Century British History' *The Review of Radical Political Economics* vol. 9, no. 3.

Hunt, Audrey, 1968, *A Survey of Women's Employment* (Office of Population Censuses and Surveys, London).

Hunt, Pauline, 1978 'Cash Transactions and Household Tasks: domestic behaviour in relation to industrial employment' *Sociological Review* vol. 26, no. 3.

Hutchins, B.L. and Harrison, A., 1911 *A History of Factory Legislation* 2nd edition (P.S. King and Son, London).
Kuhn, Annette and Wolpe, AnnMarie, 1978 *Feminism and Materialism* (Routledge and Kegan Paul, London).
Land, Hilary, 1976 'Women: Supporters or Supported?' in Barker, Diana Leonard and Allen, Sheila eds, *Sexual Divisions and Society: Process and change* (Tavistock, London).
Land, Hilary, 1978 'Who Cares for the Family?' *Journal of Social Policy* vol. 7, part 3.
Land, Hilary, 1980 *The Family Wage* (The Eleanor Rathbone Memorial Lecture for 1979) (Liverpool University Press, Liverpool).
Lloyd, C., ed., 1975 *Sex, Discrimination and the Division of Labour* (Columbia University Press, New York).
Marx, Karl, 1970 *Capital* vol. 1 (Lawrence and Wishart, London).
McIntosh, Mary, 1978 'The State and the Oppression of Women' in Kuhn and Wolpe.
Milkman, Ruth, 1976 'Women's Work and Economic Crisis: Some Lessons of the Great Depression' *Review of Radical Political Economics* vol. 8, no. 1.
Mitchell, Juliet and Oakley, Ann, 1976 *The Rights and Wrongs of Women* (Penguin, Harmondsworth).
Molyneux, M., 1979 'Beyond the Domestic Labour Debate' *New Left Review* no. 116.
Oren, Laura, 1974 'The Welfare of Women in Labouring Families: England, 1860–1950' in Hartman and Banner (1974).
Pinchbeck, Ivy, 1930 *Women Workers and the Industrial Revolution* reprinted 1969 (Frank Cass, London).
Ramelson, M., 1967 *The Petticoat Rebellion* (Lawrence and Wishart, London).
Rathbone, Eleanor, 1949 *Family Allowances* (A new edition of *The Disinherited Family*) (George Allen and Unwin, London).
Rights of Women and Women's Liberation Campaign for Financial and Legal Independence, 1979 'Disaggregation Now!' *Feminist Review* no. 2.
Royal Commission on Equal Pay, 1946 *Report* (HMSO, London, Cmd. 6937).
Smelser, Neil, 1959 *Social Change in the Industrial Revolution* (Routledge and Kegan Paul, London).
Stedman Jones, Gareth, 1975, 'Class Struggle and the Industrial Revolution' *New Left Review* no. 90.
Strachey, Ray, 1978 *The Cause* (Virago, London).
Taylor, Sandra, 1977 'The Effect of Marriage on Job Possibilities for Women and the Ideology of the Home: Nottingham 1890–1930' *Oral History* 5:1.
Thane, Pat, 1978 'Women and the Poor Law in Victorian and Edwardian England' *History Workshop Journal*, no. 6.
Tilley, Louise A. and Scott, Joan W., 1978 *Women, Work and Family* (Holt, Renehart and Winston, New York).
Vibart, H.H.R., 1926 *Family Allowances in Practice* (P.S. King, London).
Webb, Sidney and Webb, Beatrice, 1894 *The History of British Trade Unions.*
Wilmott, Peter and Young, Michael, 1973 *The Symmetrical Family* (Routledge and Kegan Paul, London).

9

Johanna Brenner and Maria Ramas

Rethinking Women's Oppression

The past decade has witnessed an extraordinary flowering of Marxist-feminist analysis and debate. Michèle Barrett's *Women's Oppression Today* is an ambitious recent attempt to present and synthesize this literature.[1] Through a dialogue with the most influential currents in socialist-feminist thought Barrett attempts to construct a Marxist analysis of the relationship between women's oppression and class exploitation in capitalism that is neither reductionist nor idealist.

. . .

Barrett views the key to women's oppression as a complex she terms the 'family-household system'. . . [it] is not seen as inherent to capitalism but has come to form a *historically constituted* element of class relations. This structure was not inevitable, but rather emerged through a historical process in which an ideology that posited women's natural connection to domesticity was incorporated into capitalist relations of production. This ideology sprang in part from precapitalist conceptions of women's place, but was predominantly a bourgeois construction that fitted with bourgeois family relations. The ideology was accepted by the organized working class in the nineteenth century and was determinant in forming craft-union political strategy. The pivot in the formation of the family-household system, Barrett contends, was the mid-nineteenth century struggle between a coalition of capitalists and male workers on the one hand, and female workers on the other, as a result of which the better organized male craft unions and the bourgeois-controlled state were able to override the interests of female workers. The expulsion of women from craft unions and the protective legislation on women's working conditions passed in Britain in the 1840s–1860s effectively forced women into the domestic sphere and laid the basis for a sex-segregated wage-labour market. Once the family-household system was in place, a sex-segregated labour market was almost inevitable. The sexual division of labour within the household and within the labour market, once established, serve to reinforce each other. Women's low wages and their segregation in a limited number of occupations effectively consolidate their position in the family, and vice versa.

Working-class men fought for the family-household system because it was in their short-term interests. However, in the long run, Barrett argues, this represented a real defeat for the class as a whole because it split the interests of working men and women...On the other hand, precisely because the family-household system divides the working class, and because the system is fundamentally a conservative social force, its adoption by the working class was in the long-term *political* interests of the bourgeoisie...

Because women's oppression is not a prerequisite for capitalism, theoretically it would not be impossible for women to achieve liberation within capitalist society...But in practice 'it is impossible to imagine that they could be extracted from the relations of production and reproduction of capitalism without a massive transformation of those relations taking place.'[2]

...

Barrett's review of the state of feminist theory is impressive, particularly because it allows her to identify in a remarkably clear, if somewhat schematic manner the impasse Marxist feminism has reached. And while we do not find that her analysis ultimately succeeds in breaking the impasse, it does indicate the direction in which we must move if we are to break through onto new terrain. Barrett's insistence that the family-household system, the crucial site of women's oppression, is not functionally determined by capitalist needs alone, and her concomitant emphasis on an historical approach which centres on how class struggle shaped the sexual division of labour, are absolutely essential to a successful Marxist-feminist analysis. Her commitment to the development of a non-reflexive but materialist theory of gender ideology is also crucial.

PROBLEMS WITH BARRETT'S APPROACH

...

Barrett's analysis, while materialist in approach, fails to identify any material basis for women's oppression in capitalism. She rejects not only explanations that root this development in capitalist exigencies of the reproduction of labour power, but also radical-feminist proposals that point to biological reproduction as a material basis. Further, Barrett fails to find this system to be unambiguously in the vital material interests of any social group. Certainly it is not in the interests of women. Nor in the class interests of working-class men,...although working-class men have some interest in the family-household system as men. But Barrett does not believe that this is as great as some feminists argue. The role of male as breadwinner (a) locks men effectively into wage labour, (b) has deprived them of access to their children, and (c) oppresses them by imposing a rigid definition of masculinity... Moreover, the system cannot be viewed as unambiguously serving the interests of the capitalist class, although, in Barrett's view, capitalists benefit more than any other social group. For while the system is not perhaps in their best economic interests, it is very advantageous politically as it 'divides and weakens the working class and reduces its militancy.'[3] ...

If the family-household system really is as tenuous a construction as Barrett's analysis suggests, it is difficult to explain why it has embedded itself so deeply in capitalist society. For, while it may be in the political interests of the bourgeoisie, it is not, at least in Barrett's analysis, essential to the survival of the bourgeoisie... Further, if the interests of working-class men, both as men and as proletarians, are not conclusively served by this system... it is hard to explain what has prevented the workers' movement from adopting a more enlightened strategy on this issue. Barrett is well aware of this problem, and her solution is to give ideology great weight in the analysis... The suggestion is that gender ideology is powerful enough to counteract or withstand the battering of the 'sex blind' tendencies of the law of capital accumulation.

Such a formulation, of course, necessitates an analysis of the production and dynamics of gender ideology itself, and the requirements for changing its content. Barrett does not address these questions in any detail in this book... As her analysis stands now we are left with an account in which the ideology of gender difference,... independently of capitalist social relations, has been powerful enough historically to have had an autonomous effect on the shaping of capitalist social relations, and remains powerful enough to reproduce this situation on an ongoing basis. Such an analysis is, of course, subject to all the criticisms of dual systems approaches that Barrett herself makes so well.

UNIONS AND PROTECTIVE LEGISLATION

We should now discuss in some detail, as it represents what may be considered an emerging Marxist-feminist consensus, Barrett's central historical account of the formation of the family-household system and the resulting ghettoization of women in low-paying sectors of capitalist production through protective legislation and trade-union exclusivism...

Barrett argues that women's precarious position in capitalist production conditioned the continuation of their domestic role within the family, and their dependence upon men. Now, it is very difficult to make a convincing case that so precarious a social-political edifice could have played a major role in conditioning the sexual division of labour or the family household system, either in England or the United States. The US example is particularly provocative because legislation barely existed until well into the twentieth century...Furthermore, not only was the enactment of protective legislation an arduous and slow-moving process, but those laws that were passed were virtually unenforced in the nineteenth century and well into the twentieth.[4]

...

In Britain the issue is somewhat more complex because protective legislation was passed at the national level and appears to have been slightly better enforced...While the evidence is limited and somewhat impressionistic, what there is to date suggests that all of this legislation did not have any determining effect on the structuring of job segregation by sex. To the extent that the Ten Hours Bill was effective, it appears to have limited men's as well as women's labour hours.[5] Insofar as this was the case, it could not have adversely affected women's chances for employment within the industry. Indeed, it was precisely because a sexual division of labour already existed in the textile industry, such that male, female and child labour were utterly interdependent, that the Ten Hours Bill could win the shortening of the working day for all through the limitation of female and child labour. Nor does this legislation appear to have resulted in any significant replacement of male for female labour, either within the industry as a whole or within particular sectors. In fact, the proportion of women to men in the textile industry continued to increase during the latter part of the nineteenth century.[6]

It is probable that the extension of protective legislation to other industries in the course of the second half of the nineteenth century also failed significantly to affect the sexual division of labour...By the time these laws became effective, skilled male workers were generally working shorter hours than those called for by such legislation; for by the 1870s many unions had succeeded in limiting the working day in their trade to nine hours...

There is no question but that trade unions followed a rigorous exclusionary policy vis-à-vis women in both Britain and the United States during the first three-quarters of the nineteenth century. It is also true that it was often justified by reference to a patriarchal ideology of gender difference. We are sceptical, however, that trade union policy had the effect Barrett suggests. Even if trade unions had been wholly successful in excluding women from their trade, which they were not, it is difficult to see how this could have significantly contributed to the capitalist sexual division of labour as a whole, as the skilled occupations controlled by trade unions in the nineteenth century represented only a very small fraction of the capitalist division of labour.

THE RECORD OF UNION STRUGGLE

The historical evidence similarly undermines Barrett's contention that the way working-class men organized in the nineteenth century was determined primarily by pre-capitalist patriarchal ideology. The realms of both legislative reform and industrial organization offer disconfirming historical cases.

...

The earliest and most consistent demand made by the working-class component of the factory movement was a call for the reduction of the working day for all. However, the bourgeoisie's adamant opposition to any restriction of adult male labour on the one hand, and the growing middle-class outcry against the condition of factory children, and later factory women, on the other, moulded the strategy which emerged from the 1830s onwards.[7] The strategy was to reduce the adult working day indirectly, through legislation that would fix the hours of child labour in such a way as to make it impossible for adults to work longer hours...

The government's bill, which was passed by Parliament in 1833, ... while providing for more stringent restrictions on child labour, actually represented a defeat for the Short-Time Movement because it allowed manufacturers to continue to employ adults for long hours by using children in relays.[8] The Short-Time Movement responded by agitating for restrictions on motive power and for a new factory act, eventually introduced by Lord Ashley in 1837, that would have restricted the labour of all under twenty-one to ten hours. Parliament rejected both bills precisely because its members recognized them to be thinly veiled attempts to restrict the labour time of all.[9]

It was at this point that the agitation for the restriction on women's hours was first voiced by the Movement, which mounted an energetic campaign in the 1840s on behalf of this new demand. The vigour of this offensive, combined with the economic depression, was substantial enough to persuade Parliament to vote the Ten Hours Bill into law in 1847. Barrett is aware of this line of interpretation, though she ignores it in *Women's Oppression Today*. In an article co-authored with Mary McIntosh,[10] ... the authors do not seem to take issue with the contention that the major motive of the factory movement was to limit all adult labour. Yet they maintain that regardless of motive the effect of the legislation was to contribute to a discriminatory sexual division of labour. Of course, the argument that protective legislation 'further differentiated men's from women's work' and 'reinforced patterns of job segregation' is quite different from the proposition of *Women's Oppression Today* – that this legislation was primarily responsible for job segregation by sex.

Trade union history poses similar problems for Barrett's analysis. While one can cite numerous cases in which trade unions practised discriminatory policies towards working women and justified them by waxing eloquent on woman's 'proper sphere', there are also many examples of trade-union support for women's organizational and strike activities, and one can even upon occasion find trade-union journals and conferences supporting feminist viewpoints. We do not point out that male trade unions often supported women as workers in order to paper over their unquestionable, substantial history of discrimination.... However it is entirely unnecessary to resort to ideology to explain why trade unions were particularly adamant in their opposition to female entry into their trades. It is quite clear that when unions were unable to exclude women, a rapid depression of wages and general degradation of work resulted. Barbara Taylor's account of the London Journeymen Tailors Union strike against homework in 1833 well illustrates this dynamic.[11] The LJTU was in fact one of the strongest unions in Britain during the eighteenth century, strictly controlling hours, prices and labour recruitment. By the early nineteenth century, the privileged position of the tailors was threatened by a reorganization of production that made it possible for capitalists to replace the relatively expensive labour of the male tailors with the cheaper labour of women working at home. The LJTU attempted to block this by preventing production outside of workshops and was fairly successful as late as the 1820s. The growth of the ready-made clothing industry, however, which centred on women engaged in homework for pitifully low wages, broke the back of the union in the 1830s. The 1833 strike against homework (female tailoresses) was the tailors' last attempt to preserve their position.[12]

...

That competition, rather than ideology, was the crucial determinant of male exclusivism is underscored by the fact that in cases where women were not competing with men, or where women were in the industry from the start, unions tended to include women and even gave substantial support to their attempts at organization and strike activity. Again, we do not wish to suggest that male trade unionists or male workers in general supported women's right to equality in work as well as in all other aspects of social life, or to deny that they held sexist ideas about women. Rather, these examples suggest that if the history of trade-union attitudes towards women is to be properly understood, we require a far more complex analysis of the social-economic background.

...

THE MATERIAL BASIS FOR THE FAMILY HOUSEHOLD SYSTEM

In sum, the problems we have identified in Barrett's interpretation can all be traced to one major lacuna in her analysis – the absence of a material basis for the historical development and reproduction of the family-household system, the sexual division of labour, and women's oppression in capitalism. We do not take issue with the contentions that such a system may serve the bourgeoisie's political interests, that working-class men (at least those in skilled jobs) wanted to exclude women from higher paying sectors of production, or that all men had an interest in maintaining control over women's lives for both practical and emotional reasons.... However, the crucial question, in our view, is how men were able to accomplish this against the opposition of women, given the 'sex-blind' tendencies of capitalist accumulation which were pushing in the opposite direction.[13]

In the remainder of this essay we would like to suggest an alternative analytical and historical interpretation that places considerable weight on the exigencies of biological reproduction. This is a somewhat heretical stance for socialist feminists. Most, Barrett among them, are extremely reluctant to acknowledge any role for biological differences in determining women's social position. Underlying this reluctance is a healthy concern that any such focus may inadvertently lead down the path to biological determinism.[14] Let us be clear at the outset. We do not wish to argue that biological facts of reproduction in themselves determine social relations, in capitalism or in any other social formation. We do propose, however, to take seriously Timpanaro's suggestion that the *relationship* between the natural and the social must be built into the analysis.[15] In our view, a materialist account of women's oppression simply must consider the way in which the class-structured capitalist system of production can incorporate the biological facts of reproduction, and the extent to which biological differences, considered in such a context, condition women's participation in economic/political life, their capacity for self-organization in defence of their interests and needs, and so forth...

Biological facts of reproduction – pregnancy, childbirth, lactation – are not readily compatible with capitalist production, and to make them so would require capital outlays on maternity leave, nursing facilities, childcare, and so on. Capitalists are not willing to make such expenditures, as they increase the costs of variable capital without comparable increases in labour productivity and thus cut into rates of profit. In the absence of such expenditures, however, the reproduction of labour power becomes problematic for the working class as a whole and for women in particular.[16]

BIOLOGICAL REPRODUCTION AND CLASS STRUCTURE IN THE NINETEENTH CENTURY

The assignment of women to reproduction and their marginalization in wage work is prior to, rather than an effect of, protective legislation or trade union policy. All studies of women's work in the nineteenth century indicate that for the most part women withdrew from full-time work in factories and shops with the birth of their first child. Long before protective legislation or union contracts, married women were shaping their employment around their domestic responsibilities. Along with their children, women made crucial economic contributions to their households. However, whereas their sons and daughters went into unskilled wage work, women with children gained income in those employments that fitted with the demands of childcare and housework: part-time work, homework, seasonal work, taking in boarders, etc.[17] The exception proves the rule: where women could work with their children, their participation rate rose – for example, Italian mothers in the New York canneries, immigrant mothers in New England textile mills and early English cotton factories.[18]...

This raises two issues. First, why did certain aspects of working-class reproduction – in particular childcare – remain outside capitalist production, so that a division of labour developed in which one person in the household became primarily responsible for this necessary labour? Secondly, why were women relegated to this position of domestic labourer rather than men?...

The increasing determination of work rhythms by complex, coordinated machine production posed difficulties in matching productive and reproductive work. However, in the abstract, the organization of production itself does not prevent the reconciliation of these two kinds of work. Barrett's contention that this particular resolution – the family-household system – was determined by an ideology of gender difference that pre-dated capitalism assumes that alternatives to locating the reproduction of labour power in the household existed – an assumption that must be addressed and justified.

The elimination of the household as a site for reproducing the labour force on a daily and inter-generational basis requires relatively cheap goods and services to be available through the market... If wages are not sufficient to purchase the whole range of these services, domestic labour has to be done in addition to wage work to make up the difference. The evidence is overwhelming that the income of several earners was necessary to provide even the bare necessities for the majority of working-class families in the first half of the nineteenth century and even in the second half when wages did rise.[19] Therefore, a sizeable amount of domestic labour remained to be done under extremely primitive conditions which made it physically arduous and time-consuming...

The determining factor, however, was the incompatibility of childcare and work outside the home. In theory it might have been possible for both husbands and wives to work and pay for childcare, but in practice, the survival of their children was jeopardized when both parents worked ... Because the nursing of infants was necessary to guarantee their survival, and because employers would not make provision for the needs of pregnant women and infants, it made sense for the woman to stay home if the family could afford it, while her husband went to work. When women spent much of their married life bearing and nursing children, as they did throughout the nineteenth century, the logic of the sexual division of labour embodied in the family-household system was overwhelming.

In order to participate fully in production, women required a range of support services – most crucially, job-site care for infants, nursing breaks for working mothers, paid maternity leave. Yet where working conditions in general were barely supportable, where employers were consistently hostile to unions, where unemployment insurance, workmen's compensation, occupational safety, etc. were unknown, the provision of such services could only be a utopian dream. A working class barely strong enough to establish simple weapons of defence was in no position to wrest these enormous concessions from capital. In the absence of these necessary supports, equal wages for women and equal access to skilled trades would not have solved women's problems, even had the labour movement adopted a much less ambiguous stance toward women's work for wages.

THE CLASS BASIS OF HIGH FERTILITY

It may be asked, of course, whether women had no choice but to have many pregnancies and many children... Up to 1920 working-class fertility appears to have remained high... in France and England as well as in America.[20] After 1920, without any substantial increase in the use of newer birth control mechanisms, American fertility rates were sharply reduced. Therefore, to understand why women did not limit the number of years in which they were bearing and nursing children, we have to take into account... how high fertility fitted into an overall strategy for survival within the working class.

Studies of fertility in relation to economic change have shown that opportunities for young couples to find work, or land in the rural economy, and the usefulness of child labour point in the direction of large families. The possibility of establishing a household independent of one's parents early in life encourages earlier marriage. The demand for child labour depresses the incentive to practise birth control during the early years of marriage. Together these factors produce high fertility levels. This pattern was especially typical of domestic industry.[21] ...

In the nineteenth century, opportunities for wage work for both men and women allowed young couples to set up house at an early age. Probably even more important in determining high fertility rates, however, was the value of child labour combined with the very high levels of infant and child mortality that prevailed in many of the urban quarters throughout the nineteenth and even into the twentieth century.[22] While the utility of very young child labour declined by the end of the nineteenth century, it seems that the labour of older children and teenagers remained an important source of family income well into the twentieth century.[23] In the absence of social security or pension systems, teenagers' wages provided crucial old-age security, perhaps allowing the parents to accumulate savings or property.[24] Since it was necessary for the family to have a large number of surviving children, and since infant and child mortality rates were high, there was little reason for couples to limit the number of births.

SEXUAL DIVISION OF LABOUR AND WAGE DIFFERENTIALS IN CAPITALIST PRODUCTION

Barrett contends that... 'because the wage-labour relation and the contradiction between labour and capital... are "sex-blind" and operate quite independently of gender,'[25] the gender division of labour can only be explained in terms of a historical development in which pre-capitalist ideology crucially conditioned the outcome: men reserved certain kinds of highly paid work for themselves and accepted women only in those jobs that reflected and reinforced their domesticity.

In our view, however, it is both possible and preferable to explain the origins and reproduction of sex segregation in the occupational structure precisely in terms of the 'sex-blind' operation of the capitalist labour market, in which capitalists compete to hire labour for the least cost and workers search for the highest-paid work available. Sex-segregation of jobs and low female wages are intimately connected. Both have their roots in the barriers women face in defending their pay and working conditions. Women are disadvantaged on the labour market because of their family responsibilities. Women's skills are less 'valued' not because of an ideological devaluation of women, but because women are less likely to be unionized, less mobile in making job searches, more constrained in general by their domestic duties.

. . .

If we remember which women were working and why, we can see how women could be utilized as cheap competitors with men. Adult women workers usually had children to support, were widows or married to men with unstable incomes. These women constituted a particularly defenceless and desperate labour pool. Their home burdens made it difficult for them to find the time or energy to organize; their lack of mobility made it difficult for them to search for better work.[26]

The other group of working women, young women living in the parental home, did not face the same constraints. And it is clear from the history of female unionization that young single women were the backbone of the union organization that did take place.[27] . . . Knowing that she was likely to leave work once married, and having opportunities for steady albeit lower-paid 'women's work', a young woman might have been reluctant to make the kind of fight required to enter and remain in skilled male work. Many working-class daughters may have preferred the feminine support of the garment factory to the hostility of the printshop. And given that women's wages were quite low even when they did factory work, young women might have reasonably chosen the new jobs in retailing and clerical work which did not pay enough to attract men.

Underlying the sex-segregation of jobs, then, are the material difficulties women face in striking a wage bargain with their employers. These difficulties are fundamentally related in turn to the sexual division of labour within the family, itself conditioned by women's role in biological reproduction. The place of ideology in this determination is secondary. Barrett contends that the ideological origins of sex-segregation are evidenced in the fact that women's jobs replicate their domestic pursuits. This, however, puts the cart before the horse. Historically, the sex-typing of jobs has been fairly flexible.

. . .

In all the instances of feminization, the availability of women as cheap workers and men's inability or disinclination to defend their jobs were key elements. For example, in the United States in 1840, 60 per cent of schoolteachers were men, but by 1860 only 14 per cent were men.[28] The redefinition of the schoolteacher as a substitute mother for young children paralleled the increasing emphasis on the mother's moral training in child development. But the major motivation for the feminization of teaching was economic...

Many jobs that are 'women's work', such as charring and dressmaking, were taken up because they could more easily be combined with family responsibilities than factory work. They remained female not because of their connection to domesticity, but because they were also among the lowest-paid jobs...Once a female job begins to pay relatively high wages, it also begins to attract male labour – for example, work in nursing or libraries.

In sum, whereas Barrett argues that a pre-capitalist ideology of female dependence played a major role in determining the household-family system, we suggest that biological facts of reproduction conditioned the sexual division of labour. Because factory production in particular, and capitalist production in general, could not accommodate childbearing and early nurturing, married women were forced to seek more marginal, lower-paying kinds of work. Already in the 1830s and 1840s – the crucial period when, according to Barrett, class struggle shaped the sexual division of labour – few married women were working in anything other than the most marginal forms of waged work.

The formation of the family-household system must be viewed within this context. Given that a sexual division of labour and wage differentials favouring men already existed, the most logical and indeed only real alternative for resolving the crisis of working-class reproduction was the family-household system. For any meaningful alternative would have demanded the wresting of substantial concessions from the capitalist class, concessions they could not afford to make. In any case, the working class was in no position to win them, given the balance of class forces prevailing during the period.

This resolution was tragic for women because it made possible the continuation of female dependence and subordination. Insofar as it amplified the tendency for women to be placed in a precarious position in the labour market, it increased the power imbalance between men and women, allowing men to exert control over women's sexuality, to shift a major portion of the burden of domestic labour onto women, and to make unreciprocated emotional demands.

THE FAMILY HOUSEHOLD SYSTEM IN THE TWENTIETH CENTURY

While the nineteenth century saw the emergence and consolidation of the family/household system, the twentieth century, especially since World War II, has witnessed a very different trend – the disappearance of the full-time housewife. This is a consequence of one side of capitalist development. The drive to accumulate pulls married women into wage labour by increasing the demand for women workers, as production expands faster than the labour supply (in, for example, clerical work after World War II), and by increasing the supply of women able to work. Increased productivity of capital allowed for higher working-class incomes without jeopardizing accumulation. Through struggle over the social and the private wage, the working class captured some of the benefits of their higher productivity. In turn, social security, pensions, improved health, etc. all encouraged lower marital fertility, both by decreasing infant mortality and by increasing old-age security, thereby decreasing the parents' need for their children's labour.

Correlatively, in the search for new markets, capital commodified reproduction and expanded the array of goods and services available and necessary for an acceptable standard of living. By cheapening commodities used in domestic production and lowering fertility, capitalist development has reduced the domestic labour time necessary for reproduction, allowing women to work at two jobs...On the other hand, the incorporation of women into wage labour on an equal basis with men has been limited by their continued responsibility for childrearing...The number of years in which women work full-time is still conditioned by the number of children they have...So long as women earn less than their husbands, they will be less able to force men to take equal responsibility for family care, reinforcing their inequality in the labour market.

In the nineteenth century, the assignment of women to domestic labour was biologically determined. But how can we account for it today, when women have few children and there are alternatives to maternal child care?

While the capitalist development of the forces of production tends to undermine the family-household system by pulling women into wage labour, capitalist class relations set up a counter-tendency reinforcing the sexual division of labour...Because individual families have to take responsibility for their dependent members, and because for most families even two incomes are not sufficient to purchase adequate substitutes on the market, a substantial amount of work remains to be done within the household. In this context, the traditional sexual division of labour retains its force. This is partly an effect of gender ideology...But in addition to this cultural and psychological inheritance, present economic realities force women into the mother role. Women earn less than men...If one person has to stay home or organize their work around children's needs, it is in the interest of both wife and husband that she, not he, subordinates wage work to home responsibilities...

Ultimately, then, the 'sex-blind' operations of the relations of capitalist production create the framework within which the working class organizes its reproduction. The decisions to have children at all, how many children to have, how to care for them, how to define their needs, are neither purely economic nor purely instrumental. On the other hand, they are not exclusively cultural or ideological. In constructing a life, in developing a strategy for survival, working-class people make choices, both individually and collectively, which have to take into account the material constraints shaped by capitalist class power.

The sexual division of labour still has a logic. But the complex of forces pressing women into their domestic role is far more contingent today than in the nineteenth century. A minority of women have already been able to break out of the vicious cycle in which home responsibilities reinforce low wages and vice versa... These women have resolved the problem on an individual basis–but the majority of women cannot. For them, a breakthrough depends on collective struggle – the self-organization of women within the working-class movement to change the conditions of daily life so that they can take men on inside the family...

The gains necessary may be difficult to win in a recession. Recessions do draw more women into work, increasing their potential for self-organization. But recessions also intensify the material pressures that reinforce the sexual division of labour. Women pay high penalties when they work, simply in order to maintain the family's previous standard of living. Their income is required to buy the same wage goods as before, so they can't afford market services to substitute for their own domestic labour.

...

WOMEN AND THE WELFARE STATE

Barrett argues that the capitalist state 'props up' the family-household system through its welfare provision, protective legislation, and other avenues of state regulation. Left to itself, the private economy tends to deprive the working class – or at least broad sections of it – of the means to establish the male breadwinner/female housewife family. By providing a material base for the working class to adopt the middle-class form of the family, the welfare state allowed the bourgeoisie to 'hegemonize the working-class family under its own rubric' and helped 'forge a major link in the chain of women's dependence'.[29] State welfare policies assume a male breadwinner and male responsibility for wife and child, thereby encouraging women to rely on men economically and reinforcing the bourgeois ideal of the family within the working class, Barrett contends.

...

We find this approach to the welfare state, the dominant one in the Marxist-feminist literature, entirely unconvincing. In the first place, the legislation and programmes which Barrett and others[30] see as the basis for the 'male breadwinner' family form did not develop until after World War II. Yet large sections of the working class had organized households around a dependent housewife long before this. In only the most abjectly poor and insecure working-class families did wives go out to full-time wage work.

Secondly, Barrett lays far too much stress on state policies which reinforce women's dependence on men and ignores the contradictory trend within the welfare state toward social responsibility for children and other dependants, freeing women who would otherwise shoulder the burden. Barrett is right that income maintenance programmes are regarded as temporary substitutes for, or supplements to, the husband's wage. It *is* assumed that the mother will stay at home to take care of the children, and that intact families rely primarily on the man's wage. On the other hand, during its rapid expansion in the fifties and sixties, the welfare state developed services to care for dependent adults and, to a lesser extent, children *outside* the family – mental hospitals, convalescent hospitals and hospitals for the physically disabled, pensions and retirement homes as well as hospitals for the elderly, pre-school and after-school programmes such as Latch-Key and Headstart in the USA.

If we compare welfare legislation before and after World War II, we see not a firmer location of responsibility for dependants within the family, but a halting, grudgingly-given movement toward the narrowing of familial responsibility. Most important, we see in the post-war years the extension of state support to husbandless mothers – a benefit which is justified on the grounds of women's special responsibility for children, but one which in fact makes women far less dependent on men than they have previously been...

Finally, Barrett's approach to the relationship between the welfare state and the family gives too much weight to functionalist and conspiratorial views. It contradicts her own conclusion that the state is a 'site of struggle'.[31] Neither Barrett nor the major sources on which she bases her claim that the bourgeoisie had a pressing political interest in remarking the working-class family in its own image[32] demonstrate that welfare reforms which helped the working class to maintain its families originated with, or found widespread political support within, capitalist circles.

...

The welfare state is a major arena of class struggle, within limits imposed by capitalist relations of production. Those limits can accommodate substantial reforms. However, these reforms have not been handed down from above as part of a strategy to impose the bourgeois family form on the working class. Welfare state policies have been achieved as political concessions to working-class movements and middle-class reformers. On the other hand, to regard the welfare state as a direct expression of working-class needs would be to ignore the constraints within which reform movements have operated...

As political outcomes, state policies have necessarily reflected the balance of power, not only between classes, but between men and women in the working class. Insofar as state policies aim to shore up rather than substitute for the family/household system, this is, in part, because men have been better organized within the working-class movement. Men's point of view, men's needs, and men's assessment of priority demands have dominated the struggle: for example, state-supported quality childcare at the bottom of the agenda, high wages for men at the top. But more fundamentally, we would argue, the capitalist class has consistently resisted expanding state responsibility for children and other dependent persons. While recognizing the need to provide for the poor in order to retain legitimacy and to control the lower orders, the ruling class is also quite concerned to maintain work incentives. State subsidy above a bare minimum threatens to draw the sting of unemployment and undermine labour discipline. Protection of capitalist accumulation demands, therefore, a welfare policy that is cheap (does not cut into profits) and minimal (does not undercut the necessity to labour).[33]

...

In the face of this array of forces, we can understand how the demand for the family wage and for a welfare policy supplementing rather than replacing the family as the primary site for the care of dependants might have arisen within the working class. State services have always been seriously underfunded and understaffed, therefore of poor quality, bureaucratic and inaccessible to their clients. As a result, working-class people have had a fundamentally ambivalent attitude toward state substitutes for home care. Moreover, because a thoroughly socialized system of care is enormously expensive and apparently out of reach, a welfare programme which substitutes for the family only temporarily appears to be a more realistic and pragmatic goal...and one that can win support from middle-class allies.

We do not wish to deny that broader ideological assumptions affected the direction of reform demands. The bourgeois ideal of individual self-reliance and the patriarchal ideal of the male breadwinner surely informed many working people's vision of the good life. Nonetheless, we would also contend that the strength of these ideals can only be accounted for in the context of the social and political forces that marginalized alternative visions – most particularly the circumstances in which very militant and generalized working-class struggles were necessary to make even small gains toward state support for the reproduction of the working class.

...

THE ROLE OF GENDER IDEOLOGY

The crux of Barrett's analysis is that the development of women's oppression in capitalism must ultimately be laid at the door of ideology. The ideology of gender, quite simply put, shaped capitalist social relations of production...As we suggested earlier, gender ideology is Barrett's *deux ex machina*, her means of escape from the vexing dilemma of the Marxist-reductionist/dual systems-idealist impasse of socialist-feminist thought ...She suggests that gender identity is created 'in an ideology of family life' rather than within actual concrete families, and is 'continually recreated and endorsed, modified or even altered substantially, through a process of ideological representation.'[34] But how exactly one appropriates gender identity and how it is reinforced or transformed in adult life, remain untheorized.

...

In our view, ideology and consciousness are processes in which individuals actively, creatively engage. The 'imaginary relationship of individuals to their real conditions of existence' is the work of human creativity.[35] Thus we would argue that gender ideology, like all ideology, is rooted in and shaped by women's and men's actual experience and practice in everyday life. We agree with Barrett that the relationship between experience and consciousness, between social relations and ideology, is not an unmediated one. To define the relative autonomy of ideology is precisely to decipher these mediations...

Historically developed social relations construct the possibilities within which women and men imagine and order their existence. For example, the determined nature of the sexual division of labour and the family-household system in the nineteenth and early-twentieth centuries entailed that the ideas of 'male breadwinner' – 'female childrearer/dependant' (the key components in Barrett's 'familial ideology') were not really negotiable. These ideas retained their force precisely because they were underpinned by an inescapable social reality. Because the family-household system imposed itself on individuals with unrelenting logic, women and men had to take these social relationships into account when forming their ideas about themselves and their world. This was true not only for the bourgeoisie but also for the working class.

However, the very intricate, complex web of ideas constituting gender ideology that was in continual process of definition and redefinition during the nineteenth century cannot be explained solely by reference to necessary social relations. This is easily seen in the case of nineteenth-century bourgeois gender ideology. Many excellent works in middle-class women's history have recently been written by feminist historians who argue that the bourgeois ideology of domesticity was not simply imposed upon women but was in good part shaped by women themselves. In this way they created a world view, out of circumstances not of their choosing, that explained their experience and was forged by their needs.[36]

. . .

Domestic ideology, rather than merely reflecting social reality, helped to transform it by widening bourgeois women's spheres of influence and activity. In this sense, the creation of gender ideology is a continual social, political act.[37] However, this formidable creativity always rested upon the bedrock of a seemingly inescapable sexual division of labour. . . Only in the twentieth century did feminists really begin to challenge the sexual division of labour itself – particularly in childrearing and domestic labour. But then again, only in this century has the possibility of transforming the sexual division of labour become real.

CONCLUSION

We have argued that historically developed capitalist class relations of production, in combination with the biological facts of reproduction, set up a powerful dynamic toward the family-household system, assuring women's continued subordination to men and their exaggerated vulnerability to capitalist exploitation. While emphasizing that women's oppression in capitalism emerged from the confrontation between the demands of capitalist accumulation and the structures of human reproduction, our analysis, nevertheless, places the self-organization of women and the development of a working-class women's movement as its centre. For while capitalist development in the twentieth century has laid the basis for alternatives to the family-household system, the implementation of these requires political struggle. Capitalist class relations, especially the drive for profit, will continue to push in the direction of privatizing reproduction and forcing the working-class family to shoulder responsibility for its dependants. It is this tendency, and the inability of the working class thus far to counter it significantly, that underlies the persistence of the sexual division of labour and gender inequality.

Thus, gender divisions are not so much embedded in the capitalist division of labour or relations of production, as produced by a complex balance of forces at a given point in the history of capitalism.

NOTES

1 Michèle Barrett, *Women's Oppression Today*, Verso Editions and NLB, London, 1980.
2 Ibid., pp. 254–5.

3 Ibid., pp. 222–3.
4 Judith A. Baer, *The Chains of Protection*, Westport Conn., 1978; Elizabeth Faulkner Baker, *Protective Legislation*, New York, 1925.
5 B.L. Hutchins and A. Harrison, *A History of Factory Legislation*, London, 1903; J.T. Ward, *The Factory Movement, 1830–1835*, London, 1962.
6 Hutchins and Harrison, p. 110.
7 Cecil Driver, *Tory Radical: the Life of Richard Oastler*, New York, 1946.
8 J.T. Ward argues that the government bill was passed only to prevent a ten hours bill that would have effectively limited adult as well as child labour. J.T. Ward, *The Factory Movement, 1830–1835*, p. 115. Also see Ward's 'The Factory Movement', in *Popular Movements*, ed. J.T. Ward, London 1970, p. 68.
9 Hutchins and Harrison, pp. 60–1.
10 Michèle Barrett and Mary McIntosh, 'The "Family Wage": Some Problems for Socialists and Feminists', *Capital and Class*, no. 11, 1980.
11 Barbara Taylor, *Eve and the New Jerusalem*, London and New York, 1983.
12 Ibid., p. 106.
13 It should be clear that *working class* women's oppression poses the key theoretical problem here; for unlike women's subordination in feudal society or within the bourgeoisie, it cannot be related to male control of property.
14 Barrett, p. 250.
15 Sebastiano Timpanaro, *On Materialism*, London 1975, pp. 29–54; but see also Barrett, p. 74.
16 For a more extended discussion of this point and its relationship to Marx's contention that labour power must be paid the cost of its reproduction, see Johanna Brenner, 'Women's Self-Organization: A Marxist Justification', *Against the Current*, vol. 1, no. 1, Fall 1980, pp. 25–7.
17 See, among others, Alice Kessler-Harris, *Women Have Always Worked*, New York 1981, p. 73; Robert Smuts, *Women and Work in America*, New York 1978, pp. 2–3, 23, 56; Louise A. Tilley and Joan W. Scott, *Women, Work and Family*, New York 1978, pp. 123–9; Carol Gronemann, 'She Earns as a Child, She Pays as a Man', in *Class, Sex and the Woman Worker*, eds Milton Cantor and Bruce Laurie, Westport, Conn., 1977, pp. 89–98; Barbara Mayer Wertheimer, *We Were There*, New York 1977, pp. 209–13; Theresa M. McBridge, 'Women's Work and Industrialization', in *Becoming Visible: Women in European History*, eds Renate Bridenthal and Claudia Koonz, Boston 1977, pp. 258–87; Mary Lynn McDougall, 'Working-Class Women During the Industrial Revolution', in *Becoming Visible*, pp. 267–8; Tamara K. Harevan, *Family Time and Industrial Time: The Relationship between the Family and Work in a New England Industrial Community*, New York 1982, p. 198; Mary P. Ryan, *Womanhood in America: From Colonial Times to the Present*, 2nd edn, New York 1979, p. 125.
18 Virginia Yans-McGalughlan, 'Italian Women and Work', in *Class, Sex and the Woman Worker*, pp. 109–11; Smuts, p. 57.
19 Susan Estabrook Kennedy, *If All We Did Was Weep At Home: A History of White Working-Class Women in America*, Bloomington 1979, p. 52; Kessler-Harris, p. 71; Susan M. Strasser, 'An Enlarged Human Existence? Technology and Household Work in Nineteenth-Century America', in *Women and Household Labour*, ed. Sarah Fenstermaker Berk, London and Beverly Hills, 1980, pp. 44–5.
20 Tilly and Scott, pp. 99–102; Ellen Ross, 'Fierce Questions and Taunts: Married Life in Working-Class London, 1870–1914', *Feminist Studies*, vol. 8, no. 3, Fall 1982, p. 578.

21 D. Levine, *Family Formation in an Age of Nascent Capitalism*, New York 1977. See also Hans Medick, 'The Proto-Industrial Family Economy: the Structural Function of Household and Family during the Transition from Peasant Society to Industrial Capitalism', *Social History*, no. 3 (October 1976), pp. 291–315.
22 Ryan, p. 129; Levine, pp. 68–71; Tilly and Scott, p. 91.
23 Hareven, pp. 189–91; Ryan, pp. 124–6.
24 Ross, p. 576.
25 Barrett, p. 99.
26 Smuts, p. 51.
27 Alice Kessler-Harris, 'Organizing the Unorganizable', in *Class, Sex, and the Woman Worker*, footnote 2, p. 161. For contemporary data see Kate Purcell, 'Militancy and Acquiescence Amongst Women Workers', in *Fit Work for Women*, ed. Sandra Burman, New York, 1979, pp. 112–33, 128–9.
28 Margery Davie, 'Woman's Place is at the Typewriter: The Feminization of the Clerical Labor Force', in *Capitalist Patriarchy and the Case for Socialist Feminism*, ed. Zillah Eisenstein, New York, 1979, p. 251.
29 Barrett, p. 229.
30 Elizabeth Wilson, *Women and the Welfare State*, London 1977; Hilary Land, 'Who Cares for the Family?', *Journal of Social Policy*, vol. 7, no. 3, 1978; Mary McIntosh, 'The Welfare State and the Needs of the Dependent Family', in Sandra Burman, ed., *Fit Work for Women*, New York 1979, for the English case.
31 Barrett, p. 246.
32 Ibid., pp. 222–3.
33 Frances Fox Piven and Richard Cloward, *Regulating the Poor: The Function of Public Welfare*, New York 1971, chs 1 and 4.
34 Barrett, p. 206.
35 The quote is, of course, Althusser's in 'Ideology and Ideological State Apparatuses' in *Lenin and Philosophy*, New York 1971, p. 162.
36 Nancy Cott, 'Passionlessness: An Interpretation of Victorian Sexual Ideology', *Signs*, 4, 1979, pp. 210–36. Also see *The Bonds of Womanhood*, New Haven, 1977; Linda Gordon, 'Voluntary Motherhood: The Beginnings of Feminist Birth Control Ideology in the US', in *Clio's Consciousness Raised*, eds Mary Hartman and Lois Banner, New York 1974 and *Woman's Body, Woman's Rights*, New York, 1976; Mary P. Ryan, *Cradle of the Middle Class*, Cambridge 1981; and Kathryn Kish Sklar's masterful *Catherine Beecher: A Study in American Domesticity*, New York, 1976.
37 It is beyond the scope of the present article to assess the potential contribution that can be made to understanding gendered subjectivity by psychoanalysis but we believe this to be underestimated by Barrett.

10

Christina Loughran

Armagh and Feminist Strategy

INTRODUCTION

Northern Ireland (NI) provides an interesting example of the conflict which can arise when two national feminisms meet. NI, caught between the more socialist British feminism and Irish concern for the 'national question', forced those who called themselves feminist to take up issues specific to the national question and for it to become the major source of division between NI women. How something becomes a feminist issue is linked to the political, social and economic experiences of those in the area in which the issue is raised. Feminism's call to unite all women revealed contradictions in the position of NI women. They are fundamentally divided in a society which does not give priority to social, let alone women's issues. Religious bigotry and ignorance also undermine attempts by more radical and lesbian feminists to publicly state their case, never mind campaign for change in their situation.

THE BACKGROUND TO THE ARMAGH PROTESTS

Armagh jail is the only women's prison in NI. Built in the late eighteenth century, it has held Republican women prisoners in every campaign against British and Unionist rule since then. Since 1969, the female prison population in the Ordinary Decent Criminal category has remained a constant nine to ten women at any one time. The vast majority of women prisoners have been charged with 'terrorist type' offences and they consider themselves to be political prisoners...Until 1976 all such prisoners had political status ...This meant that they were held with those of their own political persuasion under their own commanding officers, whom the prison authorities recognized. They wore no prison uniform and did no prison work, tasks being allotted by their own command structure.

Armagh jail had up to 120 Republican women by 1975; over sixty internees, the rest sentenced prisoners...The last internee left Armagh in mid 1975, leaving behind between sixty and seventy sentenced prisoners. In 1976 the British government...introduced the criminalization policy; all prisoners who were sentenced after 1 March 1976 were denied political status and held in separate wings from their comrades who already had it...For the women, as with the men, the loss of status also meant reduced exercise, limited food parcels and little time for handicrafts. Political papers and film shows were stopped.

...

Withdrawal of political status and the imposition of prison uniform for all incoming male prisoners sparked off the 'blanket protest'. This culminated in the hunger strike of 1980 in which three women also took part, and the 1981 hunger strike which ended in the deaths of ten H Block men. The corresponding protest in Armagh was usually in the background because the women could wear their own clothes and they were so few in number; however, the women did go on a 'no work' protest. By Easter 1978 the Governor wished to break their protest. He imposed a twenty-one-hour lock-up, reduced visits to one per month and the women lost all privileges and remission. In May 1978 male warders were used to baton charge remand prisoners on protest. But it was on 7 February 1980 that the women's protest escalated into a 'no wash' protest, similar to the dirt strike in the H Blocks. While queuing for an unusually appetizing meal, the women prisoners were attacked by warders, who also searched and stripped their cells. This was on the pretext of looking for black skirts and berets, part of a Cumman na mBann (women's branch of the IRA) uniform which would have been used on Easter parade in the prison in defiance of the authorities and as a most potent symbol of their political status. As a punishment the warden locked the women out of toilet and washing facilities and they were refused exercise. The Armagh women were therefore forced on to the dirt strike, which they used to highlight the deteriorating conditions inside the prison. Altogether this no wash protest conducted by some thirty women continued for thirteen months...

Since February 1982 the women have ended all protests and have conformed to the system. However in November 1982 the use of strip searches of women prisoners leaving the prison had increased to become yet another method of harassment. The Stop The Strip Searches Committee exclusively highlights the plight of these prisoners, usually on remand, forced to endure many strip searches. To date more than 2,000 strip searches have been carried out; one woman held on supergrass evidence was strip searched 240 times! The NI Office (1985) states that this is for security purposes, yet the men have not been searched as often and nothing has yet been found on the women to constitute a risk to security. The protests on this issue continue (Sinn Fein, 1985), but less than ten women prisoners remain.

THE HISTORICAL BACKGROUND TO THE WOMEN'S MOVEMENT IN NORTHERN IRELAND

To understand why Armagh became a feminist issue it is necessary to look at the historical background to the development of the women's movement in NI. The partition of Ireland in 1921 represented the institutionalization of historical sectarian class alliances produced by the British presence. Two very conservative church-dominated regimes came to power with the two new states, the Labour movement was split up and the Republican opposition to both states was nearly destroyed by them. Since then, all political life in NI has centred around the question of the legitimacy of the state, rather than primarily around the often appalling social and economic conditions...

From its inception, the six-county state, backed up by the British government, contained a largely protestant-dominated police force and court system; their use of the Civil Authorities (Special Powers) Act (renewed every year until made permanent in 1933) to ban meetings and publications and to arrest a suspect without warrant and trial, has made the six-county 'Ulster' very different from the rest of the UK...

In the 1960s proposed changes in divorce legislation were thrown out, and more liberal laws legalizing homosexuality and abortion in Britain in 1967 were never tabled for discussion before the fall of Stormont in 1972. So forceful was Paisley's 'Save Ulster from Sodomy' Campaign in the late 1970s that individual members of the NI Gay Rights Association had to go to Europe to obtain a ruling allowing homosexual acts between consenting adults over twenty-one in private to be made legal in 1982. Abortion to this day is a criminal act under threat of life imprisonment in NI.

While other countries developed a 'new left' and the 'women's movement', in NI the war was escalating: British troops were on the streets, emergency legislation was renewed and internment without trial again became a reality for catholic men and women. Women took up their traditional political roles inside the Nationalist and Unionist parties, or organized anti-internment street committees to set up prisoners' aid or call demonstrations in Republican areas. The women who later formed the feminist groups were involved in the Civil Rights Movement in either NICRA or People's Democracy.

HOW ARMAGH BECAME A FEMINIST ISSUE

Nell McCafferty writing in the *Irish Times* (1980) argued that the 'menstrual blood on the walls of Armagh prison smells to high heaven. Shall we (feminists) turn our noses up?' She graphically described the dirt strike and how it affected the health of prisoners who, after 200 days without toilet or washing facilities, were lying 'amid their own excreta and blood'...

In replies to Nell McCafferty in the next days, some feminists argued that the Republican Movement was 'male dominated' with a 'male-defined ideology' and that feminists should rather be concerned with the victims of violence: the Armagh women therefore could not be supported. The 'no wash' protesters replied, stating that not taking up the issue was blinding feminists to the true issue as they saw only their Republican politics:

> It is our belief that not only is our plight a feminist issue, but a very fundamental social and human issue. It is a feminist issue in so far as we are women, even though we are treated like criminals. It is a feminist issue when the network of this jail is completely geared to male domination. The Governor, the Assistant Governor and the doctor are all males. We are subject to physical and mental abuse from male screws who patrol our wing daily, continually peeping into our cells. . . If this is not a feminist issue then we feel that the word feminist needs to be redefined to suit these people who feel that 'feminist' applies to a certain section of women rather than encompassing women everywhere regardless of politically held views. (No Wash Protestors, 1980)

Women Against Imperialism (WAI), a small group of Republican and anti-imperialist left-wing women based in Belfast and Derry, organized the first pickets on Armagh attended by feminists. They highlighted the conditions and humiliations which the women suffered and gained support in Ireland, Britain and abroad. Sexual abuse, both in interrogation and while the women were held in the prison, was emphasized. They stressed the denial of medical care and sanitary protection, the petty controls and beatings by male warders . . .

WAI had found and exploited the link between the British presence and the oppression of Nationalist women. Republican and catholic women had long suffered this abuse, which to WAI was linked to their belief that women's liberation was only possible after British withdrawal . . . WAI's strategy was to campaign and work within the largely catholic areas of West Belfast and Derry to raise feminist issues in the anti-imperialist struggle, such as women's role in political organization, violence against women by men and the state, childcare, health and contraception . . .

They held a picket on Armagh on International Women's Day 1979, when eleven women, eight of whom were in WAI, were arrested. When their court cases were adjourned in October, WAI used their British and Irish contacts to bring seventy women to a picket in January 1980, following their court case. Their case was adjourned four times in all, and eventually two women went to jail for three months and two months respectively for non-payment of £10 fines. Almost 500 women attended the 8 March picket in 1980 in their support. Since then there has always been a local and foreign feminist presence outside Armagh on International Women's Day.

WAI nevertheless encountered much antagonism from Irish feminists, leading one woman to state that:

> I don't want to be called a feminist – not yet – it's remote somehow. Not earthy enough for what I'm struggling with. I want liberation from all oppression. I want the people to be free. I'm against imperialism. Feminists won't deal with that from what I can see. (McCafferty, 1981:66)

WAI were accused of neglecting the 'real' feminist issues in Ireland, such as battered women, one-parent families, divorce, contraception and abortion (D'Arcy, 1981:120). In reply, WAI stated:

> We feel this shows a lack of understanding of the situation in the six counties and the fact that the war situation cannot be ignored. Without relating to the problems that have arisen from British occupation, the women's movement will not be able to reach working-class women on other feminist issues and as such it is of central importance to the women's movement. (WAI, 1979)

After WAI fought successfully to get Armagh recognized as of similar importance as the H Blocks to the political status campaign, they fell apart... WAI argued at the time that they split owing to the 'small size of the group, the weight of the opposition, the pressures of everyday life in West Belfast and the urgent need to get rid of the Brits' (WAI, 1980b).

...

THE IMPACT OF ARMAGH ON THE REPUBLICAN MOVEMENT

For some WAI members and those on the H Block/Armagh Committee, joining Sinn Fein represented their acknowledgement that the time was not right for an autonomous feminist group in Republican areas. The strategy of raising Armagh, and feminist, consciousness on women's issues was to pay off in formal policy changes inside SF and in SF's recognition of women in a political way. Gerry Adams, president of SF, has stated:

> We have a department of women's affairs going for about two and a half years. It would see its role as politicizing women republicans to fight for their rights as women and politicizing male republicans to support equality for women. It is not a feminist department though there are strong feminists in it. They are involved in working as republicans in women's centres, rape crisis centres and so on, North and South. To be frank, it is only in the last few years that we have begun to treat women's affairs in a political way and we do stand open to criticism on that issue. (Adams, 1983:14–15)

This statement is very different from anything that Republicans might have made only ten years earlier. I intend to show that the struggles around Armagh were pivotal in bringing about this change in SF's attitudes and policies on women.

...

The period between 1974 and the emergence of WAI as a voice in Republican areas in April 1978 was one of great change inside the Republican Movement as a whole. Claire Hackett has argued that the movement to the left inside SF was crucial to the women finding a voice (1985:20). Danny Morrison, a leading member of SF,... admits that 'women started coming out of their shells, putting men under pressure and forcing them to think politically about the problems of women' (Collins, 1985:84). Women first politicized through the prison struggles, and especially around Armagh, played an important role in developing the work of advice centres and grassroots constituency work. But the adoption of new policies for women was not an easy process.

As attacks inside Armagh jail increased, a letter appeared in *Republican News* arguing that women could not wait; they had to have a worked-out party policy.

> The existing women's movements in this country offer no solution. They are dominated by the middle-class and intellectuals and are too often British orientated, so there is then little the working-class republican can relate to...there is a need for a true movement that will not reflect this 'crank' image...and the lead must come from the revolutionary party Sinn Fein. (Anon, 1978)

The press officer of WAI wrote a reply which challenged the view that the existing women's movement was 'middle-class and pro-British'. She stressed that WAI was an anti-imperialist group which supported the liberation struggle, and they had their base in West Belfast. She continued that the Republican Movement

> see women merely as supportive participants in the struggle for people's liberation...Only through constant pressure exerted by the women themselves on their own behalf, will [they] effect change. An autonomous women's movement is a necessary element in safeguarding the advances made by women in the struggle for total liberation. (WAI, 1978a)

The uneasy relationship between WAI and SF was not helped by SF's ignoring the first picket on Armagh. No coverage was given to the arrest of the Armagh eleven, even though they were protesting against the criminalization policy and for the women on the 'no wash' protest. Throughout the publicity around the court cases, women inside SF began to raise some of the feminist demands which WAI had argued for. Christine Ni Elias argued that...the Republican Movement should recognize and campaign on these issues...(Ni Elias, 1979).

Until the end of 1979 and throughout 1980 debate on these issues was evident. Recognition was given to the Armagh eleven and there was coverage of both the first anti-imperialist women's conference held in Belfast in September 1979, and the demonstrations outside Armagh after that time. At a special meeting of SF women to discuss a policy on women to be put to the next Ard Fheis (Annual Party Conference) fears were expressed that SF policies were being supplanted by WAI's activities (Ward, 1983:256). Discussion centred around violence against women in Castlereagh (the largest police interrogation centre) and Armagh, with the plight of the women prisoners outlined. Lack of childcare facilities was also highlighted, as was sex-role stereotyping in education. They also succeeded in adopting a proposal to set up a department of women's affairs, which a few years later became known as the Women's Department. However, there was a persistent uneasiness about challenging the views of the Catholic Church on moral issues. Some women pointed out that they would never use contraceptives on religious grounds but would still like to see them legalized in a New Ireland. A pro-contraception policy was, however, passed at the Ard Fheis, even though it was argued that 'divorce, like abortion, would not be necessary if there were good pre-marriage courses and if sex education was given to all children by their parents backed up by the schools' (Anon, 1979). Clearly the Women's Department had a lot of work ahead of it.

Feminists have been most concerned about SF policy on abortion.

> There is a need to face up to the problem of abortion no matter what individual opinions are. We do not judge women who have abortions but recognise that it is an indictment of society that so many women should feel the need to avail themselves of abortion. We are opposed to the attitudes and forces in society which impel women to have abortions, we are totally opposed to abortion. (Sinn Fein, 1981:5)

At the 1984 Ard Fheis the issue of abortion again came up. This time a motion condemning abortion as a means of birth control was passed. However, there was obvious confusion at the debate...During the 1983 amendment campaign on abortion, SF sat on the fence and made no statements against the 'right to life of the foetus' amendment. But change came at the 1985 Ard Fheis when a pro right-to-choose policy was passed by four votes. The resolution could easily be repealed in 1986, but it is significant that feminists in NI outside of Republican areas have failed to comment on this obvious progress. (It has since been dropped completely – Ed.)

The Women's Department has set up a women's centre on the Falls Road in the heart of West Belfast. It opened in 1982 and attempts to connect SF women to other women in the community, prioritizing such issues as prisoners' relatives, childcare, creche facilities and violence against women. Rita O'Hare stresses that the 'women working in the centre are every day making contact with ordinary women who do not see the women's movement as representing them or recognizing the things that oppress their lives because the women's movement everywhere was started by middle-class women'. She feels that it is important not only to raise demands in the party 'but [to make] women's politics and the women's movement relevant to working-class women' (Collins, 1985:116–17).

It is in this grassroots area that the strategy of working within a broader movement for change has netted gains. In contrast to the complete absence of policies from the SDLP and the Unionist parties on women, except that they are anti-abortion, progress has been made on women's issues ideologically and practically within the Republican Movement. However, where this strategy is weakest is in the eternal contradiction facing all those who put women first. For non-Republican feminists it is impossible to support SF, either because there is no security in waiting for a promised New Ireland in which a male-defined organization might give reforms to women or because this strategy totally ignores and excludes protestant women. It is to the strategies pursued by these feminists that I now turn.

THE CASE AGAINST ARMAGH AS A FEMINIST ISSUE

Two broad groups of feminists have taken the view that Armagh is not a feminist issue. The larger, more organized group centres its activities on the Northern Ireland Women's Rights Movement's (NIWRM) women's centre in Donegall Street in Belfast's city centre. (This was opened in March 1980 with Belfast City Council funding.) The strategy pursued by the NIWRM is more closely linked to the policies of the Communist Party of Ireland (CPI) and the CPI dominated Northern Ireland Civil Rights Association (NICRA), and argues that the demands won by the British women's movement could be obtained by demanding parity of rights with the UK. Just as the CPI has called for working-class unity across the sectarian divide before national unity, the NIWRM believes that women have a vital part to play in developing such a unity. In practice this group is totally opposed to republicanism and blames the Republican Movement for causing sectarian division. They also refer to the lack of reform to help women in the South as their reason for supporting the link with Britain (NIWRM, 1980).

Direct rule in 1972 gave left-wing groups a hope that the British government could be appealed to for reform over the heads of the reactionary Nationalist and Unionist parties, who had made up the old Stormont regime. (Republicans always boycotted elections to Stormont or refused to take their seats.) In 1975, International Women's Year, the CPI journal *Unity* and the PD paper *Unfree Citizen* gave news coverage to women's issues in the North and the British government's planned extension of the Equal Pay Act. A conference was called in May to set up a campaigning group to demand the extension of the Sex Discrimination Act as well. After this conference the NIWRM emerged as an umbrella group, with some fifty male and female members on paper and a core of about a dozen women. They adopted a women's charter in 1976 calling for equal opportunities in education, training and work; equal pay for work of equal value; equality of legal and financial and social rights; the right to maternity leave and childcare facilities; parity of rights for women in NI with women in England, including abortion; improved free and comprehensive family-planning services for all, including sex education; and recognition of working and non-working mothers by increasing child benefit. These loosely parallel the social democratic demands of the British women's movement. As in Britain, the NIWRM has since also recognized the problem of all forms of violence against women (Charter of the NIWRM).

Disputes over whether men could be members of the organization, the National Question and whether to seek the active support of trade unions and make abortion a sole campaigning issue led to the Socialist Women's Group (SWG) forming a separate group. The NIWRM viewed their departure as a positive step, allowing more scope for local-based groups to develop.

. . .

The Women's Law and Research Group was supported by the NIWRM in its call for reform of nursery provision, divorce law and the extension of Domestic Proceedings Orders to NI, gained in 1980. The Matrimonial Causes Order was extended in 1978, giving more scope for divorce and abolishing the concept of a guilty party, but divorce provision still lags behind the UK...

More recently, they published a report on the situation of young hairdressers, and to mark their tenth anniversary in 1985 they have published a book containing stories by women writers in NI. Since 1978 the NIWRM has represented the Women's International Democratic Federation (WIDF) in Ireland. This Soviet-influenced body of women's groups, with many Third World members, influenced NIWRM's support for nuclear disarmament and Greenham Common. They also work with the Women's Peace and Detente Group.

The Women's Committee of the Irish Congress of Trade Unions (ICTU) contains members of the NIWRM and has proved successful in getting the public service unions to push women forward. On their own initiative members of the National Union of Public Employees (NUPE) have started a women's health project, looking at their own histories.

Given this background to the NIWRM, their opposition to republicanism and their support for a strategy of uniting women across the sectarian divide, they opposed the Armagh campaigns and refused to recognize that they were the concern of feminists...Those in the CPI supported the call for political status while rejecting the tactics and strategy of the campaign and the hunger strikes; those in the Workers' Party (WP) rejected both the aims and the tactics of the political status campaign. The NIWRM avoided a split as it had always avoided the National Question, but many of its members argued elsewhere that the Armagh women 'were aping the tactics of their male counterparts in Long Kesh'. Because Republican women refused to associate with other prisoners it was further argued 'so much for...pioneering prison reform. Armagh like the Kesh is all about status, elitism and privilege' (McMahon, 1980:9).

This argument came up again and again at Irish feminist conferences all over Ireland. Because the Armagh women were Republicans and incarcerated for 'terrorist' offences, the NIWRM were able to argue that Armagh was not a feminist issue but a sectarian one, dividing catholic from protestant women. This is still their view today.

The SWG, on the other hand, wanted to pursue an anti-imperialist strategy as an autonomous feminist group. They recognized that reforms such as equal pay and contraception (made freely available under the NHS in NI in 1974) had come indirectly to NI as part of the gains made by women in Britain. However the SWG argued that they could not simply set their sights on achieving parity of rights with Britain. They published a manifesto in which they argued that while being opposed to the military campaign of the IRA, they believed 'that the effective liberation of the working class – women and men – requires the creation not of a united capitalist Ireland but of an Irish Workers State. We see the struggle for woman's liberation as an integral part of the struggle for socialism and we stress the importance of women organizing to fight for their rights' (SWG, 1976).

. . .

The SWG relationship to the RAC (Relatives Action Committee) women was to prove decisive in their splitting with the NIWRM; after their public dispute over the Peace People (who supported peace at any price – in effect, the security forces), the SWG declared that the NIWRM 'sees women's freedoms mainly in terms of legal reforms and nothing else; while we believe these to be important, we do not see them as an end in themselves' (SWG, 1977). But the SWG's use of pursuing reforms as a tactic to build up feminist support led them into dispute with the RAC women who felt that the SWG were rather 'elitist' in their approach to issues facing working-class women in Republican areas.

A debate started with the RAC women. The SWG criticized their own manifesto which the RAC women felt was a barrier. But the SWG women felt that the RAC women were reluctant to enter into discussions with them as the RAC women had only 'a basic knowledge of women's oppression' and had not yet been through a period of theoretical discussion (SWG minutes, April 1977). The SWG decided to dissolve and set up another group called the Belfast Women's Collective (BWC), in the hope that they could keep their contacts in Republican areas. It was the campaign around Armagh which proved that they could no longer hope to organize in those areas. A discussion group on feminist issues was started by the BWC and for the first time a radical voice emerged, arguing for issues such as rape and sexuality to be highlighted in their paper *Women's Action* (Interview, 7 February 1985). WAI criticized the BWC for not giving the work of the political status campaign enough emphasis: 'In our view working with anti-imperialist women in the RAC is not just another campaign. Imperialism is the major dominating force in the lives of women throughout Ireland' (WAI, 1978b). . .

In *Scarlet Woman* the BWC gave an explanation of their position:

> Because we regarded ourselves in opposition to the British we were labelled as republican by those women's groups who didn't actively oppose it [the NIWRM], at the same time because we were highly critical of the Republican Movement we were labelled as a bourgeois women's group by that section of the movement [WAI], we couldn't win either way. (BWC, 1980)

They felt that divergences of opinion on other areas of feminist activity were not being voiced, and in the end they could not support Armagh as a feminist issue because it was being translated as support for republicanism and the 'armed struggle' of the IRA. . .

Before dissolving, the collective initiated many new single-issue campaigns, based on their belief that it was now the only way forward for an autonomous women's movement. They debated lesbianism, held the first Reclaim the Night March in early 1979 and organized the first health conference provoking needed discussion on childbirth, sex education, contraception and abortion. By June 1980 an abortion campaign with the minimum demand for the extension of the 1967 Abortion Act to NI was set up. Members of the NIWRM also got involved with these.

Armagh convinced those feminists who were not working-class Republicans that ignoring the National Question and achieving some measure of women's unity was a more realistic strategy. The idea was tested in 'unity' meetings to see what issues could be agreed on, such as action on debt, rape and the cuts in social services. These meetings were attended by all feminists for a while, but disagreement over the National Question crept back into the discussions. Those most closely identified with the Armagh campaign stopped coming.

CONCLUSION

The campaigns around the Republican women prisoners in Armagh have revealed the contradictory situation facing NI feminists. Armagh highlighted the already existing strategies of avoiding the National Question and supporting the British link in the hope of attracting both catholic and protestant and, if possible, working-class women, or alternatively pursuing a strategy within the Republican Movement in the hope that if they come to power they will implement policies favourable to women.

Republicans have adopted a more sophisticated strategy of raising electoral support while still supporting the 'armed struggle' of the IRA. The idea that campaigning for reforms can raise consciousness on issues such as poverty, cuts in benefits and housing, which are of central importance to working-class life, is gaining credence, although there is still a tension in the movement. Within this strategy women have become more important, especially as it is the women who usually confront the welfare state in their daily lives. But the Women's Department still has difficulty raising those feminist issues most central to women's relationship to men, such as reproductive rights and violence against women by men. However, they have made progress on these issues in ideological terms, and through their practical work in their women's centre they are still building up their local base. Despite these obvious gains the SF women have not received any more support from other feminists in NI.

Through the Armagh campaigns, the BWC and the various non-aligned radical women realized that to gain reform now and raise consciousness on women's issues it was necessary to develop single-issue campaigns, which have brought some legislative change, though noticeably not on abortion. This strategy has also meant that they have constantly had to look to the gains of the British women's movement in order to see what could be argued for in NI. This has meant that the strains of the cuts and the recession already hard felt in NI and the rest of Britain make it doubly hard for feminist campaigns to achieve results.

The NIWRM strategy of uniting women across the sectarian divide has not been that successful. While catholic and protestant women do meet occasionally on issues such as housing, education, poverty, health and violence against women, they cannot realistically bridge the different ways in which Catholic and Protestant, middle-class and working-class women may experience deprivation, discrimination and the effects of religious ideology. They go home to largely separate lives. The women's movement is still marginal and small, concentrated in the main urban centres of Belfast and Derry. Moreover, the strong church organizations on either side still oppose women's rights. No issue is neutral in a sectarian state: Britain cannot be seen as neutral by catholic and especially by politicized Republican women. It is simply impossible to ask Republican women to support the extension of a British Act (no matter how progressive) to NI, as they do not recognize the legitimacy of that state to legislate for them.

However, working within the system to gain what they can for women has recently led to gains within Unionist areas in the form of two new women's centres funded by local councils. But Unionist women on the whole lack the political experience of Republican women, and as yet no policy changes have been made among the loyalist parties, who are essentially reactionary and would settle for a return to Stormont which offered women nothing.

Feminists are caught in division. They organize on opposite sides of the sectarian divide with mutually exclusive strategies. They hold separate International Women's Day events; one side picketing Armagh, the other holding a rally in the city centre of Belfast on the issue of cuts, health care or nursery provision; they go to separate socials and use separate women's centres. Nell McCafferty's observation that it is easier to 'feminize' Republicans than to republicanize feminists still holds true (1981:90).

Armagh has raised vital questions for feminists everywhere on the need to re-order priorities. Women can make gains while working in a broader movement for social change, yet do we lose our autonomy in doing so? Is this gamble worth the risk if even a few working-class women begin to realize that feminism exists? Do contradictory situations like NI leave feminists with no choice but to develop separate strategies, and if so does this not show the weaknesses of feminism? I will leave you to contemplate these points.

GROUPS REFERRED TO IN THE TEXT

BWC	Belfast Women's Collective, which emerged from the SWG in September 1977 and dissolved in June 1980.
CPI	Communist Party of Ireland.
IRA	Irish Republican Army.
IRSP	Irish Republican Socialist Party, formed after a split with Official Sinn Fein in 1975.
NICRA	Northern Ireland Civil Rights Association, originally a branch of the Civil Rights Movement, now dominated by the CPI.

NIWRM	Northern Ireland Women's Rights Movement, set up in May 1975.
PD	People's Democracy, originally the student wing of the Civil Rights Movement, now a Trotskyist group allied to the Fourth International.
RAC	Relatives Action Committee, a group set up in 1976 by mostly women relatives to defend the rights of Republican prisoners engaged in the political status campaign. This evolved into the National Smash H Block/Armagh Committee, in 1980.
SDLP	Social Democratic and Labour Party, emerged in 1971 from the old Nationalist Party. They believe in the use of constitutional means to obtain a united Ireland and represent Catholic middle-class and clerical viewpoints. They currently support the Anglo-Irish agreement and are led by John Hume.
SF	Sinn Fein, political wing of the provisional Republican Movement.
SWG	Socialist Women's Group, set up in October 1975, dissolved April 1977.
WAI	Women Against Imperialism, formed April 1978, dissolved early 1981.
WP	Workers' Party, formerly Sinn Fein the Workers' Party, the political wing of the Official Republican Movement.

A NOTE ON SOURCES

1 Interviews with activists, conducted between November 1983 and February 1985
2 Minutes of the NIWRM, the SWG, the BWC, WAI and 'Unity' meetings
3 Papers from the Socialist Feminist Conference, London, October 1980
4 Papers from all Irish feminist conferences 1977–84
5 Papers from Republican Ard Fheiseana (Annual Conferences)
6 **Irish feminist journals**
Saorbhean (Free Woman), journal of WAI
WICCA, Dublin-based *Wise Woman* magazine
Women's Action, journal of the SWG and the BWC
Women's News, an independent feminist magazine based in Belfast
Women's View, paper of the women's section of the WP
7 **Irish left-wing journals**
Unfree Citizen
Socialist Republic, papers of PD
Unity, the paper of the Northern Committee CPI
8 *Magill*, Irish current affairs magazine
9 **Republican publications**
Republican News, the Voice of Republican Ulster to 1979
An Phoblacht/Republican News, from 1979 covering the whole of Ireland *Iris*, the Republican magazine

REFERENCES

Adams, Gerry (1983) in *Magill*, July.
Anon (1973) *Republican News*, 26 January.

Anon (1974a) *Republican News*, 9 February.
Anon (1974b) *Republican News*, 31 August.
Anon (1978) *Republican News*, 24 June.
Anon (1979) *An Phoblacht/Republican News*, 17 November.
Anthias, Floya and Yuval-Davis, Nira (1983) 'Contextualizing Feminism – Gender, Ethnic and Class Divisions' *Feminist Review* no. 15.
Armagh Co-ordinating Group (1981) *Women Behind the Wire* (bulletin) May.
Belfast Brigade of the IRA (1974) statement in *Republican News*, 23 February.
Belfast Women's Liberation Group (1974) *Unfree Citizen*, 18 March.
BWC (1978) *Women's Action*, May–June.
BWC (1980) *Scarlet Women* no. 11, June.
Collins, Martin (1985) ed. *Ireland After Britain* London: Pluto Press with Labour and Ireland.
Collins, Patricia (1984) *Iris*, August.
Coogan, Tim Pat (1980) *On the Blanket: The H Block Story* Dublin: Ward Rivers Press.
D'Arcy, Marguretta (1981) *Tell Them Everything* London: Pluto Press.
Hackett, Claire (1985) *Sinn Fein and Feminism 1979–1984* unpublished MSc thesis, politics Department, Queen's University, Belfast.
London Armagh Group (1984) 'Strip Searches in Armagh Jail' *Women Behind The Wire* no. 2 (bulletin), February.
McCafferty, Nell (1980) *Irish Times*, 22 August.
McCafferty, Nell (1981) *The Armagh Women* Dublin: Co-op Books.
McShane, Elizabeth (1984) *Day Nursery Provision 1942–55: A Case Study of Women and Social Policy in Northern Ireland* unpublished PhD thesis, Faculty of Economics and Social Science, Queen's University, Belfast.
McMahon, Mary (1980) 'Provo Women in Armagh Treat Others As Slaves' *Women's View* no. 4, Winter.
Ni Elias, Christine (1979) *An Phoblacht/Republican News* 1 September.
NIWRM (1980) Unpublished paper.
No Wash Protestors (1980) *Irish Times* August.
Northern Ireland Office (1985) 'Armagh Prison, Strip Searching – The Facts' June.
Sinn Fein (1981) *Women in the New Ireland* (pamphlet, 2nd edn) Belfast.
Sinn Fein (1985) *This Baby is Being Body Searched in Armagh Jail* (pamphlet) Belfast.
SWG (1976) Manifesto, 8 March.
SWG (1977) *Wires* no. 25, 7 January.
Taylor, Peter (1980) *Beating the Terrorists? Interrogations in Omagh, Gough and Castlereagh* Harmondsworth: Penguin.
WAI (1978a) Press officer in *Republican News* 8 July.
WAI (1978b) *Women's Action*, May–June.
WAI (1979) paper at Anti-Imperialist Feminist Conference Belfast, 22–23 September.
WAI (1980a) *Women Campaign for Political Status in Armagh Goal* (pamphlet) Belfast.
WAI (1980b) papers at Socialist-Feminist Conference London, October.
Ward, Margaret (1983) *Unmanageable Revolutionaries: Women in Irish Nationalism* London: Pluto Press.

PART IV

Psychoanalysis and Feminism

Introduction

THEORIZING SUBJECTIVITY

Dual systems theory posited the existence of two parallel, interconnected systems of domination, consisting respectively of the social relations of production, and of sex and gender. Marxism was understood as the privileged theory of the former. The latter, irreducible to the exigencies of production, required its own, object-specific theory.

Feminists influenced by Althusserian Marxism assigned 'patriarchy' or the sex-gender system, to the domain of 'ideological practice'.[1] Althusser's account of the social formation as a complex totality opened up space for a theory of patriarchal ideology which might draw on theoretical resources outside Marxism.

Althusser distinguished between 'particular ideologies' and 'ideology in general'.[2] He drew for his understanding of the former on the work of the Italian Marxist, Antonio Gramsci. The second, 'ideology in general', was a more radical concept which provided the link which connected Marxism with theoretical developments in other fields, notably structural linguistics and psychoanalysis. The fundamental task of ideological practice, over and above the reproduction of particular ideologies, was the 'interpellation' of individual human beings as subjects, within the place assigned them in the social order. It was thus that individuals acquired, and assented to, their social identity. Althusser drew on the work of Jacques Lacan for his theory of ideology in general, using Lacan's account of the process of the infants simultaneous entry into language and social life.[3]

The widespread adoption of the Althusserian theory of ideology among Marxist feminists in the 1970s paved the way for a reassessment of Freud and psychoanalysis via Lacan. Traditionally feminism had maintained considerable hostility towards psychoanalysis. It was identified as a powerful and dangerous enemy to feminist hopes and aspirations in much of the work which inaugurated feminism's second wave in the United States and

Britain, for example Kate Millett's *Sexual Politics*, Germaine Greer's *The Female Eunuch*, and Eva Figes's *Patriarchal Attitudes*.

In 1974, when Juliet Mitchell's *Psychoanalysis and Feminism* appeared, her insistence that psychoanalysis offered what feminism sorely required, a theory of the psychic processes through which an internalized feminine identity was acquired, while going very much against the grain of this early consensus in second wave feminist thought, was yet very much of its time.[4] Mitchell taught English literature at the universities of Leeds and Reading during the 1960s. She had been working on a study of childhood in the English novel and her literary essays, many of which predate the shift into psychoanalysis, strongly presage that move, in their interest in literary psychodynamics and in the ways in which the child, in fiction, is parent to the adult.[5]

Mitchell's turn towards psychoanalysis was doubtly determined. She has part of the New Left movement of the early 1960s, an active member of the editorial board of *New Left Review* from 1963–6. Her name remained on the list of editorial board members until 1983. Her earliest writings on women appeared in the Review. Under the editorship of Perry Anderson, it was, in the 1960s, engaged in the project of introducing continental Marxist theory to a British Left diagnosed as labouring under the burden of an empiricist tradition hostile to theory, a narrow parochialism, and the lack of any strong indigenous Marxism.[6] Among the theoretical writings presented by the Review were key texts by Althusser and Lacan.[7] For a time, Anderson's own work was cast within a broadly Althusserian frame.

The *New Left Review* never wholly committed itself to either Althusserian structuralism or Lacanian psychoanalysis however. It was catholic in its presentations, and in 1975 for instance, printed Sebastiano Timpanaro's attack on Freud[8] which was described in the editorial as 'a highly original ...caustically witty counter-demonstration of the arbitrary character of Freud's own method of interpretation',[9] a description which provoked much protest.[10] And its commitment to feminism has always been strictly circumscribed by the imperatives of a class-based politics and theory.

Mitchell's seminal essay, 'Women: the Longest Revolution', likewise used an Althusserian frame. It was clear that classical Marxism could not supply any equivalent to the sociological concept of 'socialization'. What Mitchell required was a theory which could explain the psychic processes whereby the human infant acquired a sexed social identity. At this point in time she also looked to psychoanalysis for an explanation 'of the ways in which patriarchal society bequeaths its structures to each of us...gives us, that is, the cultural air we breathe.'[11] It was this transient moment in the trajectory of *New Left Review* that was the second factor in Britain which pointed towards the appropriation of psychoanalysis for feminism.

PSYCHOANALYSIS AND FEMINISM: JULIET MITCHELL

Mitchell's achievement in staking a claim for psychoanalysis as of special significance for feminism in the face of feminism's record of hostility was the more remarkable in that she resolutely refused to countenance the work of those analysts who had challenged Freud's work on female sexuality in the debates of the 1920s and 1930s. Melanie Klein and Karen Horney, on the face of it more likely candidates than either Freud or Lacan on which to found a feminist psychoanalysis, were rejected, along with those attempts to reconcile Freud and Marx which had been looked upon with favour by the Review a little earlier – Eric Fromm, Herbert Marcuse, and Wilhelm Reich, as well as the anti-psychiatry of R.D. Laing and David Cooper.[12]

The weight of Mitchell's early interpretation of the significance of psychoanalysis for feminism fell on its ability to register the strength of attachment to gender-identities. More sociologically based theories of role-learning, and popular feminist understandings of femininity as an alien identity imposed on women by men and a male-dominated social order, rang hollow in the face of the depth and strength of psychic investments in gender. Ann Oakley's scrupulous dismantling of biological arguments and evidence which rooted gender divisions in nature were of little avail when the only alternative explanation was some kind of externally imposed social conditioning.[13] Biological explanations, spurious as they are, remain persuasive not so much because of some deeply ingrained habit of interpreting what is constructed in ideology as natural, as out of a widely felt conviction that only something as fundamental as biology is commensurate with the taken-for-granted experience of gender as an essential and not an accidental component of personal identity. The acid test of feminist theories of gender is not their ability to refute biological arguments, but rather the capacity to put something as plausible in their place. What is needed is a theory which acknowledges and accounts for the depth and ubiquity of gender divisions, while yet powerfully revealing them as socially constructed and open to change. The attraction of psychoanalysis was its promise with respect to this important task.

The first article reprinted here is from a later work in which Mitchell reiterates and reformulates the importance of Lacanian psychoanalysis for feminism – her introduction to the volume of essays on female sexuality which she edited with Jacqueline Rose in 1982.[14] The project of presenting Lacan's writings on feminine sexuality was formed in the period following the publication of *Psychoanalysis and Feminism*, at a time when the French institute of psychoanalysis, the Lacanian École Freudienne, was riven by a dispute in which Lacan's theory of feminine sexuality was challenged by feminists such as Luce Irigaray. Irigaray was expelled from the school on the publication of her *Speculum de l'autre femme.*[15] It was a dispute which in some respects replayed the Freud-Jones debate of the 1930s in Britain.[16] What was immediately at stake was Freud's hypothesis of a single, undifferentiated infantile sexuality which only emerged as masculine or feminine on the resolution of the Oedipus complex, under the threat of castration. Irigaray, like Klein and Horney before her, posited a distinct and separate feminine sexuality which, she argued, was already in place in the pre-Oedipal phase. As in object-relations theory, attention was drawn back to the earliest relationship of infant to mother. It was this displacement of father and phallus from centre stage by the mother that gave this version of psychoanalytic theory its attraction for feminism.

Freud's objection to sexual dualism was reiterated by Mitchell. She argued that it undermined the notion, so central to feminism, of masculinity and femininity as *learned* identities. For the source of an infantile sexuality differentiated from birth into masculine and feminine forms, can only be biological. Yet when this objection is made and conceded, a further point remains to be met. It can be no accident, nor yet the result of some stubborn feminist refusal to see the theoretical difficulties which ensue, which has lead twice over to this particular form of feminist 'revisionism' in the short history of psychoanalysis. There remains a felt difficulty in its account of female sexuality which has twice provoked feminist analysts to embark on this particular detour. This difficulty must be addressed, for it is the locus of the continued resistance of feminists to psychoanalysis.

FEMINISM AND THE RESISTANCE TO PSYCHIC IDENTITY

While psychoanalytic theory has had a considerable impact on feminist thought in Britain it is probably true to say that the dominant response within the women's movement has been reserved at best, uncomprehending or hostile at worst. In the second article in this section Elizabeth Wilson expresses some of the reservations which have prevented feminists from embracing psychoanalysis. The very strength of the case which Mitchell made in *Psychoanalysis and Feminism* for the socio-cultural acquisition of a femininity which is 'held in the heart and the head as well as in the home'[17] must give feminists pause. She accuses Mitchell of offering a form of 'psychic essentialism' which is almost as debilitating for feminism as the biological essentialism it displaces. Janet Sayers makes a similar point in a longer work.[18] She indicts all the post-Freudians, including Lacan, the French feminists Irigaray and Montrelay,[19] Mitchell and Rose, exempting only Freud himself, on the grounds of their inability to offer a plausible explanation of women's resistance to femininity, oppression and inferiority. She insists that any feminist appropriation of psychoanalysis must explain feminism as well as femininity – the conscious and purposeful struggle of the women's movement for revolutionary change – without reducing it to a mere stubborn refusal of women to give up their desire to possess the phallus.

It was Rose rather than Mitchell herself who took up the challenge of Wilson's critique in a reply reprinted here, which is valuable for its lucidity, and for the new inflection which was given to feminist interpretations of Freud. On the face of it this would seem to answer both Sayers's and Wilson's objections. She argues that psychoanalysis is wrongly interpreted as a theory of how women are psychically induced into femininity within a patriarchal culture, for indeed, if this were the case, then 'the very effectiveness of the account as a *description*. . .leaves no possibility of change'.[20] She argues that what the unconscious, that key concept of psychoanalysis so often dispensed with in feminist revisionism, reveals is the *failure* of identity. 'Feminism's affinity with psychoanalysis rests above all... with this recognition that there is a resistance to identity at the very heart of psychic life.... Psychoanalysis becomes one of the few places in our culture where it is recognised as more than a fact of individual pathology that most women do not painlessly slip into their roles as women.'[21] Where Nancy Chodorov, drawing on the British object-relations school, argued that it is the male child's task of acquiring a masculine identity which presents the greatest psychic difficulty,[22] for Rose it is on the contrary femininity that is especially problematic. It can *never* be achieved with complete success. Women are necessarily at odds with their own psychically-acquired gender-identities.

But Rose's decentred feminine subject who cannot but have a fraught and deeply ambivalent relationship to her femininity is not on that account the more readily mobilized for feminism, as she herself recognizes. If she dangles before us the inviting prospect of the Proper Lady struggling unsuccessfully to repress the angry discontent that will out come what may, her necessary counterpart is the angry feminist struggling equally unsuccessfully to repress the desire to be the Proper Lady. Which is not to say that both figures may not be salutary for feminism. We need to be able to understand why it is so difficult to sustain a feminist identity in the face of treacherous impulses towards conformity, and equally we need to believe that feminine conformity is never complete. But while ambivalence towards femininity may provide a lever for feminist intervention, it cannot found feminism. Nor can feminism be located in the space of that insatiable and undirected *want* which Mitchell identifies as the defining characteristic of the feminine self without undermining its pretensions. For feminism can no more fill that void than can femininity. The bottom line in feminist resistance to Lacanian psychoanalysis is this: if women's oppression is rooted in the very founding of sexed identity in terms which are inescapable for language-speaking human beings, then feminist demands for the lifting of that oppression are deeply compromised.

PSYCHOANALYSIS: WOMEN LOVING WOMEN

The annexation of Lacanian psychoanalysis for feminism did little to resolve another sensitive problem within the women's movement, the need for a politically acceptable theory of lesbian sexuality. It was object-relations psychoanalysis which appeared to many lesbian feminists more promising in this respect. The writings from America, most notably those of the poet Adrienne Rich,[23] and Nancy Chodorow's *Reproduction of Mothering*, were extremely influential in Britain. In spite of Rich's criticisms of Chodorow for her neglect of lesbianism, feminist object-relations theory lends itself very well to the valorization of Rich's 'woman-related woman', part of a 'lesbian continuum' which potentially includes us all.[24] This particular use of object-relations theory is represented here by Joanna Ryan's article, 'Psychoanalysis: Women Loving Women'.

Object-relations theory has attracted criticism as well as acclaim among feminists. One objection, made for example by Lynne Segal, is that under this new banner, the familiar 'womanly woman' of anti-feminist rhetoric has re-emerged.[25] For this and other reasons, not all lesbian feminists have chosen to follow this particular route in from the cold excluded margins to lay claim to a new, warm centre of the women's liberation movement in the lesbian mother who models her relationships with lovers and children, both, on the deep satisfactions of the pre-oedipal mother-baby dyad. In this, as in much else, Elizabeth Wilson has struck an uncomfortable, dissenting note: 'I certainly never longed for the "power of woman-bonding". I always wanted my lover to be *other*, not like me. I did not want to be bathed, drowned in the great tide of womanliness.'[26] If feminist identity and demands focus on this promise of a return to that pre-social moment of the mother–baby dyad which permitted no boundaries of self: an idyllic, conflict-free 'Herland',[27] the result may paradoxically be a recurrent and bitter sense of betrayal within the women's movement as it necessarily fails to achieve this utopian dream.

PSYCHOANALYSIS AND POSTSTRUCTURALISM

The final extract in this section by Parveen Adams is taken from the journal *m/f*. *m/f* was a short-lived feminist journal which made an original contribution to British feminist psychoanalysis, where some of the potentialities as well as the difficulties of feminist psychoanalysis were explored in rigorous fashion.[28] Lacan had argued that psychoanalysis was a theory of language as well as of subjectivity, since the subject was constructed in the acquisition of language. In his account, the phallus retains pride of place as *the* privileged signifier under whose organization the sexed entry into language and culture takes place. It is easy to see why this privilege might cause problems for feminists. But other grounds for dissent related to the primacy in this account of the founding of human subjectivity accorded the early interactions within the family. Lacan had posited a fractured, decentred, non-unitary human subject. But its parameters were bounded by the vicissitudes of these early years in which language and social identity were acquired under the sign of the phallus. Theorists working within cultural studies in particular, while inclined to welcome the Lacanian recasting of psychoanalysis in terms of representation and language, were less willing to see 'culture', so recently rescued from economic reductionism, reduced yet again, this time to the endless replaying of the psychic processes of early childhood.[29]

For these reasons, many feminists looked, as did cultural studies generally, to new French theorists who had moved beyond Lacanian psychoanalysis, in particular to the 'poststructuralism' of Michel Foucault[30] and the 'deconstructionism' of Jacques Derrida and the *Tel Quel* group.[31] With these developments, the process of decentring the subject was completed. But taken to its logical conclusion, subjectivity was in danger of complete detachment from *any* social or psychic determinations, becoming the mere point of intersection of the discordant 'discourses' which, in addressing and naming the subject, constituted it. In the work of Foucault and his followers, human subjectivity was historicized,[32] but its history threatened to dissolve into the history of discourse.

In this last contribution by Parveen Adams, Jacques Donzelot's history of the transformation of family forms in France, *The Policing of Families*,[33] is critically dissected, in unfavourable contrast to the work of Foucault. Both Donzelot and Foucault displace psychoanalysis as an explanatory theory of sexuality, and the phallus as uniquely privileged signifier. Psychoanalysis is reinserted as merely one discourse, though historically of great significance, which actually produced that sexuality, placing it under close surveillance in the process. The decisive move in 'poststructuralism' was its refusal of epistemological questions concerning the adequacy of psychoanalysis as explanatory theory. Instead it asks how, in the 'discursive practices' which include, importantly, social institutions, it constituted its object. Donzelot offers a historical analysis of psychoanalysis as one of a number of 'psy-techniques' which were instrumental in the development of a regime for the regulation of families in conformity with social norms.

Adams, in her critique, faults Donzelot for his distortion of Freud. The unconscious self disappears, to give place to a conscious, calculating and rational self. In the process, Freud's theory of sexuality is lost, and not replaced. 'What he gives is a rational explanation of sexuality in the sense that desires are seen as alterable at the level of consciousness. But does such an account meet anybody's sense of sexuality?[34] This is a telling point against Donzelot, but in order to make it, it is necessary to hold on to epistemological concepts of (more or less) adequate *knowledge*. In preferring Foucault, and exempting him from these criticisms, Adams is at the same time implicitly disallowing Foucault's refusal of epistemology. This is important. For once that point is conceded, the last barrier to the radical relativism which is associated with certain forms of poststructuralism, deconstructionism and postfeminism is removed.

NOTES

1 See for example, some of the contribution to Annette Kuhn and AnnMarie Wolpe, eds, *Feminism and Materialism*, Routledge and Kegan Paul, 1978, and Centre for Contemporary Cultural Studies, *Women Take Issue*.

2 L. Althusser, 'Ideology and Ideological State Apparatuses', in L. Althusser, *Lenin and Philosophy and Other Essays*, New Left Books, 1971.

3 J. Lacan, *The Talking Cure: Essays in Psychoanalysis and Language*, ed. C. McCabe, Macmillan, 1981; J. Lacan, [Le Seminaire de Jacques Lacan, vol. 11] *The Four Fundamental Concepts of Psychoanalysis*, tr. Alan Sheridan. Hogarth, 1977. See also R. Coward and J. Ellis, *Language and Materialism* London, 1977.

4 J. Mitchell, *Psychoanalysis and Feminism*, Penguin, 1974. Part 2, section II,

'Feminism and Freud', contains her critique of the early second wave feminists hostile to Freud, noted above.

5 These literary critical essays are included in J. Mitchell, *Women: the Longest Revolution*, Virago, 1984.

6 P. Anderson, 'Origins of the Present Crisis', and T. Nairn, 'The English Working Class', *New Left Review*, 23, 1964, reprinted in P. Anderson and R. Blackburn, eds, *Towards Socialism*, Cornell University Press, 1966. See also the reply by E.P. Thompson, 'Peculiarities of the English', *Socialist Register*, 2, 1965, reprinted in E.P. Thompson, *The Poverty of Theory*, Merlin, 1978.

7 L. Althusser, 'Freud and Lacan', *New Left Review*, 55, 1969 and J. Lacan, 'The Mirror-Phase as Formative of the Functions of the I', *New Left Review*, 51, 1968.

8 S. Timpanaro, 'The Freudian Slip', *New Left Review*, 91, 1975.

9 *New Left Review*, 91, 1975, editorial comment, p. 2.

10 *New Left Review*, 94, 1975, published replies by Jacqueline Rose, Juliet Mitchell and Lucien Rey, Alan Beckett and John Howe, and David Rumney.

11 Mitchell, *Women: the Longest Revolution*, p. 232.

12 See Mitchell, *Psychoanalysis and Feminism*, part 2, section I, 'Radical Psychotherapy and Freud'.

13 Ann Oakley, *Sex, Gender and Society*, Temple Smith, 1972.

14 J. Mitchell and J. Rose, eds, *Feminine Sexuality*, Macmillan, 1982.

15 L. Irigaray, *Speculum de l'autre femme*, Paris, Minuit, 1974, translated as *Speculum of the Other Woman* by Gillian C. Gill, Cornell University Press, 1985.

16 Mitchell and Rose's collection of Lacan's essays contains one which discusses the Freud-Jones debate: 'The Phallic Phase and the Subjective Import of the Castration Complex', *Feminine Sexuality*, pp. 99–122.

17 Mitchell, *Psychoanalysis and Feminism*, p. 362.

18 Janet Sayers, *Sexual Contradictions*, Tavistock, 1986.

19 Michèle Montrelay was another feminist psychoanalyst of the Ecole Freudienne, who dissociated herself from Lacan in 1980. See her *L'Ombre et le nom. Sur la femininité*, Paris, Minuit, 1977. See also, in translation, 'Inquiry into Femininity' in Toril Moi, ed., *French Feminist Thought*, Blackwell, 1987; the presentation of Montrelay's thought in *m/f*, 1, 1978; and E. Marks and I. de Courtivron, *New French Feminisms*, Harvester, 1980. On Irigaray, see in addition Toril Moi, *Sexual/Textual Politics*, Methuen, 1985.

20 J. Rose, 'Femininity and its Discontents', *Feminist Review*, 14, 1983, p. 89.

21 Ibid., p. 91.

22 Nancy Chodorow, *The Reproduction of Mothering*, University of California, 1978.

23 Adrienne Rich, *Of Woman Born*, Virago, 1977.

24 Adrienne Rich, *Compulsory Heterosexuality and Lesbian Existence, Signs*, vol. 5, 4, 1980.

25 See Lynne Segal, *Is the Future Female?*, Virago, 1987, and Hester Eisenstein, *Contemporary Feminist Thought*, Unwin, 1984.

26 Elizabeth Wilson, 'Forbidden Love', in *Hidden Agendas*, Tavistock, 1986, p. 178.

27 The title of Charlotte Perkins Gilman's science fiction/utopian novel written in 1915. It has been reissued by The Womens Press, 1979.

28 Although the title stands for 'marxist/feminist', and the early numbers included articles on various questions within Marxist feminism, it rapidly came to focus more particularly on issues within psychoanalysis and theories of subjectivity.

29 Stuart Hall makes this point in 'Recent developments in theories of language and ideology: a critical note' in *Culture, Media, Language*, Hutchinson, 1980, p. 2. See also Chris Weedon, Andrew Tolson and Frank Mort (with help from Andrew Lowe), 'Theories of Language and Subjectivity' in the same volume.
30 Michel Foucault. *History of Sexuality, vol. I, An Introduction*, Penguin, 1981: *History of Sexuality, vol. II, The Use of Pleasure*, Penguin, 1986; *Discipline and Punish*, Penguin, 1979. For a feminist introduction to and defence of poststructuralism, see Chris Weedon. *Feminist Practice and Poststructuralist Theory*, Blackwell, 1987.
31 J. Derrida, *Of Grammatology*, Johns Hopkins, 1973. For an example of feminist deconstructionism, see Gayatri Chakravorty Spivak, *In Other Worlds*, Routledge, 1988.
32 J. Donzelot, *The Policing of Families*, Hutchinson, 1979.
33 P. Adams, 'Family Affairs', *m/f*, 7, 1982, p. 14.

11

Juliet Mitchell

Feminine Sexuality: Jacques Lacan and the Ecole Freudienne Introduction – I

. . .

Jacques Lacan dedicated himself to the task of refinding and reformulating the work of Sigmund Freud. Psychoanalytic theory today is a variegated discipline. There are contradictions within Freud's writings and subsequent analysts have developed one aspect and rejected another, thereby using one theme as a jumping off point for a new theory. Lacan conceived his own project differently: despite the contradictions and impasses, there is a coherent theorist in Freud whose ideas do not need to be diverged from; rather they should be set within a cohesive framework that they anticipated but which, for historical reasons, Freud himself could not formulate. The development of linguistic science provides this framework.

It is certainly arguable that from the way psychoanalysis has grown during this century we have gained a wider range of therapeutic understanding and the multiplication of fruitful ideas, but we have lost the possibility of a clarification of an essential theory. To say that Freud's work contains contradictions should not be the equivalent of arguing that it is heterogeneous and that it is therefore legitimate for everyone to take their pick and develop it as they wish. Lacan set his face against what he saw as such illegitimate and over-tolerant notions of more-or-less peacefully co-existent lines of psychoanalytic thought. From the outset he went back to Freud's basic concepts. Here, initially, there is agreement among psychoanalysts as to the terrain on which they work: psychoanalysis is about human sexuality and the unconscious.

Freud, and Lacan after him, are both accused of producing phallocentric theories – of taking man as the norm and woman as what is different therefrom. Freud's opponents are concerned to right the balance and develop theories that explain how men and women in their psychosexuality are equal but different. To both Freud and Lacan their task is not to produce justice but to explain this difference which to them uses, not the man, but the phallus to which the man has to lay claim, as its key term. But it is because Freud's position only clearly became this in his later work that Lacan insists we have to 're-read it', giving his theory the significance and coherence which otherwise it lacks.

Although Lacan takes no note of it, there is, in fact, much in Freud's early work, written long before the great debate, that later analysts could use as a starting-point for their descriptions of the equal, parallel development of the sexes. Divisions within writings on the subject since, in many ways, can be seen in terms of this original divergence within Freud's own work.

Freud's work on this subject can be divided into two periods. In the first phase what he had to say about female sexuality arises in the context of his defence of his theory of the fact and the importance of infantile sexuality in general before a public he considered hostile to his discoveries. This first phase stretches from the 1890s to somewhere between 1916 and 1919. The second phase lasts from 1920 until his final work published posthumously in 1940. In this second period he is concerned with elaborating and defending his understanding of sexuality in relation to the particular question of the nature of the difference between the sexes. By this time what he wrote was part of a discussion within the psychoanalytic movement itself.

In the first phase there is a major contradiction in Freud's work which was never brought out into the open. It was immensely important for the later theories of female sexuality. In this period Freud's few explicit ideas about female sexuality revolve around his references to the Oedipus complex. The essence of the Oedipus complex is first mentioned in his published writings in a passing reference to *Oedipus Rex* in *The Interpretation of Dreams* (1900), in 1910 it is named as the Oedipus complex and by 1919, without much theoretical but with a great deal of clinical expansion (most notably in the case of Little Hans), it has become the foundation stone of psychoanalysis. The particular ways in which the Oedipus complex appears and is resolved characterize different types of normality and pathology; its event and resolution explain the human subject and human desire. But the Oedipus complex of this early period is a simple set of relationships in which the child desires the parent of the opposite sex and feels hostile rivalry for the one of the same sex as itself. There is a symmetrical correspondence in the history of the boy and the girl. Thus in 'Fragment of an Analysis of a Case of Hysteria' (1905) Freud writes: 'Distinct traces are probably to be found in most people of an early partiality of this kind – on the part of a daughter for her father, or on the part of a son for his mother' (Freud, VII, 1905, p. 56), and the entire manifest interpretation of Dora's hysteria is in terms of her infantile Oedipal love for her father, and his substitute in the present, Herr K. Or, in 'Delusions and Dreams in Jensen's

Gradiva': 'it is the general rule for a normally constituted girl to turn her affection towards her father in the first instance' (Freud, IX, 1906/7, p. 33). And so on. At the root of Freud's assigning parallel Oedipal roles to girls and boys lies a notion of a natural and normative heterosexual attraction; a notion which was to be re-assumed by many psychoanalysts later. Here, in Freud's early work, it is as though the concept of an Oedipus complex – of a fundamental wish for incest – was so radical that if one was to argue at all for the child's incestuous desires then at least these had better be for the parent of the opposite sex. Thus it was because Freud had to defend his thesis of infantile incestuous sexuality so strenuously against both external opposition and his own reluctance to accept the idea, that the very radicalism of the concept of the Oedipus complex acted as a conservative 'stopper' when it came to understanding the difference between the sexes. Here Freud's position is a conventional one: boys will be boys and love women, girls will be girls and love men. Running counter, however, to the normative implications of sexual symmetry in the Oedipal situation are several themes. Most importantly there is both the structure and the argument of the *Three Essays on the Theory of Sexuality* (1905). Lacan returns to this work reading the concept of the sexual drive that he finds latent there through the light shed on it in Freud's later paper on 'Instincts and Their Vicissitudes' (1915).

The *Three Essays* is the revolutionary founding work for the psychoanalytic concept of sexuality. Freud starts the book with chapters on sexual aberration. He uses homosexuality to demonstrate that for the sexual drive there is no natural, automatic object; he uses the perversions to show that it has no fixed aim. As normality is itself an 'ideal fiction' and there is no qualitative distinction between abnormality and normality, innate factors cannot account for the situation and any notion of the drive as simply innate is therefore untenable. What this means is that the understanding of the drive itself is at stake. The drive (or 'instinct' in the Standard Edition translation), is something on the border between the mental and the physical. Later Freud formulated the relationship as one in which the somatic urge delegated its task to a psychical representative. In his paper, 'The Unconscious', he wrote:

> An instinct can never become an object of consciousness – only the idea that represents the instinct can. Even in the unconscious, moreover, an instinct cannot be represented otherwise than by an idea.... When we nevertheless speak of an unconscious instinctual impulse or of a repressed instinctual impulse...we can only mean an instinctual impulse the ideational representative of which is unconscious. (Freud, XIV, 1915, p. 177)

There is never a causal relationship between the biological urge and its representative: we cannot perceive an activity and deduce behind it a corresponding physical motive force. The sexual drive is never an entity, it is polymorphous, its aim is variable, its object contingent. Lacan argues that the *Three Essays* demonstrate that Freud was already aware that for mankind the drive is almost the *opposite* of an animal instinct that knows and gets its satisfying object. On the other hand, object-relations theorists contend that Freud suggested that the sexual drive was a direct outgrowth of the first satisfying relationship with the mother; it repeats the wish to suck or be held. The baby thus has a first 'part-object' in the breast and later an object in the mother whom it will love pre-Oedipally and then as a 'whole object' Oedipally. Later the sexual drive of the adult will seek out a substitute for this which, if it is good enough, can and will satisfy it.

Though the lack of clarity in some parts of the *Three Essays* could, perhaps, be held responsible for this diversity of interpretation and for the new dominant strand of humanism that Lacan deplores, yet there is absolutely nothing within the essays that is compatible with any notion of natural heterosexual attraction or with the Oedipus complex as it is formulated in Freud's other writing of this period. The structure and content of the *Three Essays* erodes any idea of normative sexuality. By deduction, if no heterosexual attraction is ordained in nature, there can be no genderized sex – there cannot at the outset be a male or female person in a psychological sense.

In the case of 'Dora', Freud assumed that had Dora not been an hysteric she would have been naturally attracted to her suitor, Herr K, just as she had been attracted to her father when she was a small child. In other words, she would have had a natural female Oedipus complex. But the footnotes, written subsequently, tell another story: Dora's relationship to her father had been one not only of attraction but also of identification with him. In terms of her sexual desire, Dora is a man adoring a woman. To ascribe the situation to Dora's hysteria would be to beg the whole founding question of psychoanalysis. Hysteria is not produced by any innate disposition. It follows that if Dora can have a masculine identification there can be no natural or automatic heterosexual drive.

Until the 1920s Freud solved this problem by his notion of bisexuality. 'Bisexuality' likewise enabled him to avoid what would otherwise have been too blatant a contradiction in his position: thus he argued that the too neat parallelism of the boy's and girl's Oedipal situations, the dilemma of Dora, the presence of homosexuality, could all be accounted for by the fact that the boy has a bit of the female, the girl of the male. This saves the Oedipus complex from the crudity of gender determinism – but at a price. If, as Freud insists, the notion of bisexuality is not to be a purely biological one, whence does it arise? Later analysts who largely preserved Freud's early use of the term, did relate bisexuality to the duplications of anatomy or based it on simple identification: the boy partly identified with the mother, the girl partly with the father. For Freud, when later he reformulated the Oedipus complex, 'bisexuality' shifted its meaning and came to stand for the very uncertainty of sexual division itself.

Without question during this first period, Freud's position is highly contradictory. His discovery of the Oedipus complex led him to assume a natural heterosexuality. The rest of his work argued against this possibility as the very premise of a psychoanalytic understanding of sexuality. There is no reference to the Oedipus complex or the positions it assumes in the *Three Essays* and by this omission he was able to avoid recognising the contradiction within his theses, though the essays bear its mark within some of the confusing statements they contain.

By about 1915 it seems that Freud was aware that his theory of the Oedipus complex and of the nature of sexuality could not satisfactorily explain the difference between the sexes. Freud never explicitly stated his difficulties (as he did in other areas of work), but in 1915, he added a series of footnotes to the *Three Essays* which are almost all about the problem of defining masculinity and femininity. Other writers – notably Jung – had taken Freud's ideas on the Oedipus complex as they were expressed at the time, to their logical conclusion and in establishing a definite parity between the sexes had re-named the girl's Oedipal conflict, the Electra complex. Whether or not it was this work – Freud rejected the Electra complex from the outset – or whether it was the dawning awareness of the unsatisfactory nature of his own position that provoked Freud to re-think the issue cannot be established; but something made him look more intensively at the question of the difference between the sexes.

One concept, also added in 1915 to the *Three Essays*, marks both the turning point in Freud's own understanding of the differences between men and women, and also the focal point of the conflict that emerges between his views and those of most other analysts on the question. This concept is the castration complex.

During the first phase of Freud's work we can see the idea of the castration complex gradually gain momentum. It was discussed in 'On the Sexual Theories of Children' (1908), crucially important in the analysis of Little Hans (1909), yet when he wrote 'On Narcissism: An Introduction' in 1914 Freud was still uncertain as to whether or not it was a universal occurrence. But in 1915 it starts to assume a larger and larger part. By 1924, in the paper on 'The Dissolution of the Oedipus Complex' the castration complex has emerged as a central concept. In his autobiography of 1925, Freud wrote: 'The *castration complex* is of the profoundest importance in the formation alike of character and of neurosis' (Freud, XX, 1925, p. 37). He made it the focal point of the acquisition of culture; it operates as a law whereby men and women assume their humanity and, inextricably bound up with this, it gives the human meaning of the distinction between the sexes.

The castration complex in Freud's writings is very closely connected with his interest in man's prehistory. It is unnecessary to enumerate Freud's dubious anthropological reconstructions in this field; what is of relevance is the importance he gave to an *event* in man's personal and social history. It is well known that before he recognised the significance of fantasy and of infantile sexuality, Freud believed the tales his hysterical patients told him of their seductions by their fathers. Although Freud abandoned the particular event of paternal seduction as either likely or, more important, causative, he retained the notion of an event, prehistorical or actual. Something intruded from without into the child's world. Something that was not innate but came from outside, from history or prehistory. This 'event' was to be the paternal threat of castration.

That the castration complex operates as an external event, a law, can be seen too from a related preoccupation of Freud's. Some time around 1916, Freud became interested in the ideas of Lamarck. This interest is most often regarded, with condescension, as an instance of Freud's nineteenth-century scientific anachronism. But in fact by 1916 Lamarck was already outmoded and it is clear that Freud's interest arose not from ignorance but from the need to account for something that he observed but could not theorize. The question at stake was: how does the individual acquire the whole essential history of being human within the first few short years of its life? Lamarckian notions of cultural inheritance offered Freud a possible solution to the problem. In rejecting the idea of cultural inheritance, Freud's opponents may have been refusing a false solution but in doing so they missed the urgency of the question and thereby failed to confront the problem of how the child acquires so early and so rapidly its knowledge of human law. Karen Horney's 'culturalist' stress – her emphasis on the influence of society – was an attempt to put things right, but it failed because it necessitated an implicit assumption that the human subject could be set apart from society and was not constructed solely within it: the child and society were separate entities mutually affecting each other. For Horney there are men and women (boys and girls) already there; in this she takes for granted exactly that which she intends to explain.

Freud's concept of the castration complex completely shifted the implications of the Oedipus complex and altered the meaning of bisexuality. Before the castration complex was given its full significance, it seems that the Oedipus complex dissolved naturally, a passing developmental stage. Once the castration complex is postulated it is this alone that shatters the Oedipus complex. The castration complex institutes the superego as its representative and as representative thereby of the law. Together with the organizing role of the Oedipus complex in relation to desire, the castration complex governs the position of each person in the triangle of father, mother and child; in the way it does this, it embodies the law that founds the human order itself. Thus the question of castration, of sexual difference as the product of a division, and the concept of an historical and symbolic order, all begin, tentatively, to come together. It is on their interdependence that Lacan bases his theories in the texts that follow.

When Freud started to elevate the concept of castration to its theoretical heights, resistance started. It seems that infantile sexuality and the Oedipus complex were unpalatable ideas for many outside the psychoanalytical movement, yet it would appear that there was something even more inherently unacceptable about the notion of a castration complex and what it assumed in the girl child, penis envy, even for psychoanalysts. After this point, Freud's emphasis on the importance of the castration complex comes not only from his clinical observations, his growing awareness of the contradictions of his own work, his increasing interest in the foundations of human history, but to a degree as a response to the work of his colleagues.

Lou Andreas-Salomé, van Ophuijsen, then Karl Abraham and Auguste Starcke in 1921 initiate the response to the notion. Franz Alexander, Otto

Rank, Carl Müller-Braunschweig, and Josine Müller continue it until the names that are more famous in this context – Karen Horney, Melanie Klein, Lampl-de Groot, Helene Deutsch, Ernest Jones – are added in the mid-twenties and thirties. Others join in: Fenichel, Rado, Marjorie Brierley, Joan Rivière, Ruth Mack Brunswick, but by 1935 the positions have clarified and the terms of the discussion on sexual differences do not change importantly, though the content that goes to fill out the argument does so.

Karl Abraham's work is crucial. He died before the great debate was in full flow, but his ideas, though often not acknowledged, were central to it – not least because most of Freud's opponents believed that Abraham's views were representative of Freud's. As Abraham is ostensibly amplifying Freud's work and writing in support of the concept of the castration complex, this was an understandable but completely mistaken assumption. In their letters Freud and Abraham are always agreeing most politely with one another and this makes it rather hard to elucidate the highly significant differences between them. One difference is that Freud argues that girls envy the phallus, Karl Abraham believes that both sexes in parallel fashion fear castration – which he describes as lack of sexual potency. In Abraham's thesis, boys and girls – because they are already different – respond differently to an identical experience; in Freud the same experience distinguishes them. By implication for Abraham, but not for Freud, by the time of the castration complex there must already be 'boys' and 'girls'. This important distinction apart, the real divergence between Abraham's arguments and those of Freud can best be glimpsed through the shift of emphasis. In the work of both writers incest is taboo ('castration'); but only for Freud must there be someone around to forbid it: prohibition is in the air.

In Freud's work, with its emphasis on the castration complex as the source of the law, it is the father who already possesses the mother, who metaphorically says 'no' to the child's desires. The prohibition only comes to be meaningful to the child because there are people – females – who have been castrated in the particular sense that they are without the phallus. It is only, in other words, through 'deferred action' that previous experiences such as the sight of female genitals become significant. Thus, for Freud, contained within the very notion of the castration complex is the theory that other experiences and perceptions only take their meaning from the law for which it stands. In Abraham's work, to the contrary, the threat of castration arises from an actual perception that the child makes about a girl's body: no one intervenes, there is no prohibiting father whose threat is the utterance of a law; here it is the 'real' inferiority of the female genitals that once comprehended initiates the complex in both sexes.

Here, however, within Freud's work, we come across a further and most important contradiction; it was one he did not have time fully to resolve. It is a contradiction that explains subsequent readings of Abraham's and Freud's work as coincident. Freud is clear that the boy's castration complex arises from the penis being given significance from the father's prohibition; but sometimes he suggests that the girl's penis envy comes from a simple perception that she makes; she sees the actual penis, realizes it is bigger and better and wants one. Clearly such inequity in girls' and boys' access to meaning is untenable: why should the girl have a privileged relationship to an understanding of the body? In fact there is evidence that Freud was aware of the discrepancy in his account; his published statements tend to be confusing, but in a letter he wrote: 'the sight of the penis and its function of urination cannot be the motive, only the trigger of the child's envy. However, no one has stated this' (Freud, 1935, 1971, p. 329). Unfortunately neither Freud nor any subsequent analyst stated this clearly enough in their published writings.

Freud referred to Abraham's article on the female castration complex (1920) as 'unsurpassed'. But absolutely nothing in the theoretical framework of Freud's writing confirmed Abraham's perspective. Freud certainly talks of the woman's sense of 'organ-inferiority' but this is never for him the *motive* for the castration complex or hence for the dissolution of the Oedipus complex; it is therefore not causative of female sexuality, femininity or neurosis. For Freud the absence of the penis in women is significant only in that it makes meaningful the father's prohibition on incestuous desires. In and of itself, the female body neither indicates nor initiates anything. The implication of the different stress of Freud and Abraham is very far-reaching. If, as in Abraham's work, the actual body is seen as a motive for the constitution of the subject in its male or female sexuality, then an historical or symbolic dimension to this constitution is precluded. Freud's intention was to establish that very dimension as the *sine qua non* of the construction of the human subject. It is on this dimension that Lacan bases his entire account of sexual difference.

If Freud considered that the actual body of the child on its own was irrelevant to the castration complex, so too did he repeatedly urge that the actual situation of the child, the presence or absence of the father, the real prohibition against masturbation and so on, could be insignificant compared with the ineffable presence of a symbolic threat (the 'event') to which one is inevitably subjected as the price of being human. Unable to accept the notion of cultural inheritance, other analysts, agreeing with Freud that an actual occurrence could not account for the omnipresent castration anxiety they found in their clinical work, had to look elsewhere for an explanation. In all cases, they considered the castration complex not as something essential to the very construction of the human subject but as a fear that arises from the internal experiences of a being who is already, even if only in a primitive form, constituted as a subject. As a consequence, in none of these alternative theories can castration have any fundamental bearing on sexual difference.

Thus Starcke found the prevalence of castration anxiety in the loss of the nipple from the baby's mouth, so that daily weaning accounted for the universality of the complex. As a further instance he proposed the baby's gradual ability to see itself as distinct from the external world: 'The formation of the outer world is the original castration; the withdrawal of the nipple forms the root-conception of this' (Starcke, 1921, p. 180). Franz Alexander and Otto Rank took castration back to the baby's loss of the womb, which was once part of itself. Freud took up his colleague's ideas on separation anxiety (as he termed it) most fully in *Inhibitions, Symptoms and Anxiety* written in 1925, but two years earlier he had added this footnote to the case of Little Hans:

> While recognizing all of these roots of the complex, I have nevertheless put forward the view that the term 'castration complex' ought to be confined to those excitations and consequences which are bound up with the loss of the *penis*. Any one who, in analysing adults, has become convinced of the invariable presence of the castration complex, will of course find difficulty in ascribing its origin to a chance threat – of a kind which is not, after all, of such universal occurrence; he will be driven to assume that children construct this danger for themselves out of the slightest hints. (Freud, x, 1909, p. 8, n, 1923)

There is a fundamental distinction between recognizing that the castration complex may refer back to other separations and actually seeing these separations as castrations. To Freud the castration complex divided the sexes and thus make the human being, human. But this is not to deny the importance of earlier separations. Freud himself had proposed that the loss of the faeces constituted the possibility of a retrospective referral; the castration complex could use it as a model. Freud's account is retroactive: fearing phallic castration the child may 'recollect' previous losses, castration gives them their relevance. In the other accounts it is these separations that make castration relevant; here the scheme is prospective: early losses make the child fear future ones. For Freud, history and the psychoanalytic experience is always a reconstruction, a retrospective account: the human subject is part of such a history. The other explanations make him grow developmentally. If one takes castration itself back to the womb, then the human subject was there from the outset and it can only follow that what makes him psychotic, neurotic or 'normal' is some arbitrarily selected constitutional factor or some equally arbitrary environmental experience.

Once more, Lacan underlines and reformulates Freud's position. The castration complex is *the* instance of the humanization of the child in its sexual difference. Certainly it rejoins other severances, in fact it gives them their meaning. If the specific mark of the phallus, the repression of which is the institution of the law, is repudiated then there can only be psychosis. To Lacan all other hypotheses make nonsense of psychoanalysis. For him they once again leave unanswered the question whence the subject originates, and, he asks, what has happened to the language and social order that distinguishes him or her from other mammals – is it to have no effect other than a subsidiary one, on formation? Above all, how can sexual difference be understood within such a developmental perspective?

If it is argued that there is nothing specific about the threat of phallic castration; if birth, weaning, the formation of the outer world are all castrations, then something else has to explain the difference between the sexes. If castration is only one among other separations or is the same as the dread of the loss of sexual desire common to men and women alike (Jones's *aphanisis*), then what distinguishes the two sexes? All the major contributors to this field at this period, whether they supplemented or opposed Freud, found the explanation in a biological predisposition. This is the case with Freud's biologistic defender, Helene Deutsch, as it is with his culturalist opponent, Karen Horney.

The demoting of the castration complex from its key role in the construction of sexual difference, and the subsequent reliance on biological explanations, was accompanied by a further change. In the mid-twenties the focus of discussion shifted and a new epoch began. The crisis of the concept of the castration complex may well have contributed to a change of emphasis away from itself and towards a preoccupation with female sexuality. When the well-known names associated with the discussion – Horney, Deutsch, Lampl-de Groot, Klein, Jones – join in, their concern is less with the construction of sexual difference than it is with the nature of female sexuality. It is from this time that we can date what has become known as the 'great debate'. The debate was to reach its peak when in 1935, Ernest Jones, invited to Vienna to give some lectures to elucidate the fast growing differences between British and Viennese psychoanalysts, chose as his first (and, as it turned out, only) topic, female sexuality. While female sexuality of course is central to our concerns, we can see that something highly important was lost in the change of emphasis. Retrospectively one can perceive that the reference point is still the distinction between the sexes (the point of the castration complex) but by concentrating on the status and nature of female sexuality, it often happens that this is treated as an isolate, something independent of the distinction that creates it. This tendency is confirmed within the theories of those opposed to Freud. The opposition to Freud saw the concept of the castration complex as derogatory to women. In repudiating its terms they hoped both to elevate women and to explain what women consisted of – a task Freud ruled as psychoanalytically out-of-bounds. But from now on analysts who came in on Freud's side also saw their work in this way. Women, so to speak, had to have something of their own. The issue subtly shifts from what distinguishes the sexes to what has each sex got of value that belongs to it alone. In this context, and in the absence of the determining role of the castration complex, it is inevitable that there is a return to the very biological explanations from which Freud deliberately took his departure – where else could that something else be found?

For Freud it is of course never a question of arguing that anatomy or biology is irrelevant, it is a question of assigning them their place. He gave them a place – it was outside the field of psychoanalytic enquiry. Others put them firmly within it. Thus Carl Müller-Braunschweig, assuming, as did others, that there was an innate masculinity and femininity which corresponded directly with the biological male and female, wrote of a 'masculine and feminine id'. There is now not only an original masculinity and femininity but a natural heterosexuality. In 1926, Karen Horney spoke of the 'biological principle of heterosexual attraction' and argued from this that the girl's so-called masculine phase is a defence against her primary feminine anxiety that her father will violate her. Melanie Klein elaborated the increasingly prevalent notion that because of her primordial infantile feminine sexuality, the girl has an unconscious knowledge of the vagina. This naturalist perspective, exemplified in the work of Ernest Jones, posits a primary femininity for the girl based on her biological sex which then suffers vicissitudes as a result of fantasies brought into play by the girl's relations to objects. The theorists of this position do not deny Freud's notion that the girl has a phallic phase, but they argue that it is only a reaction-formation against her natural feminine attitude. It is a secondary formation, a temporary state in which the girl takes refuge when she feels her femininity is in danger. Just as the boy with his natural male valuation of his penis fears its castration, so the girl with her natural femininity will fear the destruction of her insides through her father's rape. The presence or absence of early vaginal sensations becomes a crucial issue in this context – a context in which impulses themselves, in a direct and unmediated way, produce psychological characteristics. Freud argued strenuously against such a position. In a letter that, read in this context, is not as cryptic as it at first appears, he wrote to Müller-Braunschweig:

> I object to all of you (Horney, Jones, Rado, etc.,) to the extent that you do not distinguish more clearly and cleanly between what is psychic and what is biological, that you try to establish a neat parallelism between the two and that you, motivated by such intent, unthinkingly construe psychic facts which are unprovable and that you, in the process of doing so, must declare as reactive or regressive much that without doubt is primary. Of course, these reproaches must remain obscure. In addition. I would only like to emphasize that we must keep psychoanalysis separate from biology just as we have kept it separate from anatomy and physiology. (Freud, 1935, 1971, p. 329)

However, there were those opponents of Freud's position who did not want to lean too heavily or too explicitly on a biological explanation of sexual difference; instead they stressed the significance of the psychological mechanism of identification with its dependence on an object. In both Freud's account and those of these object-relations theorists, after the resolution of the Oedipus complex, each child hopefully identifies with the parent of the appropriate sex. The explanations look similar – but the place accorded to the castration complex pushes them poles apart. In Freud's schema, after the castration complex, boys and girls will more or less adequately adopt the sexual identity of the appropriate parent. But it is always only an adoption and a precarious one at that, as long ago, Dora's 'inappropriate' paternal identification had proved. For Freud, identification with the appropriate parent is an *result* of the castration complex which has already given the mark of sexual distinction. For other analysts, dispensing with the key role of the castration complex, identification (with a biological prop) is the *cause* of sexual difference. Put somewhat reductively, the position of these theorists can be elucidated thus: there is a period when the girl is undifferentiated from the boy (for Klein and some others, this is the boy's primary feminine phase) and hence both love and identify with their first object, the mother; then, as a result of her biological sex (her femininity) and because her love has been frustrated on account of her biological inadequacy (she has not got the phallus for her mother and never will have), the little girl enters into her own Oedipus complex and loves her father; she then fully re-identifies with her mother and achieves her full feminine identity.

It can be seen from this that the question of female sexuality was itself crucial in the development of object-relations theory. This understanding of femininity put a heavy stress on the first maternal relationship; the same emphasis has likewise characterized the whole subsequent expansion of object-relations theory. When the 'great debate' evaporated, object-relations theorists concentrated attention on the mother and the sexually undifferentiated child, leaving the problem of sexual distinction as a subsidiary that is somehow not bound up with the very formation of the subject. This is the price paid for the reorientation to the mother, and the neglect of the father, whose prohibition in Freud's theory, alone can represent the mark that distinguishes boys and girls. The mother herself in these accounts has inherited a great deal of the earlier interest in female sexuality – her own experiences, the experiences of her, have been well documented, but she is already constituted – in all her uncertainty – as a female subject. This represents an interesting avoidance of the question of sexual difference.

Freud acknowledged his serious inadequacies in the area of the mother–child relationship. In fact his blindness was dictated not so much by his personal inclinations or his own masculinity – as he and others suggested – but by the nature of psychoanalysis as he conceived it. To Freud, if psychoanalysis is phallocentric, it is because the human social order that it perceives refracted through the individual human subject is patrocentric. To date, the father stands in the position of the third term that *must* break the asocial dyadic unit of mother and child. We can see that this third term will always need to be represented by something or someone. Lacan returns to the problem, arguing that the relation of mother and child cannot be viewed outside the structure established by the position of the father. To Lacan, a theory that ignores the father or sees him embodied within the mother (Klein) or through her eyes, is nonsense. There can be nothing *human* that pre-exists or exists outside the law represented by the father; there is only either its denial (psychosis) or the fortunes and misfortunes ('normality' and neurosis) of its terms. Ultimately for Kleinian and non-Kleinian object-relations theorists (despite the great differences between them) the distinction between the sexes is not the result of a division but a fact that is already given; men and women, males and females, *exist*. There is no surprise here.

The debate with his colleagues also led Freud himself to make some crucial reformulations. Again these can be said to stem from his stress on the castration complex. Time and again in the last papers of his life he underscored its significance. In rethinking his belief that the boy and the girl both had a phallic phase that was primary, and not, as others argued, reactive and secondary, he re-emphasized, but more importantly, reformulated his earlier positions. The Oedipus complex as he had originally conceived it led to what he considered the impasses and mistakes of the arguments he opposed. The natural heterosexuality it assumed was untenable but its simple reversal with its stress on the first maternal relation was equally unsatisfactory. Without an ultimate reliance on a biologically induced identificatory premise, such a position does not account for the difference between the boy and the girl. Lacan would argue that it is at this juncture that Freud – his earlier positions now seen to be leading in false directions – brings forward the concept of desire. 'What', asks Freud, 'does the woman [the little girl] want?' All answers to the question, including 'the mother' are false: she simply *wants*. The phallus – with its status as potentially absent – comes to stand in for the necessarily *missing* object of desire at the level of sexual division. If this is so, the Oedipus complex can no longer be a static myth that reflects the real situation of father, mother and child, it becomes a structure revolving around the question of where a person can be placed in relation to his or her desire. That 'where' is determined by the castration complex.

In his 1933 essay 'Femininity', Freud puts forward the solutions of his opponents on the issue of female sexuality as a series of questions. He asks 'how does [the little girl] pass from her masculine phase to the feminine one to which she is biologically destined?' (Freud, XXII, 1933, p. 119) and contrary to the answers of his opponents, he concludes that: 'the constitution will not adapt itself to its function without a struggle' (Freud, XXII, 1933, p. 117) and that though 'It would be a solution of ideal simplicity if we could suppose that from a particular age onwards the elementary influence of the mutual attraction between the sexes makes itself felt and impels the small woman towards men...we are not going to find things so easy.' (Freud, XXII, 1933, p. 119). The biological female is destined to become a woman, but the question to which psychoanalysis must address itself, is *how*, if she does manage this, is it to happen? His colleagues' excellent work on the earliest maternal relationship, from a psychoanalytic point of view, leaves unanswered the problem of sexual differentiation. As Freud puts it: 'Unless we can find something that is specific for girls and is not present or not in the same way present in boys, we shall not have explained the termination of the attachment of girls to their mother. I believe we have found this specific factor...in the castration complex' (Freud, 1933, p. 124).

Freud ended his life with an unfinished paper: 'Splitting of the Ego in the Process of Defence' (XXIII, 1940). It is about the castration complex and its implication for the construction of the subject. It describes the formation of the ego in a moment of danger (of threatened loss) which results in a primary split from which it never recovers. Freud offers the reaction to the castration complex when a fetish is set up as its alternative, as an exemplary instance of this split. In this paper we can see clearly the position of Freud's to which Lacan is to return. A primordially split subject necessitates an originally lost object. Though Freud does not talk of the object as a lost object as Lacan does, he is absolutely clear that its psychological significance arises from its absence, or as he put it in the essay on 'Femininity' from the fact that it could never satisfy: 'the child's avidity for its earliest nourishment is altogether insatiable. . .it never gets over the pain of losing its mother's breast' (Freud, XXII, 1933, p. 122). Even the tribal child, breastfed well beyond infancy, is unsatisfied: pain and lack of satisfaction are the point, the triggers that evoke desire.

Freud's final writings are often perceived as reflecting an old man's despair. But for Lacan their pessimism indicates a clarification and summation of a theory whose implications are and must be, anti-humanist. The issue of female sexuality always brings us back to the question of how the human subject is constituted. In the theories of Freud that Lacan redeploys, the distinction between the sexes brought about by the castration complex and the different positions that must subsequently be taken up, confirms that the subject is split and the object is lost. This is the difficulty at the heart of being human to which psychoanalysis and the objects of its enquiry – the unconscious and sexuality – bear witness. To Lacan, a humanist position offers only false hopes on the basis of false theories.

It is a matter of perspective – and Lacan would argue that the perspective of post-Freudian analysts is ideological in that it confirms the humanism of our times. In the view of Kleinians and other object-relations theorists, whether it is with a primitive ego or as an initial fusion with the mother from which differentiation gradually occurs, the perspective starts from an identification with what seems to be, or ought to be, the subject. The problem these theorists address is: what does the baby/person do with its world in order for it to develop? Then the question is inverted: has the human environment been good enough for the baby to be able to do the right things? In these accounts a sexual identity is first given biologically and then developed and confirmed (or not) as the subject grows through interaction with the real objects and its fantasies of them, on its complicated road to maturity.

Lacan takes the opposite perspective: the analysand's unconscious reveals a fragmented subject of shifting and uncertain sexual identity. To be human is to be subjected to a law which decentres and divides: sexuality is created in a division, the subject is split; but an ideological world conceals this from the conscious subject who is supposed to feel whole and certain of a sexual identity. Psychoanalysis should aim at a destruction of this concealment and at a reconstruction of the subject's construction in all its splits. This may be an accurate theory, it is certainly a precarious project. It is to this theory and project – the history of the fractured sexual subject – that Lacan dedicates himself.

REFERENCES

K. Abraham, 'Manifestations of the Female Castration Complex', (1920) *International Journal of Psychoanalysis*, III, 1922.

Sigmund Freud, *The Interpretation of Dreams*, (Standard Edition (SE), V, 1900).

—— *Three Essays on the Theory of Sexuality*, (SE, VII, 1905).

—— 'Fragment of an Analysis of a Case of Hysteria ('Dora') (1901) (SE, VII, 1905).
—— 'Delusions and Dreams in Jensen's *Gradiva*', (SE, IX, 1906–7).
—— 'On the Sexual Theories of Children' (SE, IX, 1908).
—— 'Analysis of a Phobia in a Five Year Old Boy' ('Little Hans') (SE, X, 1909).
—— 'On Narcissism: an Introduction' (SE, XII, 1914).
—— 'The Unconscious' (Papers on Metapsychology (SE, XIV, 1915).
—— 'An Autobiographical Study', (SE, XX, 1925).
—— 'Femininity', Lecture XXXIII, New Introductory Lectures, (1932), (SE, XXII, 1933).
—— 'Letter to Carl Muller-Braunschweig' (1935), published as 'Freud and female sexuality: a previously unpublished letter', *Psychiatry*, 1971.
—— 'Splitting of the Ego in the Process of Defence' (1938) (SE, XXIII, 1940).
A. Starcke, 'The Castration Complex', *International Journal of psychoanalysis*, II, 1921.

12

Elizabeth Wilson

Psychoanalysis: Psychic Law and Order?

INTRODUCTION

What are the political implications of psychoanalysis for feminists? What follows is an attempt to explore some of my own doubts whether the psychoanalytic path taken by many feminists and Marxists in recent years is really as fruitful as is claimed. Nor am I convinced that the *politics* of this theoretical position has really been thought through in any coherent way.

I am aware that I am taking up an unpopular position in questioning this new orthodoxy, and that my criticisms will be open to the charge that my stance is purely negative – the implication being that there is no point, or one is not justified, in criticizing the use of psychoanalysis unless one has something better to offer in its place. But although I, on the whole, think that a positive view is preferable, this cannot always be the only or the overriding imperative. In any case the debate around ideas should not be seen as negative, and I see this piece as inviting a debate that I hope will be taken up in the pages of *Feminist Review* and perhaps elsewhere.

FREUD

Although I would agree that all accounts of 'what Freud really said' are themselves interpretations – because of the contradictions and gaps in his own writings – I shall begin with a brief outline of some aspects of Freudian theory in order to point up what I see as certain ambiguities. A fuller and far more adequate (although rather densely written) account of the theoretical controversies surrounding Freud and Lacan may be found in 'Psychoanalysis and the cultural acquisition of sexuality and subjectivity' by Steve Burniston, Frank Mort and Christine Weedon (1978).

Freud's work offers an explanation of the creation of individual identity based on the child's changing relationship to its own body (and particularly its sexual impulses, or drives), the early discovery of the boundary between 'self' and 'not self', and the limitations imposed on desire by reality. For Freud, the individual is socially constructed, albeit on a biological basis. At the beginning of its life the infant is dominated by the 'pleasure principle' and has virtually no Ego or conscious self as we understand it. This initial state is constantly modified by the incessant demands of reality, and it is this that creates what Freud came to call the Ego.

Although the Ego is the organizing and rationalizing part of the psyche, and although it is the most integrated part of the 'self' it remains the site of struggle between the pleasure demands of the Id or unconscious and the reality demands of the external world. It remains defensive, fluctuating and contradictory, and parts of it also remain cut off from consciousness; so that in the adult there is an Ego that has in many ways mastered or come to terms with reality, yet this adult psyche still consists also of an Id of which a large part consists of childish, repressed desires. These remain infantile because they have not been modified by the demands of reality, but have been dealt with in early life by being repressed – made unconscious – and thus placed beyond the reach of reality. Parts of the unconscious may however 'return' in certain circumstances. This notion of an unconscious hinterland to the 'personality' (for want of a better word), that somehow contains unresolved conflicts and wishes, explains our often irrational behaviour as adults, our own internal sense of conflict and contradiction, inappropriate feeling states, and indeed neurotic symptoms and dreams.

In his discussion of the development of identity Freud placed primary emphasis on the body and the role played in particular by the child's biological sex. For Freud the Ego was a bodily Ego; and since the infant was for Freud essentially a pleasure seeker, and since the child's bodily and soon enough specifically genital sensations provide him with his greatest sources of pleasure, sexuality and Ego must be complexly bound together. In the satisfaction of his needs the child is dependent upon others; usually primarily his mother, and a need for what the mother can give him eventually develops into a feeling with a momentum of its own: love. The relationship between the satisfaction of sensual needs and this love for another being leads directly in Freud's view to that love being eroticized. Indeed it is *because* of this that the child's sexual feelings can be directed towards another human being; otherwise he would remain locked within masturbatory auto-eroticism.

The infant initially loves his mother in a dual and symbiotic relationship. His feeding relationship with her breast was described by Freud as the prototype of all erotic satisfactions, and the bliss of the hunger-satisfied child asleep at the breast as reminiscent of the bliss of the satisfied lover asleep on the breast of his beloved. The crisis of the child's infant erotic life comes later with the Oedipus complex. By the age of three of four the child has realized that he does not have his mother all to himself, but shares her with another, his father, who has more comprehensive and explicitly sexual access to her. Thus he is caught in the most painful of love triangles, since he also loves his father.

Threats of castration as a punishment for masturbation take on a new and terrifying meaning. Not only has he by this time seen the female genital, and thus realized that some individuals *are* 'castrated', but the castration threat is interpreted as an expression of the father's jealousy. The little boy has both a narcissistic *and* a realistic attachment to his genital, so in order to preserve it he renounces his sexual love for his mother and instead he *identifies* with his father:

> the authority of the father. . . is introjected into the ego, and there it forms the nucleus of the super-ego which takes over the severity of the father and perpetuates the prohibition against incest. (Freud, 1977:319)

So far, it is the development of the little boy that has been discussed. Freud at first described the Oedipus complex in terms of the little boy and assumed that the little girl's development was the same in reverse. Later he recognized that the development of the little girl is both more complicated and more obscure. The little boy retains the same love object – a woman – throughout his life; his primary sexual organ is and remains the penis. The little girl, on the other hand, has to achieve a change of both organ and object. She, like the baby boy, begins life with an attachment to the breast and hence to the mother; yet she must transfer her affections to her father/men. The only sexual organ of which she is aware (according to Freud, although here he was challenged by other psychoanalysts in the 1920s) is the clitoris: 'the little girl is a little man': yet she must transfer her sexual excitability from clitoris to vagina.

So Freud was forced to the conclusion that the Oedipus complex in girls is different from the boy's experience. The little boy's Oedipus complex is dissolved or 'smashed' when he gives up his love for his mother and identifies with paternal authority in order to avoid the dreaded retaliation of castration. But the little girl does not fear castration because she *is* castrated; this recognition for her initiates rather than demolishes the Oedipus complex. Only then can she move from the dual relationship with her mother into the triangular relationship in which she takes her father as the object of her desire, giving up her wish for the penis and replacing it by a wish for the baby the father could give her.

Three important consequences of this are that the little girl and the woman is dominated by penis-envy; that the female's super-ego is not so developed as the male's because she has not had to internalize the father; and:

> a third consequence of penis-envy seems to be a loosening of the girl's affectionate relation with her maternal object. The situation as a whole is not very clear, but it can be seen that in the end the girl's mother, who sent her into the world so insufficiently equipped, is almost always held responsible for her lack of a penis. (Freud, 1977:338)

Freud was always careful to insist on the fragmentary, indeterminate and unsatisfactory nature of his conclusions:

> It must be admitted...that in general our insight into these developmental processes in girls is unsatisfactory, incomplete and vague. (Freud, 1977:321)

At the same time, and this is presumably where Freud's own ambivalence emerges, he often slips into vulgar stereotypic generalizations. He allows himself to talk of woman as Enigma (as in his famous question: 'Was will das Weib?' – 'What does Woman want?'). He sees women as a problem because they deviate from the male model. For him, women *are* more vain and narcissistic than men; have less super-ego or 'conscience'; less sense of justice; less sexual libido; and less capacity to love another human being.

Yet there is more to Freud's account of women than this. His notorious statement 'anatomy is destiny', which even Juliet Mitchell describes as 'disastrous' is by no means as downright as most feminists have supposed. He was discussing the differences between the Oedipus complex in the little girl and little boy and all he said was:

> the feminist demand for equal rights for the sexes does not take us far, for the morphological distinction is bound to find expression in differences of psychical development. (Freud, 1977:320)

To say that anatomical differences between the sexes are 'bound to' have some echo in psychological differences does not in itself seem an objectionable statement. Where there is disagreement is when psychological attributes of narcissism, stupidity, frivolousness and the rest are taken as inexorably and inevitably 'feminine'.

Freud was perfectly clear that to be anatomically 'male' or 'female' was no simple matter. Bisexuality was central to his theory, and moreover he realized that there was no one-to-one correspondence between anatomical maleness and 'masculinity' on the one hand, and anatomical femaleness and 'femininity' on the other. Although the male alone produces semen and the female alone ova (except in very rare cases):

> Science...draws your attention to the fact that portions of the male sexual apparatus also appear in women's bodies, though in an atrophied state, and vice versa in the alternative case. It regards their occurrence as indicators of *bisexuality*, as though an individual is not a man or a woman but always both – merely a certain amount more the one than the other. (Freud, 1973:147)

So bisexuality itself had an anatomical basis. It was also, for Freud, a part of mental or psychical life. He argues that really, when we speak of 'masculine' or 'feminine' behaviour, we are usually merely making a distinction between 'active' and 'passive'. He goes on to say that this analogy does have a biological basis since:

> The male sex-cell is actively mobile and searches out the female one, and the latter, the ovum, is immobile and waits passively. This behaviour of the elementary sexual organisms is indeed a model for the conduct of sexual individuals during intercourse. The male pursues the female for the purpose of sexual union, seizes hold of her, and penetrates her. (Freud, 1973:48)

We might quarrel with this description, and it has been pointed out that the ovum is just as active as the sperm in biological fact. Yet Freud himself goes on to point out that in some species this active/passive distinction is not assigned according to the male/female division in the expected way, but is reversed, so that the male cares for the young, in others the female pursues the male sexually, and so on. And Freud says:

> I shall conclude that you have decided in your own minds to make 'active' coincide with 'masculine' and 'passive' with 'feminine'. But I advise you against it. It seems to me to serve no useful purpose and adds nothing to our knowledge. (Freud, 1973:148)

Yet he often slips back into this terminology himself. He did believe that women must give preference to 'passive aims', and in the very paper in which he argues for bisexuality one of his not infrequent digs at 'feminists' reveals how his own thinking remained stamped with the very usages of which he seemed so critical:

> For the ladies, whenever some comparison seemed to turn out unfavourable to their sex, were able to utter a suspicion that we, the male analysts, had been unable to overcome certain deeply-rooted prejudices against what was feminine, and that this was being paid for in the partiality of our researches. We, on the other hand, had no difficulty in avoiding impoliteness. We had only to say: 'This doesn't apply to *you*. You're the exception; on this point you're more masculine than feminine'. (Freud, 1973:150)

A final, and interesting point about Freud's theory of sexuality is his conviction, (of which he spoke in one of his last papers, and which applied equally to men and women, although it had different consequences for each) of the existence at the core of the individual of a 'bedrock' that rendered sexual satisfaction and the reconciliation of both men and women to their bisexuality virtually impossible. It is as if men are condemned to protest forever against any kind of passivity, particularly in relation to men, while women must mourn forever the penis they cannot have.

Freud's work is shot through with the consciousness of biology and its importance. This gives his work at times a contradictory and ambiguous character. Sometimes he seems to be addressing the problem of the psychological consequences of biology and how the psyche of the individual is built on a biological base; at others he seems rather to use biological analogies and metaphors. The difficulties that arise sometimes have to do with the absence of an adequate recognized language, and Freud himself refers to the problems of conceptualizing his thought within the then existing scientific language. Richard Wollheim (1971) has suggested that Freud's theory is built round a 'form of biological learning, in which unpleasure is the teacher'. Frank Sulloway (1979), another recent interpreter of Freud, has emphasized Freud's Darwinian and evolutionist legacy. In Darwinian vein Freud was highly teleological (that is he saw processes in terms of their ends or purposes), and he was constantly mindful of the fact that although sexuality is for the individual simply a source of personal pleasure and the satisfaction or relief of desire, it also serves a racial purpose, the continuation of the species:

> Since the penis...owes its extraordinarily high narcissistic cathexis[1] to its organic significance for the propagation of the species, the catastrophe of the Oedipus complex (the abandonment of incest and the institution of conscience and morality) may be regarded as a victory of the race over the individual. (Freud, 1977:331)

Of course this means that the clitoris becomes a total mystery:

> The clitoris, with its virile character, continues to function in later female sexual life in a manner which is very variable and which is certainly not yet satisfactorily understood. We do not, of course, know the biological basis of these peculiarities in women; and still less are we able to assign to them any teleological purpose. (Freud, 1977:374)

So part of Freud's attitude to the clitoris may be because for him it served no 'racial' purpose; although it is doubtful whether this kind of socio-biological argument may legitimately be used to explain the development of the individual psyche.

JULIET MITCHELL

I hope that the above section will have indicated the kinds of ambiguity that arise in Freud's work around the issue of the relationship between the biological and the psychic. Burniston, Mort and Weedon have gone further than I have done in insisting that in Freud's own work 'the structuring of the Oedipal triangle is...based on anatomical rather than social privilege' (1978:111). Richard Wollheim (1971) and Frank Sulloway (1979) have based their readings on the more biologistic side of Freud's work. Juliet Mitchell in *Psychoanalysis and Feminism* (1974) on the other hand sought to retrieve Freud from biologism by using the structuralism of Louis Althusser and the work of Jacques Lacan, a French psychoanalyst who emphasized the importance of language and of the symbolic in his approach to Freud.

Why was it important for her as a Marxist and a feminist, to move away from a biologistic interpretation of Freud? 'Biologism' must be unacceptable to the progressively minded because it denies, or is usually used as an argument to deny, the possibility of change. Women, or the black races, or the Jews are said to possess certain characteristics that derive from their biology. So, for example, women were said to be prone to hysteria *because* they have wombs. Juliet Mitchell effected the rehabilitation of Freud by presenting him as the theorist of the way in which the infant, 'a small human animal', achieves the entry into *culture*. A *social* not a biological process occurs. This process is the social construction of gender, whereby the infant internalizes the characteristics of 'masculinity' or 'femininity'. This gender identity has no one-to-one relation to biological sex differences, and so – to take an extreme example – it is possible for trans-sexual men to experience a fundamental conviction of their 'femininity'.

But, whereas there are many passages in Freud's work that are hard to read as anything other than assertions that the actual little boy is threatened with an actual loss of a real penis, and that the little girl is objectively inferior because her clitoris is actually an inferior penis, for Louis Althusser (following Lacan) and for Juliet Mitchell (following them both) the penis is not a penis but is the symbolic Phallus: 'the very mark of human desire', a phallus that represents the very notion of exchange itself' (Mitchell, 1974:395). In this way she appears to transform Freud's theory from a theory about how things are biologically *and* socially, into a theory of the way things are in 'patriarchal society'. Yet since she also accepts the view of both Freud and Engels that equates human civilization with this same patriarchy, she does in effect universalize both the theory and women's oppression. Forever and a day the Phallus is and must be the dominating *symbol of power* around which the creation of sexual difference is organized.

This is perhaps a difficult concept that deserves further attention. Juliet Mitchell argues that the 'anatomical distinction' between the sexes is not biologically significant. But:

> to Freud society demands of the psychological bisexuality of both sexes that one sex attain a preponderance of femininity, the other of masculinity: man and woman are made in culture. (Mitchell, 1974:131)

Juliet Mitchell has developed this line of argument in a book review (Mitchell, 1980) and to me it seems a strange one. Firstly it is *assumed* as something that need not be proven or argued that the biological differences (which do exist) between women and men are somehow insufficient to ensure the reproduction of the species. Secondly, '*masculinity and feminity only exist by virtue of their difference from one another*' (Mitchell, 1980). This statement translates the linguistic theory which Lacan imports into Freud very directly into the realm of the psychic. To see a system (of whatever kind) as a structure is to emphasize the relationship of one part to another. Structural linguistics stresses also the *arbitrary* nature of the linguistic sign. (A word – for example the name for a quality such as 'red' – is arbitrary. Moreover, just as the colour 'red' can be defined only in relation to other colours, yellow, orange, brown, so words have meaning only in relation to other words.) When Juliet Mitchell translates this arbitrary nature of the sign from the sphere of linguistics to that of psychology, the differences between men and women completely float away from biology and become purely social constructs. This happens because society 'needs' it to (a trace of Juliet Mitchell's functionalism here):

> So long as we reproduce ourselves as social beings *through a heterosexual relationship*, human society must distinguish between the sexes. It is because of this fundamental social situation that we need to feel ourselves as predominantly men or women. . .*for human society to exist at all*, men and women must be marked as different from each other. [my italics] (Mitchell, 1980:234-5)

Yet the logic of this locks us as securely within the structures of phallic power as does 'biologism'. Instead of simply accepting certain biological distinctions between the sexes, of which the psychological and cultural consequences are not necessarily very great (we do not really know how important they are) we appear condemned perpetually and for all time to recreate – or to *create* – the distinction *culturally* because otherwise we could not survive *biologically*, or could not survive at least as distinctively human. Thus the touchstone of human culture itself becomes the difference between 'masculine' and 'feminine'. Strangely, this is both wholly arbitrary and absolutely inevitable. It seems odd to demolish the tyranny of biology only to put in its place an imperative equally tyrannical and unalterable. And I question whether the whole of human culture should necessarily be seen as resting primarily and predominantly on the creation of heterosexuality in this way.

Psychoanalysis and Feminism is both a polemic and a theoretical work. Just as Freud deceivingly slips from detailed theoretical investigation to speculative generalization, so Juliet Mitchell fluctuates between polemic and theory in a fashion that masks some of the weaknesses in her arguments. There is a slippage, for example, from her account of the Oedipus complex to a contentious ideological statement when she writes:

> The women's task is to *reproduce* society, the man's to go out and *produce* new developments. There is an obvious link between the security of Oedipal father-love (the girl's destiny) and the happy hearth and home of later years. (Mitchell, 1974:118)

To say this is to argue that the sexual division of labour as we know it in an industrial capitalist society has some *permanent* correspondence with the creation of 'masculinity' and 'femininity'.

Both Burniston, Mort and Weedon (1978) and Cora Kaplan in her brilliant article on Kate Millett (Kaplan, 1979) criticize *Psychoanalysis and Feminism* on two major points. On the one hand there is Juliet Mitchell's determinism:

> Freudian theory, with its emphasis on repetition and reproduction of ideological positions, emphasizes, perhaps too heavily, the unalterable distance between gender positions so that they remain rather like Marvell's 'Definition of Love' stuck at distant poles, 'begotten by Despair/Upon Impossibility'. (Kaplan, 1979:9)

Secondly, ideology and the economy are radically separated; the feminist struggle is against ideology, the socialist struggle against the capitalist infrastructure. There is a further point to be made about the political conclusions to *Psychoanalysis and Feminism:* that is, that they are characterized by voluntarism. Juliet Mitchell wrenches an optimistic, 'revolutionary' conclusion from her arguments when they do not support it. She asserts that a cultural revolution is just around the corner – patriarchy like capitalism is in its death-throes. The arguments to support this prediction appear to run as follows: in capitalism the patriarchy is mediated through the nuclear family, which is all that remains of the formerly elaborate kinship structures (in this respect she follows Talcott Parsons and other mainstream – and right-wing – functionalist sociologists). Yet capitalism also hastens the disintegration of the nuclear family. This in turn implies that patriarchy itself is disintegrating since it cannot survive without the structural support of the nuclear family. (This last assumption is never argued through and Mitchell does not explain why patriarchy could not be mediated through other institutions such as schools and the law.) She argues that patriarchy is disintegrating because the exchange of women and the old kinship relations are no longer *needed* and her political conclusion is that therefore the time is ripe for their overthrow in an autonomous struggle of women against ideology.

Yet Juliet Mitchell recognizes that the arrival of socialism does not necessarily ensure the demise of patriarchy, hence her insistence on the autonomy of the struggle against ideology. At the same time this recognition weakens the logic of the earlier part of her argument which suggested that capitalism and the partriarchy were so intertwined that they would fall together. And this optimistic scenario is supported by 'evidence' from the experience of the Second World War in Britain, which, she asserts, saw the virtual (temporary) cessation of the nuclear family with the socialization of the means of survival. This is just wrong historically. Whatever the heightening of neighbourliness and communal living amongst evacuated workmates, in the army, and so on, I know of no evidence that family ties were correspondingly weakened. On the contrary, family support (for instance, grandmothers looking after children for mothers who went out to work) was often of vital importance, while the *idea* of family life as something the British were fighting to preserve was a very important one – hence the popularity of the Beveridge Report (Wilson, 1980).

THE POLITICAL CONSEQUENCES OF PSYCHOANALYSIS

The underlying assumption never really questioned by feminists who have followed Juliet Mitchell in exploring the relevance of psychoanalysis for feminist theory has been this: since the subordination of women is so heavily mediated through and in the private realm of marriage and other sexual relationships, in the family, in the reduction of women to sexual stereotypes, and in the threat of rape and generalized sexual violence, the overriding political imperative for feminists must be the immediate struggle against these practices.[2] Part of the Marxist heritage is the belief that political struggles have to be informed by a theory that will enable us to understand the nature of our exploitation/oppression/subordination. It is argued by feminists sympathetic to psychoanalysis that psychoanalysis is *the* theory of the construction of the sexual identity and gender relations; since it emphasizes the social construction of gender it must be the theory feminists need.

It is implied that psychoanalysis enables us to understand how we internalize an oppressive ideology. This is turn assumes (and Juliet Mitchell certainly *does* seem to assume) that women are in general *successfully* constructed as 'feminine' in our society. Women, according to her, *do* end up narcissistic, masochistic and the rest. This is rather curious since Freud himself laid great stress on the difficulty of this process and its incomplete success in many women. This appears to me an unproven, certainly an under-researched area. Feminists who have talked with young teenage working-class girls appear to reach contradictory conclusions (McRobbie, 1978; Cowie and Lees) but it does seem as if girls experience heterosexuality and marriage as inevitable rather than desirable. Social pressures of a direct kind as much as the internalization emphasized by psychoanalysis seem to ensure heterosexuality,[3] as well as a desire to be 'normal' which is not quite the same as 'feeling' feminine. But I hesitate to interpret the small amount of evidence available, and would simply suggest that it is a more unknown quantity than psychoanalytic theorists allow.

Even to the extent that women *do* internalize 'femininity', psychoanalysis, while of some use in explaining how this comes about, certainly does not give us much idea how we might escape. In this respect, psychoanalytic theory is odd in its mingling of the highly particular (the details of an individual's biography to elucidate an individual's current psychological state) with the universal and general (the general 'law' of the Phallus, and the necessity for the individual – and for all individuals – of entering culture via the Oedipus complex enacted in the nuclear family). At both these levels it misses the historically specific; that is, it can be 'true' of one individual and of all human history; it has little to say about one particular historical period. This makes it especially difficult to integrate with Marxism, since Marxism precisely deals with what is socially particular at a given historical period (Burniston, Mort and Weedon, 1978:127). Although many such attempts at integration have been made, this latest feminist one seems, like the rest, destined to failure. The result has often been in recent years an effective withdrawal from or abandonment of Marxism. (I am not making a value judgement on this score; simply suggesting that it has happened.)

Lacanian theory does not confront the problem of what happens to the individual psyche when family patterns change. Freud's work was at least solidly based on clinical studies of the then contemporary nineteenth-century bourgeois nuclear family. But the family changes constantly. The generalizing abstractions of Lacan simply do not help us to understand these profound changes which must surely have some significance for the social construction of the individual. This appears to me another fascinating area unexplored by psychoanalysis. May we not be living in a period in which the construction of sexed identity is altering in important ways?

More generally feminist interest in psychoanalysis has not in practice led to a sharpening of feminist political struggle. On the contrary it has validated reactionary positions amongst feminists. I've already given an example of how these surface in *Psychoanalysis and Feminism*. It also appears to me that psychoanalysis has been the justification for some feminists to assert anew that the sexual division of labour presents no problems for feminists; that what is needed is to reassert the value of women's work (i.e. domestic labour) rather than seeking to socialize it; that careers for women may be irrelevant to feminism, even a result of penis-envy. I cannot cite written evidence for this. The statement may therefore be open to the criticism that it is unfair, contentious, distorted, or reliant on a kind of gossip of the women's movement to which only some are privy and that it is therefore elitist. But I am anxious to share with others my fear that such positions are returning; to me they seem to remark a return to constricting images of women accepted by feminists and non feminists alike after 1945 and before women's liberation (Wilson, 1980). If my fears are unfounded, I hope that women will refute them. If they are justified I hope that women who hold such views will commit them to paper and argue them out in open debate. So far they have surfaced only as a kind of unease; for example, in discussions of divisions between mothers and non-mothers. Liz Heron in a succinct and wholly sisterly discussion of her similar worries on this score writes:

> In the early days of the (women's) movement, feminists with children discovered their oppression and had the support of their sisters in throwing off guilt and finding independence. Those founding mothers were striving to challenge the mystique – and the material realities – that made them prisoners, to live like those of us who weren't hemmed in by maternity. But their counterparts of today appear to be reversing the process, moving away from us and melting back into motherhood... Will we move motherhood back to centre-stage? Bathe it in the glow of that old insidious prestige, that status of 'real womanhood'? Will we again pick up the ideological baggage we've fought for the last decade to discard? (Heron, 1980:5)

Another rather different yet related problem about the appropriation by feminists of psychoanalytic theory is that it is used to close up further investigation into the construction of gender:

> From a feminist reading of antropology we learned that the social meaning of maleness and femaleness is constructed through kinship rules which prescribe patterns of sexual dominance and subordination. From psychoanalysis we learned how these kinship rules become inscribed on the unconscious psyche of the female child via the traumatic re-orientation of sexual desire within the Oedipal phase away from the mother and towards the father ('the law of the father'). (Alexander and Taylor, 1980:161)

If we have really 'learned' this with such finality, there seems nothing more to be done about it, and further theoretical discussion seems pointless. I, though, hope I have demonstrated that we cannot really give psychoanalysis this doctrinal status. I would also argue that this kind of determinism can only have pessimistic implications for feminism, suggesting as it does unchanging, static patterns of human psychic development.

I suggest that a more interesting point to discuss might be how we *are* to engage in struggle around issues to do with consciousness and its formation. Feminists drawing on a psychoanalytic perspective have had little to say about this. But what forms of political struggle does psychoanalysis suggest for feminism?

Another point, and an important one for feminists, is that feminist theoretical writings drawing on psychoanalysis have had remarkably little to say about homosexuality and lesbianism. If anything, psychoanalysis seems to have been used implicitly to justify heterosexual relationships at a period in the women's movement when women who wanted to relate to men sexually felt under pressure from feminists who were lesbians. It is of interest in this context that Juliet Mitchell fudges the issue of Freud's attitude to homosexuality. In seeking to reassure feminists that Freud's attitude was not one of hostility she quotes this famous letter to the mother of a homosexual son. This is certainly a very kind and sensible letter, in which Freud tries to comfort the unhappy mother:

> Homosexuality is assuredly no advantage, but it is nothing to be ashamed of, no vice, no degradation; it cannot be classified as an illness; we consider it to be a variation of the sexual function, *produced by a certain arrest of the sexual development*. [my italics] (Freud, 1961:277)

But in omitting the significant last phrase Juliet Mitchell might be taxed with evasion of an admittedly difficult issue.[4]

Another important question not being asked by Lacanian feminists is, what is the role of the orthodox institutions of psychoanalysis; and what is the role of the psychoanalytic therapy, and can it be changed. Another point of interest: there is a strong interest among feminists today in 'radical' and 'feminist' therapy, but this interest and the ongoing work of, for example, the Women's Therapy Centre, has remained apart from the body of theory I have been discussing; indeed the very concept of feminist therapy has been severely criticized by at least one Freudian feminist (Lipschitz, 1978; and in reply, Women's Therapy Centre Study Group, 1979). Yet after all, the issue of therapy is an important one. As Rosalind Delmar wrote:

> The prevalence of psychic distress in our society, which reproduces neurosis on a mass scale – the figures speak for themselves, represent...what could be interpreted as a massive 'flight into illness'. Any political movement struggling to change society has to confront this striking phenomenon. (Delmar, 1975:21)

CAN THE IRON LAW OF THE PHALLUS BE OVERTHROWN?

Even the most meticulous critics of Freud within the contemporary debate (for example Burniston, Mort and Weedon) usually back off at the last moment from a wholesale dismissal of Freud. I too believe, following Michèle Barrett (1980:58) that since Freud's work is not internally consistent or coherent, but is, as some would say, a very 'fractured' body of work, we can if we wish retain some of his insights without buying the whole package, although I do feel there are dangers in this eclecticism. I accept the psychoanalytic account of the way in which sexual identity gets constructed – haltingly and with difficulty – and that, as we know it, it is constructed in the context of male power. Freud often describes very accurately the construction of that male power at the psychic level. But in the Freudian, and even more fatally in the Lacanian account, the organization of difference not only does but *must* occur around the dominant symbol of the Phallus, which also represents male power; although in many of these discussions, the Phallus becomes no more than a metaphor, be it for male power or for desire. Yet it is possible to imagine that personal identity could be, in a society in which male power did not dominate, organized around some other principle. There could be an adult sexual identity that was constructed around a different symbolic differentiator.

In conclusion, I wish to look again at some of the weaknesses of recent feminist psychoanalytic perspectives in a general way; and to suggest some possible political directions the debate might more usefully take.

I suggested earlier that because the subordination of women occurs in a privatized way it has often been assumed that the struggle against it necessarily consists of for the most part private struggles – to change men, to change relationships with men, or (an entirely different but equally problematic solution) to abandon all relationships with men and sexualize relationships with other women. Or else, individual children should be reared differently. And/or collective living relationships should be set up. Such attempts represent an important part of the feminist struggle. They will nonetheless remain privatized themselves unless the women's movement as a political movement socializes and collectivizes this struggle. This would mean a return to the largely abandoned arena of the family and the construction of campaigns to change the family at different levels and in different ways; social policy, income maintenance, child care provision, obstetric practices are areas in which such a campaign could operate (and campaigns do flourish in these areas, although they are not ideologically linked to the extent that they might be).

The experience of Woman's Aid suggests that social provision may often come before individual change, or that certainly the two go together. It's hard even to say it in the current economic climate, but today we need more than ever nonsexist social provision for many needs currently catered for by the family. Unless the family *is* radically changed (not abolished) I do not see how we can develop different child rearing practices in which a sexual identity is constructed that gives more conscious and creative control to the child than s/he currently enjoys, and which is not so hysterically obsessed with one particular form of difference – an unstable form, moreover, since the cultural construction of 'masculine' and feminine' is a massive edifice elevated on an arguably insignificant base. In other words, I am arguing for social solutions to the oppression we experience as private.

This does not mean that I reject in individual given circumstances the individual solution of psychoanalysis or therapy. Mental disorder is a serious problem. Even those of us who have no crippling 'symptoms' must often experience a loss of energy, a paralysis of the will and an apathy generated by the kind of society in which we live. But feminists who take psychoanalysis seriously will have at some stage to confront the sexism of the psychoanalytic movement and its institutional practices far more radically than has yet been done, just as feminist doctors have had to confront the medical hierarchy, and feminist social workers the social services hierarchy. One of the most serious weaknesses of the contemporary feminist psychoanalytic debate has been its failure for the most part (so far as I know) to engage in therapeutic practice.

Perhaps precisely the attraction of Lacan's 'law of the father' has been the sense that it *is* inescapable.[5] It has seemed that only through the gate of the Oedipal trauma could we become adult women and men and save ourselves either from a perpetuation of 'polymorph perverse' infantile sexuality; or from the psychotic symbiosis of the pre-Oedipal mother-infant relationship, at best a narcissistic mirroring. There is a sinister ring to the language used by Althusser to discuss this point:

> (the little girl) doubly accepts that she has not the same right (phallus) as her father, since her mother has not this right (no phallus)...But she gains ...the promise of a large right, the full right of a woman when she grows up, if she will grow up accepting the Law of Human Order. (Althusser, 1971:197)

There are similarities here to the language used in political debate since time immemorial, whereby anarchy on the one hand and law and order on the other are posed as antagonistic opposites in order to discredit anarchy, i.e. chaos. Feminists should know better than to be taken in by this kind of language which constantly seeks to mask the progressive or revolutionary implications of rebellion; rebellion is always stigmatized as flouting law and order and producing chaos.

The last thing feminists need is a theory that teaches them only to marvel anew at the constant recreation of the subjective reality of subordination and which reasserts male domination more securely than ever within theoretical discourse. Psychoanalysis is of interest in its account of sexual identity and its construction – indeed, in many ways it is fascinating. More useful to contemporary feminists may be theories of social change that speak to aspects of the self not harnessed to the Phallic taskmaster. To change the conditions of work – in the world and in the home – might do more for our psyches as well as for our pockets than an endless contemplation of how we came to be chained.

NOTES

1 Freud nowhere gave a rigorous theoretical definition of 'cathexis' (Laplanche and Pontalis, 1973:63). Broadly speaking, it means the loading with nervous energy of an idea, symbol or event. We may say that the infant 'cathects' the mother when he invests her with the eroticized love arising out of his sensual satisfaction at the breast. A foot fetishist 'cathects' feet, or shoes. Or we may say that cathexis is the disposition of energy, or its distribution, in relationships with objects and with the self.

2 In their editorial to an issue of *m/f* Parveen Adams, Beverly Brown and Elizabeth Cowie appear to be raising a rather similar question (Adams, Brown and Cowie, 1981:3).
3 See Mary McIntosh (1981), who makes a similar point in relation to income maintenance.
4 It is noteworthy that Paul Hirst uses the same quotation in an article in *m/f*, perpetuating the crucial omission (Hirst, 1981:112).
5 I am indebted to Angie Mason in this section.

Thanks to those who read and commented on this article for me when it was in draft form: Angie Mason, Julia Naish, Marie Zaphiriou, Maxine Molyneux, Michèle Barrett, Victoria Greenwood and Wendy Hollway.

REFERENCES

Adams, Parveen, Brown, Beverly and Cowie, Elizabeth (1981) Editorial *m/f* nos 5 and 6.
Alexander, Sally and Taylor, Barbara (1980) 'In Defence of Patriarchy' *New Statesman* February 1.
Althusser, Louis (1971) 'Freud and Lacan' in *Lenin and Philosophy* London: New Left Books.
Barrett, Michèle (1980) *Women's Oppression Today: Problems in Marxist Feminist Analysis* London: New Left Books.
Burniston, Steve, Mort, Frank and Weedon, Christine (1978) 'Psychoanalysis and the Cultural Acquisition of Sexuality and Subjectivity', in Women's Studies Group, Centre for Contemporary Cultural Studies (1978).
Cowie, Celia and Lees, Susan (1981) 'On the Slagheap: The Oppression of Working Class Girls' (unpublished paper).
Delmar, Rosalind (1975) 'Psychoanalysis and Feminism' *Red Rag* no. 8, February.
Freud, Sigmund (1961) *Letters of Sigmund Freud 1973–1939* edited by Ernst Freud London: The Hogarth Press.
Freud, Sigmund (1973) *New Introductory Lecutres on Psychoanalysis* Harmondsworth: Penguin.
Freud, Sigmund (1977) *On Sexuality* Harmondsworth: Penguin.
Heron, Liz (1980) 'The Mystique of Motherhood' *Time Out* November 21.
Kaplan, Cora (1979) 'Radical Feminism and Literature: Rethinking Millett's *Sexual Politics*' *Red Letters* no. 9.
Laplanche, J. and Pontalis, J-B (1973) *The Language of Psychoanalysis* London: The Hogarth Press.
Hirst, Paul (1981) 'Psychoanalysis and Social Relations' *m/f* nos 5 and 6.
Lipschitz, Susan (1978) '"The Personal is Political": The Problem of Feminist Therapy' *m/f* no. 2.
McIntosh, Mary (1981) 'Feminism and Social Policy' *Critical Social Policy* no. 1.
McRobbie, Angela (1978) 'Working Class Girls and the Culture of Femininity' in Women's Studies Group, Centre for Contemporary Cultural Studies (1978).
Mitchell, Juliet (1974) *Psychoanalysis and Feminism* London: Allen Lane.
Mitchell, Juliet (1980) 'On the Differences between Men and Women' *New Society* 12 June.
Sulloway, Frank J. (1979) *Freud: Biologist of the Mind* London: Burnett Books.

Wilson, Elizabeth (1980) *Only Halfway to Paradise* London: Tavistock Publications.
Wollheim, Richard (1971) *Freud* London: Fontana.
Women's Studies Group, Centre for Contemporary Cultural Studies (1978) *Women Take Issue* London: Hutchinson.
Women's Therapy Centre Study Group (1979) Letter in Reply to Susan Lipschitz *m/f* no. 3.

13

Jacqueline Rose

Femininity and its Discontents

Is psychoanalysis a 'new orthodoxy' for feminism? Or does it rather represent the surfacing of something difficult and exceptional but important for feminism, which is on the verge (once again) of being lost? I will argue that the second is the case, and that the present discarding of psychoanalysis in favour of forms of analysis felt as more material in their substance and immediately political in their effects (Wilson 1981, 1982; Barrett 1980; Sayers 1982) is a *return* to positions whose sensed inadequacy for feminism produced a gap in which psychoanalysis could – fleetingly – find a place. What psychoanalysis offered up in that moment was by no means wholly satisfactory and it left many problems unanswered or inadequately addressed, but the questions which it raised for feminism are crucial and cannot, I believe, be approached in the same way, or even posed, from anywhere else. To ask what are the political implications of psychoanalysis for feminism seems to me, therefore, to pose the problem the wrong way round. Psychoanalysis is already political for feminism – political in the more obvious sense that it came into the arena of discussion in response to the internal needs of feminist debate, and political again in the wider sense that the repudiation of psychoanalysis by feminism can be seen as linking up with the repeated marginalization of psychoanalysis within our general culture, a culture whose oppressiveness for women is recognized by us all.

Before going into this in more detail, a separate but related point needs to be made, and that is the peculiarity of the psychoanalytic object with which feminism engages. Thus to ask for effects from psychoanalysis in the arena of political practice (Wilson 1981) is already to assume that psychoanalytic practice is a-political. Recent feminist debate has tended to concentrate on theory (Freud's theory of femininity whether or not psychoanalysis can provide an account of women's subordination). This was as true of Juliet Mitchell's defence of Freud (Mitchell 1974) as it has been of many of the more recent replies. The result has been that psychoanalysis has been pulled away from its own practice. Here the challenge to psychoanalysis by feminists has come from alternative forms of therapy (feminist therapy and co-counselling). But it is worth noting that the way psychoanalysis is engaged with in much recent criticism already divests it of its practical effects at this level, or rather takes this question as settled in advance (the passing reference to the chauvinism of the psychoanalytic institution, the assumption that psychoanalysis depoliticizes the woman analysand). In this context, therefore, the common theory/practice dichotomy has a very specific meaning in that psychoanalysis can only be held accountable to 'practice' if it is assumed not to be one, or if the form of its practice is taken to have no purchase on political life. This assumes, for example, that there is no politics of the psychoanalytic institution itself, something to which I will return.

Both these points – the wider history of how psychoanalysis has been placed or discarded by our dominant culture, and the detaching of psychoanalysis from its practical and institutional base – are related, inasmuch as they bring into focus the decisions and selections which have already been made about psychoanalysis before the debate even begins. Some of these decisions I would want to argue are simply wrong; such as the broad accusation of chauvinism levelled against the psychoanalytic institution as a whole. In this country at least, the significant impetus after Freud passed to two women – Anna Freud and Melanie Klein. Psychoanalysis in fact continues to be one of the few of our cultural institutions which does not professionally discriminate against women, and in which they could even be said to predominate. This is not of course to imply that the presence of women inside an institution is necessarily feminist, but women have historically held positions of influence inside psychoanalysis which they have been mostly denied in other institutions where their perceived role as 'carers' has relegated them to a subordinate position (e.g. nursing), and it is the case that the first criticisms of Freud made by Melanie Klein can be seen to have strong affinities with later feminist repudiation of this theory.

For those who are hesitating over what appears as the present 'impasse' between feminism and psychoanalysis, the more important point, however, is to stress the way that psychoanalysis is being presented for debate, that is, the decisions which have already been made before we are asked to decide. Much will depend, I suspect, on whether one sees psychoanalysis as a new form of hegemony on the part of the feminist intelligentsia, or whether it is seen as a theory and practice which has constantly been relegated to the outside of dominant institutions and mainstream radical debate alike – an 'outside' with which feminism, in its challenge to both these traditions, has its own important forms of allegiance.

COMPONENTS OF THE CULTURE

In England, the relationship between the institution of psychoanalysis and its more general reception has always been complex, if not fraught. Thus in 1968, Perry Anderson could argue (Anderson 1968) that major therapeutic and theoretical advances inside the psychoanalytic institutions (chiefly in the work of Melanie Klein) had gone hand in hand with, and possibly even been the cause of, the isolation of psychoanalysis from the general culture, the slowness of its dissemination (until the Pelican Freud started to appear in 1974, you effectively had to join a club to read *The Standard Edition* of Freud's work), and the failure of psychoanalysis to effect a decisive break with traditions of empiricist philosophy, reactionary ethics, and an elevation of literary 'values', which he saw as the predominant features of our cultural life. Whether or not one accepts the general 'sweep' of his argument, two points from that earlier polemic seem relevant here.

Firstly, the link between empiricist traditions of thought and the resistance to the psychoanalytic concept of the unconscious. Thus psychoanalysis, through its attention to symptoms, slips of the tongue and dreams (that is, to what *insists* on being spoken against what is *allowed* to be said) appears above all as a challenge to the self-evidence and banality of everyday life and language, which have also, importantly, constituted the specific targets of feminism. If we use the (fairly loose) definition which Anderson provided for empiricism as the unsystematic registration of things as they are and the refusal of forms of analysis which penetrate beneath the surface of observable social phenomena, the link to feminism can be made (Anderson 1966). For feminism has always challenged the observable 'givens' of women's presumed natural qualities and their present social position alike (especially when the second is justified in terms of the first). How often has the 'cult of common sense', the notion of what is obviously the case or in the nature of things, been used in reactionary arguments against feminist attempts to demand social change? For Anderson in his article of 1968, this espousal of empiricist thinking provided one of the chief forms of resistance to Freud, so deeply committed is psychoanalysis to penetrating behind the surface and conscious manifestations of everyday experience.

Secondly, the relationship between this rejection of psychoanalysis and a *dearth* within British intellectual culture of a Marxism which could both theorize and criticize capitalism as a social totality. This second point received the strongest criticism from within British Marxism itself, but what matters here is the fact that both Marxism *and* psychoanalysis were identified as forms of radical enquiry which were unassimilable to bourgeois norms. In the recent feminist discussion, however – notably in the pages of *Feminist Review* – Marxism and psychoanalysis tend to be posited as antagonistic; Marxism arrogating to itself the concept of political practice and social change, psychoanalysis being accused of inherent conservatism which rationalizes and perpetuates the subordination of women under capitalism, or else fails to engage with that subordination at the level of material life.

In order to understand this, I think we have to go back to the earlier moment. For while the argument that Marxism was marginal or even alien to British thought was strongly repudiated, the equivalent observation about psychoanalysis seems to have been accepted and was more or less allowed to stand. This was perhaps largely because no-one on the left rushed forward to claim a radicalism committed to psychoanalytic thought.

New Left Review had itself been involved in psychoanalysis in the early 60s, publishing a number of articles by Cooper and Laing (Cooper 1963, 1965; Laing 1962, 1964); and there is also a strong tradition, which goes back through Christopher Caudwell in 1930s, of Marxist discussion of Freud. But the main controversy unleashed by Anderson's remarks centred around Marxism; Anderson himself in an earlier article had restricted his own critique to the lack of Marxism and classical sociology in British culture making no reference to psychoanalysis at all (Anderson 1964; see also Thompson 1965). After 1968, *New Left Review* published Althusser's famous article on Lacan (Althusser 1969, 1971) and one article by Lacan (Lacan 1968), but for the most part the commitment to psychoanalysis was not sustained even by that section of the British Left which had originally argued for its importance.

Paradoxically, therefore, the idea that psychoanalysis was isolated or cut off from the general culture could be accepted to the extent that this very marginalization was being *reproduced* in the response to the diagnosis itself. Thus the link between Marxism and Freudian psychoanalysis, as the twin poles of a failed radicalism at the heart of British culture, was broken. Freud was cast aside at the very moment when resistance to his thought had been identified as symptomatic of the restrictiveness of bourgeois culture. Juliet Mitchell was the exception. Her defence of freud in 1970 and 1974 (Mitchell 1970, 1974) needs, I think, to be placed first in this context, as a claim for the fundamentally anti-empiricist and radical nature of Freudian thought. That this claim was made via feminism (could perhaps *only* be made via feminism) says something about the ability of feminism to challenge the orthodoxies of both left and right.

Thus the now familiar duo of 'psychoanalysis and feminism' has an additonal and crucial political meaning. Not just psychoanalysis *for* feminism or feminism *against* psychoanalysis, but Freudian psychoanalysis and feminism *together* as two forms of thought which relentlessly undermine the turgid resistance of common sense language to all forms of conflict and political change. For me this specific sequence has been ironically or negatively confirmed (that is, it has been gone over again backwards) by one of the most recent attempts to relate psychoanalysis to socialism (Rustin, 1982) through a combination of F.R. Leavis and Melanie Klein – the very figures whose standing had been taken as symptomatic of that earlier resistance to the most radical aspects of Freudian thought (Klein because of the confinement of her often challenging ideas to the psychoanalytic institution itself, Leavis because of the inappropriate centrality which he claimed for the ethics of literary form and taste). I cannot go into the details of Rustin's argument here, but its ultimate conservatism for feminism is at least clear: the advancement of 'mothering' and by implication of the role of women as mothers, as the psychic basis on which socialism can be built (the idea that psychoanalysis can *engender* socialism seems to be merely the flip side of the argument which accuses psychoanalysis of producing social conformity).

This history may appear obscure to many feminists who have not necessarily followed the different stages of these debates. But the diversion through this cultural map is, I think, important in so far as it can illustrate the ramifications of feminist discussion over a wider political spectrum, and also show how this discussion – the terms of the argument, the specific oppositions proposed – have in turn been determined by that wider spectrum itself.

Thus it will have crucial effects, for instance, whether psychoanalysis is discussed as an addition or supplement to Marxism (in relation to which it is then found *wanting*), or whether emphasis is laid on the concept of the unconscious. For while it is indeed correct that psychoanalysis was introduced into feminism as a theory which could rectify the inability of Marxism to address questions of sexuality, and that this move was complementary to the demand within certain areas of Marxism for increasing attention to the ideological determinants of our social being, it is also true that undue concentration on this aspect of the theory has served to cut off the concept of the unconscious, or at least to displace it from the centre of the debate. (This is graphically illustrated in Michèle Barrett's book, *Women's Oppression Today*, in which the main discussion of psychoanalysis revolves around the concept of ideology, and that of the unconscious is left to a note appended at the end of the chapter (Barrett, 1980).)

FEMININITY AND ITS DISCONTENTS

One result of this emphasis is that psychoanalysis is accused of 'functionalism', that is, it is accepted as a theory of how women are psychically 'induced' into femininity by a patriarchal culture, and is then accused of perpetuating that process, either through a practice assumed to be *prescriptive* about women's role (this is what women *should* do), or because the very effectiveness of the account as a *description* (this is what is demanded of women, what they are *expected* to do) leaves no possibility of change.

It is the aspect of Juliet Mitchell's book which seems to have been taken up most strongly by feminists who have attempted to follow through the political implications of psychoanalysis as a critique of patriarchy or, by extension, as a means of explaining how women internalize their role. Thus Gayle Rubin, following Mitchell, uses psychoanalysis for a general critique of a patriarchal culture which is predicated on the exchange of women by men (Rubin 1975: for criticisms of the use of Levi-Strauss on which this reading is based see Cowie 1978 and MacCormack and Strathern 1980). Nancy Chodorow shifts from Freud to later object-relations theory to explain how women's childcaring role is perpetuated through the earliest relationship between a mother and her child, which leads in her case to a demand for a fundamental change in how childcare is organized between women and men in our culture (Chodorow 1978). Although there are obvious differences between these two readings of psychoanalysis, they nonetheless share an emphasis on the social exchange of women, or the distribution of roles for women, across cultures: 'Women's mothering is one fo the few universal and enduring elements of the sexual division of labour' (Chodorow 1978:3).

The force of psychoanalysis is therefore (as Janet Sayers points out, Sayers, 1982) precisely that it gives an account of patriarchal culture as a trans-historical and cross-cultural force. It therefore conforms to the feminist demand for a theory which can explain women's subordination across specific cultures and different historical moments. Summing this up crudely, we could say that psychoanalysis adds sexuality to Marxism, where sexuality is felt to be lacking, and extends beyond Marxism where the attention to specific historical instances, changes in modes of production etc., is felt to leave something unexplained.

But all this happens at a cost, and that cost is the concept of the unconscious. What distinguishes psychoanalysis from sociological accounts of gender (hence for me the fundamental impasse of Nancy Chodorow's work) is that whereas for the latter, the internalization of norms is assumed roughly to work, the basic premise and indeed starting point of psychoanalysis is that it does not. The unconscious constantly reveals the 'failure' of identity. Because there is no continuity of psychic life, so there is no stability of sexual identity, no position for women (or for men) which is ever simply achieved. Nor does psychoanalysis see such 'failure' as a special-case inability or an individual deviancy from the norm. 'Failure' is not a moment to be regretted in a process of adaptation, or development into normality, which ideally takes its course (some of the earliest critics of Freud, such as Ernest Jones, did, however, give an account of development in just these terms). Instead 'failure' is something endlessly repeated and relived moment by moment throughout our individual histories. It appears not only in the symptom, but also in dreams, in slips of the tongue and in forms of sexual pleasure which are pushed to the sidelines of the norm. Feminism's affinity with psychoanalysis rests above all, I would argue, with this recognition that there is a resistance to identity which lies at the very heart of psychic life. Viewed in this way, psychoanalysis is no longer best understood as an account of how women are fitted into place (even this, note, is the charitable reading of Freud). Instead psychoanalysis becomes one of the few places in our culture where it is recognized as more than a fact of individual pathology that most women do not painlessly slip into their roles as women, if indeed they do at all. Freud himself recognized this increasingly in his work. In the articles which run from 1924 ('The Dissolution of the Oedipus Complex', Freud, 1924) to 1931 ('Female Sexuality', Freud, 1931), he moves from that famous, or rather infamous, description of the little girl struck with her 'inferiority' or 'injury' in the face of the anatomy of the little boy and wisely accepting her fate ('injury' as the *fact* of being feminine), to an account which quite explicitly describes the process of becoming 'feminine' as, 'injury' or 'catastrophe' for the complexity of her earlier psychic and sexual life ('injury' as its *price*).

Elizabeth Wilson (Wilson, 1981) and Janet Sayers (Sayers, 1982) are, therefore, in a sense correct to criiticize psychoanalysis when it is taken as a general theory of patriarchy or of gender identity, that is, as a theory which explains how women wholly internalize the very mode of being which is feminism's specific target of attack; but they have missed out half the (psychoanalytic) story. In fact the argument seems to be circular. Psychoanalysis is drawn in the direction of a general theory of culture or a sociological account of gender because these seem to lay greater emphasis on the presures of the 'outside' world, but it is this very pulling away from the psychoanalytic stress on the 'internal' complexity and difficulty of psychic life which produces the functionalism which is then criticized.

The argument about whether Frend is being 'prescriptive' or 'descriptive' about women (with its associated stress on the motives and morals of Freud himself) is fated to the extent that it is locked into this model. Many of us will be familiar with Freud's famous pronouncement that a woman who does not succeed in transforming activity to passivity, clitoris to vagina, mother for father, will fall ill. Yet psychoanalysis testifies to the fact that psychic illness or distress is in no sense the prerogative of women who 'fail' in this task. One of my students recently made the obvious but important point that we would be foolish to deduce from the external trappings of normality or conformity in a woman that all is in fact well. And Freud himself always stressed the psychic costs of the civilizing process for all (we can presumably include women in that 'all' even if at times he did not seem to do so).

All these aspects of Freud's work are subject to varying interpretation by analysts themselves. The first criticism of Freud's 'phallocentrism' came from inside psychoanalysis, from analysts such as Melanie Klein, Ernest Jones and Karen Horney who felt, contrary to Freud, that 'femininity' was a quality with its own impetus, subject to checks and internal conflict, but tending ultimately to fulfilment. For Jones, the little girl was 'typically receptive and acquisitive' from the outset (Jones, 1933, pp. 265); for Horney, there was from the beginning a 'wholly womanly' attachment to the father (Horney, 1924, 1967,[1] p. 53). For these analysts, this development might come to grief, but for the most part a gradual strengthening of the child's ego and her increasing adaptation to reality, should guarantee its course. Aspects of the little girl's psychic life which were resistant to this process (the famous 'active' or 'masculine' drives) were defensive. The importance of concepts such as the 'phallic phase' in Freud's description of infantile sexuality is not, therefore, that such concepts can be taken as the point of insertion of patriarchy (assimilation to the norm). Rather their importance lies in the way that they indicate, through their very artificiality, that something was being *forced*, and in the concept of psychic life with which they were accompanied. In Freud's work they went hand in hand with an increasing awareness of the difficulty, not to say impossibility, of the path to normality for the girl, and an increasing stress on the fundamental divisions, or splitting, of psychic life. It was those who challenged these concepts in the 1920s and 1930s who introduced the more normative stress on a sequence of development, and a coherent ego, back into the account.

I think we go wrong again, therefore, if we conduct the debate about whether Freud's account was developmental or not entirely in terms of his own writing. Certainly the idea of development is present at moments in his work. But it was not present *enough* for many of his contemporaries, who took up the issue and reinstated the idea of development precisely in relation to the sexual progress of the girl (her passage into womanhood).

'Psychoanalysis' is not, therefore, a single entity. Institutional divisions within psychoanalysis have turned on the very questions about the phallocentrism of analysts, the meaning of femininity, the sequence of psychic development and its norms, which have been the concern of feminists. The accusations came from analysts themselves. In the earlier debates, however, the reproach against Freud produced an account of femininity which was more, rather than less, normative than his own.

The politics of Lacanian psychoanalysis begins here. From the 1930s, Lacan saw his intervention as a return to the concepts of psychic division, splitting of the ego, and an endless (he called it 'insistant') pressure of the unconscious against any individual's pretension to a smooth and coherent psychic and sexual identity. Lacan's specific target was 'ego-psychology' in America, and what he saw as the dilution of psychoanalysis into a tool of social adaptation and control (hence the central emphasis on the concepts of the ego and identification which are often overlooked in discussions of his ideas). For Lacan, psychoanalysis does not offer an account of a developing ego which is 'not *necessarily* coherent' (Wilson, 1982). but of an ego which is 'necessarily *not* coherent', that is, which is always and persistently divided against itself.

Lacan could therefore be picked up by a Marxist like Althusser not because he offered a theory of adaptation to reality or of the individual's insertion into culture (Althusser added a note to the English translation of his paper on Lacan criticizing it for having implied such a reading. Althusser, 1969, 1971), but because the force of the unconscious in Lacan's interpretation of Freud was felt to undermine the mystifications of a bourgeois culture proclaiming its identity, and that of its subjects, to the world. The political use of Lacan's theory therefore stemmed from its assault on what English Marxists would call bourgeois 'individualism'. What the theory offered was a divided subject out of 'synch' with bourgeois myth. Feminists could legitimately object that the notion of psychic fragmentation was of little immediate political advantage to women struggling for the first time to find a voice, and trying to bring together the dissociated components of their life into a political programme. But this is a very different criticism of the political implications of psychoanalysis than the one which accuses it of forcing women into bland conformity with their expected role.

PSYCHOANALYSIS AND HISTORY/THE HISTORY OF PSYCHOANALYSIS

What, therefore, is the political purchase of the concept of the unconscious on women's lived experience and what can it say to the specific histories of which we form a part?

One of the objections which is often made against psychoanalysis is that it has no sense of history, and an inadequate grasp of its relationship to the concrete institutions which frame and determine our lives. For even if we allow for a moment the radical force of the psychoanalytic insight, the exclusiveness of limited availability of that insight tends to be turned, not against the culture or state which mostly resists its general (and publicly funded) dissemination,[2] but against psychoanalysis itself. The 'privatization' of psychoanalysis comes to mean that it only refers to the individual as private, and the concentration on the individual as private is then seen as reinforcing a theory which places itself above history and change.

Again I think that this question is posed back to front, and that we need to ask, not what psychoanalysis has to say about history, but rather what is the history of psychoanalysis, that is, what was the intervention of psychoanalysis into the institutions which, at the time of its emergence, were controlling women's lives? And what was the place of the unconscious, historically, in that? Paradoxically, the claim that psychoanalysis is a-historical dehistoricizes it. If we go back to the beginnings of psychoanalysis, it is clear that the concept of the unconscious was radical at exactly that level of social 'reality' with which it is so often assumed to have nothing whatsoever to do.

Recent work by feminist historians is of particular importance in this context. Judith Walkowitz, in her study of the Contagious Diseases Acts of the 1860s (Walkowitz, 1980) shows how state policy on public hygiene and the state's increasing control over casual labour, relied on a category of women as diseased (the suspected prostitute subjected to forcible examination and internment in response to the spread of venereal disease in the port towns). Carol Dyhouse has described how debates about educational opportunity for women constantly returned to their evidence of the female body (either the energy expended in their development towards sexual reproduction meant that women could not be educated, or education and the overtaxing of the brain would damage their reproductive capacity (Dyhouse, 1981).) In the birth control controversy, the Malthusian idea of controlling the reproduction, and by implication the sexuality, of the working class served to counter the idea that poverty could be reduced by the redistribution of wealth (MacLaren, 1978). Recurrently in the second half of the nineteenth century, in the period immediately prior to Freud, female sexuality became the focus of a panic about the effects of industrialization on the cohesion of the social body and its ability to comfortably reproduce itself. The importance of all this work (Judith Walkowitz makes this quite explicit) is that 'attitudes' towards women cannot be consigned to the sphere of ideology, assumed to have no purchase on material life, so deeply implicated was the concept of female sexuality in the legislative advancement of the state (Walkowitz, 1980).

Central to all of this was the idea that the woman was wholly responsible for the social well-being of the nation (questions of social division transmuted directly into the moral and sexual responsibility of subjects), or where she failed in this task, that she was disordered or diseased. The hysteric was either the over-educated woman, or else the woman indulging in non-procreative or uncontrolled sexuality (conjugal onanism), or again the woman in the lock hospitals which, since the eighteenth century, had been receiving categories refused by the general hospitals ('infectious diseases, fevers, children, maternity cases, mental disorders, venereal diseases', Walkowitz, 1980, p. 56). It was these hospitals which, at the time of the Contagious Diseases Acts, became the place of confinement for the diseased prostitute in a new form of collaborative relationship with the state.

This is where psychoanalysis begins. Although the situation was not identical in France, there are important links. Freud's earliest work was under Charcot at the Salpetrière Clinic in Paris, a hospital for women: 'five thousand neutrotic indigents, epileptics, and insane patients, many of whom were deemed incurable' (Veith, 1965, 1970, p. 229). The 'dregs' of society comprised the inmates of Salpetrière. (Psychoanalysis does not start in the Viennese parlour.) Freud was working under Charcot whose first contribution to the study of hysteria was to move it out of the category of sexual malingering and into that of a specific and accredited neurological disease. The problem with Charcot's work is that while he was constructing the symptomatology of the disease (turning it into a respected object of the medical institution), he was reinforcing it as a special category of behaviour, visible to the eye, and the result of a degenerate hereditary disposition.

Freud's intervention here was two-fold. Firstly, he questioned the visible evidence of the disease – the idea that you could know a hysteric by looking at her body, that is, by reading off the symptoms of nervous disability or susceptibility to trauma. Secondly (and this second move depended on the first), he rejected the idea that hysteria was an 'independent' clinical entity, by using what he uncovered in the treatment of the hysterical patient as the basis of his account of the unconscious and its universal presence in adult life.

The 'universalism' of Freud was not, therefore, an attempt to remove the subject from history; it stemmed from his challenge to the category of hysteria as a principle of classification for certain socially isolated and confined individuals, and his shifting of this category into the centre of everybody's psychic experience: 'Her hysteria can therefore be described as an acquired one, and it presupposed nothing more than the possession of what is probably a very wide-spread proclivity – the proclivity to acquire hysteria' (Freud, 1893–95, p. 121,[3] *p. 187*). The reason why the two moves are interdependent is because it was only by penetrating behind the visible symptoms of disorder and asking what it was that the symptom was trying to *say*, that Freud could uncover those unconscious desires and motives which he went on to expose in the slips, dreams and jokes of individuals paraded as normal. Thus the challenge to the entity 'hysteria', that is, to hysteria *as* an entity available for quite specific forms of social control, relies on the concept of the unconscious. 'I have attempted', wrote Freud, 'to meet the problem of hysterical attacks along a line other than *descriptive*' (my emphasis) (Freud, 1892–94, p. 137). Hence Freud's challenge to the visible, to the empirically self-evident, to the 'blindness of the seeing eye' (Freud, 1893–95, p. 117, *p. 181*). (Compare this with Charcot's photographs offered as the evidence of the disease.) It is perhaps this early and now mostly forgotten moment which can give us the strongest sense of the force of the unconscious as a concept against a fully social classification relying on empirical evidence as its rationale.

The challenge of psychoanalysis to empiricist forms of reasoning was therefore the very axis on which the fully historical intervention of psychoanalysis into late nineteenth-century medicine turned. The theories of sexuality came after this first intervention (in *Studies on Hysteria*, Freud's remarks on sexuality are mostly given in awkward footnotes suggesting the importance of sexual abstinence for women as a causal factor in the aetiology of hysteria). But when Freud did start to investigate the complexity of sexual life in response to what he uncovered in hysterical patients, his first step was a similar questioning of social definitions, this time of sexual perversion as 'innate' or 'degenerate', that is, as the special property of a malfunctioning type (Freud, 1905). In fact if we take dreams and slips of the tongue (both considered before Freud to result from lowered mental capacity), sexuality and hysteria, the same movement operates each time. A discredited, pathological, or irrational form of behaviour is given by psychoanalysis its psychic value. What this meant for the hysterical woman is that instead of just being looked at or examined, she was allowed to *speak*.

Some of the criticisms which are made by feminists of Freudian psychoanalysis, especially when it is filtered through the work of Lacan, can perhaps be answered with reference to this moment. Most often the emphasis is laid either on Lacan's statement that 'the unconscious is structured like a language', or on his concentration of mental representation and the ideational contents of the mind. The feeling seems to be that the stress on ideas and languages cuts psychoanalysis off from the materiality of being, whether that materiality is defined as the biological aspects of our subjectivity, or as the economic factors determining our lives (one or the other and at times both).

Once it is put like this, the argument becomes a version of the debate within Marxism over the different instances of social determination and their hierarchy ('ideology' versus the 'economic') or else it becomes an accusation of idealism (Lacan) against materialism (Marx). I think this argument completely misses the importance of the emphasis on language in Lacan and of mental representation in Freud. The statement that 'the unconscious is structured like a language' was above all part of Lacan's attempt to establish a continuity between the seeming disorder of the symptom or dream and the normal language through which we recognize each other and speak. And the importance of the linguistic sign (Saussure's distinction between the signifier and the signified. Saussure, 1915, 1974) was that it provided a model internal to language itself of that form of indirect representation (the body speaking because there is something which cannot be said) which psychoanalysis uncovered in the symptomatology of its patients. Only if one thing can stand for another is the hysterical symptom something more than the logical and direct manifestation of physical or psychic (and social) degeneracy.

FEMINISM AND THE UNCONSCIOUS

It is, however, this concept which seems to be lost whenever Freud has been challenged on those ideas which have been most problematic for feminism, in so far as the critique of Freudian phallocentrism so often relies on a return to empiricism, on an appeal to 'what actually happens' or what can be *seen* to be the case. Much of Ernest Jones' criticism of Freud, for example, stemmed from his conviction that girls and boys could not conceivably be ignorant of so elementary a fact as that of sexual difference and procreation (Jones, 1933, p. 15). And Karen Horney, in her similar but distinct critique, referred to 'the manifestations of so elementary a principle of nature as that of the mutual attraction of the sexes' (Horney, 1926, 1967, p. 68). We can compare this with Freud: 'from the point of view of psycho-analysis the exclusive sexual interest felt by men for women is also a problem that needs elucidating and is not a self-evident fact based upon an attraction that is ultimately of a chemical nature' (Freud, 1905, p. 146 n, *p. 57 n*). The point is not that one side is appealing to 'biology' (or 'nature') and the other to 'ideas', but that Freud's opening premise is to challenge the self-evidence of both.

The feminist criticism of Freud has of course been very different since it has specifically involved a rejection of the evidence of this particular norm: the normal femininity which, in the earlier quarrel, Freud himself was considered to have questioned. But at this one crucial level – in the idea of an unconscious which points to a fundamental division of psychic life and which therefore challenges any form of empiricism based on what is there to be observed (even when scientifically tested and tried) – the very different critiques are related. Juliet Mitchell based at least half her argument on this point in *Psychoanalysis and Feminism*, but it has been lost. Thus Shulamith Firestone in *The Dialectic of Sex* (Firestone 1970, 1979) arguing that the girl's alleged sense of inferiority in relation to the boy was the logical outcome of the observable facts of the child's experience, had to assume an unproblematic and one-to-one causality between psychic life and social reality with no possibility of dislocation or error. The result is that the concept of the unconscious is lost (the little girl rationally recognizes and decides her fate) and mothering is deprived of its active components (the mother is seen to be only subordinate and in no sense powerful for the child) (see Mitchell, 1974, 2, II, 5) for all its more obvious political appeal, the idea that psychic life is the unmediated reflection of social relations locks the mother and child into a closed subordination which can then only be broken by the advances of empiricism itself:

> Full mastery of the reproductive process is in sight, and there has been significant advance in understanding the basic life and death process. The nature of ageing and growth, sleep and hibernation, the chemical functioning of the brain and the development of consciousness and memory are all beginning to be understood in their entirety. This acceleration promises to

> continue for another century, or however long it takes to achieve the goal of Empiricism: total understanding of the laws of nature (Firestone, 1970, 1979, p. 170).

Shulamith Firestone's argument has been criticized by feminists (Delmar, Introduction to Firestone, 1979) who would not wish to question, any more than I would, the importance of her intervention for feminism. But I think it is important that the part of her programme which is now criticized (the idea that women must rely on scientific progress to achieve any change) is so directly related to the empiricist concept of social reality (what can be *seen* to happen) which she offers. The empiricism of the goal is the outcome of the empiricism at the level of social reality and psychic life. I have gone back to his moment because, even though it is posed in different terms, something similar seems to be going on in the recent Marxist repudiation of Freud. Janet Sayers' critique of Juliet Mitchell, for example, is quite explicitly based itself on the concept of 'what actually and specifically happens' ('in the child's environment' and 'in the child's physical and biological development') (Sayers cit. Wilson 1982).

UTOPIANISM OF THE PSYCHE

Something else happens in all of this which is probably the most central issue for me: the discarding of the concept of the unconscious seems to leave us with a type of utopianism of psychic life. In this context it is interesting to note just how close the appeal to biology and the appeal to culture as the determinants of psychic experience can be. Karen Horney switched from one to the other, moving from the idea that femininity was natural quality, subject to checks, but tending in its course, to the idea that these same checks, and indeed most forms of psychic conflict, were the outcome of an oppressive social world. The second position is closer to that of feminism, but something is nonetheless missing from both sides of the divide. For what has happened to the unconscious, to that divided and disordered subjectivity which, I have argued, had to be recognized in us all if the category of hysteria as a peculiar property of one class of women was to be disbanded? Do not both of these movements make psychic conflict either an accident or an obstacle on the path to psychic and sexual continuity – a continuity which, as feminists, we recognize as a myth of our culture only to reinscribe it in a different form on the agenda for a future (post-revolutionary) date?

Every time Freud is challenged, this concept of psychic cohesion as the ultimate object of our political desires seems to return. Thus the French feminist and analyst, Luce Irigaray, challenges Lacan not just for the phallocentrism of his arguments, but because the Freudian account is seen to cut women off from an early and untroubled psychic unity (the primordial state of fusion with the mother) which feminists should seek to restore (Irigaray 1978). Irigaray calls this the 'imaginary' of women (a reference to

Lacan's idea of a primitive narcissism which was for him only ever a fantasy). In a world felt to be especially alienating for women, this idea of psychic oneness or primary narcissism has its own peculiar force. It appears in a different form in Michèle Barrett's and Mary McIntosh's excellent reply to Christopher Lasch's thesis that we are witnessing a regrettable decline in the patriarchal family (Barrett and McIntosh, 1982). Responding to his accusation that culture is losing its super-ego edge and descending into narcissism, they offer the particularly female qualities of mothering (Chodorow) and a defence of this very 'primary narcissism' in the name of women against Lasch's undoubtedly reactionary lament. The problem remains, however, that whenever the 'feminine' comes into the argument as a quality in this way we seem to lose the basic insight of psychoanalysis – the failure or difficulty of femininity for women, and that fundamental psychic division which in Freud's work was its accompanying and increasingly insistent discovery.

If I question the idea that psychoanalysis is the 'new orthodoxy' for feminists, it is at least partly because of the strong political counterweight of this idea of femininity which appears to repudiate both these Freudian insights together.

To return to the relationship between Marxism and psychoanalysis with which I started, I think it is relevant that the most systematic attack we have had on the hierarchies and organization of the male Left (*Beyond the Fragments*, Rowbotham et al., 1979) gives to women the privilege of the personal in a way which divests it (*has* to divest it) of psychic complexity at exactly this level of the conflicts and discontinuities of psychic life. Like many feminists, the slogan 'the person is political' has been central to my own political development; just as I see the question of sexuality, as a political issue which *exceeds* the province of Marxism ('economic', 'ideological' or whatever) as one of the most important defining characteristics of feminism itself. But the dialogue between feminism and psychoanalysis, which is for me the arena in which the fully complexity of that 'personal' and that 'sexuality' can be grasped, constantly seems to fail.

In this article, I have not answered all the criticisms of psychoanalysis. It is certainly the case that psychoanalysis does not give us a blueprint for political action, nor allow us to deduce political conservatism and radicalism directly from the vicissitudes of psychic experience. Nor does the concept of the unconscious sit comfortably with the necessary attempt by feminism to claim a new sureness of identity for women, or with the idea of always conscious and deliberate political decision-making and control (psychoanalysis is *not* a voluntarism, Sayers, 1982). But its challenge to the concept of psychic identity is important for feminism in that it allows into the political arena problems of subjectivity (subjectivity *as* a problem) which tend to be suppressed from other forms of political debate. It may also help us to open up the space between different notions of political identity – between the idea of a political identity for feminism (what women require) and that of a feminine identity for women (what women are or should be), especially given the problems constantly encountered by the latter and by the sometimes too easy celebration of an identity amongst women which glosses over the differences between us.

Psychoanalysis finally remains one of the few places in our culture where our experience of femininity can be spoken as a problem that is something other than the problem which the protests of women are posing for an increasingly conservative political world. I would argue that this is one of the reasons why it has not been released into the public domain. The fact that psychoanalysis cannot be assimilated directly into a political programme as such does not mean, therefore, that it should be discarded, and thrown back into the outer reaches of a culture which has never yet been fully able to heed its voice.

NOTES

A draft of this article was presented in discussion with Elizabeth Wilson at the first of a series of seminars – 'Psychoanalysis and Feminism, Re-Opening the Case' – organized in London in 1982–83. It has been rewritten for *Feminist Review*. Thanks are due to Ann Whitehead, Cora Kaplan and Juliet Mitchell for their comments. Many of the ideas finally came together during discussion with my students on the 'Studies in Feminism' course at Sussex University 1982–83. I would like to dedicate the article to them.

1 Where two dates are given, the first is to the original date of publication: page references are to the more easily available editions (e.g. English translation, collections of articles, where possible.)
2 For more detailed discussion of the relative assimilation of Kleinianism through social work in relation to children in this country (especially through the Tavistock Clinic in London) see Rustin 1982 p. 85 and n. As Rustin points out, the State is willing to fund psychoanalysis where it is a question of helping children to adapt, but less so when it is a case of encouraging adults to remember.
3 References to Freud are to the Standard Edition and to the Pelican edition where available (in italics).

REFERENCES

Althusser, Louis, (1969, 1971) 'Freud and Lacan', *Lenin and Philosophy and other essays* London: New Left Books.

Anderson, Perry (1964) 'The Origins of the Present Crisis', *New Left Review* no. 23.

Anderson, Perry (1966) 'Socialism and Pseudo-Empiricism', *New Left Review* no. 35.

Anderson, Perry (1968) 'Components of the National Culture', *New Left Review* no. 50.

Barrett, Michèle (1980) *Women's Oppression Today* London: Verso and NLB.

Barrett, Michèle and McIntosh, Mary (1982) 'Narcissism and the Family: a Critique of Lasch', *New Left Review* no. 135.

Chodorow. Nancy (1978) *The Reproduction of Mothering* London: University of California Press.
Cooper, David (1963) 'Freud Revisited' *New Left Review*' no. 20.
Cooper, David (1965) 'Two Types of Rationality' *New Left Review* no. 29.
Cowie, Elizabeth (1978) 'Woman as Sign' *m/f* no. 1.
Dyhouse, Carol (1981) *Girls Growing Up in Late Victorian and Edwardian England* London: Routledge and Kegan Paul.
Firestone, Shulamith (1970, 1979) *The Dialectic of Sex* introduced by Rosalind Delmar, London: The Women's Press.
Freud, Sigmund (1892–94) 'Preface and Footnotes to Charcot's *Tuesday Lectures*', *The Standard Edition of the Complete Psychological Works of Sigmund Freud* vol. 1.
Freud, Sigmund (1893–95) *Studies on Hysteria, Standard Edition* vol. II, *Pelican Freud* vol. 3.
Freud, Sigmund (1905) *Three Essays on the Theory of Sexuality, Standard Edition* vol. II, *Pelican Freud* vol. 7.
Freud, Sigmund (1924) 'The Dissolution of the Oedipus Complex' *Standard Edition* vol. XIX, *Pelican Freud* vol. 7.
Freud, Sigmund (1925) 'Some Psychical Consequences of the Anatomical Distinction Between the Sexes'. *Standard edition* vol. XIX, *Pelican Freud* vol. 7.
Freud, Sigmund (1931) 'Female sexuality', *Standard Edition* Vol. XXI, *Pelican Freud* vol. 7.
Horney, Karen (1924, 1967) 'On the Genesis of the Castration Complex in Women', *Feminine Psychology* London: Routledge and Kegan Paul.
Horney, Karen (1926, 1967) 'The Flight from Womanhood', *Feminine Psychology* London: Routledge and Kegan Paul.
Irigaray, Luce (1978) 'Women's Exile: Interview with Luce Irigaray', *Ideology and Consciousness* no. 1.
Jones, Ernest (1933) 'The Phallic Phase', *International Journal of Psychoanalysis* vol. XIV, part I.
Lacan, Jacques (1936, 1968) 'The Mirror Phase', *New Left Review* no. 51.
Laing, R.D. (1962) 'Series and Nexus in the Family', *New Left Review*' no. 15.
Laing, R.D. (1964) 'What is Schizophrenia?' *New Left Review* no. 28.
MacCormack, Carol and Strathern, Marilyn (1980) eds *Nature, Culture and Gender* Cambridge: University Press.
MacLaren, Angus (1978) *Birth Control in the Nineteenth Century* London: Croom Helm.
Mitchell, Juliet (1970) 'Why Freud?' *Shrew* November-December 1970.
Mitchell, Juliet (1974) *Psychoanalysis and Feminism* London: Allen Lane.
Rowbotham, Sheila, Segal, Lynne and Wainwright, Hilary (1979) *Beyond the Fragments* London: Merlin Press.
Rubin, Gayle (1975) 'The Traffic in Women' in Reiter, Rayna M. ed., *Towards an Anthropology of Women* New York: Monthly Review Press.
Rustin, Michael (1982) 'A Socialist Consideration of Kleinian Psychoanalysis', *New Left Review* no. 131.
Saussure, Ferdinand de (1915, 1974) *Course in General Linguistics* London: Fontana.
Sayers, Janet (1982) 'Psychoanalysis and Personal Politics: A Response to Elizabeth Wilson', *Feminist Review* no. 10.
Thompson, E.P. (1965) 'The Peculiarities of the English', *Socialist Register* 1965.
Veith, Ilza (1965, 1970) *Hysteria, the History of a Disease* London: University of Chicago Press.

Walkowitz, Judith (1980) *Prostitution and Victorian Society, Women, Class and the State* Cambridge: University Press.
Wilson, Elizabeth (1981) 'Psychoanalysis: Psychic Law and Order', *Feminist Review* no. 8.
Wilson, Elizabeth (1982) 'Psychoanalysis and Feminism, Re-Opening the Case', opening seminar presentation, London 1982.

14

Joanna Ryan

Psychoanalysis and Women Loving Women

In this chapter I want to look at some ways in which psychoanalysis can be helpful in understanding our sexuality. Clearly the scope of such a discussion is enormous, and I can only pick out some specific feminist uses of psychoanalysis and indicate the limits of these. I want to consider the central question of attraction in relation to the now widespread experience of change in sexual orientation from heterosexual to lesbian.

Our sexual relationships stand out in our lives as areas of felt irrationality, the focus of our strongest and most conflicting feelings. The phrase 'turned on', with its suggestions of switches and electricity, captures the seemingly absolute nature of attraction – how remote from conscious control our sexual feelings are, how forceful when they come, how total in their absence when they do not. There is often a tremendous difference in our feelings between people we feel sexual towards and those we don't, between lovers and friends, with little continuity between the two. This split, whilst experienced as quite natural, is itself part of the social formation of our sexuality, of the way in which it has been channelled, associated with some people and some emotions, and not with others. Sex is often written about as if it were an absolute and irreducible category of human experience, as if we knew without doubt what it is or isn't. But in fact this in itself is an assumption, a product of how our sexuality is formed and lived, that it should appear to have this discreteness from other forms of contact between people.

The notion of attraction has often been attacked as mystified and oppressive. There is a persisting tradition within libertarian and some feminist politics of trying to make sexual relationships less involuntary and exclusive, more rational. One means of doing this has been to blur the distinction between friends and lovers by substituting political sisters and comrades as sexual partners, in defiance of 'fancying'. Hence the sleeping rotas of some 1960s communes, where the justification for sharing sex, if not the result, was the same as for other areas of domestic life: the creation of alternative structures which would allow different, less oppressive relationships to grow. Similarly now, there is a strong body of opinion that heterosexual women can decide to stop their sexual involvement with men and become, if not lesbian, at least more woman-identified. And some heterosexual feminists are insisting that men change their sexual inclinations, away from an obsessive focus on penetraton and orgasm to one which accords more with what women might like or want. In all these instances sexuality is seen as subject to quite a degree of conscious control. The demand that it be so is posed not only as a challenge about who or what is attractive, but also about the nature of attraction itself. Does this have to remain a mysterious force in our lives?

Some people have been able to accommodate their sexuality in these ways, others have become confused, uncertain and often asexual, and yet others have remained stuck with familiar patterns of attraction and non-attraction, with varying degrees of guilt and compromise. Whilst we may disagree with the most voluntaristic politics as completely underestimating the strength, complexity and depth of our feelings, are we just to be stuck with old and mystified notions of attraction, or a complete collapse into the unconscious? What is the scope for understanding the sources of sexual attraction in a way that allows us some possibility of change and control in our lives and of opposition to prevailing norms, but which doesn't negate the reality of our emotions or result in untenable arrangements? One of the points at issue here is what does constitute the reality of our emotions. Are they as absolute and irreducible as it is often assumed? Or is the common assumption of their fixity another way in which we construct ourselves and are constructed?

We could view the process of sexual fetishism as only an extreme example of what happens 'normally'. There, the same objects or activities are needed over and over again for sexual excitement or release with a consequent severe restriction in the kind of relationship involved (if any), and with a rigid lack of capacity for change. Parts of the body, specific acts or scenarios, clothes, etc. are substituted for whole persons, images for actual peole. It is striking that massively more men than women are involved in fetishistic or 'perverse' practices of some kind – indeed most books on the subject really are about male sexuality.[1] And from a wider point of view the whole culture of compulsory heterosexuality seems fetishistic and suited primarily to male 'needs': women have to be of a certain shape, size, age and appearance in order to be desired; certains parts of the female body are at a premium as sexual stimuli, and certain repetitive patterns of behaviour (seductiveness, passivity) are required for the stereotypically satisfying sexual act. The cultural imposition of norms and stereotypes of sexuality, and the hypervalution of specific forms of attractiveness, represent an enormous restriction of our sexual potential and diversity. It excludes vast numbers of women from being seen as sexual at all, and elevates a few to impossible or untenable standards of attractiveness. With this comes a very specific oppression of women: a deep-seated self-hatred and dislike of our own bodies, a minefield of competitiveness with other women about appearance, all of which are surprisingly hard to eradicate even with the creation of alternative values and norms. It is within this context, as well as that of the immediate family, that our specific sexualities are formed.

The supposedly absolute nature of sexual attraction extends to common ideas of sexual orientation, the assumption that we have to be one or the other – homo- or heterosexual – and that there is an identity that is our real one, whatever our actual behaviour. It is clear that the construction of a discrete homosexual identity is a relatively recent development, for both sexes,[2] and that this has necessitated the invention of a problematic third category, 'bisexual'. Although we cannot avoid using the terms involved (and often there are important reasons why, with a different valuation, we should do so), we should not adopt these categories uncritically, especially as regards the assumptions involved about sexual identity and attraction.

One of the major achievements of the women's movement has been its facilitation of sexual relationships between women. It is important that we try to understand this transformation, not only for its personal and political importance, but also because it can clarify our ideas about how sexuality is formed more generally. It certainly is not sufficient to see the process of change as only one of political choice, even though this may be a contributing factor. We have as well to look at the deeper emotional changes involved, and the basis on which our previous heterosexuality was constructed. Many psychological and psychoanalytic theories, including some feminist ones,[3] would predict that such an extensive change of sexual orientation as has occurred through the women's movement would not be possible or would only be 'superficial', and behaviourist attempts to condition adults (always of course into heterosexuality) have not been conspicuously successful.

The phrase most often used by feminists to describe this process is 'coming out'. Whilst this contains the suggestive imagery of blooming and flowering, and of needing the ground and the sun to do so, it also carries the implication, sometimes explicit sometimes not, of revealing previously hidden and unknown identities, our real or true selves. The enormous sense of self-discovery and self-realization that can accompany a long denied acknowledgement of sexual attraction to other women is not to be ignored or underrated: nor, even now, the courage required to do so. However, to describe this as the discovery of one's real identity begs too many questions about the processes involved and what was experienced beforehand. Not only does it imply a fixed (albeit hidden) identity of one or the other kind, it also is in danger of dismissing past engagement with heterosexuality as false consciousness, an unknowing or unwilling compliance, certainly not one's real self. For women with periods of substantial heterosexuality this problem is particularly acute: however painful and unsatisfactory these relationships may have been, they cannot be disowned. To do so is to deny a part of ourselves, the needs and hopes invested, however mistakenly, in such relationships, which may well carry over into present lesbian ones.

There is, though, a problem about how to describe the change involved, without it seeming chameleon-like and mysterious on the one hand, or excessively rational on the other. We need a way of sufficiently validating the enormous leap involved without losing all sense of continuity within ourselves. Whereas there *is* a complete discontinuity in lesbian and heterosexual existence in terms of social acceptability, discrimination and the possibilities for self-disclosure with all that this means for any one woman, it does not have to be a political cop-out to consider the substantial continuities that do exist, at least for some women, in the primary emotions involved – love, dependency, jealousy, trust, for example.

Psychoanalysis as a whole does not have much to say about lesbianism that is unpejorative or illuminating, but it does contain a form of understanding that is at least adequate to the complexity of our sexual feeling, and which can contribute to our understanding of what is involved in such a change of sexual relationships.

Psychoanalysis is far from being one unified body of theory and practice, and since Freud it has developed into many distinct schools of thought. These developments have taken place in different ways: as a result of clinical and therapeutic practice in different settings, and through the introduction of new concepts and theoretical developments. The psychoanalysis that has been introduced into the women's movement represents two very different traditions and two very different sets of interest: Freudo-Lacanian theoretical writings about the construction of femininity and female identity, and the use of post-Kleinian, 'object-relations' theory in feminist therapy and writings about this. Here I shall consider some specific uses of object-relations theory, as it has been written about in the women's movement, without attempting to discuss the differences between the two approaches.

Feminist therapy has developed from quite pragmatic origins. It has had to tread a complex methodological and political path in understanding how what is social creates the individual, and what the limits of therapy are. It is no accident that feminist psychoanalytic therapy, as well as some more practical Marxist approaches[4] have turned to object-relations theory in attempting this. This branch of psychoanalysis, associated originally with Balint, Fairbairn, Guntrip and Winnicott, contains a decisive break with certain aspects of Freudian theory, with its inherent biologism, its notions of instinct and gratification, and its anatomically-based conceptions of sexuality. It contains a more inherently social view of psychological development, seeing individuals as formed in relation to, and seeking connection with others. It replaces the notion of libidinal stages with an account of the gradual differentiation of the self, through the formation of internal 'objects – reflections of our experience of real persons from earliest infancy which then form and structure our later relationships. I am not claiming that this school of thought is uncontentious for feminists – its perspective on mothering, for example, is very problematic – but feminist development of it has been extremely fruitful, particularly in its emphasis on the early mother–daughter relationship and the development of a sense of self within this.

Whilst disputing the Freudian notion of sexuality or libido as central to mental life, object-relations theory does not really contain a theory of sexuality as such. Instead sexuality is seen as stemming from the whole developement of the personality rather than as determining it, and the goal of sexual activity is viewed as object rather than pleasure seeking. Recent feminist development of object-relations theory contains as much of a theory of sexuality and sexual identity as is to be found in previous writings.

E.S. Person argues that sexuality expresses many aspects of personality and motivation, originating in both infantile and later experiences, and varying between individuals as to its role and importance in their lives.[5] She also argues for the critical importance of early tactile experience in mediating the relationship between infant and caretaker, and assumes that later sexuality develops out of this early sensuality: 'Because sensual pleasure is the vehicle of object relations in the real world, sexuality expresses an enormous variety of motives, predominantly dependent or hostile, and the force of sexuality exists precisely because sexuality is linked to other motives.' In particular, because of the real dependence of a helpless child on a relatively powerful adult, 'it is unlikely that sexuality will ever be completely free of submission–dominance connotations.'

Chodorow, in her far-reaching book,[6] assumes that a main goal of adult sexuality is a return to a kind of 'oneness' or merging with the other. In this she is following Balint's notion of primary love and the attempts of adults to recapture it: 'This primary tendency, I shall be loved always, everywhere, in every way, my whole body, my whole being – without any criticism, without the slightest effort on my part – is the final aim of all erotic striving.[7] Sexual intercourse, according to Annie Reich, is the 'temporary relinquishment of the separating boundaries',[8] or, according to Alice Balint, 'the situation in which the reciprocal interdependence as experienced in early childhood is recreated.[9] Eichenbaum and Orbach express a similar idea: 'Because adult sexuality echoes aspects of mother–infant pre-verbal sensuality in its very unique communication, sexuality and merger may stir up deeply resonant early physical experience before there was a definite sense of self and before language.[10]

Merging with another is also described in non-psychoanalytic writings, though more as a peak of sexual experience than a common occurrence, and not as an echo of childhood experience. The Hite investigation included questions on why sexual intercourse was important to women, and many of the answers referred not just to closeness and intimacy, but also to various forms of merging: 'complete contact', 'breaking down barriers between self and others', 'we are one', 'becoming one in love', 'ultimate human closeness where a person can express and understand more than the mind can conceive of.'[11] (Other themes mentioned were: reassurance of being loved, becoming desirable, feeling like a woman, giving pleasure, feeling needed and special.) It is as well to remember that most sexual intercourse does not approximate to these descriptions of merging: feeling disconnected from oneself or the other person, ambivalent, alienated, or only in contact sporadically, are also frequent experiences which may well be accompanied by other forms of satisfaction and pleasure apart from merging (conquest, reassurance, for example).

The idea that adult sexual activity can stir up infantile feelings in adults is basic to any psychoanalytic approach. Whilst problematic in some ways (because it is not entirely clear what is meant or why it should happen), it does point to some common predicaments in sexual relationships. That infants first of all experience themselves as totally merged with their mother (or other primary person) and then gradually differentiate separating boundaries is now a common conception. The symbiosis of early infancy is very different for infant and mother. For the infant it is a reflection of its limited consciousness and actual total dependence, without regard for the mother as a separate person with her own interests. Mother-love, on the other hand, involves an often overwhelming sense of 'reality' as regards concern for the interests of the child, to an extent that can become self-loss.

The re-experiencing of infantile states in sexual relationships is described above as though it was a relatively safe and satisfying experience, if hard to achieve. In fact, this 'merging' can only be partial and temporary (whereas the infantile state is total and timeless), since we actually are adults and retain some awareness of this and our capacity to return to our adult state should we desire to do so. And frequently it is painful and full of conflict, partly because we cannot actually become infants, and partly because of all the unmet needs, defences and fantasies stimulated by just this possibility. . . It seems it is the emotions associated with the infantile state that are stirred up so strongly rather than the state itself. The other person is felt as all-powerful, the self as needy, exposed and vulnerable (or sometimes the other way round). How acceptable such feelings are, how much trust or despair they evoke about about being loved, depend on each person's history and current situation. Further, in adult–adult relationships we are also trying to be adults: both in reaction to our own child-like feelings of dependency and vulnerability, which may be too threatening, and also to care for the other person, both as adult and as child.

Despite these difficulties there are some interesting implications that have been drawn aboaut this notion of merger. The first, described by Eichenbaum and Orbach, is that sexual connection can bring with it a fear of loss of self, and that this is particularly acute for women given the difficulties they have with developing a secure and separate sense of self as children. They describe women as either overwhelmed by sexual merger or as unable to 'let go' emotionally and physically, both consequences of an unclear sense of self and the false boundaries developed to cope with it. They maintain that in order to let go fully a defined sense of self is needed to return to, which thereby makes the experience not like an infantile state at all. Such fear of loss of self may keep women removed from sexual relations altogether or participating in them in a limited way: the result of either conscious or unconscious choices.

The implication that Chodorow draws is that heterosexual intercourse reproduces the infantile situation much more nearly for a man than for a woman, given the usual gender division of parenting: 'Men cannot provide the kind of return to oneness that women can.' Instead men come nearer to an experience of fusion with the mother in heterosexual sex than women can do, both because of the historic situation of female mothering and the fantasies and emotions associated with it, and also because of men's actual inabilities to be sensitive, caring and containing, to 'mother' in short. This creates an unequal situation in heterosexual relationships, where women can only recreate the experience of oneness at secondhand – either by identifying with the man's experience of fusion with her, or by becoming the mother to the man (child). Both are ways in which women can fail to experience either themselves as centre stage, or the great lack involved in this. The implication that Chodorow rather obviously does not draw is the absence of these particular structural inequalities from lesbian relationships, and the emotional possibilities that this opens out.

'Merging' is only one thread amongst many in sexual relationships. Loaded as it is with notions of caring and infancy, it does not convey anything very specifically erotic: for this we have to turn to discussions of sexual orientation.

A strength of most psychoanalytic accounts is that they do not see a girl's pathway to heterosexuality as either straightforward or inevitable. Chodorow particularly, in that she is trying to break from all ideas of reproductive instinct or innate heterosexuality, emphasizes the complex and highly contingent developmental processes that are involved and how heterosexuality is never established without considerable pain and ambivalence, conscious and unconscious. Her focus, like much of psychoanalytic theory, is the so-called 'change of object' that girls have to effect in order to become heterosexual, given that their first and most powerful experience of love and physical care is with a woman, that is homosexual. To become heterosexual as an adult a girl has to transfer her primary affections to someone of a different sex, a boy only to a different member of the same sex. There are many different psychoanalytic versions of this transfer, but what is widely recognized is its problematic nature, and also how incompletely, at an internal level, it ever happens.

Chodorow sees the nature of a girl's early relationship with her mother as motivating her to look elsewhere for a primary person other than the mother, and argues that the roots of eventual heterosexuality lie in the early mother–daughter relationship. She describes in some detail what she thinks happens in this early relationship, drawing on both psychoanalytic and observational literature, and contrasting it with the mother–son relationship. She argues that mothers relate to their daughters with a greater sense of symbiosis and identification than they do to their sons, to the extent that daughters may be felt as extensions of or identical to the mother. Eichenbaum and Orbach, although they have a less overridingly functionalist account than Chodorow of the effects of social roles, also emphasise the importance of gender similarity in creating identification between mother and daughter. Both appoaches concur in how this poses specific difficulties for girls in differentiating and separating themselves as individuals, and how these issues become connected to ones of loss of love and rejection.

Maternal identification does not guarantee that a daughter will feel adequately loved – quite the opposite is often the case, since, as Eichenbaum and Orbach describe, the identification is based on the culturally devalued attribute of femaleness and also mothers may perceive in their daughters, or project onto them, all the attributes of themselves that they least like (including their femaleness). Given the massive cultural preference for boys, it is hardly surprising that one common experience of women is of being inadequately loved and certainly less so than their brothers.

Chodorow adds to her account the tendency of mothers right from birth to sexualize their relationship with their sons but not with their daughters. Quite what this sexualization of mother–son relationships consists of is not so clear, although she describes how sons become emotional substitutes for relatively absent husbands. Nor is it clear why Chodorow is so categorical about the absence of any sexualization between mother and daughter. For one thing this differentiation assumes (which Chodorow acknowledges) the mother's exclusive heterosexuality and that this applies across the board to infants. Secondly it underplays any element of physical sensuality between mothers and daughters, which often, as Eichenbaum and Orbach point out, is an important aspect of women's memories of their mothers, but one which is largely ignored and devalued on all sides. They tend rather to emphasize the physical and erotic nature of the involvement of mothers with their daughters, but describe how this is curtailed, contained and cut off. The other aspect of sexualization between mother and daughter they emphasize is not with the daughter as possible object of the mother's feelings, but as similar subject, in which a mother's feelings about herself, her body and sexuality in general are transmitted to a daughter with strong undercurrents of anxiety, approval and disapproval.

Chodorow argues that a girl's 'change of object' rests on these prior developments, and is motivated by a need to get away emotionally from the mother, a form of defence against even greater primary identification and dependence. The father or other parent-figure, regardless of gender or any other attribute, becomes a symbol of independence, of separation from the mother. 'The turn to the father . . . whatever its sexual meaning, also concerns emotional issues of self and other.' This underlines how non-gender processes (dependence, separation) become related to gender through the typical parenting practices of our society where women are primary and men secondary parents. As well, the girl's very love for her mother may be a problem for her: if she feels inadequately loved and not preferred, she may look for a kind of special love from her father she cannot get from her mother. And to this we may add, as do Eichenbaum and Orbach, and many writers before them, the girl's attempts to reject the inferiority and powerlessness of women, and acquire the power that men have in the world, as personified in her father.

Chodorow also describes the father's role in encouraging his daughter to look elsewhere than her mother to fulfil some of these needs, and, crucially for her account, describes this encouragement as 'sexualized in tone', which is where the father's gender is important. This allegedly consists in the father not only encouraging the girl in role-appropriate behaviour but also making her in some way an object of his sexual interest – encouraging flirtatious and seductive behaviour but not making himself actually available sexually (though of course this does happen much more often than is generally supposed). Eichenbaum and Orbach emphasize how mothers actively push their daughters in the direction of their fathers, or men in general, as sources of emotional involvement, but at the same time convey the disappointments and frustrations of such relationships.

Along with many other writers, Chodorow emphasizes that this 'turn to the father' is seldom absolute, girls remain strongly attached (internally if not externally) to their mothers, and fathers never become emotionally so dominant. The typically late and insubstantial role they actually play in a child's life may mean they are the target of much idealization and, as Eichenbaum and Orbach recount, bitterness.

In her account of adulthood Chodorow distinguishes three components: conscious heterosexual erotic orientation to men in general; heterosexual love or emotional attachment to a man with whom there is sexual involvement; and non-sexual emotional attachments; thus propounding a split between eroticism and emotional attachment. She views women as 'getting' the first from their fathers, who are seen as 'activating ' genital sexuality but not the other two components because of their unavailability as satisfying love objects in most families. We are left with a view of women as pushed and pulled out of their original homosexual intimacy into an ambivalent and very incomplete heterosexuality, where men may be the exclusive and primary erotic objects but are for the most part emotionally secondary to women: 'a girl never gives up her mother as an internal and external love object, even if she does become heterosexual.'

Chodorow makes a girl's relationship to her father crucial to her eventual heterosexuality, albeit in the context of her prior relationship to her mother. She leaves undiscussed what happens if the father is not present, or does not behave in the way described. Her notion that fathers 'activate' genital sexuality is extremely problematic: it assumes a separate category of the sexual, defined in terms of eventual orientation, that comes only via the father. A girl's pre-existing sexuality, and erotic feelings between her and her mother, are unmentioned or denied. Despite her intention to avoid any form of biological determinism. Chodorow still invokes the 'broadening of innate sex drives' as one contributing factor in the girl's interest in her father, to fill this gap in her account.

What Chodorow leaves us with in terms of heterosexuality is a deep split between eroticism and emotional attachment, explicable in terms of the fact that sexuality is developed not in relation to the person with whom the deepest attachment is formed, but with one who is relatively unavailable for a close and caring relationship. Thus eroticism and emotional unavailability are closely connected, and men (for other reasons as well) are frequently extremely unsatisfactory love objects for women. Certainly this has been one of the collective realizations of the women's movement.

Chodorow provides us with a vivid account of the fertile emotional ground on which relationships between women can grow. Her account makes the attainment of heterosexuality seem at once inevitable and profoundly precarious, never achieved without major ambivalence and built upon primary feelings of attachment to women. Heterosexuality is seen to involve as much a rejection and denial of attachment to women, in the form of the mother, as a positive attachment to men. In this sense heterosexuality is a defence against homosexuality, at both a personal and a social level. The early need to separate and individuate from a primary parent figure, so often a woman, to attain some measure of independence and selfhood, interacts with the cultural disparagement of women and the hypervaluation of men as this is mediated both via the mother–daughter relationship, and in many other ways. The fear and shame that most women can experience about sexually loving other women is as much witness to the desire to do so as it is to the social stigma and personal cost involved.

What is extraordinary is that Chodorow does not herself consider the implications of her arguments for the possibility of sexual relationships between women – extraordinary because she is so insistent on the persistent importance of women in women's emotional lives, and the problematic and contradictory nature of sexual relationships with men. Her practical conclusions all concern the transforming of men to become primary parental figures and more satisfactory love objects for women, rather than the facilitation of lesbian relationships, which she virtually ignores. Her questionable account of the mother – daughter relationship as basically asexual (compared to father–daughter, or mother–son) supports this bias, given her overall framework in which sexuality is seen as 'coming from' one or other parental relationship. Though it can be very helpful to look at adult sexuality in terms of the sensual and erotic nature of particular parental relationships, and though the idea that some of these are more or differently sexualized than others has considerable meaning, we cannot let the whole understanding of where our sexuality 'comes from' rest on these ideas. To do so is to create an account that is too closed and too inevitable. Chodorow, despite her insistence on the complexity and ambivalence with which social roles are internalized via parent–child relationships, does not allow enough space for the mass of other influences that can shape sexuality (peer group pressure, the media, for example) particularly during adolescence and later. The contradictory nature of our expectations and experience which has often been the impetus for feminism; the fact that we do change from generation to generation and do not only reproduce our mothers' oppression, is as much in need of explanation as is the internalization of patriarchal ideology. What the women's movement has shown is how powerful later experiences can be, given the rich emotional ground that Chodorow describes. It has set out to counter the cultural disparagement of women, both as this exists in the world at large and within and between ourselves, and has thereby facilitated all kinds of relationship between women that would not have been possible before, both sexual and otherwise. It has also prompted an enormous re-evaluation of our mothers and our relationships with them.

It has always been considered pejorative to consider lesbian relationships in terms of mother-love, and not surprisingly considering the use that has been made of this: the Freudo-medical stigmatizing of lesbianism as immature and hence only partially satisfactory and to be grown out of: and Wolff's[12] ambivalent interpretation of lesbian relationships as basically 'incest' with the mother – ambivalent because incest is a pathologizing term, and because, despite her considerable empathy, she can only see lesbians as a stigmatized group with ultimately barren relationships. The imposition of heterosexuality is seen at its starkest: what men are allowed in terms of suitably displaced union with the mother is disallowed to women and made taboo. There has also been the argument amongst feminists that for too long women have been 'mother' to men – why should we now wish to be mothers to each other with all the connotations of powerlessness and dreaded omnipotence that this conveys? However precisely such emotions are involved in our sexual relationships, as we have seen, and often they are even more overwhelming with women than men, just because of where they 'come from'. Perhaps what we can do now is recognize the threads in our adult relationships that connect with our earliest homosexual affections without the necessity of defending ourselves against yet another invalidation of lesbian relationships, and without denying either the sexuality or the ambivalence involved.

ACKNOWLEDGEMENTS

I would like to thank Sheila Ernst, Sue Cartledge and Lynne Segal for many helpful comments.

NOTES

1 Robert Stoller, *Perversion: The Erotic Form of Hatred,* Delta, New York, 1975.
2 Mary McIntosh, 'The Homosexual Role', in K. Plummer ed., *The Making of the Modern Homosexual,* Hutchinson, London, 1981.
3 Ethel Person, 'Sexuality as the mainstay of identity: Psychoanalytic perspectives', in C.R. Stimpson and E.S. Person eds, *Women: Sex and Sexuality,* University of Chicago Press, 1980.
4 Paul Hoggett and Sue Holland, People's Aid and Action Centre, *Humpty Dumpty,* no. 8, 1978.
5 Person, 'Sexuality as the mainstay of identity'.
6 Nancy Chodorow, *The Reproduction of Mothering,* University of California Press, Berkeley, 1978.
7 Michael Balint, 'Critical notes on the theory of pregenital organization of the libido' (1935), in M. Balint ed., *Primary Love and Psychoanalytic Technique,* Tavistock, London, 1952.
8 Quoted in M. Balint, *The Basic Fault,*Tavistock, London, 1968.

9 A Balint, 'Love for the mother and mother love' (1939), in Balint, *Primary Love and Psychoanalytic Technique*.
10 Louise Eichenbaum and Susie Orbach, *Outside In...Inside Out*, Penguin, Harmondsworth, 1982.
11 S. Hite, *The Hite Report*, MacMillan, New York, 1976.
12 Charlotte Wolff, *Love Between Women*, Duckworth, London, 1971.

15

Parveen Adams

Family Affairs

Feminism has been particularly concerned with two different sorts of problem. The first is an analytical problem and concerns the relative weight to be assigned to biological as against non-biological determinations of the destiny of women. The second problem is the working out of the implications of the slogan 'The personal is political'. These two important questions are often run together in the assertion that gender and its consequences are socially constructed and therefore that personal life and its transformation are questions of social transformation. It should be noted here that this running together of all that is non-biological with the social gives rise to a form of analysis which is exclusively posed in social and historical terms. The exception to this approach has been the importance within feminism of psychoanalysis and it is worth reflecting why psychoanalysis was ever thought relevant to the concerns of feminism. Why not, for example, academic psychology? The redundancy of the question provides the answer. Feminism looked to psychoanalysis because of the particular way in which it links sexuality and the unconscious. Both of which problems soon appeared central to anybody who was concerned with the forms and conditions of possibility of change in personal life. These psychoanalytic objects, sexuality and the unconscious, were welcomed then, as being consistent with feminist concerns. But the invocation of the psychoanalytic unconscious leads to more problems than the invocation of any old unconscious. It designates a particular psychical apparatus which calls into question the usual function assigned to non-biological explanation, that is, determination by the social. Let us state bluntly that this problem is quite unresolved both at an analytic and at a political level.

Various strategies have been adopted to get round this difficulty. At one extreme, the contents of the unconscious are declared to be an effect of the mode of production. But this really abolishes the unconsious as such and merely extends the grip of a mode of production. The changes that are rung on the problem of the relation between a form of society and its form of subjectivity are always structured by an assertion of the isomorphism between that society and its subjects which, in the end, functions only to destroy the category of unconscious life.

At the other extreme, a form of feminine subjectivity has been advanced, eternal in its content, subversive (and oppressed) in its effects – the excessive, the transgressive, etc, which reduce social relations and history to the local manifestations of this feminine essence.

A third possibility has opened up and appears to be consistent with the original assertion that gender is socially and historically constructed. It also appears to deal with the question of sexuality. It takes the form of asserting that sexuality is the effect of particular discourses which emerge in a particular historical and social conjunction. One must suppose that this includes the Freudian unconscious insofar as that is defined in terms of sexuality. Of particular note in this context is Michel Foucault's *History of Sexuality* vol. 1 (Allen Lane 1978) [1976] and Jacques Donzelot's account of the transformation of family forms in France in *The Policing of Families* (Hutchinson 1979 [1977]). These are both works which sustain a peculiar ambiguity towards psychoanalysis. Schematically they may both be said to accept the eternity of the unconscious. But both of them are concerned to qualify psychoanalysis' concept of sexuality. They wish to do so by specifying the ways in which its concept of sexuality is complicit with a range of theories and social practices which are used to manage social problems.

This paper will examine the different ways in which Foucault and Donzelot conceptualize sexuality and will show that Donzelot's *The Policing of Families* evades the problems posed by psychoanalysis in respect to sexuality in a way which Foucault cannot be directly accused of, while and at the same time no particular confirmation of Foucault is implied. It will be the contention of this paper that the problems for feminist analysis raised by psychoanalysis are not so easily displaced as might appear from Donzelot's work.

We will now consider *the Policing of Families.* The first point to recognise is that in no sense is this a conventional history of the family, as if it were a question of measuring the changes which happened to a social unit. Donzelot is concerned with the 'family' as a nexus of scientific knowledges, political concern, institutional arrangements, legal provisions, architectural forms, philanthropic strategies. In short, the whole area in which the human sciences are implicated in forms of administration. So, for example, Donzelot's history refers to medical treatises on the weaning, clothing and care of children as one element in the constitution of the modern mother as an ally of the doctor. Or again, it treats the existence of healthy families which are founded on legal marriage and a prudential attitude towards saving as, in part, a consequence of philanthropic practices. Or yet again, how the management of children is inflected by the influence of psychoanalysis on psychiatric theory and classification thus enabling the latter in turn to produce radical effects on the distribution of juvenile justice.

However, I restrict myself to only one of these discursive practices as they traverse the family – the way in which Donzelot holds that psychoanalytic theory and practice are responsible for changes in the sexual life and relations of the family such that it increasingly becomes subject to forms of normalizing intervention. Donzelot appears to side-step the question of psychoanalytic theory and practice as such and attempts to analyse their effects. It should be noted that this involves an assessment of the effects of psychoanalytic theory as well as practice. Donzelot eschews the common psychoanalytic tactic of denouncing certain effects of the practice as a deformation of psychoanalysis, a tactic employed frequently by Jacques Lacan. Donzelot is concerned to demonstrate the particular historical modes of operation through which psychoanalysis has had effects. In particular, he is concerned with the relation which psychoanalysis establishes with the family through the Trojan horse of the school.

Nonetheless, it should not be thought that such an analysis can be a straightforward task. Donzelot himself recognises a major difficulty quite explicitly. In 'The Poverty of Political Culture' (*Ideology and consciousness* no. 5, 1979) he writes

> Before Freud, sexuality was reduced to sex. The problem was how to contain it, to tame it, to correct it, make it serve the well-being of the individual and the ordered functioning of society. Freud demonstrates the existence of sexuality as an entity which affects the whole of behaviour and whose specific variations relating to the history of each individual subject can provide explanations for the different manifestations of the human psyche. This is thus a discovery which goes beyond all the operationalizations of psychoanalysis, all the orthopaedics which the techniques of interpretation enables specialists to utilize, in other words, every attempt to collapse sexuality to the category of sex.

While he recognizes all this, Donzelot still believes he can analyse something he calls the operationalization of psychoanalysis. We will suggest that his conclusions are extremely reductionist.

For Donzelot, the pertinence of psychoanalysis is to be located in the question of the management of sexuality. He gives a historical analysis which seeks both to explain this and to question a conventional opposition which many on the Left and in the Women's Movement make between the family on the one hand and sexual liberation on the other. Till the first decades of this century perhaps this was true as an opposition, but he claims that what psychoanalysis does is to overcome this opposition, converting the theme of sexual liberation to familial ends. Donzelot isolates two tendencies in the management of sexuality around the turn of the century. The first broad strategy was concerned with the nation and the family and consisted of a network of family-oriented organizations which were concerned with maintaining the level of population and which fought against contraception, abortion and divorce, in order to preserve the strength of the family. The second was a neo-Malthusian movement which combined a defence of co-habitation and the distribution of contraceptive devices with a concern for social hygiene. They argued that the freedom of families to act as they wished produced a social pathology (illegitimacy rates that led to sickness, prostitution and the spread of venereal disease, marriages that were medically unsound) and thus this second tendency also supported programs of eugenics. Donzelot argues that we no longer work within the opposition set up between the family and the theme of sexual liberation: 'Who would still make sexualization out to be a pure and simple tactic of destruction of the family, when the latter takes from this sexualization, at least in equal part, the means of its reinforcement?'

It is psychoanalysis that is credited with reducing the gap between these two strategies of the management of sexuality. One represented the goal of strengthening the family and maintaining its system of marriage alliances, the other represented a social normalization of sexuality, the organization of sexuality in relation to public welfare. Psychoanalysis was able to link these and resolve their contradiction. How? For Donzelot, what is at stake is the social normalization of the family's relation to sexuality. Throughout the nineteenth century Donzelot identifies transformations in family life that have come about through the general concern with the health and welfare of the child, with its socialization within the family. Since the family's relation to children is so crucial to Donzelot's account of transformations in the family, it is not surprising that the influence of psychoanalysis is located within the school-family relationship.

He identifies three stages in this relationship between school and family and claims that psychoanalysis is the instigator of each new stage. The first stage is marked by a systematic interchange between three major agencies concerned with children: The Child Neuropsychiatry Clinic which dealt with maladjusted children and delinquent children from the lower classes, the Medico-psycho-pedagogical Centre established in 1945, which was psychoanalytic in orientation and dealt with middle-class children and their problems at school and the Parent's School founded in 1929 with a program for improving parents and for safeguarding the rights of the family over the child in the context of all the modern innovations that required the family to readjust itself. The links between these agencies resulted in a shift from the problems of pupils in school to the problems in the family. So the next stage involves an intervention in sexual and family life. The child's problems are increasingly treated as symptoms of the parents' problems. If a mother invests too much in a child it is because she is frustrated in the conjugal relation; if a mother invests too little in a child it is because she did not want it, perhaps because she had no love for the father or because he had deserted her. The child with a problem is either wanted too much or too little; in either case desire becomes an area of intervention. Donzelot claims that it is psychoanalysis that authorised this shift from the problems of scholastic performance to the relations within the family. The third stage involves the introduction of sex education into the schools, an issue over which there had been much debate and disagreement. Sex education, now conceived as a discussion of personal matters, would prevent scholastic maladjustment and would prepare the child for its individual, conjugal and parental functions in later life. Again, Donzelot claims that it is psychoanalysis that instigated the new stage. The argument is that psychoanalysis provided a theory of sexuality which made it a problem of mental and emotional balance; sexuality was thus made relevant to the harmonious development of the child. This had not been true of the old psychiatric theories organized around the themes of heredity, degenerescence and perversion.

The danger constituted by universal schooling and sex education taught in schools to parental rights over the child, is now mitigated by assigning to the family the possibility of improving the child's behaviour. The sorts of personal problem that arise from this create a space for psychoanalysis to organize. For the particular types of disturbance and their resolution which might be involved suit psychoanalysis in a way that clearly, for example, excludes psychiatry. Psychoanalysis suggests a flexibility in the relational structures of the family and by utilizing the educational role of the family as I have just described, psychoanalysis introduces a concern with the observance of social norms into the family. In others words, for Donzelot, psychoanalysis is the conduit through which the family becomes attached to the educational progress of the child in the sense that this progress is experienced as a consequence of the internal sexual health of the family.

Not only had psychoanalysis been instrumental in the constitution of the family as a relational space within which its own concerns with the education of its children could be handled, but Donzelot claims that psychoanalytic techniques were called upon by the family, to deal with failure. This is the moment when the defence of the autonomy of the family couples with the social management of family relations. And for Donzelot, this is the moment when the familial management of sexuality and the social management of sexuality meet. Before psychoanalysis intervened, the mechanisms of the management of the family and its sexuality had come from religion and the confession, or from medicine and its expertise. Donzelot argues that psychoanalytic intervention makes the family amenable to social norms by a combination of confession and expertise. About the mechanism of confession, Donzelot tells us only that it furnished the family with a way of coping with the split within the *ancien regime*, that is, between matrimonial choice and sexual desire and temptations of the flesh. Expertise appears to refer to the use of diagnoses, tests, inventories of individual potential and advice and opinions that can be referred to special knowledges. Now however, the new technicians, the 'psy' technicians formed, it seems, under the influence of psychoanalysis, set up a process whereby expertise and confession do not merely co-exist. (Donzelot uses a general notion of 'psy' to unify practices of intervention as different as marital counselling, child therapy and parental consultations under the sign of psychoanalysis.) The 'psy' allows the subject itself to take responsibility for expertise in the sense that the initial diagnosis can be called into question through the subject's own 'confessions'. So that finally it is the subject's own judgement and not a social judgement that is at stake. Hence it need have no fears of being manipulated.

Donzelot writes: 'The individual's resistance to norms. . . is thus no longer anything but an *internal* resistance to a process whose outcome can be a greater well-being for him and for it. *The resistance to norms becomes a resistance to analysis,* a purely negative and blind blockage in the way of one's own welfare.' Relational technology does not manipulate; it allows old moral rules and new social norms to *'float in relation to one another until they find their equilibrium'*. Flotation is a general mechanism governing adjustment to norms. More characteristically, Donzelot talks of the flotation of *images,* a term which is nowhere defined and which is often used interchangebly with 'desires'. Desires here covers both what human subjects may desire and what, to put it figuratively, social norms may desire of human subjects. Images, then, are objects of identification through the mobilization of desire. An equilibrium achieved between images is thus an equilibrium between familial desires and social desires.

The conditions for psy intervention, then, are states of disequilibrium. And while such a disequilibrium is often marked and identified through the child's problems, since the proper socialization of the child demands that the family subject itself to social norms, family relations come in for interrogation. The right parental images are crucial to the child's socialization and these parental images can be changed by working on the parents themselves. Psy intervention brings the parents' own images 'to the fore' and by virtue of the fact that the subject is in charge, this results both in a revelation and in an acceptance of that which was refused before – the subject can 'accept what he was refusing to hear, to see, to do, since it no longer has to do with morality, laws or merits', but has to do with his own relational equilibrium, his psychical and sexual fulfilment. It is in this way that psy technique brings social norms into the family. This is a pretty long way round of saying that psychoanalysis gets people to accept respectable social values.

That is the account of how parents regulate their own images. An example from Donzelot will show how these relate to the child's problems and the child's images of the parent. It concerns a child's instability as a result of the lack of a paternal image in the mother's discourse. The child's difficulty highlights the difficulties of the couple. Their satisfactions and dissatisfactions are opened up to investigation and they have to adjust to one another by acquiring the images proper to parents. This will no doubt rectify the mother's lack of representation of the paternal image. The good parent will then produce a good child. Psy techniques then, induce a form of rationality in the subject by providing images of identification which, if the subject chooses to adopt them, will have the effect of rectifying a malfunction in the family.

Is it possible to recognize even the vestiges of psychoanalysis in this account of technique? Donzelot's account is governed ultimately by an individual's rationality, a rationality which exists as a capacity to choose those images which bring advantage and to discard those which bring trouble. But this overlooks the fact that such a rationality of behaviour is radically challenged by psychoanalysis. I shall return to this point later. For the moment it is sufficient to state that Donzelot's invocation of rationality is directed towards explaining the effectivity of norms. But he rejects any notion of ideology as a general mechanism for impregnating human subjects with social norms. The notion of ideology, he says, 'comes down to saying, in less delicate language, that these individuals are imbeciles'. For Donzelot, the contrast with ideology is a mechanism of choice as a path of decisions to which benefits attach. What Donzelot is presumably attempting to identify is that social norms do not enter individuals like a virus, through a general but unnoticed means of transmission, but that they function in a relation in which the subject need only adopt as much of them as it derives benefit from them. The degree to which it adopts them will strike a balance, an equilibrium, between those benefits and the costs which it incurs in changing. It is in this sense that norms float. They are a process of adjustment. Choice here is not, of course, a question of freedom, but is called such to mark the fact that it is neither usefully conceived as coercion nor as ideology.

Donzelot himself is quite explicit on this question of choice and his argument implies the production of a general form of subject, the subject who adjusts his interests through choice. This is clear in the analogies he sets up between the operations of philanthropy and those of psy agencies. He writes: 'The relation...established...between the family and the agencies of relational counselling, like the relations to the savings plan, was one of *enticement*.' Both relations were served by a notion of the freedom to choose. Just as the family is free to adopt or reject the advice proffered to it by philanthropy, so the family's relation to psy agencies can be a 'free' choice and what is offered to them in the space of consultation is seen to be free of social judgement. Furthermore, when talking about philanthropic practices, he claims that they work because saving, marrying, etc. are one term of an 'everyday alternative', the other being less favourable. There is a similarity between this and the mechanism which determines the outcome of the flotation of images, which removes the resistance to norms and the 'blind blockage' through choosing one's welfare or one's children's welfare. For Donzelot, all the procedures of philanthropy and psychoanalysis do indeed appear to produce a subject who adjusts to its interests through choice. In relation to psychoanalysis, at least, the postulation of such a subject appears strange.

Donzelot might argue that this form of the subject we are dealing with indeed results from the effects of psychoanalysis on the sexuality of the family insofar as it produces a relational space of the family through the part it plays in the school-family circuit. The argument might proceed: this is a space of communication between family members and when there are gaps in communication, psy intervention can resolve the problem. Since psychoanalysis is credited with the production of a communication network, it follows that psychoanalytic tecnique is the example, *par excellence*, of all the techniques that deal with communication problems. But why should we accept that psychoanalysis has to do with communication? And in any case, what has happened to sexuality?

It is true that Donzelot speaks of psy intervention in the case of the impotent husband, the frigid wife, the disturbed child, that is, of family pathology. But if the psy technician furnishes the impotent husband with images of what parents should be, how is that going to help? The latter might well consciously wish to be a good parent and husband and wish to be potent. But how does achieving an equilibrium of images help the problem, indeed how is it connected with the problem at all? We will see later how the account of sexuality collapses.

Even if it is asserted that some forms of therapeutic intervention explicitly attempt to convert sexuality into a relational, communicational matter, that fact does not license Donzelot to subsume psychoanalysis within it. It must be remembered that psychoanalysis proper does not deal with the analysand's relation to real parents in the sense that they might be brought onto the scene to verify a relationship or be psychoanalysed themselves. The incidence of psychoanalysis is on particular human subjects, not on that relational space of the family. The analysand is not reducible to one point of a family network. And while the parent's actual behaviours will undoubtedly figure in the analysand's fantasies, they cannot be said to determine those fantasies. Precisely what intervenes between what is actual and its effects is a psychical domain, the domain of unconscious processes, without which psychoanalysis is not psychoanalysis.

It is not just a question of rehearsing well-known theses of psychoanalysis in order to protect it from the threat of Donzelot's argument. Rather, I want to show that *The Policing of Families,* although it puts forward an account of the management of sexuality, actually avoids the question of sexuality. In order to demonstrate this I will use Foucault's work as a contrast, for he has at least addressed the question of sexuality directly. Foucault and Donzelot both use the notion of police and the notion of bio-politics. Since the eighteenth century sexuality has come to be policed. It is important to note that this notion of police refers not at all to a coercive power armed with a truncheon but to an extension of that century's conception of police as the inspection and administration of public welfare. This involves a concern with the species body, with the population, the national stock, and thus with questions of propagation, births and mortality, the level of health, etc. and the conditions which affect them. Public welfare thus requires the *regulation* of individual bodies, desires and pleasures at the level of the social aggregate. This regulation of the species body is what constitutes bio-politics. And we have already seen how Donzelot uses the social concern with children in his account of the management of sexuality. But alongside the regulation of bio-politics and equally important for Foucault is the notion of an anatamo-politics of the human body governed by *discipline.* Disciplinary techniques centre on the body as a machine, optimizing its capabilities and integrating it into systems of surveillance. Discipline is crucial to modern sexualities. Both disciplinary techniques and regulative methods, then, are crucial modes of modern administration. But discipline does not figure in Donzelot's book.

How does a policing of the sexuality of individuals operate for Foucault? This question of policing, it must be stressed, is not a question of damping down the burgeoning effects of a natural order. Foucault is precisely concerned to demonstrate the effective link between the policing of sexuality and the production of the very forms of sexuality which are governed by discipline. To speak of the production of forms of sexuality, for example, infantile masturbation, homosexuality, does not imply, of course, that before a certain date children did not masturbate or that sodomy did not exist. For Foucault, the reference is to the effects of a different kind of attention paid to peripheral sexualities in the course of the nineteenth century. Peripheral sexualities being precisely perversions such as masturbation and homosexuality. In that century, sexuality becomes medicalized. Where previously sodomy was a category of forbidden acts, now homosexuality became a 'species'. Foucault explains this: 'The nineteenth century homosexual became a personage, a past, a case-history, and a childhood, in addition to being a type of life, a life-form, and a morphology, with an indiscrete anatomy and possibly a mysterious physiology. Nothing that went into his total composition was unaffected by his sexuality.' This medicalization of sexuality operates first on peripheral sexualities in order to deploy a whole technology of sexual health and pathology. These entities are no longer a classification of acts, they are rather, sexualities described *in* individuals. Through observation, examination and questioning which function as specific forms of surveillance, these entities are isolated, intensified and solidified in individual bodies. The very techniques of surveillance are themselves a constant incitement. For the curiosity and pleasure of the questioner elicits the pleasure in the answer or the evasion of the answer. The oddities of sex are drawn out, worked upon and become productive of pleasure. This form of surveillance uses the physical proximity of psychiatrist and patient and it is these proximities that produce an intensification of the patient's sexuality through a circulation of sexuality. The intensification of sexualities in the family comes about in the same way: all the techniques of surveillance therein are mechanisms of incitement and intensification. The family is thus saturated with sexuality and one result of this is to produce a greater threat than before to the prohibition on incest.

This problem of incest, heightened as it is by the effects of discipline which have just been described, raises the question of how disciplinary and regulatory techniques are combined in families. For Foucault, one way in which this was done was through the normalizing influence of psychoanalysis. The effect of discipline has been to proliferate forms of sexuality which, while they enlarge the domain of surveillance, have the counterpart of marginalizing the law and the juridical notion of matrimonial alliance. The normalization of sexualities, then, concerns the relation between sexuality as desire, the affective intensification of the family space and the old system of alliance. Insofar as the effects of the former threaten the latter, sexuality has to be recoded. Foucault accords psychoanalysis a central role in this recodification. Outside the law of the land it makes the unconscious a land of the law. Firstly, it conceptualizes desires and their development by reference to the incest taboo as a law, obedience to which is the price for entering culture. Secondly, as a practice, it is in part a technique for relieving the pathogenic effects of the subject's relation to that law, lived as sexuality. It should be noted that this description of the normalizing effects of psychoanalysis, although it is constructed largely in a play on the term 'law', could at least be said to retain a specific reference to psychoanalytic technique, the putting into speech of incestuous desires, to retain a semblance of psychoanalysis insofar as it is about sexuality, the incest taboo and language.

For Foucault, then, desires of family members are produced *in and through* discipline and regulation. However, it does not follow that the procedures of normalization are necessarily successful. Nor, for psychoanalysis, does the person who has been 'cured' and who in this sense may be considered to be normal by virtue of a freedom from the disabling effects of pathology, necessarily meet the demands of social norms. In Donzelot we are dealing with a problem occasioned by the use of the term norm which appears to cover both the inculcation of norms and the quite separate problem of the achievement of normality.

Donzelot is inattentive to the production of forms of sexuality and appears to conflate normalization procedures with the inculcation of norms. As a consequence of this he fails to address himself to anything that is recognizable as psychoanalytic technique. The fact that he sets up a technique whose success is the inculcation of norms dictates his account of what the problem was in the first place. Since there has been no elaboration of familial sexualities as they are produced in and through the social, failure is ascribed to a stubborn desire born out of family interests, interests which are themselves an obstacle to normality. For Donzelot, there is on the one hand, familial desire and on the other hand, social desire. He writes: 'The difference between the power regime of the family and that of society as a whole is sufficiently great that all attempts at a precise codification of familial behaviour are doomed ultimately to fail.' The idea of a 'power regime of the family' presumably means that the family has a certain autonomy and a certain freedom from coercion. Certainly, discipline and regulation, the modern forms of power do not work primarily through coercive techniques, through the law. But his autonomy cannot refer to an autonomous domain of desires *outside* discipline and regulation.

In Donzelot, the reference to familial desire is completely ambivalent and it is at this point that his account of sexuality collapses. Familial desire refers merely to those desires of family members that mark the failure in normality, desires which lead to impotence, frigidity, disturbances in children. Now in Foucault it is true that the 'frigid wife', the 'impotent husband' and the 'homosexual' are figures through which sexual normalization works – they are, as he puts it, 'the combined figures of an alliance gone bad and an abnormal sexuality'. For Donzelot, however, they are actual conditions which mark a family's active opposition to norms. It is as though there really was a family desire which would explain the failure. But how can a familial desire which is itself unexplained, explain the production of these abnormal sexualities? Especially as, and contradictorily, it is in the family's interest for the conjugal couple to change their images and their desires. For Donzelot this is achieved through psy intervention which, he says, brings about change through a mechanism of choice governed by interest. This term 'family interest' is being used, then, to explain both the family's stubborn difference from and then its incorporation into general social norms.

In setting up an opposition between two registers, the familial and the social, which he can only do by failing to account for sexuality as anything other than a ground for psy intervention, Donzelot has merely produced a version of the problem of all traditional theories of socialization, the problem of the junction between the individual and society. The subject with the will to choose and the capacity to make a choice in its own interests reappears. It is this singular and homogeneous form of the subject that must be questioned. Even were philanthropy to work on a subject of choice, is sexuality regulated through such a subject, does psychoanalysis work on such subject and has Donzelot shown that it does? Surely, psychoanalysis with its concept of unconscious wishes challenges any notion of a match between society and the individual. To say the least, the author of *Civilization and its Discontents* (*SE* XX 1930) was quite clear on this. Nor could one easily imagine the psychoanalytic concept of the subject being a particularly suitable vessel for the type of manoeuvering which Donzelot assigns to it.

Donzelot's reduction, then, of psychoanalytic theory and practice to a question of images equilibrated by choice between interests, cannot be accepted. This reduction involves two further misconceptions about the effects psychoanalytic practice can achieve and these should be pointed out. First, for Donzelot, since images impinge on sexuality and are a matter of choice, it is implied that individual sexual desires can be radically altered, that particular desires can be eliminated and replaced by others. But if we take up the example of incestuous desires we see that what is at stake for Foucault is a desire embodied in individuals, drawn out, intensified and sustained through the effects of discipline. Neither discipline nor normalization imply the disappearance of the desire. Neither, of course, does psychoanalysis claim to remove the injunction against incest. It may alleviate troubled sexualities by reorganizing the significance and individual meanings that formed historically around the desire for the mother and father, but it does not claim to eliminate the desires.

Secondly, in Donzelot the choice of images is governed by public norms. But it is clear that the outcome of psychoanalytic intervention is not necessarily that of a sexuality in line with juridical forms of alliance, still less with social norms. A homosexual is an obvious example of this. Furthermore, far from the intervention producing an adjustment to social norms in Donzelot's sense, psychoanalysis shows precisely that freedom from neurosis and adjustment to social norms do *not* coincide; meeting the stringent requirements of a society's code of conduct might well generate neurosis. Psychoanalysis then, is neither about a radical substitution of desires, nor about adjustment to norms. If Donzelot is to talk about psychoanalytic technique and its effects he must take notice of the nature of sexual desires and hence of the limits on their alteration.

By this I do not mean that he must share psychoanalysis' view of sexuality. Rather, that he must have some explanation of forms of sexuality, given that he does not subscribe to either a biological or a psychoanalytic or for that matter, Foucault's account of sexuality. For he does claim that sexuality has become a relational matter that can be operated on by relational technology. What he gives is a rational explanation of sexuality in the sense that desires are seen as alterable at the level of consciousness. But does such an account meet anybody's sense of sexuality? Has he convinced us that family members come to *live* this relational space and live it as sexuality? Can interest and choice lead to alterations in the forms of lived sexuality?

That a relational space, for example, of desire, is discursively produced and can function as a space of intervention is easily understood. But must not the actual desire for a child or the lack of desire for a child itself be explained? This is not to say that one is seeking an explanation of individual cases; rather, the contrast is with the simple having of a child, or having a child as a source of support in old age. Of course, the question of the conditions of desire is a meaningless one for psychoanalysis. But it is an important one for Foucault and for Donzelot for whom a social and historical explanation is required.

That there are treatises on the relational space of the family that may invoke psychoanalysis, that there are psy interventions that work at a rational level, that there are alterations in the behaviour of parents and children as a result of those interventions; all that is not in doubt. But the existence of treatises and techniques must be demonstrated to have some purchase on individuals and their desires. In the question of sexuality the mechanism of this cannot be rationality. The experience of the politics of feminism demonstrates that it is simply too easy to speak of changing images. If our sexualities are organised in a relation to images, that relation is certainly no simple one of recognition and acceptance. Sexuality is stubborn and excessive.

The reduction of psychoanalysis to Donzelot's account of psy technique is finally unacceptable, not because it fails to take psychoanalysis at its word, but because while treating of the contemporary management of sexuality and psychoanalysis' role in it, he reduces the problem of sexuality to a question of choice and psychoanalysis to a decision technique. This does not advance feminism's engagement with the question of sexuality which prompted its original concern with psychoanalysis.

PART V

Feminist Criticism and Cultural Studies

Introduction

FEMINIST LITERARY CRITICISM, CULTURAL STUDIES, AND THE ACADEMY

Two schools of feminist literary criticism are often distinguished in contemporary discussions, the French and the Anglo-American. Marilyn Butler, in a recent review of no fewer than fifteen volumes of feminist criticism and theory, commented that while 'British-born and British-based critics can join in the debate...it is pointless to pretend that feminist criticism in English is as international as the frequently used adjective "Anglo-American" suggests.'[1] Such a judgement is difficult to contest in the face of the quality as well as the sheer quantity of feminist criticism currently being produced in the United States. Clearly Butler is correct when she observes that American departments of literature and language have offered feminist scholars 'an institution to harbour and focus a scholarship of their own'.[2] It is true that English departments in British institutions of higher education have produced some distinguished feminist critics, for example, Gillian Beer[3] and Mary Jacobus.[4] But it is perhaps significant that the two the most influential British feminists of the second wave, Germaine Greer and Juliet Mitchell, were refugees from English. Greer left the University of Warwick following the publication of *The Female Eunuch*, and Mitchell left her teaching post at the University of Reading at much the same time. Greer's subsequent work drew as much upon anthropology as on literary criticism, while Mitchell went on to train as a psychoanalyst.

Comparative studies of the institutionalization of literary criticism are rare, and throw little light on the differences in the fortunes of feminist criticism in Britain and America. Paul Lauter argues that the construction of the American literary canon in the 1920s pushed it towards a masculine identity. Cultural authority accrued to the professoriat in the newly professionalized discipline; an almost exclusively male authority, but one deeply troubled over its masculinity. The discipline had inherited a distinctly feminine identity, and moreover attracted a high proportion of female students. Finally, the study of a national literature in America, as elsewhere, took upon itself the task of defining the nation in cultural terms. The construction of the literary canon claimed a masculine identity for that canon and for the nation, both: 'as professors and male novelists seemed to perceive it, the problems of the United States were not to be encountered over a cup of proverbial tea, in reading novelists at once genteel and sensual, or in fretting over village life in Maine or Louisiana. America needed the grand encounters with nature of Melville or even Thoreau.'[5] Lauter notes the decline in the representation of women in higher education generally in the United States from about 1930, which was not to be recovered until the 1960s. The institutionalization of the discipline of literary criticism in America, it would seem, coincided with a major setback in the fortunes of women scholars and students in higher education.

There are differences in the history of the construction of the canon and the associated professionalization of English literature in Britain, but also some striking similarities. We see the same decline in the numbers of women in higher education from this time, and a similar anxiety within the discipline and among male novelists about the 'taint' of femininity which attached to writing and literature.[6] One notable difference lies in the literary constructions of class. The imagery drawn upon by Lauter – cups of tea in Maine, women's literary societies discussing the novels of Jane Austen – is replete with class as well as gender-meanings, encapsulated in the term 'genteel'. The myth of classlessness so dear to the heart of capitalist America, is more readily sustained in a literature which, casting off the 'effeminate' trappings of class refinement, embraces the manly grand encounter. It is not a myth which has ever had much purchase within British culture and society. While the literary canon in Britain constituted a set of humane values which claimed validity over and above their class provenance, such humanism did not entail or require the repudiation of class distinction. Rather it purported to offer universal values in terms of which those differences and identities might be negotiated.

Two rather different institutional and cultural contexts, then; but in neither case could we expect the claims of feminist scholarship to provoke anything but bitter resistance, which indeed they did.

The explanation for the relatively greater success of feminist criticism in establishing itself within the American setting may emerge when the alternatives on offer, and the characteristic cast taken by feminism in each national culture, are taken into account. Several of the British feminist critics mentioned by Butler (including the present writer) are sociologists.[7] But it is in cultural studies that questions of gender, culture and representation have been most fully explored in Britain. And within cultural studies as it developed over the years, the literary text has been on principle denied any special privileges.

The new discipline found a (contested) place within the university with the founding of the Centre for Contemporary Cultural Studies (CCCS) at Birmingham in 1964. The CCCS was the end result of earlier developments in adult and in teacher education which at that time had not been integrated into the degree level sector of higher education.

Following the Robbins Report of 1962,[8] higher education entered a period of rapid expansion in Britain. (See table 1.) This was a propitious moment at which to launch a new area of study.[9] Propitious, too, for feminism: the second wave began to rise during this brief period of expansion, and at a time when the gap in the representation of men and women in higher education was at last beginning to close. (See tables 2 and 3.) The first generation of university and polytechnic-educated feminist scholars were embarking on careers in higher education in the early 1970s, when the new universities which were founded in the mid-sixties were expanding most rapidly. But the profile created by the lines of penetration of feminism

Table 1 Full-time undergraduates: increase in student numbers, 1968–9 to 1976–7

	Home		*Overseas*		*Total*		
	Number	*Percentage increase*	*Number*	*Percentage increase*	*Number*	*Percentage increase*	*Overseas as a percentage of total*
1968–9	166,993	5.4	6,517	5.0	173,510	5.4	3.8
1969–70	173,484	3.9	6,695	2.7	180,179	3.8	3.7
1970–1	178,722	3.0	7,150	6.8	185,872	3.2	3.8
1971–2	182,678	2.2	7,817	9.3	190,495	2.5	4.1
1972–3	184,543	1.0	8,706	11.4	193,249	1.4	4.5
1973–4	187,187	1.4	10,072	15.7	197,259	2.1	5.1
1974–5	190,981	2.0	11,714	16.3	202,695	2.8	5.8
1975–6	197,517	3.4	13,951	19.1	211,468	4.3	6.6
1976–7	205,771	4.2	15,714	12.6	221,485	4.7	7.1

Table 2 Trends in the numbers of recent women home postgraduates, 1968–9 to 1976–7

	Men		*Women*		
	Number	*Percentage increase*	*Number*	*Percentage increase*	*Women as a percentage of total*
1968–9	21,734	8.6	6,929	12.3	24.2
1969–70	22,254	2.4	7,125	2.8	24.3
1970–1	23,447	5.4	7,847	10.1	25.1
1971–2	24,377	4.0	8,274	5.4	25.3
1972–3	24,297	−0.3	8,717	5.4	26.4
1973–4	23,154	−4.7	9,048	3.8	28.1
1974–5	22,388	−3.3	9,438	4.3	29.7
1975–6	22,695	1.4	9,882	4.7	30.3
1976–7	22,160	−2.4	10,172	2.9	31.5

Table 3 Trends in the numbers of recent women home undergraduates, 1968–9 to 1976–7

	Men		*Women*		
	Number	*Percentage increase*	*Number*	*Percentage increase*	*Women as a percentage of total*
1968–9	118,052	5.1	48,941	6.1	29.3
1969–70	121,904	3.3	51,580	5.4	29.7
1970–1	124,004	1.7	54,718	6.1	30.6
1971–2	124,880	0.7	57,798	5.6	31.6
1972–3	123,884	−0.8	60,659	4.9	32.9
1973–4	123,512	−0.3	63,675	5.0	34.0
1974–5	123,545	0.0	67,436	5.9	35.3
1975–6	126,352	2.3	71,165	5.5	36.0
1976–7	130,795	3.5	74,976	5.4	36.4

Source: Department of Education and Science, *Statistics of Education 1976: Universities, vol. 6 University Grants Committee, HMSO 1979*

within the academy was to become prematurely fixed as expansion was swiftly followed by cuts: frozen, not in intellectual terms, but contained within those spaces which it had chosen, or had managed to carve out for itself within and between established disciplines before the cuts began to bite. Women's studies had to make itself at home as best it could within these given contours.

Women's studies courses with titles such as 'women in society', 'women and literature', 'women and the Law' etc. were incorporated as options, not without resistance, within degree programmes in sociology, English and other disciplines. But there was never any real prospect of its being founded in the manner of cultural studies at Birmingham or the Polytechnic of East London, in a space all of its own. By the time that academic feminism had mustered enough force to make possible such a bid for autonomy, the period of expansion of higher education was over. Women's studies has typically become established at postgraduate level in interdisciplinary graduate schools offering taught MA and diploma programmes. Where such schools cut across disciplinary boundaries to draw for their pool of teachers on feminists dispersed across the institution within different subject departments, they are also typically askew the normal hierarchies of governing bodies such as Boards of Faculty, and therefore poorly placed to command resources.

The age-profile of full-time academics, including feminists, in higher education at present is very unbalanced. There are few below age forty and in the new universities, few above age fifty-five.[10] A whole generation of women who might in the normal course of events have embarked on academic careers over the past ten years or so in Britain have been obliged to camp out on the margins in part-time temporary posts, or in casual hourly-paid teaching, or in fringe institutions of various kinds. All of these marginal forms of academic work carry exceptionally heavy work-loads, and call for a willingness to teach on different courses from year to year as and when required. They allow precious little time for completing doctorates or publishing books. Younger feminists who might change the contours of feminist thought, and who might be interested in the further development of feminist literary criticism and theory, lack the modern equivalent of £500 a year and a room of one's own – a secure academic post with built-in time for research.

If we wish to pursue the question why feminists working in the broad area of culture and gender were drawn in Britain towards the social sciences and cultural studies rather than towards English in those early founding years we will have to take a closer look at cultural studies as it carved out a place within the territory to which these adjacent disciplines laid claim even where they did not actually occupy or colonize it.

CULTURAL STUDIES AND THE DISPLACEMENT OF THE LITERARY TEXT

Cultural studies in Britain was effectively founded on the ground staked out by Raymond Williams and by the man with whom his name was closely linked in the late 1950s, Richard Hoggart. Both men had been working class 'scholarship boys'; both were involved in adult education; both came from a base in literary criticism. Hoggart founded the CCCS at Birmingham University in 1964. Its second director, Stuart Hall, was another key figure of the New Left at that time. He was one of the founders of *Universities and Left Review* at Oxford in 1958, the journal which merged with E.P. Thompson and John Saville's *New Reasoner* in 1960 to become the *New Left Review* (NLR). Hall edited *NLR* from 1960 to 1962.

The CCCS was to provide the focal institution for the development and definition of cultural studies in Britain. The method on which Hoggart drew in defining the early work of the Centre came from English studies – close textual analysis in the style of F.R. Leavis. The departure from orthodoxy lay in the nature of the texts under scrutiny: 'lived' working-class culture. The prototype was Hoggart's *Uses of Literacy.*[11]

In Williams's work the literary text was never so radically displaced. Rather it was contextualized and politicized. In spite of his insistence that culture was 'ordinary', the literary text continued to take a high profile within his analysis of culture. In 1961, after fourteen years in adult education, Williams returned to the conservative heartlands of the British academic world on accepting a post at Cambridge, where he continued to teach and write literary criticism, albeit with a difference. Where Williams challenged the orthodoxy was less in his choice of text, as was the case with the CCCS, than in his manner of reading it. Works of literature were not to be treated and understood outside of the relations of society at large, and the common culture of which they were a part. They were not repositories of transcendent and threatened values preserved by an educated elite, as T.S. Eliot would have it, nor yet were they merely superstructural, as in simplistic Marxist base-superstructure models. They were part of a general shared culture which was 'ordinary'.

Cultural studies then, provided a forum within which society and history could be given full weight in the analysis of texts, and where the symbolic, meaningful nature of social relations could also be registered. Unlike for example the forms of 'content analysis' developed within media sociology,[12] cultural studies recognized the need for as great a sensitivity to nuances of meaning in the analysis of 'neglected materials drawn from popular culture and the mass media,[13] or of aspects of everyday life, as any deployed in literary critical analysis.

It is not part of my argument that cultural studies in its founding moment was any more conscious of gender issues than was the case within either conventional or more radical forms of literary criticism. In Hoggart's *Uses of Literacy* the working-class woman features in his northern industrial landscape as 'our Mam', an emotionally charged, romanticized figure, flinty and stoical, that Carolyn Steedman challenges and deconstructs from the point of view of the daughter in the first extract here from her *Landscape for a Good Woman.*[14]

In William's early work, with the exception of the novel *Second Generation,* women are barely visible at all, although Jenny Bourne Taylor argues in our second extract that Williams's categories nevertheless lend themselves to feminist analysis.[15] Rather it was the convergence of textual with socio-historical analysis that made cultural studies congenial to British feminism. The whole range of interests which define feminism in general and socialist feminism in particular might be contained within its broad remit, from ethnographic studies of housebound housewives to the history of sexuality and studies of paid employment, as well as more orthodox forms of textual analysis. The volume entitled *Women Take Issue* published by the Women's Studies Group at the CCCS in 1978 exemplifies this range.[16] None of the concerns of feminism are excluded here, as they would be in the more narrowly defined field of literary criticism and theory. It might be argued that the narrower focus may bring gains as well as losses. But it is clear that cultural studies offered a peculiarly appropriate institution 'to harbour and focus a scholarship of its own' to a feminism which had always found itself crossing disciplinary boundaries, and whose distinctive claim among varieties of feminisms had been that the oppression of women could not be understood apart from and outside of its intersection with the dynamics of the capitalist social order. Cultural studies, in locating a wide variety of types of text and of meaning as integral to contemporary society and culture, opened up a space where feminists could study women's lives as well as women's texts as part of the broad socio-cultural construction of gender in capitalist society.

CULTURAL STUDIES AND THEORY

In 1980, following the departure of Stuart Hall for the Open University, the CCCS published a volume entitled *Culture, Media, Language* which was composed of pieces produced during the period of Hall's directorship.[17] In his introduction Hall mapped out the intellectual history of the Centre as it struggled to achieve a theoretically viable definition of cultural studies. He identified as the key originating texts Hoggart's and Williams's early work, mentioned above, and E.P. Thompson's *Making of the English Working Class.*[18] These texts founded a concept of culture not as a reflection of something outside itself, but as an irreducible component of the social formation. Following a detour through certain recent developments in sociology, Hall identified the next significant 'break' in the intellectual trajectory of the Centre as one which took it 'into a complex Marxism' associated with George Lukács and Lucien Goldmann, with which Williams had also become engaged in his own work by this time.[19] In a further 'break' these forms of humanist Marxism were cast aside for the structuralist embrace: the theories of Althusser, Lacan, Levi-Strauss and contemporary cultural linguistics, some of which we have already had occasion to discuss.

The excitement generated by this enthusiastic leap into 'theory' cannot be missed in the work of the CCCS, and must be registered alongside the occasional excesses. This was a fruitful period in the history of the Centre, whose style of work was refreshingly open and collective. The diverse interests represented within the Centre located themselves in different ways within the broad spectrum of theories taken on board during this time. There was no 'party line' – not even a changing one – which defined the work as a whole. This must have provided optimal conditions for feminist scholarship. Gramsci, Althusser, Lacan, Barthes, Derrida, Foucault, and others were raided, appropriated, and tried out for size in relation to the problems faced by socialist-feminist cultural studies. The engagement with (mainly French) theory has had lasting effects on British feminist thought. The short piece included here by Rosalind Coward, who has made major contributions to British feminist thought in the areas of psychoanalysis and semiotics,[20] shows how fruitfully this range of theoretical interests might be brought to bear on 'neglected materials drawn from popular culture and the mass media'.

There was of course a debit side in the CCCS's engagement with 'theory'. There is a distinct tendency in the writings generated through this engagement to move on with lightening speed. Some of the positions occupied by the Centre may have been abandoned with undue haste before their full implications had been explored. In this category I would include the work of the humanist Marxists, continental and British. The work of Lukács and Goldman had only recently begun to be known in Britain when it was upstaged by Althusserianism and an associated critique of humanism has acquired the status of an unquestionable verity. A reopening of the question of the relationship between socialism, feminism and humanism is long overdue.

One effect of the swing against left humanism was that the later writings of Raymond Williams were neglected in cultural studies. We find little engagement with it of the kind that took place in the pages of *NLR*. The one exception in *Culture, Media, Language* is the contribution by the English Studies Group, and it is worth quoting their assessment: 'For a while his work was partly eclipsed by the prestige of more 'rigorously' theoretical accounts. As that prestige wanes or is qualified by a sense of sharpening political urgencies, his work looks more and more compelling.'[21]

One consequence of feminism's engagement with 'theory' has been the reinstatement of textual analysis, including analysis of the literary text. The earlier withdrawal of privileges from 'literature' was in part determined by the recognition that 'great literature', like the American Express credit card, has a rather exclusive circulation. Socialist feminists were particularly liable to feel the force of the rhetorical 'so what?' addressed by the American materialist feminist critic Lillian Robinson to feminist analysis of literature.[22] But just as a feminist poststructuralism which has up-anchored itself from materialism is in danger of drifting over into an apolitical postfeminism, so on the other hand Marxist or materialist criticism which has not felt the full force of the debate over subjectivity and language, is in danger of being pulled back into reductionism.

THE SOCIALIST-FEMINIST SYNTHESIS

What we are beginning to see signs of is a synthetic appropriation of 'theory' which is neither an unprincipled eclecticism nor a mere capitulation to the latest fashion. The synthesis in question is between socialist history and the theory of human subjectivity historicized. It may be seen in a double movement which is registered throughout this volume: on the part of socialist historians and historical sociologists towards the recasting of socialist history to incorporate the history of human subjectivity, and on the part of feminist critics placing the literary and other texts as integral components of that history. This may be seen at best in the next two extracts in this section, Alison Light's study of Daphne Du Maurier's *Rebecca,* and Cora Kaplan's essay of socialist-feminist criticism, 'Pandora's Box'. Kaplan reinstates the literary text without losing sight of its class parameters. She makes claims for it which places it alongside the 'discourses' of socialist history, sociology, economics, as a 'central site of class meaning'. Not all the advantages, she insists, lie with these other discourses, for 'fiction refuses the notion of a genderless class subjectivity, and resists any simple reduction of class meaning and class identity to productive forces.[23] Yet at the same time we are warned that the 'appropriation of modern critical theory – semiotic with an emphasis on the psychoanalytic – . . . must engage fully with the effects of other systems of difference than the sexual or they too will produce no more than an anti-humanist avant-garde version of romance.'[24]

This volume closes, appropriately, with a contribution by a Norwegian feminist who has played a major part in ensuring the circulation of French feminist thought in Britain, and who has taught feminist criticism in Scandinavia, Britain, America and elsewhere.[25] Toril Moi yet insists, quite properly, on locating herself within the traditions of British socialist and feminist thought. She rehearses many of the arguments whose course has been plotted in this volume, in her critical analysis of the recent 'transatlantic *pas de deux*' entered into by American feminists such as Alice Jardine. The repressed third term of this dyad, which returns to disrupt the text, is, Moi argues, British materialist feminism.

NOTES

1 Marilyn Butler, 'Feminist criticism, late-80s style', *Times Literary Supplement,* 11-17, March 1988, p. 285.
2 Ibid., p. 285.
3 Gillian Beer, *Darwins Plots: Evolutionary Narrative in Darwin, George Eliot and Nineteenth-Century Fiction,* Routledge, 1983; and *George Eliot,* Harvester, 1986.
4 Mary Jacobus, ed., *Women Writing and Writing About Women,* Croom Helm, 1979; and *Reading Women,* Methuen, 1986.
5 Paul Lauter, 'Race and gender in the shaping of the American literary canon: a case study from the twenties' in J. Newton and D. Rosenfelt, eds, *Feminist Criticism and Social Change,* Methuen, 1985, p. 31.
6 For a discussion, see Terry Lovell, *Consuming Fiction,* Verso, 1987.
7 For example, Michéle Barrett and Annette Kuhn.
8 Cmnd. 2154. Committee on Higher Education, *Report of the Committee appointed by the Prime Minister under the Chairmanship of Lord Robbins, 1961-3,* HMSO, 1963.
9 The case of film studies is particularly interesting in this respect. The British Film Institute sponsored a number of posts in British Universities for limited periods, which led to the development of several film studies departments. Unfortunately the cuts began to bite while these new departments were still in fledgling state, and as a result, they have tended to remain small, in spite of the large numbers of highly-qualified students who seek admission.
10 In 1983, the University Grants Committee founded a number of 'new blood' posts in universities to redress this imbalance. But new blood, it soon transpired, runs more often in male veins. There is an upper age-limit which tells against women with gaps in their careers for child-rearing, and the posts tend to be concentrated in sciences, technology and business studies. Meanwhile ordinary posts falling vacant in arts and social sciences, where women are more likely to be found, have been frozen.
11 Richard Hoggart, *The Uses of Literacy,* Allen Lane, 1958.
12 For examples of content analysis, see Bernard R. Berelson, *Content Analysis in Communications Research,* Free Press of Glencoe, 1951; I. de Sola Pool, ed., *Trends in Content Analysis,* University of Illinois Press, 1959; George Gerbner et al., eds, *The Analysis of Communication Content,* Wiley, 1969.
13 Stuart Hall, 'Introduction', in S. Hall et al., eds, *Culture, Media, Language,* Hutchinson, 1980, p. 21.

14 Carolyn Steedman, *Landscape for a Good Woman*, Virago, 1986
15 Jenny Bourne Taylor, 'Gender and Generation in Raymond Williams's Cultural Politics' (below, pp. 329-47). See also Carol Watts, 'Reclaiming the Border Country: Feminism and the Work of Raymond Williams', in *News From Nowhere*, 6, 'Raymond Williams: Third Generation', Oxford English Limited, 1989.
16 Women's Studies Group, Centre for Contemporary Cultural Studies, *Women Take Issue*, Hutchinson, 1978.
17 S. Hall et al., eds, *Culture, Media, Language*, Hutchinson, 1980.
18 E. P. Thompson, *The Making of the English Working Class*, Allen Lane, 1963.
19 Raymond Williams, 'Literature and Sociology: in Memory of Lucien Goldmann', *New Left Review*, 67, 1971.
20 Rosalind Coward, *Patriarchal Precedents: Sexuality and Social Relations*, Routledge and Kegan Paul, 1983; R. Coward and J. Ellis, *Language and Materialism: Developments in Semiology and the Theory of the Subject*, Routledge and Kegan Paul, 1977; R. Coward, *Female Desire*, Paladin, 1984, and *The Whole Truth: The Myth of Alternative Health*, 1989.
21 English Studies Group, 1978–9, 'Recent developments in English Studies at the Centre', in S. Hall et al., eds, *Culture, Media, Language*, Hutchinson, 1980, p. 230.
22 Lillian Robinson, 'Criticism: Who Needs It?' in Robinson, *Sex, Class and Culture*, Methuen, 1978, p. 92.
23 Cora Kaplan, 'Pandora's Box: Subjectivity, Class and Sexuality in Socialist Feminist Criticism', in Gayle Green and Coppelia Kahn, eds, *Making a Difference*, Methuen, 1985, p. 164. The essay was reprinted in Cora Kaplan, *Sea Changes*, Verso, 1986.
24 Ibid., p. 148.
25 Toril Moi, *Sexual/Textual Politics: Feminist Literary Theory*. Methuen, 1985.

16

Carolyn Steedman

Stories

This book is about lives lived out on the borderlands, lives for which the central interpretative devices of the culture don't quite work. It has a childhood at its centre – my childhood, a personal past – and it is about the disruption of that fifties childhood by the one my mother had lived out before me, and the stories she told about it. Now, the narrative of both these childhoods can be elaborated by the marginal and secret stories that other working-class girls and women from a recent historical past have to tell.

This book, then, is about interpretations, about the places where we rework what has already happened to give current events meaning. It is about the stories we make for ourselves, and the social specificity of our understanding of those stories. The childhood dreams recounted in this book, the fantasies, the particular and remembered events of a South London fifties childhood do not, by themselves, constitute its point. We all return to memories and dreams like this, again and again; the story we tell of our own life is reshaped around them. But the point doesn't lie there, back in the past, back in the lost time at which they happened; the only point lies in interpretation. The past is re-used through the agency of social information, and that interpretation of it can only be made with what people know of a social world and their place within it. It matters then, whether one reshapes past time, re-uses the ordinary exigencies and crises of all childhoods whilst looking down from the curtainless windows of a terraced house like my mother did, or sees at that moment the long view stretching away from the big house in some richer and more detailed landscape. All children experience a first loss, a first exclusion; lives shape themselves around this sense of being cut off and denied. The health visitor repeated the exclusion in the disdainful language of class, told my mother exactly what it was she stood outside. It is a proposition of this book that specificity of place and politics has to be reckoned with in making an account of anybody's life, and their use of their own past.

My mother's longing shaped my own childhood. From a Lancashire mill town and a working-class twenties childhood she came away wanting: fine clothes, glamour, money; to be what she wasn't. However that longing was produced in her distant childhood, what she actually wanted were real things, real entities, things she materially lacked, things that a culture and a social system withheld from her. The story she told was about this wanting, and it remained a resolutely social story. When the world didn't deliver the goods, she held the world to blame. In this way, the story she told was a form of political analysis, that allows a political interpretation to be made of her life.

Personal interpretations of past time – the stories that people tell themselves in order to explain how they got to the place they currently inhabit – are often in deep and ambiguous conflict with the official interpretative devices of a culture. This book is organized around a conflict like this, taking as a starting point the structures of class analysis and schools of cultural criticism that cannot deal with everything there is to say about my mother's life. My mother was a single parent for most of her adulthood, who had children, but who also, in a quite particular way, didn't want them. She was a woman who finds no place in the iconography of working-class motherhood that Jeremy Seabrook presents in *Working Class Childhood*, and who is not to be found in Richard Hoggart's landscape. She ran a working-class household far away from the traditional communities of class, in exile and isolation, and in which a man was not a master, nor even there very much. Surrounded as a child by the articulated politics of class-consciousness, she became a working-class Conservative, the only political form that allowed her to reveal the politics of envy.

Many of these ambiguities raise central questions about gender as well as class, and the development of gender in particular social and class circumstances. So the usefulness of the biographical and autobiographical core of the book lies in the challenge it may offer to much of our conventional understanding of childhood, working-class childhood, and little-girlhood. In particular, it challenges the tradition of cultural criticism in this country, which has celebrated a kind of psychological simplicity in the lives lived out in Hoggart's endless streets of little houses. It can help reverse a central question within feminism and psychoanalysis, about the reproduction of the desire to mother in little girls, and replace it with a consideration of women who, by refusing to mother, have refused to reproduce themselves or the circumstances of their exile. The personal past that this book deals with can also serve to raise the question of what happens to theories of patriarchy in households where a father's position is not confirmed by the social world outside the front door. And the story of two lives that follows points finally to a consideration of what people – particularly working-class children of the recent past – come to understand of themselves when all they possess is their labour, and what becomes of the notion of class-consciousness when it is seen as a structure of feeling that can be learned in childhood, with one of its components a proper envy, the desire of people for the things of the earth. Class and gender, and their articulations, are the bits and pieces from which psychological selfhood is made.

I grew up in the 1950s, the place and time now located as the first scene of Labour's failure to grasp the political consciousness of its constituency and its eschewal of socialism in favour of welfare philanthropism.[1] But the Left had failed with my mother long before the 1950s. A working-class Conservative from a traditional Labour background, she shaped my childhood by the stories she carried from her own, and from an earlier family history. They were stories designed to show me the terrible unfairness of things, the subterranean culture of longing for that which one can never have. These stories can be used now to show my mother's dogged search, using what politics came to hand, for a public form to embody such longing.

Her envy, her sense of the unfairness of things, could not be directly translated into political understanding, and certainly could not be used by the Left to shape an articulated politics of class. What follows offers no account of that particular political failure. It is rather an attempt to use that failure, which has been delineated by historians writing from quite different perspectives and for quite different purposes, as a device that may help to explain a particular childhood, and out of that childhood explain an individual life lived in historical time. This is not to say that this book involves a search for a past, or for what really happened.[2] It is about how people use the past to tell the stories of their life. So the evidence presented here is of a different order from the biographical; it is about the experience of my own childhood, and the way in which my mother re-asserted, reversed and restructured her own within mine.

Envy as a political motive has always been condemned: a fierce morality pervades what little writing there is on the subject. Fiercely moral as well, the tradition of cultural criticism in this country has, by ignoring feelings like these, given us the map of an upright and decent country. Out of this tradition has come Jeremy Seabrook's *Working Class Childhood* and its nostalgia for a time when people who were 'united against cruel material privations...discovered the possibilities of the human consolations they could offer each other', and its celebration of the upbringing that produced the psychic structure of 'the old working class'.[3] I take a defiant pleasure in the way that my mother's story can be used to subvert this account. Born into 'the old working class', she wanted: a New Look skirt, a timbered country cottage, to marry a prince.

The very devices that are intended to give expression to childhoods like mine and my mother's actually deny their expression. The problem with most childhoods lived out in households maintained by social class III (manual), IV and V parents is that they simply are not bad enough to be worthy of attention. The literary form that allows presentation of working-class childhood, the working-class autobiography, reveals its mainspring in the title of books like *Born to Struggle; Poverty, Hardship, But Happiness; Growing Up Poor in East London; Coronation Cups and Jam Jars* – and I am deeply aware of the ambiguities that attach to the childhood I am about to recount. Not only was it not very bad, or only bad in a way that working-class autobiography doesn't deal in, but also a particular set of emotional and psychological circumstances ensured that at the time, and for many years after it was over and I had escaped, I thought of it as *ordinary*, a period of relative material ease, just like everybody else's childhood.

I read female working-class autobiography obsessively when I was in my twenties and early thirties (a reading that involved much repetition: it's a small corpus), and whilst I wept over Catherine Cookson's *Our Kate* I felt a simultaneous distance from the Edwardian child who fetched beer barefooted for an alcoholic mother, the Kate of the title (I have to make it very clear that my childhood was really *not* like that). But it bore a relationship to a personal reality that I did not yet know about: what I now see in the book is its fine delineation of the feeling of being on the outside, outside the law; for Catherine Cookson was illegitimate.[4]

In 1928, when Kathleen Woodward, who had grown up in not-too-bad Peckham, South London, wrote *Jipping Street*, she set her childhood in Bermondsey, in a place of abject and abandoned poverty, 'practically off the map, derelict', and in this manner found a way, within an established literary form, of expressing a complexity of feeling about her personal past that the form itself did not allow.[5]

The tradition of cultural criticism that has employed working-class lives, and their rare expression in literature, had made solid and concrete the absence of psychological individuality – of subjectivity – that Kathleen Woodward struggled against in *Jipping Street*. 'In poor societies,' writes Jeremy Seabrook in *Working Class Childhood*,

> where survival is more important than elaboration of relationships, the kind of ferocious personal struggles that lock people together in our own more leisured society are less known.[6]

But by making this distinction, the very testimony to the continuing reverberation of pain and loss, absence and desire in childhood, which is made manifest in the words of 'the old working-class' people that makes up much of *Working Class Childhood*, is actually denied.

It would not be possible, in fact, to write a book called 'Middle-Class Childhood' (this in spite of the fact that the shelves groan with psychoanalytic, developmental and literary accounts of such childhoods) and get the same kind of response from readers. It's a faintly titillating title, carrying the promise that some kind of pathology is about to be investigated. What is more, in *Working Class Childhood* the discussion of childhood and what our society has done to the idea of childhood becomes the vehicle for an anguished rejection of post-War materialism, the metaphor for all that has gone wrong with the old politics of class and the stance of the labour movement towards the desires that capitalism has inculcated in those who are seen as the passive poor. An analysis like this denies its subjects a particular story, a personal history, except when that story illustrates a general thesis; and it denies the child, and the child who continues to live in the adult it becomes, both an unconscious life, and a particular and developing consciousness of the meanings presented by the social world.

Twenty years before *Working Class Childhood* was written, Richard Hoggart explored a similar passivity of emotional life in working-class communities, what in *The Uses of Literacy* he revealingly called 'Landscape with Figures: A Setting' – a place where in his own memories of the 1920s and 1930s and in his description of similar communities of the 1950s, most people lacked 'any feeling that some change can, or indeed ought to be made in the general pattern of life'.[7] All of Seabrook's corpus deals in the same way with what he sees as 'the falling into decay of a life once believed by those who shared it to be the only admissible form that life could take'.[8] I want to open the door of one of the terraced houses, in a mill town in the 1920s, show Seabrook my mother and her longing, make him see the child of my imagination sitting by an empty grate, reading a tale that tells her a goose-girl can marry a king.

Heaviness of time lies on the pages of *The Uses of Literacy*. The streets are all the same; nothing changes. Writing about the structure of a child's life, Seabrook notes that as recently as thirty years ago (that is in the 1950s, the time of my own childhood) the week was measured out by each day's function – wash-day, market-day, the day for ironing – and the day itself timed by 'cradling and comforting' ritual.[9] This extraordinary attribution of sameness and the acceptance of sameness to generations of lives arises from several sources. First of all, delineation of emotional and psychological selfhood has been made by and through the testimony of people in a central relationship to the dominant culture, that is to say by and through people who are not working class. This is an obvious point, but it measures out an immensely complicated and contradictory area of historical development that has scarcely yet been investigated. Superficially, it might be said that historians, failing to find evidence of most people's emotional or psychosexual existence, have simply assumed that there can't have been much there to find. Such an assumption ignores the structuring of late nineteenth- and early twentieth-century psychology and psychoanalysis, and the way in which the lived experience of the majority of people in a class society has been pathologized and marginalized. When the sons of the working class, who have made their earlier escape from this landscape of psychological simplicity, put so much effort into accepting and celebrating it, into delineating a background of uniformity and passivity, in which pain, loss, love, anxiety and desire are washed over with a patina of stolid emotional sameness, then something important, and odd, and possibly promising of startling revelation, is actually going on. This refusal of a complicated psychology to those living in conditions of material distress is a central theme of this book, and will be considered again in its third section.

The attribution of psychological simplicity to working-class people also derives from the positioning of mental life within Marxism:

> Mental life flows from material conditions. Social being is determined above all by class position – location within the realm of production. Consciousness and politics, all mental conceptions spring from material forces and the relations of production and so reflect these class origins.

This description is Sally Alexander's summary of Marx's 'Preface to a Contribution to the Critique of Political Economy', and of his thesis, expressed here and elsewhere, that 'the mode of production of material life conditions the general process of social, political and mental life'.[10] The attribution of simplicity to the mental life of working people is not, of course, made either in the original, nor in this particular critique of it. But like any theory developed in a social world, the notion of consciousness as located within the realm of production draws on the reality of that world. It is in the 'Preface' itself that Marx mentions his move to London in the 1850s as offering among other advantages 'a convenient vantage point for the observation of bourgeois society', and which indeed he did observe, and live within, in the novels he and his family read, in family theatricals, in dinner-table talk: a mental life apparently much richer than that of the subjects of his theories. Lacking such possessions of culture, working-class people have come to be seen, within the field of cultural criticism, as bearing the elemental simplicity of class-consciousness and little more.

Technically, class-consciousness has not been conceived of as *psychological* consciousness. It has been separated from 'the empirically given, and from the psychologically describable and explicable ideas that men form about their situation in life', and has been seen rather as a possible set of reactions people might have to discovering the implications of the position they occupy within the realm of production.[11] Theoretical propositions apart though, in the everyday world, the term *is* used in its psychological sense, is generally and casually used to describe what people have 'thought, felt and wanted at any moment in history and from any point in the class structure'.[12] Working-class autobiography and people's history have been developed as forms that allow the individual and collective expression of these thoughts, feelings and desires about class societies and the effect of class structures on individuals and communities. But as forms of analysis and writing, people's history and working-class autobiography are relatively innocent of psychological theory, and there has been little space within them to discuss the *development* of class-consciousness (as opposed to its expression), nor for understanding of it as a *learned* position, learned in childhood, and often through the exigencies of difficult and lonely lives.

Children present a particular problem here, for whilst some women may learn the official dimensions of class-consciousness by virtue of their entry into the labour market and by adopting forms of struggle and understanding evolved by men,[13] children, who are not located directly within the realm of production, still reach understandings of social position, exclusion and difference. At all levels, class-consciousness must be learned in some way, and we need a model of such a process to explain the social and psychological development of working-class children (indeed, of all children).

When the mental life of working-class women is entered into the realm of production, and their narrative is allowed to disrupt the monolithic story of wage-labour and capital and when childhood and childhood learning are reckoned with, then what makes the old story unsatisfactory is not so much its granite-like *plot*, built around exploiter and exploited, capital and proletariat, but rather its *timing*: the precise how and why of the development of class-consciousness. But if we do allow an unconscious life to working-class children, then we can perhaps see the first loss, the earliest exclusion (known most familiarly to us as the oedipal crisis) brought forward later, and articulated through an adult experience of class and class relations.

An adult experience of class does not in any case, as Sally Alexander has pointed out, 'produce a shared and even consciousness', even if it is fully registered and articulated.[14] This uneven and problematic consciousness (which my mother's life and political conviction represents so clearly) is one of the subjects of this book. A perception of childhood experience and understanding used as the lineaments of adult political analysis, may also help us see under the language and conflicts of class, historically much older articulations – the subjective and political expressions of radicalism – which may still serve to give a voice to people who know that they do not have what they want, who know that they have been cut off from the earth in some way.[15]

The attribution of psychological sameness to the figures in the working-class landscape has been made by men, for whom the transitions of class are at once more ritualized than they are for women, and much harder to make. Hoggart's description of the plight of the 'scholarship boy' of the thirties and forties, and the particular anxiety afflicting those in the working class

> who have been pulled one stage away from their original culture and have not the intellectual equipment which would then cause them to move on to join the 'declassed' professionals and experts[16]

makes nostalgic reading now in a post-War situation where a whole generation of escapees occupies professional positions that allow them to speak of their working-class origins with authority, to use them, in Seabrook's words 'as a kind of accomplishment'.[17] By the 1950s the divisions of the educational establishment that produced Hoggart's description were much altered and I, a grammar-school girl of the 1960s, was sent to university with a reasonably full equipment of culture and a relative degree of intellectual self-awareness. Jeremy Seabrook, some eight years older than me and at Cambridge in the late fifties, sat with his fellow travellers from working-class backgrounds 'telling each other escape stories, in which we were all picaresque heroes of our own lives'.[18]

But at the University of Sussex in 1965, there were no other women to talk to like this, at least there were none that I met (though as proletarianism was fashionable at the time, there were several men with romantic and slightly untruthful tales to tell). And should I have met a woman like me (there must have been some: we were all children of the Robbins generation), we could not have talked of escape except within a literary framework that we had learned from the working-class novels of the early sixties (some of which, like *Room at the Top*, were set books on certain courses); and that framework was itself ignorant of the material stepping-stones of our escape: clothes, shoes, make-up. We could not be heroines of the conventional narratives of escape. Women are, in the sense that Hoggart and Seabrook present in their pictures of transition, without class, because the cut and fall of a skirt and good leather shoes can take you across the river and to the other side: the fairy-tales tell you that goose-girls may marry kings.

The fixed townscapes of Northampton and Leeds that Hoggart and Seabrook have described show endless streets of houses, where mothers who don't go out to work order the domestic day, where men are masters, and children, when they grow older, express gratitude for the harsh discipline meted out to them. The first task is to particularize this profoundly a-historical landscape (and so this book details a mother who was a working woman and a single parent, and a father who wasn't a patriarch). And once the landscape is detailed and historicized in this way, the urgent need becomes to find a way of theorizing the result of such difference and particularity, not in order to find a description that can be universally applied (the point is *not* to say that all working-class childhoods are the same, nor that experience of them produces unique psychic structures) but so that the people in exile, the inhabitants of the long streets, may start to use the autobiographical 'I', and tell the stories of their life.

There are other interpretative devices for my mother which, like working-class autobiographies of childhood, make her no easier to see. Nearly everything that has been written on the subject of mothering (except the literature of pathology, of battering and violence) assumes the desire to mother; and there are feminisms now that ask me to return Persephone-like to my own mother, and find new histories of my strength. When I first came across Kathleen Woodward's *Jipping Street*, I read it with the shocked astonishment of one who had never seen what she knows written down before. Kathleen Woodward's mother of the 1890s was the one I knew: mothers were those who told you how hard it was to have you, how long they were in labour with you ('twenty hours with you', my mother frequently reminded me) and who told you to accept the impossible contradiction of being both desired and a burden; and not to complain.[19] This ungiving endurance is admired by working-class boys who grow up to write about their mother's flinty courage. But the daughter's silence on the matter is a measure of the price you pay for survival. I don't think the baggage will ever lighten, for me or my sister. We were born, and had no choice in the matter; but we were burdens, expensive, never grateful enough. There was nothing we could do to pay back the debt of our existence. 'Never have children dear,' she said; 'they ruin your life.' Shock moves swiftly across the faces of women to who I tell this story. But it is *ordinary* not to want your children, I silently assert; normal to find them a nuisance.

I read the collection *Fathers: Reflections by Daughters*, or Ann Oakley's *Taking It Like a Woman*[2] and feel the painful and familiar sense of exclusion from these autobiographies of middle-class little-girlhood and womanhood, envy of those who belong, who can, like Ann Oakley, use the outlines of conventional romantic fiction to tell a life story. And women like this, friends, say: but it was like that for me too, my childhood was like yours; my father was like that, my mother didn't want me. What they cannot bear, I think, is that there exists a poverty and marginality of experience to which they have no access, structures of feeling that they have not lived within (and would not want to live within: for these are the structures of deprivation). They are caught then in a terrible exclusion, an exclusion from the experience of others that measures out their own central relationship to the culture. The myths tell their story, the fairy-tales show the topography of the houses they once inhabited. The psychoanalytic drama, which uses the spatial and temporal structures of all these old tales, permits the entry of such women to the drama itself. Indeed, the psychoanalytic drama was constructed to describe that of middle-class women (and as drama it does of course describe all such a woman's exclusions, as well as her relationship to those exclusions, with her absence and all she lacks lying at the very heart of the theory). The woman whose drama psychoanalytic case-study describes in this way never does stand to one side, and watch, and know she doesn't belong.

What follows is largely concerned with how two girl children, growing up in different historical periods, got to be the women they became. The sense of exclusion, of being cut off from what others enjoy, was a dominant sense of both childhoods, but expressed and used differently in two different historical settings. This detailing of social context to psychological development reveals not only difference, but also certain continuities of experience in working-class childhood. For instance, many recent accounts of psychological development and the development of gender, treat our current social situation as astonishingly new and strange:

> On the social/historical level. . . we are living in a period in which mothers are increasingly living alone with their children, offering opportunities for new psychic patterns to emerge. Single mothers are forced to make themselves subject to their children; they are forced to invent new symbolic roles. . . . The child cannot position the mother as object to the father's law, since in single parent households her desire sets things in motion.[21]

But the evidence of some nineteenth- and twentieth-century children used in this book shows that in their own reckoning their households were often those of a single female parent, sometimes because of the passivity of a father's presence, sometimes because of his physical absence. Recent feminisms have often, as Jane Gallop points out in *The Daughter's Seduction*, endowed men with 'the sort of unified phallic sovereignty that characterises an absolute monarch, and which little resembles actual power in our social, economic structure'.[22] We need a reading of history that reveals fathers mattering in a different way from the way they matter in the corpus of traditional psychoanalysis, the novels that depict the same familial settings and in the bourgeois households of the fairy-tales.

A father like mine dictated each day's existence; our lives would have been quite different had he not been there. But he didn't *matter*, and his singular unimportance needs explaining. His not mattering has an effect like this: I don't quite believe in male power; somehow the iron of patriarchy didn't enter into my soul. I accept the idea of male power intellectually, of course (and I will eat my words the day I am raped, or the knife is slipped between my ribs; though I know that will not be the case: in the dreams it is a woman who holds the knife, and only a woman can kill).

Fixing my father, and my mother's mothering, in time and politics can help show the creation of gender in particular households and in particular familial situations at the same time as it demonstrates the position of men and the social reality represented by them in particular households. We need historical accounts of such relationships, not just a longing that they might be different.[23] Above all, perhaps, we need a sense of people's complexity of relationship to the historical situations they inherit. In *Family and Kinship in East London*, the authors found that over half the married women they interviewed had seen their mothers within the preceding twenty-four hours, and that 80 per cent had seen them within the previous week. Young and Willmott assumed that the daughters wanted to do this, and interpreted four visits a week on average as an expression of attachment and devotion.[24] There exists a letter that I wrote to a friend one vacation from Sussex, either in 1966 or in 1967, in which I described my sitting in the evenings with my mother, refusing to go out, holding tight to my guilt and duty, knowing that I *was* her, and that I must keep her company; and we were certainly not Demeter and Persephone to each other, nor ever could be, but two women caught by a web of sexual and psychological relationships in the front room of a council house, the South London streets stretching away outside like the railway lines that brought us and our history to that desperate and silent scene in front of the flickering television screen.

Raymond Williams has written about the difficulty of linking past and present in writing about working-class life, and the result of this difficulty in novels that either show the past to be a regional zone of experience in which the narrator cancels her present from the situation she is describing, or which are solely about the experience of flight. Writing like this, comments Williams, has lacked 'any sense of the continuity of working class life, which does not cease just because the individual [the writer] moves out of it, but which also itself changes internally'.[25]

This kind of cancellation of a writer's present from the past may take place because novels – stories – work by a process of temporal revelation: they move forward in time in order to demonstrate a state of affairs. The novel that works in this way employs contingency, that is, it works towards the revelation of something not quite certain, but *there*, nevertheless, waiting to be shown by the story,[26] and the story gets told without revealing the shaping force of the writer's current situation.

The highlighting not just of the subject matter of this book, but also of the possibilities of written form it involves, is important, because the construction of the account that follows has something to say about the question that Raymond Williams has raised, and which is largely to do with the writing of stories that aren't central to a dominant culture. My mother cut herself off from the old working class by the process of migration, by retreat from the North to a southern country with my father, hiding secrets in South London's long streets. But she carried with her her childhood, as I have carried mine along the lines of embourgeoisement and state education. In order to outline these childhoods and the uses we put them to, the structure of psychoanalytic case-study – the narrative form that Freud is described as inventing – is used in this book.[27] The written case-study allows the writer to enter the present into the past, allows the dream, the wish or the fantasy of the past to shape current time, and treats them as evidence in their own right. In this way, the narrative form of case-study shows what went into its writing, shows the bits and pieces from which it is made up, in the way that history refuses to do, and that fiction can't.[28] Case-study presents the ebb and flow of memory, the structure of dreams, the stories that people tell to explain themselves to others. The autobiographical section of this book, the second part, is constructed on such a model.

But something else has to be done with these bits and pieces, with all the tales that are told, in order to take them beyond the point of anecdote and into history. To begin to construct history, the writer has to do two things, make two movements through time. First of all, we need to search backwards from the vantage point of the present in order to appraise things in the past and attribute meaning to them. When events and entities in the past have been given their meaning in this way, then we can trace forward what we have already traced backwards, and make a history.[29] When a history is finally written, events are explained by putting them in causal order and establishing causal connections between them. But what follows in this book does not make a history (even though a great deal of historical material is presented). For a start, I simply do not know enough about many of the incidents described to explain the connections between them. I am unable to perform an act of historical explanation in this way.

This tension between the stories told to me as a child, the diffuse and timeless structure of the case-study with which they are presented, and the compulsions of historical explanation, is no mere rhetorical device. There is a real problem, a real tension here that I cannot resolve (my inability to resolve it is part of the story). All the stories that follow, told as this book tells them, aren't stories in their own right: they exist in tension with other more central ones. In the same way, the processes of working-class autobiography, of people's history and of the working-class novel cannot show a proper and valid culture existing in its own right, underneath the official forms, waiting for revelation. Accounts of working-class life are told by tension and ambiguity, out on the borderlands. The story – my mother's story, a hundred thousand others – cannot be absorbed into the central one: it is both its disruption and its essential counterpoint: this is a drama of *class*.

But visions change, once any story is told; ways of seeing are altered. The point of a story is to present itself momentarily as complete, so that it can be said: it does for now, it will do; it is an account that will last a while. Its point is briefly to make an audience connive in the telling, so that they might say: yes, that's how it was; or, that's how it could have been. So now, the words written down, the world is suddenly full of women waiting, as in Ann Oakley's extraordinary delineation of

> the curiously impressive image of women as always waiting for someone or something, in shopping queues, in antenatal clinics, in bed, for men to come home, at the school gates, by the playground swing, for birth or the growing up of children, in hope of love or freedom or re-employment, waiting for the future to liberate or burden them and the past to catch up with them.[30]

The other side of waiting is wanting. The faces of the women in the queues are the faces of unfulfilled desire; if we look, there are many women driven mad in this way, as my mother was. This is a sad and secret story, but it isn't just hers alone.

What historically conscious readers may do with this book is read it as a Lancashire story, see here evidence of a political culture of 1890–1930 carried from the North-west, to shape another childhood in another place and time. They will perhaps read it as part of an existing history, seeing here a culture shaped by working women, and their consciousness of themselves as workers. They may see the indefatigable capacity for work that has been described in many other places, the terrifying ability to *get by*, to cope, against all odds. Some historically conscious readers may even find here the irony that this specific social and cultural experience imparted to its women: 'No one gives you anything', said my mother, as if reading the part of 'our mam' handed to her by the tradition of working-class autobiography. 'If you want things, you have to go out and work for them.' But out of that tradition I can make the dislocation that the irony actually permits, and say: 'If no one will write my story, then I shall have to go out and write it myself.'

The point of being a Lancashire weaver's daughter, as my mother was, is that it is *classy*: what my mother knew was that if you were going to be working class, then you might as well be the best that's going, and for women, Lancashire and weaving provided that elegance, that edge of difference and distinction. I'm sure that she told the titled women whose hands she did when she became a manicurist in the 1960s where it was she came from, proud, defiant: look at me. (Beatrix Campbell has made what I think is a similar point about the classiness of being a miner, for working-class men.)[31]

This is a book about stories; and it is a book about *things* (objects, entities, relationships, people), and the way in which we talk and write about them: about the difficulties of metaphor. Above all, it is about people wanting those things, and the structures of political thought that have labelled this wanting as wrong. Later in the book, suggestions are made about a relatively old structure of political thought in this country, that of radicalism, and its possible entry into the political dialogue of the North-west; and how perhaps it allowed people to feel desire, anger and envy – for the things they did not have.

The things though, will remain a problem. The connection between women and clothes surfaces often in these pages, particularly in the unacknowledged testimony of many nineteenth- and twentieth-century women and girls; and it was with the image of a New Look coat that, in 1950, I made my first attempt to understand and symbolize the content of my mother's desire. I think now of all the stories, all the reading, all the dreams that help us to see ourselves in the landscape, and see ourselves watching as well. 'A woman must continually watch herself,' remarked John Berger some years ago.

> She is almost continually accompanied by her own image of herself. Whilst she is walking across a room or whilst she is weeping at the death of her father, she can scarcely avoid envisioning herself walking and weeping.[32]

This book is intended to specify, in historical terms, some of the processes by which we come to step into the landscape, and see ourselves. But the *clothes* we wear there remain a question. Donald Winnicott wrote about the transitional object (those battered teddies and bits of blanket that babies use in the early stages of distinguishing themselves from the world around them) and its usefulness to the young children who adopt it. The transitional object, he wrote, 'must seem to the infant to give warmth, or to move, or to have texture, or to do something that seems to show it has vitality or reality of its own.'[33] Like clothes: that we may see ourself better as we stand there and watch; and for our protection.

NOTES

The place of publication is London, unless otherwise specified. The abbreviation PP stands for the Parliamentary Paper Series.

1 Gareth Stedman-Jones, 'Why is the Labour Party in a Mess?' in *Languages of Class: Studies in English Working Class History, 1832–1982*, Cambridge University Press, Cambridge, 1983, pp. 239–56. Beatrix Campbell surveys critiques of the 1950s in *Wigan Pier Revisited*, Virago, 1984, pp. 217–34. See also James Hinton, *Labour and Socialism: A History of the British Labour Movement, 1867–1974*, Wheatsheaf, Brighton, 1983, pp. 182–7.

2 'What actually happened is less important than what is felt to have happened. Is that right?' says Ronald Fraser to his analyst, and his analyst agrees. Ronald Fraser, *In Search of a Past*, Verso, 1984, p.95.

3 Jeremy Seabrook, *Working Class Childhood*, Gollancz, 1982, pp. 23–7, 33.

4 Catherine Cookson, *Our Kate*, Macdonald, 1969.

5 Kathleen Woodward, *Jipping Street (1928)*, Virago, 1983.

6 Seabrook, *Working Class Childhood*, p. 140.

7 Richard Hoggart, *The Uses of Literacy,* Penguin, 1959, p. 91.
8 Jeremy Seabrook, *The Unprivileged* (1967), Penguin, 1973, Foreword.
9 Ibid., pp. 202–3.
10 Sally Alexander, 'Women, Class and Sexual Difference', *History Workshop Journal*, 17 (1984), pp. 125–49. Karl Marx, 'Preface to "A Contribution to the Critique of Political Economy"' (1859), *Early Writings*, The Pelican Marx Library, Penguin, 1975, pp. 424–8.
11 George Lukács, *History and Class Consciousness*, Merlin Press, 1968, pp. 46–82, especially pp. 50–5. See also Eric Hobsbawm, 'Notes on Class Consciousness', in *Worlds of Labour*, Weidenfeld and Nicolson, 1984, pp. 15–32.
12 Lukács, *History and Class Consciousness*, p. 51.
13 Pauline Hunt, *Gender and Class Consciousness*, Macmillan, 1980, pp. 171–9. A direct and simple learning isn't posited here; but it is the workplace and an existing backdrop of trade-union organization that provides for the expression of women's class consciousness.
14 Alexander. 'Women, Class and Sexual Difference', p. 131.
15 See Carolyn Steedman, *Landscape for a Good Woman*, 'Exclusions', pp. 119–21; and Gareth Stedman-Jones, 'Rethinking Chartism' in Stedman-Jones, *Languages of Class*, pp. 90–178.
16 Hoggart, *The Uses of Literacy*, p. 293.
17 Jeremy Seabrook, *What Went Wrong?*, Gollancz, 1978, pp. 260–1.
18 Ibid., p. 262.
19 To be told how difficult it was to give birth to you is an extremely common experience for all little girls, and as John and Elizabeth Newson point out in *Seven Years Old in the Home Environment*, Allen and Unwin, 1976, pp. 186–7, chaperonage, and the consequent amount of time girls spend in adult company, is likely to make such topics of conversation accessible to them. But the punishment and the warning involved in telling girl children about the difficulties their birth presented to their mother is rarely written about. But see Carolyn Steedman, *The Tidy House: Little Girls Writing,* Virago, 1982, pp. 34–5, 145–7.
20 Ursula Owen ed., *Fathers: Reflections by Daughters,* Virago, 1983. Ann Oakley, *Taking It Like a Woman,* Cape, 1984.
21 E. Ann Kaplan, 'Is the Gaze Male?', in Ann Snitow et al., eds, *Desire: The Politics of Female Sexuality,* Virago, 1984, p.335.
22 Jane Gallop, *Feminism and Psychoanalysis: The Daughter's Seduction,* Macmillan, 1982, p. xv.
23 For recent arguments concerning the necessity of historicization, see Jane Lewis, 'The Debate on Sex and Class', *New Left Review*, 149 (1985), pp. 108–20.
24 Michael Young and Peter Willmott, *Family and Kinship in East London*, Penguin, 1962, pp. 44–61.
25 Raymond Williams, *Politics and Letters,* NLB/Verso, 1979, pp. 271–2. See also Seabrook, *What Went Wrong?*, p. 261, where the same process is described: a working-class life, ossified by time, enacted in 'symbolic institutional ways, by those who teach in poor schools, or who write novels and memoirs about a way of life which they have not directly experienced since childhood'.
26 Seymour Chatman, *Story and Discourse: Narrative Structure in Fiction and Film,* Cornell University Press, 1978, pp. 45–8.
27 See Steven Marcus, 'Freud and Dora: Story, History, Case-History', in *Representations,* Random House, New York, 1976, pp. 247–310 for the argument that Freud invented a new narrative form in his writing of the 'Dora' case. See also below, pp. 130–4.

28 For a brief discussion of the way in which historical writing masks the processes that brought it into being, see Timothy Ashplant, 'The New Social Function of Cinema', *Journal of the British Film Institute*, 79/80 (1981), pp. 107–9, and Hayden White, 'The Value of Narrativity in the Representation of Reality', *Critical Inquiry*, 7:1 (1980), pp. 5–27.
29 Paul Ricoeur, *Time and Narrative*, University of Chicago Press, Chicago, 1984, pp. 118, 157.
30 Ann Oakley, *From Here to Maternity: Becoming a Mother*, Penguin, 1981, p. 11.
31 Campbell, *Wigan Pier Revisted*, pp. 97–115.
32 John Berger, *Ways of Seeing*, BBC/Penguin, 1972, p. 46.
33 Donald Winnicott, *Playing and Reality*, Penguin, 1974, p. 6.

17

Jenny Bourne Taylor

Raymond Williams: Gender and Generation

At one stage in *Politics and Letters*, the book of Raymond Williams's long interview with *New Left Review* of 1979, the *NLR* team probe the implications of his concept of 'structure of feeling' in *The Long Revolution* by discussing how it relates to the analysis of different kinds of social transformation across time as it is lived by different generations. Then, in 1961, he had defined 'structure of feeling' as being:

> as firm and definite as 'structure' suggests, yet it operates in the most delicate and least tangible parts of our activity. In one sense, this structure of feeling is the culture of a period: it is the particular living result of all the elements in the general organization...I do not mean that the structure of feeling, any more than the social character, is possessed in the same way by all the individuals in the community...One generation may train its successor, with reasonable success, in the social character or the general cultural pattern, but the new generation will have its own structure of feeling, which will not appear to have come 'from' anywhere. For here, most distinctly, the changing organization is enacted in the organism: the new generation responds in its own ways to the unique world which it is inheriting, taking up many continuities that can be traced, and reproducing many aspects of the organization, which can be separately described, yet feeling its whole life in certain ways differently, and shaping its creative response to a new structure of feeling.[1]

NLR challenge this definition, and the implied notion of a common experience and identity that it suggests. How does this take into account the fact that any given moment in history is made up not of one but at least three generations – can any one be said to give a distinct 'character' to the age they ask? And then, 'how can the concept be articulated to a plurality of classes? Victorian England, for example, was composed of at least three major social classes: landed aristocracy, industrial bourgeoisie and urban proletariat, not to speak of agricultural labourers, rural small-holders as well as a heterogeneous petit-bourgeoisie.'[2] A few pages later they pose the problem differently: how can the concept of 'structure of feeling' be mapped on to different kinds of time-scales which might work in various determining ways on a particular historical moment or process? A structure of feeling is described as a decade – the 1840s – in *The Long Revolution*; in *Marxism and Literature* is linked to the rise of an entire class from 1700–1760. Williams stresses

> The problem of generations is certainly a very tricky one: perhaps we need another term distinct from the biological category. I have been particularly conscious of this myself, since I have not since 1945 worked contemporarily with my own generation, and I think that these asymmetries always happen. Should one speak in this sort of cultural analysis of a generation of work rather than a generation of birth? I'm trying to resolve this now, with some new methodology of cultural formations.[3]

This scrap of dialogue stresses the continual sense of tension that underlies most of his writing. The many tributes to Raymond Williams have tended to focus on his work's extraordinary consistency and continuity; yet he was always revising and rethinking his project – 'I am the most critical reader of my own books', he wrote in *Politics and Letters*. Equally his influence worked in quite uneven and discontinuous ways. I read *Culture and Society*, for example, as a set text in the early 1970s, part of a syllabus I primarily wanted to challenge and rethink in beginning to think about what a feminist literary criticism might look like. Williams then was a crucial reference point, but reading him often involved projecting meaning back into his work, which often went completely against the grain of the way that it was actually moving. Ten years later, having read *Politics and Letters* and rethought much of the earlier writing, I encountered him in a totally different context while helping to set up the Socialist Society. What struck me in the early and mid-eighties was his balancing of an assessment of structural shifts in contemporary political and economic processes – the arms race, the ecological crisis, the consequences of the reversal of the post-war social democratic consensus and the political logic of Thatcherism – with an insistence that we always put this in a longer-term perspective in order to gather the 'resources for a journey of hope'. His sense, too, that we never let the necessary awareness of contemporary political and technological complexity and domination undercut the necessity to fight for control over defining the future. 'Emotions don't alter the hard relations of power', he wrote at the end of *Towards 2000*,

> but where people actually live, what is specialised as emotioal, has an absolute and primary significance. . . . There are very strong reasons why we should challenge what now most controls and constrains us: the idea of such a world as an inevitable future. . . It is not in staring at these blocks that there is any chance of movement past them. . . The decisive movement lies elsewhere, in the difficult business in gaining confidence in our own energies and capacities.[4]

I want to take this sense of the uneveness of intellectual and political transmission between different generations, using Williams's remarks that I opened with as one starting point in thinking about the interconnections between his own writings and socialist-feminist theory and practice in Britain. Contemplating the different lines of transmission and transformation between Williams's work and socialist feminism involves different kinds of processes. Initially it means considering how far his work provides a framework that can be extrapolated for a feminist analysis of social and cultural forms – and how much its underlying premises and conceptual categories would need to be reassessed if 'gender' was to be made as central an analytic category as the other markers of cultural identity – 'class', 'region', 'nationality', 'ethnicity', 'generation'. But beyond these it also involves setting up a series of interlocking frameworks that can intersect in divergent ways across lines of gender and generation, and this can mean that what may start out as a feminist critique of Williams soon turns into another set of questions which emphasize that his work can provide a means of getting beyond the kinds of binary divisions of identity that have become increasingly restrictive for feminism. The very diffuseness of Williams's influence is crucial here – he shapes the terms through which we think about him far more pervasively by not offering an identifiable paradigm that can simply be applied to different situations.

It means, too, suggesting that feminism, along with the rest of the Left in Britain, currently faces a crisis that is at once theoretical and strategic, about how to define itself – a crisis that hinges most obviously on the terms *identity and difference*. Various factors are at work here. In an immediate and material sense there's the fundamental matter of the conditions of production of intellectual work. During the 1970s and through the main part of the 1980s there has been an enormous proliferation of feminist intellectual work ranging across the disciplines whose boundaries it challenges: social theory, history, psychology, cultural studies, literature. In Williams's terms this can be seen as a identifiable 'generation of work' – emerging through journals such as *History Workshop*, Feminist Review and *Screen*, – expressing the various concerns of a particular group of predominently metropolitan intellectuals, emerging out of the renaissant women's movement of the late sixties, in the space for radical interdisciplinary work that Williams own generation of work had opened up, both of which were made possible by the post-war expansion of higher education.

Thus, while much feminist cultural theory defined itself in the late 1970s in a rather simplistic opposition to what was percieved as an earlier naive humanism, replacing 'women's experience' with 'gender difference', drawing self-consciously on structuralist and poststructuralist models – more on Althusser, Gramsci, Lacan and Foucault than explicitly on Williams – it could do so precisely because it was able to gain a circumscribed toehold in dominant educational structures. Though it might be marginalized it could still to some extent take the institutional space itself in universities and polytechnics for granted even though it might contest and subvert those dominant forms. Feminist intellectual work has always to a large extent been marginal – often indeed defining itself in opposition to the mainstream canon. Yet it was able to flourish at a time when it has been generally acknowledged that the margins were the places that the most exciting things were happening, making it, paradoxically, able to gain enormous influence while remaining structurally peripheral. But how will a new generation of work emerge now that those preconditions in educational institutions – however power-laden and partial they might remain – are being systematically restructured? Will it be possible to talk of developing and extending an intellectual project in any meaningful way, when the very cultural and political tensions that it emerged from have been radically redefined?

I've raised this problem because I want to suggest that the connections between the social position of a particular intellectual generation and the way it defines its own project and identity is a particularly fraught one in feminist work at the moment, and this has a bearing on my argument about Williams's varied kinds of relationship to the shifting focus of this work. For the question that has recently dominated the women's movement is this: is it possible to take 'women' as some sort of theoretical or strategic starting point any more, since gender identity is never pure but is always shaped by, as it shapes, other specific identities – of class, ethnicity, sexuality, region, age, and so on. This has a simultaneously strategic and epistemological dimension. Strategically, it's been argued that 'feminism' is currently in an impasse: that it paradoxically undermines and is undermined by actual contingent and local struggles for progressive change. Feminism, the case goes, only has meaning in so far as it is both a theory and a political practice – not that it should provide a detailed and exhaustive political programme, but that it should pose some sense of radically reforming change based on a notion of a coherent political subjectivity and a methodology that transcends immediate and local struggles and identities. This, however, runs counter to the particular experience and practice of actual social movements, where resistance arises precisely from the local and the relative. But this in turn can only have meaning within 'feminism' as a meaningful political discourse if it makes sense in the context of a wider framework of power, agency and change. Epistemologically, this contradiction between feminism as a universal theory and the notion of difference or otherness in specific social groups and movements leads to the paradoxes posed by poststructuralism and postmodernism that Toril Moi has explored. Firstly, feminism as any kind of coherent theory, linked to any notion of grand narrative or rationality based on the liberal values of progress and equality, is itself deconstructed by a feminine difference that is at once, by extension, associated with other forms of otherness, yet remains, by this process of representation, parasitically dependent on the very notion of rationality that it seeks to subvert. Secondly these two versions of difference and identity – the one primarily based on historical and local experience, the other on symbolic and linguistic constructions, themselves don't match up, implicitly accusing each other of essentialism and ahistoricism respectively.

How does this affect the way one reads Williams? Does his own method and his notion of cultural materialism ofter any way through this impasse, not obviously in explicitly engaging with these questions, but in exploring issues that are broadly compatible and extending them in new contexts and groupings? Might it provide a means of acknowledging the local and the historically specific and particular forms of power without collapsing into a postmodern pluralism? What are the specific implications of this for developing a socialist feminist critique of cultural forms while retaining a sense of agency and political strategy? How would Williams's own work then need to be taken up and transformed in the light of this critique? I want to explore these questions by taking apart that early concept of *structure of feeling,* while holding on to the terms 'gender' and 'generation' as relative constants. Using two texts from around 1960 and two from around 1980 as reference-points – *The Long Revolution* and *Towards 2000*, the novels *Border Country* and *Loyalties* – I want to raise distinct kinds of questions about the relationship between social and historical structures and subjectivity; the way that social relationships are enacted within the self.

STRUCTURES OF *FEELING*

What are the main components of Williams's analysis of the ways in which identity is formed through experience, and how does this shape his conception of the emergence of political consciousness through the study of cultural and social formations? In the first place, there's an increasingly complex set of connections and tensions in his work between insisting on the primacy of ordinary everyday experience as it is lived through detailed local relationships, and the structural forces – national, global, economic, military – within which those identities exist, but which never absolutely determine them. There are clearly close connections between the stress on lived experience and the density and texture of everyday life in feminist writing in the early 1970s (the work of Sheila Rowbotham, for example) and Williams's own sense much earlier in the 1950s of the 'ordinariness' of culture as a closely-knit fabric of relationships. At the time that this perspective was emerging within feminism Williams had already developed his account, stressing:

> I can see that my appeal to experience, in those earlier definitions, was problematic. What I said in effect was that we know this to be so about our own lives – hence we can take it as a theoretical assumption. The difficulty with that argument, however, is that it is precisely experience in its weakest form that appears to block any realization of the unity of this process, concealing the connections between the different structures – not to mention the unnoticed relations of domination and subordination, disparity and unevenness, residue and emergence, which lend their particular nature to these connections.[5]

Yet *by* being historical, Williams *does* take his own formative experience as the point of reference of the ways in which consciousness changes, though he never explicitly universalizes it. And this slippage – consistent throughout his writing, though it manifests itself in different ways – suggests that his analysis smuggles in a set of uncontested assumptions, a set of unexplored power relationships, within the 'indissoluble element of a single social-material process' most crucially in the ubiquitous yet strangely absent status that the family (the fundamental meeting point of gender and generation) holds in his work. On the initial level of 'experience' itself, it also means that by not locating a particular encounter of cultural transformation as being bound up in various specific ways with the particular formation of a masculine identity, though elements of it always might of course apply to women's experience as well, these power relationships are silently written in as natural – but now a 'natural' that has undegone a further stage of repression.

Consider Williams's complex critical reappraisal of what was set up as the protoypical structure of feeling of his own generation: the experience of the scholarship boy, retrospectively constructing a working-class childhood and sense of community that is intensified by the splits in the self generated by the move from customary to educated forms of life; identity reshaped through the experience of dislocation and crisis. There's a telling moment in *Politics and Letters* when Williams describes winning the County scholarship from the village school: 'there was a group photograph taken because it was such an exceptional event – six girls and me. But the girls – several of them were farmers' daughters – would usually only go as far as the sixth form and then leave' – the implications are at once acknowledged and passed over.[6] At no point, not even in his early writing, can Williams's work be grouped with the image of the working class community put out by such as Richard Hoggart or Jeremy Seabrook – the image which Carolyn Steedman's *Landscape for a Good Woman* has explored as being bound up with the formation of a particular kind of masculine identity that was able to negotiate its class transition precisely by retrojecting an image of community onto the home that is left – particularly the figure of the working-class mother eternally inhabiting that mythologized landscape of endless streets of northern terraces. Clearly Williams's writing cannot at any point be assimilated to the Hoggart/Seabrook perspective. Throughout his work there is a constant impulse to view those relationships of domination and subordination that take various dichotomous forms (between region and metropolis, country and city, private and public) from the standpoint of the subordinate term, yet at the same time to take apart the discourse and the material relations through which those kinds of marginality and exclusion are founded. This means that up to a point 'community' itself is a continually shifting signifier through Williams's writing; it is always made up of the combination of relations of place, of mutual recognition and class identity.

Yet the question remains, is the family itself on a continuum with these other relations of flux and transformation? Or does it hold a particularly privileged relation to the notion of community by being the clearest manifestation of a set of bonds that one is born into? Williams continually stresses the centrality of familial genealogy in the reproduction of dominant class wealth and power – it's a crucial theme, for example, in *The Country and the City*. But is 'community' counterposed to this? And is the working-class family assigned a familiar unity, on the one hand occluding both the sexual division of labour, and its pattern of psychic relationships that shape it? Hoggart pastoralizes the working class mother. Steedman rewrites that story of class and cultural transformation in a way that emphasizes how the lines of both break and continuity between generations and the perception of class that follows from it take on different meanings in the light of a fraught mother/daughter relationship. Does Williams focus on the generational divisions and connections between father and son as *the* primary significant relationship, but always as an internal mirror of 'wider' social and cultural transformations?[7]

It's partly a matter of how one reads him. *Border Country* and *Loyalties* both strike me as being in many ways essentially paradoxical novels, in that while they are both concerned to represent regional affiliations as an intricate web of historical and geographical locations, the forms available to do this continually pull one back into feeling that 'community' is centred on the figure of the working-class father. Similarly the family itself is apparantly never naturalized or essentialized, but always seen to be formed out of shared necessities or common loyalties. Yet at the same time the illusion is created, again through the figure of the working class father (in the case of *Loyalties*, quite deliberately, *not* the biological father) that certain figures are, through particular class experience and political affiliations, rooted in a particular identity and thus are without contradiction. Harry Price is the obvious example of this in *Border Country*; in *Loyalties* it's Bert Lewis – the dark working-class Welsh miner set clearly in opposition to middle-class nineteen-Thirties communist, blond bombshell Norman (as in 'yoke') Braose. *Loyalties* starts by subverting the 'fairy tale' conventions of the discovery of noble origins through illegitimacy and thus sets various kind of commitment against each other, looking at what Edward Said has called the relationship between filiation and affiliation: class affiliation, sexual commitment, political allegiance with the break-up of a clearly defined communist movement, national and political loyalties via this basic opposition.

At the same time Norman's history is set against that of Gwyn, his 'natural' son, and this means that the narrative simultaneously depends on yet scrutinizes its own terms of reference. Norman's seduction and betrayal of working class Nesta Pritchard is on a continuum with his abandonment of an indiginous British socialist movement in favour of the machinations of espionage. Although his closing confrontation with Gwyn, his illegitimate son, qualifies this, Bert, the social father, and Norman, the biological father, are set finally in a binary opposition, as shadowy reference points who are always seen out of the corner of the eye. This in turn smuggles various other connotations in its train – though explicitly heterosexual Norman is unmistakably effete; both political authenticity and masculinity are called into question with his evasion of active service in Spain. Although Bert is never sentimentalized – his life is seen as a continual set of difficult struggles, missed opportunities, physical disabilities – his political allegiance and his 'doing the right thing by Nesta' make him unmistakeably a 'real man'. Thus it's not only the next generation – the son Gwyn affiliating himself with his social father in coming to terms with his double paternity – but also the two women, Nesta and Emma, Norman's sister, who act as a link between past and present and the two social worlds; and who are the contradictory, liminal figures, implicitly calling those implied oppositions into question. But in each case the stresses and strains within the self are through the internalization of social relations: relations defined as those of economic and political power, not as the social relations – including those formed in very early childhood – within the family.

Williams is here posing a nexus of basically continuous connections between the self, community and political affilation which does not seem to offer space for conflict or contradiction either within the community or family as its metonymic paradigm. In the section on 'The Culture of Nations' in *Towards 2000* he elaborates this by emphasizing that at any one time, identities are formed through what seems to be contradictory social structures that inherently contain stresses and divisions; but that often the contradiction emerges because we do not have an adequate framework of analysis rather than because the structures themselves are intrinsically incoherent. One can use this argument as a starting point in relating gender identity to other kinds of social forms, but only if it is seen as being on a direct continuum with other kinds of local identity that is shaped by a common relationship and set of interests. However if one defines 'women's experience' by extrapolating from the concept of community the forms of living which seem closest to it, one also needs to see those forms of family structure and gender division as historically and locally variable in order to avoid falling back into the old essentialist trap. Yet in the terms that Williams offers, this means looking primarily at economically structured class relations – seeing how they might exist in a mutually determining tension with divisions based on gender, perhaps, but in a way that always renders gender the subordinate term.

The implications of this conception of experience and consciousness as formed within and through communities and relationships becomes more paradoxical when one relates it to Williams's analysis of actual changes in consciousness, particularly those forms of consciousness that might subvert or oppose the dominant forms that shaped their social identity in the first place. As a self-conscious political movement, even as a form of liberalism, feminism is certainly extraordinarily absent in most of Williams's historical work, though not so much in *Politics and Letters* and *Towards 2000*. Clearly this is partly, though not entirely, because he was writing much of it at a time when feminism itself was marginalized. In spite of this though his analysis of dominant, residual and emergent identities can still be a very useful reference point for exploring how transformations in consciousness might develop within the dominant culture, breaking doen the idea of 'the dominant culture' itself as a monolithic entity. It can be used to explore, for example, how nineteenth-century feminism was simultaneously able to develop within the discourse of liberal ideology that was in the process of becoming dominant, as an emergent force that at the same time challenged it. It can help one to think about why there might be long periods of history in which an oppressed group might not experience itself as such, might actively collude in its own subordination; how 'a dominant set of forms or conventions – and in that sense structures of feeling – can represent a profound blockage for subordinated groups in a society...In these cases it is very dangerous to presume that an articulate structure of feeling is necessary equivalent to inarticulate experience.'[8]

It can help one, too, think about how the growing consciousness of particular interests within a wider subordinate oppositional group can reshape the framework of that group beyond its immediate concerns, yet not in a way that completely negates the original set of needs; how, for example the emergence of the 'women against pit closures' groups during the 1984 miners' strike, by taking as starting point their own particular position as women within that specific situation, completely redefined the initial defensive posture of the strike set by the male-dominated union – opening up instead much wider questions about the nature of work, of the relationship between productive work and domestic labour, the sexual division of labour and men and women's identity within the family, including their identity as parents. Yet there's still a problem here, for this kind of emergent consciousness precisely makes sense only if it's primarily located in this particular economic and social community, which implies that the analysis itself is dependent on that specific social form, that can't be extrapolated to other situations. The limits of this framework are set by seeing difference simply as diversity within a common framework, never as a more radical otherness that challenges its terms. Williams's analysis doesn't simply privilege cetain forms of 'native' identity over others – it is unable to perceive those forms of control than cannot be assimilated into that mould. How do homophobia, sexual abuse, racism figure in this community, except simply as 'false consciousness'? What bearing does this have more generally on Williams's implied conception of *power*?

STRUCTURES OF FEELING

I've identified a particular paradox in Williams's concept of identity and community that hinges particularly on the slippery status of the family as both a social form and a site of identity. Is this paradox compounded by the more structural analysis of the development of social formations? How useful is the perspective he develops for socialist-feminist historical and sociological work that implicitly takes as its starting point the point that Williams himself continually emphasizes about the inextricability of different kinds of economic, reproductive and cultural relationships?

Williams's own work was oddly invisible, not in cultural studies as such but in the main tendency of socialist-feminist sociology and economic theory in the mid-seventies. Its determination to transcend classic Marxism and all the implications of the base/superstructure metaphor – to relate production to reproduction, and to see both as simultaneously mental and material, as both economic and cultural – owed more to a direct engagement with Althusser's work, although Williams had already worked many of these questions through in *The Long Revolution*. But when one attempts to extrapolate further from his analysis it becomes incredibly frustrating, as the very 'inextricability' of the 'social-material process', and beyond that the notion of culture itself that at first is so attractive becomes self–defeating – everything collapses into everything else, so that it becomes impossible to get a purchase on any specific element. Thus in *The Long Revolution* he writes:

> The truth about a society, it would seem, is to be found in the actual relations, always exceptionally complicated , between the system of decision, the system of communication and learning, the system of maintenance and the system of generation and nurture. It is not a question of looking for the absolute formula, by which the structure of these relations can be invariably determined. The formula that matters is that which, first, makes the essential connections between what are really separable systems, and second, shows the historical variability of each of these systems, and therefore of the real organizations within which they operate and are lived.[9]

But this is never really borne out in the actual analysis, and developing the point in *Politics and Letters* it is possible to see why. Here Williams emphasizes that 'in the whole gamut of Marxism, the material-physical importance of the human reproductive process has been generally overlooked. Correct and necessary points have been made about the exploitation of women or the role of the family, but no major account of this whole area is available'. He develops the point by arguing:

> Human reproduction, seen as a historico–material process, clearly has complex relations to other forms of production. If you were to say to me, can a change in the nature of the family cause the sort of change in the nature of society that a change in the production of energy, or of clothing has generated? – the answer is no, it cannot...But at the same time I think the category of production is itself an expression of the capitalist specialization of production to commodities, which then poses to us precisely these problems about forms of production that are not commodities.... The particular difficulty is to integrate that kind of truth with an analysis of advanced capitalist societies where commodity production has become so much more extensive, where central areas of human life have become excluded from the category of production altogether.[10]

Yet the very process of undercutting the distinction between public and private worlds, the rigour with which he demonstrates how those most personal identities and patterns of consumption are shaped by a split between production and reproduction which is itself determined by changes in the economy and commodity production, means that the 'system of generation and nurturance' is never given the kind of historical analysis that is accorded to other cultural forms – education or the press for example. In the end it is even implicitly excluded from culture itself. I don't mean that Williams simply falls back into some prelapsarian view of family life, but that he tends to locate the forms of oppression and exploitation that exists inside it in economic relationships as part of seeing it as a model of community defined as 'the place one is born into'.

> On the one hand, it is clear the system of generation and nurture has continued to retain certain distinct priorities in human energy and attention: here is an area where people really do struggle to retain certain absolutes against a capitalist order.... On the other hand...there is also frequent evidence of the break-up of relations under the strain of poverty or unemployment, and of the very ugly reproduction inside certain families of the repressions and cruelties of the work situation, of which women and children are the primary victims.[11]

But it is always as the mirror of an external situation, not because of its own internal social relations.

PSYCHIC AND SOCIAL IDENTITY

I don't want to carp at absences in Williams's past analysis from some supposed position of wisdom in the present, but to point to a more intractable aspect of the relationship between his work and feminist thought. So far I've been suggesting that both on the level of 'identity' and of 'structure' Williams's work offers a crucial set of terms for feminism, in so far as they can be rewritten in ways that foreground gender divisions and relations. Yet at the same time, one comes up against a strange kind of resistance in the process of pushing this project forward within Williams's terms. While the means to analyse the historical and cultural construction of gender identity seem to be there, where one tries to pin them down, they slip away.

Does elaborating his analysis in this way mean moving into another framework of reference that completely overturns the previous one? I could take the straightforward way out here and set Williams's methodology against another – work in cultural studies and literary and film theory that has developed out of his perspective by drawing on those various forms of poststructuralism that precisely focus on difference as otherness, that develop an analysis of representation and the cultural acquistion of femininity, emphasizing the role of fantasy, exploring the social tensions of the family as a psychic institution. Here it could be argued that the divergence of interest and method of analysis between Williams's work and feminist critical theory can basically be explained as a *paradigm shift* – that it is not really meaningful to compare their accounts because they ask different questions, use different methods, have a completely different conception about what constitutes knowledge, truth and reality. But this implies not only incommensurability between Williams and feminism, but that different areas of feminist work are just doing their own thing within their self-referential worlds, in the process often falling back into redefined disciplinary boundaries they set out to challenge.

Earlier I asked whether Williams's work provides a means of looking at structures historically, without falling into complete relativism. I want to use this question to underpin my final point that there is an area of constructive, though difficult debate within that very terrain that he seems to resist – the interconnections between psychic and social identity. That isn't to say that one can build up some grand narrative or totalizing theory, but that it is possible to bring Williams's work to bear on an interpretion of psychoanalyis and come up with something that is different from either of them; to look at the interconnections between psychic and social forces without seeing one purely as the effect of the other. This means taking elements of Williams's method and using them against the grain of what he actually argues, transforming them, but not out of all recognition, in the process.

It's true that Williams is explicitly hostile to psychoanalysis as an adequate mode of explanation and that in many respects his criticisms correspond closely to those of some sceptical feminists. He sees it as universalizing human drives and desires; as being fundamentally repressive by turning the subject into a bundle of symptoms rather than as having the means of self-knowledge through collective action and social relationships; as contributing to a process of private individualism rather than seeing that private realm itself as socially constructed. Yet too often, as has been noted, his response has been to leave those difficult areas within the self or family simply in shadow, so that in an odd kind of way he ends up implicitly doing the same kind of thing that he accuses psychoanalysis of – by not subjecting those forms of subjectivity to 'social' analysis he perpetuates the split between the public and the private, the personal and the political that in other areas he so thoroughly takes to pieces. This could be described as a kind of return of the repressed or as a set of displacements; the absences of childhood conflict in the novels, particularly the relationship between father and son in *Loyalties* for example, is particularly significant. In effect, too, there has to be some sort of working psychology in order to write about novels at all and Williams inevitably does draw on certain psychoanalytic terms out of a culture steeped in psychoanalytic assumptions. But this misses the point, for Williams does discuss psychoanalysis as a range of varied discourses on individual identity in *The Long Revolution* – though he never develops this analysis. He argues that Freud's work should be read like a text, drawing on the conventions of the confessional novel, and so on. In some respects his critique of psychoanalysis takes what is in fact a very limited aspect of a diverse intellectual tradition and generalizes from it.

This notion of the historical nature of psychoanalysis as a language of the self is one way that feminists can use Williams's work without being bounded by its terms. Of course it doesn't encompass all the issues that debates on psychoanalysis has opened up over the last ten or fifteen years, but it does make it possible to see psychoanalysis itself as a varied and complex discourse, one that raises different kinds of questions about the social structuring of subjectivity – the difference between Lacanian and Kleinian interpretations is one case in point. It doesn't resolve many problems, including the vexed question of whether one should read the history of those languages of the self within the framework of one of those languages, but it can be a means of collapsing the boundary between the psychic and the social, taking Williams's method further in breaking down the distinction between forces 'in' the self and 'in' society, which his own scepticism of psychoanalysis to some extent perpetuates. It can be a means of relating it to other social discourses and structures some of which may seem to be extraordinarily resistant, yet still retaining, at some level, a notion of historical determination. And it can become part of the difficult business of balancing historical complexity with hopeful strategies for the future – of appreciating the power of the 'blocks' (including those within his work) in order to move past them.

NOTES

1 Raymond Williams, *The Long Revolution*, (1961) Pelican Books, 1975, pp. 64–5.
2 Raymond Williams, *Politics and Letters*, Verso, 1979, p. 158.
3 Ibid., p. 162
4 Raymond Williams, *Towards 2000*, Chatto and Windus, 1983, pp. 266–8.
5 *Politics and Letters*, p. 138.
6 Ibid., p. 28.
7 Williams's review of *Landscape for a Good Woman* ('Desire', *London Review of Books* 8, April 17, 1986) condones Carolyn Steedman's critique of Hoggart, but suggests that her analysis substitutes the concept of desire itself for an appraisal of the social and economic forces that structured it.
8 *Politics and Letters*, p. 164.
9 *The Long Revolution*, p. 36.
10 *Politics and Letters*, p. 147
11 Ibid., pp. 148–9.

18

Rosalind Coward

Naughty but Nice: Food Pornography

There's a full-page spread in a woman's magazine. It's captioned Breakfast Special, and shows a picture of every delicious breakfast imaginable. The hungry eye can delight in croissants with butter, exquisitely prepared bacon and eggs, toasted waffles with maple syrup. But over the top of the pictures there's a sinister message: 430 calories for the croissants; 300 for the waffles. The English breakfast takes the biscuit with a top score of 665 calories. It must be a galling sight for the readers of this particular magazine. Because it's *Slimmer* magazine. And one presumes the reader looks on these pleasures in the full knowledge that they had better not be indulged.

This pleasure in looking at the supposedly forbidden is reminiscent of another form of guilty-but-indulgent looking, that of sexual pornography. Sexual pornography as a separate realm of imagery exists because our society defines some explicit pictures of sexual activity or sexual parts as 'naughty', 'illicit'. These images are then made widely available through a massive and massively profitable industry.

The glossy pictures in slimming magazines show in glorious Technicolor all the illicit desires which make us fat. Many of the articles show almost life-size pictures of the real baddies of the dieting world – bags of crisps, peanuts, bars of chocolate, cream puddings. Diet foods are advertised as sensuously as possible. The food is made as appetizing as possible, often with explicit sexual references: 'Tip Top. For Girls who used to say No': 'Grapefruits. The Least Forbidden Fruit'.

Pictures in slimming magazines and those circulated around the slimming culture are only the hard core of food pictures which are in general circulation in women's magazines. Most women's magazines carry articles about food, recipes or advertising. All are accompanied by larger-than-life, elaborate pictures of food, cross sections through a cream and strawberry sponge, or close-ups of succulent Orange and Walnut Roast Beef. Recipe books often dwell on the visual impact of food. Robert Carrier has glossy cards showing the dish in question and carrying the recipe on the back – just the right size for the pocket. In the street, billboards confront us with gargantuan cream cakes.

But it is only the unfortunate readers of the slimming magazines who are supposed to use the pictures as a substitute for the real thing. While other forms of food photography are meant to stimulate the desire to prepare and eat the food, for the slimmers it is a matter of feasting the eyes only.

Like sexual pornography, pictures of food provide a photographic genre geared towards one sex. And like sexual pornography, it is a regime of 'pleasure' which is incomprehensible to the opposite sex. This is because these pornographies are creating and indulging 'pleasures' which confirm or trap men and women in their respective positions of power and subordination.

Sexual pornography is an industry dealing in images geared towards men. Sexual pornography is dominated by pictures of women. It shows bits of women's bodies, women engaged in sex acts, women masturbating, women supposedly having orgasms. When the women look at the camera, it is with an expression of sexual arousal, interest and availability. The way in which women are posed for these images presupposes a male viewer, behind the camera, as it were, about to move in on the act.

Pornography is only the extreme end of how images of women are circulated in general in this society. Pornography is defined as being illicit, naughty, unacceptable for public display (though definitions of what is acceptable vary from one epoch to the next). It shows things which generally available images don't – penetration, masturbation, women's genitals. The porn industry then thrives on marketing and circulating these 'illicit' images. But if pornography is meant to be illicit, and hidden, the kinds of images it shows differ little from the more routinely available images of women. Page three nudes in daily papers, advertisements showing women, the representation of sex in non-pornographic films, all draw on the conventions by which women are represented in pornography. Women are made to look into the camera in the same way, their bodies are arranged in the same way, the same glossy photographic techniques are used, there is the same fragmentation of women's bodies, and a concomitant fetishistic concentration on bits of the body.

Many women now think that the way male arousal is catered for in these images is a problem. These images feed a belief that men have depersonalized sexual needs, like sleeping or going to the lavatory. Pornography as it is currently practised suggests that women's bodies are available to meet those needs. Men often say that porn is just fantasy, a harmless way of having pleasure as a substitute for the real thing. But women have begun to question this use of the term 'pleasure'. After all, the pleasure seems conditional on feeling power to use women's bodies. And maybe there's only a thin line between the fantasy and the lived experience of sexuality where men do sometimes force their sexual attentions on women.

If sexual pornography is a display of images which confirm men's sense of themselves as having power over women, food pornography is a regime of pleasurable images which has the opposite effect on its viewers – women. It indulges a pleasure which is linked to servitude and therefore confirms the subordinate position of women. Unlike sexual pornography, however, food porn cannot even be used without guilt. Because of pressures to diet, women have been made to feel guilty about enjoying food.

The use of food pornography is surprisingly widespread. All the women I have talked to about food have confessed to enjoying it. Few activities it seems rival relaxing in bed with a good recipe book. Some indulged in full colour pictures of gleaming bodies of Cold Mackerel Basquaise lying invitingly on a bed of peppers, or perfectly formed chocolate mousse topped with mounds of cream. The intellectuals expressed a preference for erotica, Elizabeth David's historical and literary titillation. All of us used the recipe books as aids to oral gratification, stimulants to imagine new combinations of food, ideas for producing a lovely meal.

Cooking food and presenting it beautifully is an act of servitude. It is a way of expressing affection through a gift. In fact, the preparation of a meal involves intensive domestic labour, the most devalued labour in this society. That we should aspire to produce perfectly finished and presented food is a symbol of a willing and enjoyable participation in servicing other people.

Food pornography exactly sustains these meanings relating to the preparation of food. The kinds of pictures used always repress the process of production of a meal. They are always beautifully lit, often touched up. The settings are invariably exquisite – a conservatory in the background, fresh flowers on the table. The dishes are expensive and look barely used.

There's a whole professional ideology connected with food photography. The *Focal Encyclopaedia of Photography* tells us that in a 'good food picture', 'the food must be both perfectly cooked and perfectly displayed' if it is to appeal to the magazine reader. The photographer 'must decide in advance on the correct style and arrangement of table linen, silver, china, flowers. Close attention to such details is vital because the final pictures must survive the critical inspection of housewives and cooks.' Food photographers are supposed to be at the service of the expert chef, but sometimes 'the photographer learns by experience that certain foodstuffs do not photograph well'. And in such circumstances, 'he must be able to suggest reasonable substitutes'. Glycerine-covered green paper is a well-known substitute for lettuce, which wilts under the bright lights of a studio. And fast-melting foods like ice-cream pose interesting technical problems for the food photographer. Occasionally, they do get caught out – I recently saw a picture of a sausage dinner where a nail was clearly visible, holding the sausage to its surroundings! Virtually all meals shown in these photos are actually inedible. If not actually made of plaster, most are sprayed or treated for photographing. How ironic to think of the perfect meal destined for the dustbin.

Food photographs are the culinary equivalent of the removal of unsightly hairs. Not only do hours of work go into the preparation of the settings and the dishes, but the finished photos are touched up and imperfections removed to make the food look succulent and glistening. The aim of these photos is the display of the perfect meal in isolation from the kitchen context and the process of its production. There are no traces of the hours of shopping, cutting up, preparing, tidying up, arranging the table and the room which in fact go into the production of a meal. Just as we know that glamorous models in the adverts don't really look as they appear, so we know perfectly well about the hours of untidy chaos involved in the preparation of a meal. We know that photos of glamour models are touched up, skin blemishes removed, excess fat literally cut out of the picture. And – subconsciously at least – we probably realize the same process has been at work on the Black Forest Gâteau. But the ideal images still linger in our minds as a lure. A meal should really look like the pictures. And that's how the images produce complicity in our subordination. We aim at giving others pleasure by obliterating the traces of our labour.

But it is not as if, even if we could produce this perfect meal, we could wholeheartedly enjoy it. Because at the same time as food is presented as the one legitimate sensual pleasure for women we are simultaneously told that women shouldn't eat too much. Food is Naughty but Nice, as the current Real Dairy Cream advertisement announces.

This guilt connected with eating has become severe over the last few decades. It's a result of the growing pressure over these years towards the ideal shape of women. This shape – discussed in 'The Body Beautiful' – is more like an adolescent than a woman, a silhouette rather than a soft body. There's a current dictum in slimming circles: 'If you can pinch an inch, you may need to lose weight.' This seems a particularly vicious control of female contours in a society obsessed with eating and uninterested in physical exertion. Dieting is the forcible imposition of an ideal shape on a woman's body.

The presentation of food sets up a particular trap for women. The glossy, sensual photography legitimates oral desires and pleasures for women in a way that sexual interest for women is never legitimated. At the same time, however, much of the food photography constructs a direct equation between food and fat, an equation which can only generate guilt about oral pleasures. Look at the way advertising presents food, drawing a direct equation between what women eat and what shape they will be. Tab is the low-calorie drink from Coca-Cola. Its advertising campaign shows a glass of the stuff which is in the shape of a woman's body! Beside the glass are the statistics 35″ 22″ 35″. A Sweetex advertisement shows two slender women and exhorts 'Take the lumps out of your life. Take Sweetex'! Heinz promotes its 'Slimway Mayonnaise' with a picture of a very lurid lobster and the caption 'Mayonnaise without guilt'. Tea even 'adds a little weight to the slimming argument'. Another soft-drink company exhorts: 'Spoil yourself, not your figure', which is a common promise for slimming foods. Nor is this phenomenon confined to slimming foods. Women's magazines have articles about whether 'your taste buds are ruining your figure', and creamy foods are offered as wicked but worth it.

An equation is set up in this kind of writing and these pictures between what goes into the mouth and the shape your body will be. It is as if we swallow a mouthful and it goes immediately, without digestion, to join the 'cellulite'. If we give this a moment's thought, we realize it is nonsense. There's no direct correlation between food into the mouth and fat; that's about the *only* thing on which all the diet experts agree. People have different metabolisms, use food differently. Different things in different people's lives affect what they eat and what effect that eating has on overall health. But the simplistic ideologies behind food and dieting cultures reinforce the guilt associated with food for women. Oral pleasures are only really permissible when tied to the servicing of others in the production of a meal. Women are controlled and punished if they indulge themselves.

The way images of food are made and circulated is not just an innocent catering for pleasures. They also meddle in people's sense of themselves and their self-worth. In a sexually divided and hierarchical society, these pleasures are tied to positions of power and subordination.

19

Felly Nkweto Simmonds

SHE'S GOTTA HAVE IT: The Representation of Black Female Sexuality on Film

The black man...particularly since the Black Movement has been in a position to define the black woman. He is the one who tells her whether or not she is a woman and what it is to be a woman. And therefore, whether he wishes it or not, he determines her destiny as well as his own.

Michelle Wallace, *Black Macho and the Myth of the Superwoman*

I think this film should be the antidote to how the black male is perceived in 'The Colour Purple'...the film's black men...are just one-dimensional animals...because if you read Alice Walker, that's the way she feels about black men. She really has problems with them.... To me, it's justifying everything they say about black people and black men in general that we are animals.

Spike Lee, *Film Comment*

INTRODUCTION

She's Gotta Have It (SGHI) has been hailed as the new face of black American cinema by critics both in America and Europe. Its writer and director, Spike Lee, young, gifted and black, has been dubbed the black Woody Allen and, in 1986, *SGHI* won the Prix de Jeunesse at Cannes. *Film and Filming* concluded its review of the film with the words:

> Only time will tell if he is going to make it as a mainstream American film-maker. But if he does and can do it without compromising, then he won't only become the first important Black film-maker America has produced, but the first of any colour, to tell it as it really is in Black America. (*Film and Filming*, 1987:42–3)

Spare Rib, while acknowledging some of the film's more obvious limitations, called it a

> well observed and humorous film...about a sexually liberated woman... [which] offers a refreshing alternative to the stereotyped and peripheral roles and concerns which have become the domain of Black people. (Alexander, 1987:32)

My concern in this article is not primarily with the film narrative, nor with the question of whether the character Nola Darling represents a realistic image of a black American woman. I am more concerned with the messages and definitions that accumulate in the film around black sexuality and, in particular, black female sexuality. The analysis will therefore examine not only the totality of the film, its construction and method, but also the political context in which the film has been made and in which it will be viewed. This will include the examination, not only of who constructs film, and for whom, but also who is excluded from such a framework. Finally, the article examines the construction of women in the narrative and asks whose interests are served by such a construction.

THE FILM

The focus of the film is the sexual life of a young black American woman, Nola Darling. She is economically independent and works as a graphic artist. She has her own apartment in Brooklyn. Nola Darling wishes to remain a sexually free woman. She has three male lovers: Jamie Overstreet, Mars Blackmon (played by Spike Lee) and Greer Childs. There is also a woman, Opal Gilstrap, who would like to have Nola Darling as her lover.

In various ways – its use of black and white photography, direct address to camera and so on – the film departs in form from the conventional feature. This, combined with the fact that it has an all-black cast, gives *SGHI* the air of being a different, and more acceptable film about black experience in America.

Throughout, *SGHI* is a humorous film. An early sequence, for example, shows a series of stereotyped male figures making direct, comical sexual advances to women. The same play on sexual behaviour as a source of humour is returned to throughout the film, especially by Mars Blackmon. The characters use humour to maximum advantage, since each is given the opportunity directly to address the camera, and thus the audience. We are invited to laugh with them.

Nola Darling's three male lovers spend most of the film trying to convince her, and us, why each is best for Nola, and why she should give up her other lovers. In defence of their own positions, they spend much time telling us what they think is wrong with her because she refuses to choose between them. Nola is presented to us as odd because she chooses to have more than one lover. Even her father agrees she is odd. Most of the time, the lovers' attempts to persuade Nola to give up their rivals are light and playful. Towards the end, however, one of Nola's lovers rapes her, to teach her a lesson.

The majority of the scenes are shot in Nola's apartment, where her lovers come to her. The central feature in her apartment is her bed. It is from here that she addresses the camera at the beginning of the film. In the opening sequence, Nola states what for her is the purpose of the film. She wants to clear her name. Her position, however, has already been undermined by the title of the film, *She's Gotta Have It,* which frames our subsequent perceptions of Nola. The 'it' that she has to have is sex. Lots of it. Spike Lee as the writer and director defines Nola's sexuality, exercising what Andrea Dworkin defines as the male power of naming:

> Men have the power of naming, a great and sublime power. This power of naming enables men to define experience, to articulate boundaries and values, to designate to each thing its realm and qualities, to determine perception itself. (Dworkin, 1981:17)

By naming the film in the way that he has, the writer invites the viewer – even if she is a black woman herself – to view Nola Darling from the outside. The title is value-laden, for the word 'it' carries male-defined sexual meaning:

> Commonly referred to as 'it', sex is defined in action only by what the male does with his penis. Fucking – the penis thrusting – is the magical, hidden meaning of 'it', the reason for sex, the expansive experience through which the male realizes his sexual power. (Dworkin, 1981:23)

Spike Lee's use of 'it' in his title demonstrates his assent to the notion that all a woman really needs is a man who can fuck her. *SGHI*, then, is not a woman-centered film, and it is a mistake to classify it, as *City Limit's* Saskia Baron has done, as a 'feminist sex-comedy' (Baron, 1987:15).

Spike Lee is quite specific in his reasons for making the film. In the summer of 1985 he had failed to make a different film, *The Messenger*, and, in his own words, 'out of that devastation and disaster...out of desperation...we came up with the idea to do *SGHI*. I was determined to do another film for as little money as possible' (Lee, 1986:47). He therefore needed to make a film that would guarantee some return. Sex, it seemed, was not a bad place to start. He also wanted to make a film that would appeal to black men, and counter what he saw as the exploitation of black men by black women writers such as Alice Walker and Ntozake Shange:

> Within recent years, the quickest way for a black playwright, novelist or poet to get published had been to say that black men are shit. If you say that, then you are definitely going to get media, your book published, your play done... that's why they put Alice Walker out there. That's why she won the Pulitzer Prize. That's why Hollywood leaped the pond to seize this book and had it made. (Lee, 1986:47)

Thirdly, Spike Lee wanted to make a film about black sexuality:

> I think a lot of people, particularly black Americans, have been waiting for a film like this for a long time. They never saw black people kissing on the screen or making love. (Lee, 1987)

Spike Lee, as a black film director, wanted to challenge the notion that white film directors, such as Spielberg, could define the black experience on film. He used down-to-earth Brooklyn humour to make his audience accept the sexual experiences of a black woman and her three male lovers at face value.

The use of an all-black cast is significant. It releases the film from the race issues that surface in any film with a black and white cast. The lack of racial tension in *SGHI*, and the humour of the film, give it a fresh, relaxed air, and help us to swallow what would otherwise be bitter and painful messages about black sexual politics.

Spike Lee alone created the film. He wrote, directed and edited it. It is exactly as he labels it in the humorous credits: a 'Spike Lee Joint'. It is therefore safe to assume that the views and messages of the film are predominantly his. Yet, he admits himself that, as a black man, he can never be a spokesperson for black women: 'To me this film is about various men's views on this type of woman... [it is] not meant to represent every single black woman in the United States' (Lee, 1987). As he (alias Mars Blackmon) would have said, it is mighty black of him to acknowledge that he can neither speak for, nor represent, black female experience. And yet, the very expression 'this type of woman' starts to define categories of women. The film explicitly defines one particular woman and classifies her experience as unnatural. The words 'freak', 'nympho' and 'bogus' are all used in the film to define and categorize. Whether or not it was so intended, the film has been received as a film about a sexually promiscuous black woman, and this is what brings the crowds to the cinemas. Spike Lee could not have been unaware of the attraction a black woman on the screen, presented as an erotic being, would have for an American audience. This is why he makes Nola the central figure. It is around Nola, not around male sexuality, and certainly not around black women's views on sexually promiscuous young men, that the film revolves.

To understand the attraction of *SGHI*, we have to move beyond the image of Nola Darling on screen, and examine the combination of black + woman + sex in the context of the politics of gender and race, both in the historical and current political context. These, then, are the questions on which the following section focuses.

THE BLACK WOMAN AND SEXUALITY

Black sexuality has historically been defined by white racism to justify its perception of the inferiority of black people. That perception has always been explicit. Blacks, considered lower on the evolutionary ladder, have always been considered more sexually active than whites. In the United States that notion of black sexuality has its roots in the history of slavery. Black sexuality was used to the economic advantage of white slavers, particularly after the banning of direct importation of enslaved Africans, when the reproduction of an enslaved workforce had to be ensured. The image of the black woman as breeder played a crucial role in the reproduction of the workforce. As T.F. Gossett suggests:

> The market required that a brutal emphasis be placed upon the stud capabilities of the black man and upon the black woman's fertility...she was labeled sexually promiscuous because it was important that her womb supply the labor force. (Gossett, 1965:48)

Black women were, therefore, subjected to ruthless exploitation of their sexuality. The rape of black women by white slavers was one of the more acute manifestations of this exploitation. The perception of a black woman's sexuality was damaged for all time, and out of this exploitation grew the image of a black woman as 'not only emotionally callous but physically invulnerable' (Wallace, 1979:138).

Through history, the image of the black female as breeder has remained dominant. Even black resistance movements have failed to address, let alone unseat, this view. In the 1960s the black power movement never challenged dominant images of black female sexuality. Black power was explicitly expressed as the pursuit of black manhood. The manhood that black male activists like Malcolm X proclaimed was black patriarchy, and the black woman had only one place in it – on her back. Even the young George Jackson wrote from his prison cell: 'Black Mama, you're going to have to stop making cowards...Black Mama, your overriding concern with the survival of our sons is mistaken if it is a survival at the cost of their manhood' (Jackson, 1971:220). He talked of a manhood that excluded women, for he too had heard Malcolm X, Stokely Carmichael and Eldrige Cleaver all proclaim black manhood as the essence of black power. The black woman was asked not to do anything that would stand in his way and, more importantly, not to threaten his manhood. As Michelle Wallace points out:

> The message of the Black Movement was that I was being watched, on probation as a Black woman, that any signs of aggressiveness, intelligence or independence would mean I'd be denied even the one role still left open to me – my man's woman.... Black men were threatening me with being deserted, with being alone. (Wallace, 1979:138)

This message produced its own antagonisms, within black sexual politics, between black men and black women. This position remains largely unchanged in the 1980s. It is, however, a position that has started to change as black women, influenced by feminist politics, are trying to define their own reality as black women. A reality that can be uncomfortable for black men and which requires a re-examination of black sexual politics, a task which the black power movement of the 1960s singularly failed to address. Women were defined then as men's possessions and 'as a possession, the black woman was of little use to the revolution except as a performer of drudgery' (Wallace et al., 1982:7).

Today, black women such as Alice Walker are trying to redefine black sexual politics, and it is in this context that the film *SGHI* has been made, in an attempt once again to restrict a black woman's ability to assert her independence. Nola Darling, beautiful, independent and black, is the very embodiment of a black woman's threat to black manhood. Spike Lee speaks of his film as being 'an antidote' to Alice Walker, and it is on this basis that he justifies making *SGHI*.

THE CONSTRUCTION OF WOMAN

Nola Darling is constructed as a sensuous body. She is, in fact, what Spike Lee condemns others for creating: a one-dimensional animal. She only seems to be able to make relationships through her sexuality. Her three male lovers, the stable Jamie Overstreet, the narcissistic Greer Childs and the humorous Mars Blackmon, all want her body. Each of them tries to persuade us – and Nola – that he is the best lover for her. The film is structured so that we hear more of the men's voices, reasoning and pleading, than Nola's reasons for being a sexually free woman. The male voice is given more actual time in the film. Even when Nola invites all three men together to her apartment for Thanksgiving, it is the men who are given space to express their feelings.

Throughout most of the film, Spike Lee presents Nola to us on the bed. It is from here that she addresses us, both at the start and the end of the film. In her own bed she is at ease. Outside it she feels awkward. It is the only bed in which she makes love. 'I can only do it in my bed', she tells Jamie. The bed is constructed as an altar, illuminated by scented candles, to which the lovers come to worship the sex goddess herself. We are encouraged to view these acts of worship, not only as outsiders, but as male observers. The lovemaking scenes are shown in a context where they are part of the men's stories. We too are thus forced into the position of trying to work out which man is the best for Nola. We are invited to look at Nola's body through male eyes. The voyeuristic, erotic scenes, the lingering camera shots over Nola's naked body, Nola making love and the slowing down of the film to make the moment last longer, are constructed to excite the (male) audience.

Nola seems obsessed with men. She spends most of her time with them. Even when alone in her apartment (which is not very often) she works on a collage of male political figures. She shares a birthday with Malcolm X, to whom the collage is dedicated. The images also include that supreme male patriarch, Jesse Jackson. Even Nola's politics cannot include women. In fact, the only image of a woman is from an advertisement that she is working on. The caption proclaims: 'She is fresh!'

Nola is curiously isolated, not only from other aspects of her life – her job, her family – but also from genuine female friendships. Her independence excludes female solidarity and female politics. The film does not allow us to establish why she chooses not to have female friendships. What comes through, however, is that she cannot handle female friendships because they threaten her relationships with men. It is not from a very secure position that she defends her independence. Both her position as a woman and her independence are isolated. The film only allows the men to define her relationships with other women.

One relationship is made particularly pathological. 'It was bad enough with Nola and her male friends, but there was one particular female friend' states Jamie Overstreet as the film's way of introducing Opal Gilstrap. We, as the observers (male?) are expected to sympathize with him. What ensues is a male fantasy of what a lesbian relationship is like. Opal is portrayed in the same way as Nola's male lovers, in active pursuit of Nola's body, like a lioness about to pounce on her prey. The very words she uses to introduce herself confirm this image: 'From an early age I knew what my preference was, and I pursued it'. Opal is also portrayed as more sexually threatening to Nola. Nola is more uncomfortable with her and feels that this is a situation that she might not be able to control. This threat is never extended to her male lovers. Even when Jamie rapes her, the threat and danger are minimized by the way the scene is constructed.

All Nola's relationships with other women are underscored with mistrust. Opal threatens her sexuality. Her room-mate, Clorinda Bradford, threatens her independence. The men's other lovers (real and imagined) also threaten her sexual independence. Nola rejects even the one woman who can help her understand her sexuality – the analyst, Dr Jamison, who tries to make Nola realize that whatever her male lovers tell her, her sexuality is not warped. She offers her the potential to recognize that sexuality is only one dimension of her life. 'The beautiful sex organ is between your ears, not between your legs', she advises Nola.

Conveniently for the film, Nola has no sisters (or brothers) and even her mother is absent. This allows us to relate to Nola in isolation from other women and only in relation to men. The film denies Nola women friends, because male language and meaning devalues female friendship and emphasizes sexual relationships with men. As Debbie Alicen has noted:

> The absence of overt sexual behaviour in a relationship makes it deficient and worth less than being 'lovers' [but] a friend is someone who allows us the space and freedom to be, while relationships with lovers often feel binding. (Alicen, 1985:170)

It is men who occupy the privileged position in the film, silencing women's voices. Nola is a lonely woman. By constructing Nola Darling as a woman, free and independent, yes, but one who has no need for female friendship and solidarity, the film forces us to view all the other women in terms of the positions they occupy in relation to men. It is this isolation that undermines Nola's professed independence. It also makes her vulnerable to male violence.

THE RAPE

Without the rape scene, the film could have remained what most reviewers have chosen to see it as, an erotic sex comedy. The rape, however, is the climax of the film. It cuts through the comedy and exposes the very meaning of the film, which justifies rape as a legitimate tool that a man can use to punish a woman. Nola Darling is punished for trying to define her own sexuality. She is punished not only because one man, Jamie, rapes her, but because the structure of the scene allows him to punish her for the other men, as he subjects her not only to physical but also to psychological rape. The scene must also have taken considerable time to film. All three main male characters had to be filmed acting out the rape to make the sequence of Jamie's fantasy. In a low-budget film it is a curious decision to make since the scene could have been made much more cheaply if filmed in other ways. Why then does the director make the decision to capture male sexual fantasy so elaborately? It is easier to understand this decision if we examine how rape functions for some men. It is the ultimate tool, not only for female subjugation, but also over women's sexuality. It is used to punish Nola and to excite other men, the spectators. The very positioning of Nola, on her knees, evokes an air of punishment and submission for her, and power and domination for Jamie. The very words he uses – 'Is this how you like it?' – confirms what Andrea Dworkin classifies as one of the most enduring sexual 'truths' in pornography, that 'sexual violence is desired by the normal female, needed by her, suggested and demanded by her' (Dworkin, 1981: 166). The preceding scenes in the film illustrate and confirm this 'truth'. Nola Darling, in need of sex, rings up Jamie and asks him to come over. 'I need you', she says to him. Jamie, angry at having to leave his other lover, is even more angry when he finds out that nothing is wrong and that what she wants is sex. He rapes her, not just to teach her an immediate lesson, but also for all the times he has been trying to get her to reject other men. Throughout the film, he has tried to reason with her, offering her love and protection which she has rejected. Finally, as he rapes her, he says, 'Is this what you want?' and concludes, 'I am trying to "dog" you as best as I can and what bothers me is that I enjoyed it!' What are we meant to understand by this ending? Is it that she has made him rape her? Is it what she has really been asking for? What makes her especially vulnerable at this point is that we know she is sexually promiscuous and likes sex. The underlying message is that a woman who needs so much sex and, as the title suggests 'has gotta have it', deserves whatever she gets from men.

Spike Lee, as a black director, is treading dangerous ground by using his first film to be the teller of this 'truth' about black women's sexuality. He has joined the ranks of men, themselves products of white racist views of a black woman's sexuality, who have contributed to this myth about black women. More important, since it is a black man who articulates this 'truth', his word will be taken more seriously. The black woman is silenced and there is no place for her to express anger, or she will be accused of undermining all black men. She must accept this violence at the hand of a black man in silence and alone. Nola Darling is made to do just this. She cannot even admit that anger, even to herself. When she goes to her old room-mate, she actually says, 'I think I have fucked up this time . . . Jamie hates me.' Why is she not angry with him? She is supposed to be an independent person, in control of her body. Why does she return to Jamie and, in fact, goes to look for him, not to challenge him, but to justify to him what she intends to do next? Towards the end of the film, she tells Jamie that she intends to give up all her lovers and stay celibate. Significantly, she fails to keep her word and Jamie persuades her to return to him without too much trouble. The fact that he is the man who raped her makes no difference to her. When in the final scene of the film, she starts by saying 'that celibacy thing didn't last long' it is the final undermining of the character Nola by her creator. Whatever she says subsequently from her bed in the last scene sounds hollow to us as spectators, for we have seen her humiliated and beaten. We are left with a lingering doubt about the strength of her intention to stay an independent woman. Even the final words, 'I am not a one-man woman, there you have it', do not leave much room for a positive future for Nola Darling unless she can define more clearly what she means by being a sexually liberated woman.

CONCLUSION. A CHALLENGE FOR BLACK WOMEN: REDEFINING FEMALE SEXUALITY FOR OURSELVES

She's Gotta Have It chooses to leave black women silent in discussion about sexuality, by omission (the absent mother), by isolation (Nola is isolated from Opal and from her room-mate Clorinda) and by overemphasizing competition for men as one of the most important factors in black female sexuality (the men's other lovers). Our sexuality continues to be defined by others. Spike Lee labels Nola 'that kind of woman' and even more negatively, Opal Gilstrap, the lesbian, as a 'freak'. Yet no one needs to have their sexuality labelled by, or justified to, other people. Any valid discussion needs to hear what black women have to say about themselves. A position has to be found that gets strength from both black politics and women's politics, for we are *black women.* That position has been identified and used by many women: Alice Walker, Bell Hooks, Michelle Wallace and many more, to articulate black women's priorities. It is not only a feminist position but a black feminist position; Alice Walker has specifically named it a 'womanist' position. It is not a comfortable position because it has to identify both gender and race as primary sources of oppression for black women. It means we have to recognize the limitations of both black male politics and white female politics, since we are neither black men nor white women. We have to recognize that although we share common oppressions with both, as black people and as women, we constitute another quite specific group of people as black women. To do this effectively, we need to find and talk to each other. We need to transform both black politics and female politics if we are to define black female sexuality for ourselves. As long as men like Spike Lee continue to define it for us, the emphasis will be on phallic sex. We need a wider definition of sexuality and its relationship to other aspects of our lives. As Molly Haskell says:

> It is a mistake in any event, and an oversimplification that does great injustice to female sensibility to isolate orgasmic sexual fulfilment as the supreme. . . it excludes a wide range of effective feelings and behaviour. (Haskell, 1975:340)

We cannot allow sexual promiscuity to be the sole defining factor in our liberation. In fact, it pinpoints the basic contradiction for women in an overemphasis on sex. By treating sex as the supreme, defining quality of the self, we trap ourselves in male-dominated society's moral stance, that classifies sexual freedom as pathological. It traps us into positions where this freedom becomes the ultimate symbol of control and independence, and leaves us vulnerable to society's sanctioned punishments for such behaviour – verbal and physical abuse. It also simplifies and belittles the struggle for women's total liberation – sexual, political and economic: 'if we are to accept the screen version. . . there is only sexual liberation or non-liberation, either/or' (Haskell, 1975:340). However, we have learnt with hindsight that the 1960s sexual revolution only gave men more access to women's bodies, while women continued to be responsible for contraception and taking care of unwanted babies. Women have decided that the sexual revolution has to go beyond sex as defined by men. We also have to recognize that the closer women come to claiming their rights and achieving independence in real life, the more loudly and stridently films tell us it's a man's world' (Haskell, 1975:363). To change the meaning of sexual liberation, or any other liberation, women have to challenge the very language of film – the narrative and the meanings. The woman's voice has to be heard, and it is only in the context of female-defined liberation that the control of our bodies and minds can be explored. Film has to get away from evoking only male pleasure in looking at women on film, whatever the message of the film, and especially if the film is trying to establish woman as in control of her body. This is the challenge for black women. In the words of Martina Attille and Maureen Blackwood, we need

> to establish an ongoing forum for discussion around the social and political implications of the fragmentation of black women in film. . . as well as a forum to talk about the kind of images we want to construct ourselves, in an attempt to offer a more complete picture of our lives/politics. (Attille and Blackwood, 1986:203)

The need for such a forum becomes even more urgent as black film-making begins to grow. If the black woman's voice is silent once more, we cannot ensure that the new image is not just the same old one, but without its racist overtones.

NOTES

This article arises out of initial discussions in Birmingham in March 1987: discussions about whether issues of black female sexuality have a place in black politics. As part of the International Women's Day celebrations, Vokani Film Circuit showed a series of films on and about women. *She's Gotta Have It* was one of the films shown. Since then it has gone into general circulation and beyond all-women viewings, but has been discussed privately by many women, especially black women.

I could not have written this article without the support of my friends, Helle Johansen and especially Inge Blackman, who in the end bore the brunt of some of the anger aroused in some men by our daring to discuss black female sexuality in public.

REFERENCES

Alexander, Karen (1987) review of *She's Gotta Have It* in *Spare Rib* no. 176 (March) p. 32.

Attille, Martina and Blackwood, Maureen (1986) 'Black Women and Representation' in Brunsdon (1986).

Baron, Saskia (1987) 'Kiss Me in Black and White' *City Limits* no. 282 (26 February–5 March) pp. 15, 17.

Brunsdon C. (1986) ed., *Films for Women* London: BFI.

Dworkin, Andrea (1981) *Pornography: Men Possessing Women* London: The Women's Press.

Gossett, T.F. (1965) *Race: The History of an Idea in America* New York: Schocken Books.

Haskell, Molly (1975) *From Reverence to Rape: The Treatment of Women in the Movies* London: New English Library.

Jackson, George (1971) *Soledad Brother: The Prison Letters of George Jackson* Harmondsworth: Penguin.

Kramarae, C. and Treichler, P.A. (1985) *A Feminist Dictionary* London: Pandora Press.

Lee, S. (1986) *Film Comment* (October) Film Society of Lincoln.

Lee, S. (1987) *Ebony* BBC 1: transcript ref. 1/NBM JH 646T.

Wallace, Michelle (1979) *Black Macho and the Myth of the Superwoman* London: John Calder.

Wallace, M., Tull, G., Scott P.B. and Smith, B. (1982) *But Some of Us Are Brave* New York: The Feminist Press.

20

Alison Light

'Returning to Manderley' – Romance Fiction, Female Sexuality and Class

Last night I dreamt I went to Manderley again.

Thus opens Daphne du Maurier's *Rebecca,* published in 1938. With thirty-nine impressions and translations into twenty languages in as many years, *Rebecca* was and still is an enormous bestseller. Hitchcock made a film of the novel in 1940, its latest TV serialization was only a couple of years ago and even more recently it has been the subject of an opera. Whilst one study of its initial success claims that 'every good historian should read it in tandem with contemporary newspapers' (Beauman, 1983:178), its clear that *Rebecca* speaks as much to readers in the 1980s as it did to those in the 1940s. The story of the plain, genteel orphan girl – we never learn her name – who marries the aristocratic widower has got everything a romance needs and more: jealously, mystery, adultery and murder.

Jealousy and envy of her husband's first wife – the beautiful, upper-class Rebecca – propels the nameless heroine down the dark corridors of Rebecca's past. But in unlocking the secrets of Rebecca's character, the girl gets more than she bargained for: her husband turns out to have murdered Rebecca himself. All is not lost, however, for the heroine's bourgeois virtue triumphs and in the end she manages to save both her husband and her marriage. *Rebecca* is a rewrite of *Jane Eyre* amidst a nostalgia for the waning of the British Empire and the decline of its aristocracy. It's a lingering farewell to the world of Monte Carlo and of paid companions, to splendid breakfasts and devoted servants, the ease and arrogance of life in a stately home like Manderley, the Cornish mansion of the suave gentleman-hero, Maximilian de Winter. Obviously, it is a ripping yarn. But apart from that how do feminists and socialists account for the continued popularity and appeal of a book like this?

In the aftermath of Charles and Di, a lot of critical attention has been turned toward romance and its fictions, from Mills and Boon to 'bodice rippers' and the latest high-gloss consumerist fantasies (see, for example, Batsleer, 1981; Margolies, 1982; Harper, 1982). At the centre of the discussion has been the question of the possible political effects of reading romances – what, in other words, do they do to you? Romances have on the whole, been condemned by critics on the Left (although Janet Batsleer's piece is a notable exception). They are seen as coercive and stereotyping narratives which invite the reader to identify with a passive heroine who only finds true happiness in submitting to a masterful male. What happens to women readers is then compared to certain Marxist descriptions of the positioning of all human subjects under capitalism.[1] Romance thus emerges as a form of oppressive ideology, which works to keep women in their socially and sexually subordinate place.

I want to begin by registering the political dangers of this approach to romance fiction and then to suggest that we should come at the question of its effects rather differently. David Margolies, for example, (Margolies, 1982:9) talks in highly dubious ways when he refers to women readers being 'encouraged to sink into feeling' and 'to feel without regard for the structure of the situation'. 'Romance', he continues, 'is an opportunity for exercising frustrated sensitivity. . .inward-looking and intensely subjective', it is 'retrogressive' as a form of 'habitual reading for entertainment'. Such an analysis slides into a puritanical Left-wing moralism which denigrates readers. It also treats women yet again as the victims of, and irrational slaves to, their sensibilities. Feminists must baulk at any such conclusion which implies that the vast audience of romance readers (with the exception of a few up-front intellectuals) are either masochistic or inherently stupid. Both text and reader are more complicated than that. It is conceivable, say, that reading Barbara Cartland could turn you into a feminist. Reading is never simply a linear con-job but a process of interaction, and not just between text and reader, but between reader and reader, text and text. It is a process which helps to query as well as endorse social meanings and one which therefore remains dynamic and open to change.[2]

In other words, I think we need critical discussions that are not afraid of the fact that literature is a source of pleasure, passion *and* entertainment. This is not because pleasure can then explain away politics, as if it were a panacea existing outside of social and historical constraints. Rather it is precisely because pleasure is experienced by women and men within and despite those constraints. We need to balance an understanding of fictions as restatements (however mediated) of a social reality, with a closer examination of how literary texts might function in our lives as imaginative constructions and interpretations. It is this meshing of the questions of pleasure, fantasy and language which literary culture takes up so profoundly and which makes it so uniquely important to women. Subjectivity – the ways in which we come to express and define our concepts of our selves – then seems crucial to any analysis of the activity of reading. Far from being 'inward-looking' in the dismissive sense of being somehow separate from the realities of the state or the marketplace, subjectivity can be recognized as the place where the operations of power and the possibilities of resistance are also played out.

A re-emphasis on the imaginative dimensions of literary discourse may then suggest ways in which romance, as much because of its contradictory effects as despite them, has something positive to offer its audience, as readers and as *women* readers. It must at the very least prevent our 'cultural politics' becoming a book-burning legislature, a politics which is doomed to fail since it refuses ultimately to see women of all classes as capable of determining or transforming their own lives.

Romance fiction deals above all with the doubts and delights of heterosexuality, an institution which feminism has seen as problematic from the start. In thinking about this 'problem' I myself have found the psychoanalytic framework most useful since it suggests that the acquisition of gendered subjectivity is a process, a movement towards a social 'self', fraught with conflicts and never fully achieved. Moreover, psychoanalysis takes the question of pleasure seriously, both in its relation to gender and in its understanding of fictions as fantasies, as the explorations and productions of desires which may be in excess of the socially possible or acceptable. It gives us ways into the discussion of popular culture which can avoid the traps of moralism or dictatorship.

What I want to do in this article is to focus some of these points by a close study of du Maurier's *Rebecca,* a text which seems to me to provide a classic model of romance fiction while at the same time exposing many of its terms. Crucially, because, *Rebecca* concentrates on femininity as it is regulated and expressed through class difference, it illustrates and also investigates the psychic, social and fictive conditions necessary for a successful bourgeois romance.

A ROMANTIC THRILLER

Rebecca is in fact a tale in two genres – crime and romance. Both of these have been dominated by women writers in this last century (interestingly, Agatha Christie – 'the Queen of Crime' – also wrote romance fiction under the name of Mary Westmacott). The girl's romance and whirlwind marriage, however, only occupy about one eighth of *Rebecca.* Although this is the chronological starting point of the girl's story – the plot – it is not the starting point of the novel, or narrative proper. The opening chapter and a half of *Rebecca* are chronologically the story's epilogue, an epilogue in which the girl narrator and her unnamed husband are in exile abroad, homeless and disinherited.[3] The entire novel and clearly the romance take the form of a flashback. *Rebecca* takes the conventional romance story as its setting and as its own prologue; all the rest of the action takes place *after* marriage, after what traditionally constitutes the happy ending of romance fiction. Instead, the bulk of the text revolves around the girl's jealous pursuit of Rebecca's character and of her death. Once these enigmas have been solved they will explain the curious situation of the couple as expatriates which opens the story and will bring it full circle. I want to follow this structural movement of displacement and return, as it is narrated by the girl. I want to argue that through it *Rebecca* can investigate the terms and conditions of romance for women, both fictionally and socially. The novel becomes a thriller which goes behind the scenes of the romance drama.

'I'm asking you to marry me, you little fool.' This irresistible proposal (du Maurier, 1975:36) is the climax of the romance between the 'red-elbowed and lanky haired' girl (20) and 'the man who owns Manderley', as Maxim is first designated in the dining-room of the Monte Carlo hotel where they meet. Their marriage – which takes place against all odds, and much to everyone's amazement – would itself have furnished the standard plot of a contemporary Berta Ruck or Barbara Cartland romance (Anderson, 1974). Yet it is this category of romance that the girl immediately begins to question and that is as troubling as it is reassuring:

> Romantic, that was the word... Yes, of course, Romantic. That was what people would say. It was all very sudden and romantic. (61)

From here she is led on to compare her 'raw ex-schoolgirl' dream to the adult love-story she imagines took place between Maxim and Rebecca. What makes the girl insecure about 'romance' is not simply her youth and lack of sexual experience, but crucially its expression in the class difference between her and Maxim, her and Rebecca. Much is made of her dowdy and inelegant clothes, of exactly how much she earns, of her down-at-heel middle-class niceness. Obviously their marriage is not one of social equals. Maxim makes this explicit in a comparison which demonstrates how class interprets and regulates sexual behaviour and expections:

> instead of being companion to Mrs. Van Hopper you become mine, and your duties will be almost exactly the same. (58)

Not surprisingly, the girl finds this both comforting and profoundly depressing. Thus her initial jealousy of Rebecca is one of her confident social and sexual place, since for women the one must secure and define the other. Where Rebecca was 'mistress of Manderley' the girl 'is no great lady' (79). And more importantly the girl begins to imagine that Rebecca's aristocratic lineage allowed her a passionate and equal sexuality which her own bourgeois model of femininity, with its stress on companionship and duty, does not. Rebecca's class difference makes her seem more mature, more adult, both socially and sexually. In the course of the novel the girl idealizes her as the expression of all the other possible versions of female sexuality which her own middle-classness excludes. Rebecca disrupts the girl's romantic model and leads her to search for a 'successful' marriage which will also legitimize female sexual desire. For the girl to find a secure social identity (a name) as Maxim's wife, Rebecca's difference must be reinterpreted. From being the girl's imaginary ideal, she has to become her nightmarish enemy. No longer the perfect wife, hostess and lover, she is to branded by the end of the novel as lesbian and whore.

So the key question of romance that the girl asks – does Maxim really love her? – comes to depend on the answer to an earlier question – did

Maxim love Rebecca? If so, how can he love both, so different? This then raises the question of the nature of Rebecca's difference – what was Rebecca like? On returning to Manderley, the girl begins to pick up clues which lead to the discovery of Rebecca's mysterious death. It is no coincidence that the exploration of Rebecca's sexuality is imaginatively recast in the novel as a crime story. The text shifts between a fiction which idealizes and constructs harmonious models for human relations – romance – and one which starts from the violent disruption of the social – crime. This shifting marks out the distance which the girl and the reader have to travel in coming to understand Rebecca's significance as a seductive but ultimately tabooed expression of femininity. What is more *Rebecca* is a who-dunnit with a difference. Not only does the culprit get away with murder and ostensibly with the reader's approval too, but the innocent witness is called upon to become an accomplice. The girl agrees to keep secret the facts of Rebecca's murder in order to find true romance with the criminal, finally to get her man.

The problem is that in pursuing Rebecca the girl has identified with her as a positive alternative to herself. What then is dramatized is a scenario of extraordinary force and suspense. It is nothing less than an enactment of the power relations upon which successful bourgeois marriage depends, upon which the institution of its oppressed female heterosexuality turns. What the girl has to attempt, and what she must compulsively repeat in the telling of the tale, is a kind of self-murder. It is a violent denial of those other versions of female sexuality which Rebecca has come to represent.

Rebecca, then, is the focus of the novel's conflicting desires for and descriptions of the feminine. She is the character through whom the fiction of romance is undermined and whose murder will rescue and re-establish its norms. She jeopardizes the given social categories by existing outside them. And it is from this point of social and sexual disruption that the novel and its narrator must always draw back. From the outset, the novel acknowledges that the regulation of female sexuality finds its weapon in the expression of class difference. In so doing, it threatens to expose the social construction of all sexuality and the inherent instability of *all* those class and gender definitions. The narrative's circular structure thus tries to mop up and gloss over the disorder at its centre. It constantly disproves the girl's opening assertion – we can never go back' (8). Going back is precisely what *Rebecca* is all about: returning to Manderley, to the primal scene of the acquisition of femininity.

Becoming a good bourgeois woman is shown in *Rebecca* to be a perilous process, one which can never be either fictionally or socially completed. *Rebecca* begins with the dream of a return and so it anticipates its own narrative strategies. It gestures too toward the dream of all romance fiction: toward a resolution of all the tensions within fictionality itself. It gestures to an imaginary realm in which the conflicts of class and gender differences might be transcended by an unproblematic and full female subjectivity. But as the story of *Rebecca* comes full circle it is doomed to expose as a failure the myth, which is at the centre of all bourgeois ideology, and is its ultimate romance – that of a unified and coherent self.

WHO IS REBECCA?

As the girl finds out about Rebecca in the first part of the novel, she herself begins to fade. Her fragile security as married woman, and indeed as woman, crumbles until she is brought to the point of collapse and almost of self-destruction. This is the first movement of the plot and it charts Rebecca's ascendancy. Slowly the girl collects the signs of Rebecca's difference: the raincoat (Rebecca's height and slendeness), the handwritten cards and accounts (Rebecca's elegance and efficiency as wife), the cambric handkerchiefs, silk lingerie and perfume which suggest her sensual and delicate nature, as well as her expensive tastes. Maxim's grandmother testifies to Rebecca's amiability and Frank Crawley testifies to her beauty. Rebecca was fearless and energetic, rode difficult horses and sailed boats single-handed, even in rough weather. The girl, who doesn't hunt, shoot or sail, likes sewing and doing the odd sketch. Gradually the text sets up a binary opposition between the two kinds of femininity which the girl and Rebecca represent. Virginal Lily and sensuous dark-haired Rose; the girl occupies the East wing overlooking the domesticated flower garden whilst the West wing, Rebecca's, is dominated by the sight and sound of the sea, restless and disturbing. Rebecca emerges as an aristocratic mix of independent and 'essential' femininity, a strong physical presence, a confident and alluring sexuality. The girl emerges as literally a girl, immature by Rebecca's standards.

But these conventional oppositions are recast in an important way. For it is crucial that Rebecca is wholly a figment of the girl's imagination, invented from a sense of her own social and sexual limitations. 'Rebecca' is a projection of her own desires which both help to produce and to ratify the girl's feelings of inadequacy. Rebecca is in fact only the most complete moment and expression of the girl's longing for a secure place, socially and sexually. The narrative is made up of a series of fantasies which the girl projects, all of which function as an imaginary commentary on her lack of a fixed identity. She constantly slides away from her real location in time and space to invent scenarios, for example, between Maxim and the servants, which points up her failure to become a proper grown woman and wife, to be a Mrs de Winter.

But whilst the reader is invited to share this process of disintegration which the young romantic undergoes, she is also offered something else. There is another twist. The girl herself is only a remembered and invented persona – relayed back to us by the older-woman narrator with whom we started the novel. The narrator is already projecting back into the feelings and thoughts of an imaginary younger self. The reader knows then from the beginning that the girl makes it, becomes that adult woman, 'older, more mature' (49). But this twist means also that we can be given clues about Rebecca which the girl misses and which come from the hindsight of the older woman. Thus 'Rebecca' the novel and 'Rebecca' the woman, are being simultaneously written and revised. The 'editorial' position of the older self and the insecure persona of the young girl are both available for the reader.

Our very first intimations of an alternative Rebecca come from the opening pages of the novel, from that dream-return to Manderley which finds it overgrown and wild. 'Nature', we are told,

> had come into her own again...things of culture and grace...had gone native now, rearing to monster height without a bloom, black and ugly...The rhododendrons...had entered into an alien marriage with a host of nameless shrubs, poor, bastard things...conscious of their spurious origin. (5–6)

The English garden has been overrun by natives in a kind of horticultural anarchy in which the proper order of class, family and Empire has been flouted. The passage neatly expresses social and racial disruption in terms of sexual – 'natural' – excess. This symbolism is given more force when the heroine is startled by the same rampant rhododendrons on arrival at Manderley. This time her homily on the politics of gardening is clearly linked to definitions of femininity. The shrubs are

> slaughterous red, luscious and fantastic...something bewildering, even shocking...To me a rhododendron was a homely, domestic thing, strictly conventional...these were monsters...too beautiful I thought, too powerful; they were not plants at all. (70)

It turns out that these had been planted by Rebecca, her pride and joy. The lesson of an 'over-natural' and therefore deviant female sexuality is being mapped out.

Two processes are at work then in the narrative. As the appeal of Rebecca mounts, the girl begins to be dissatisfied with the romance between her and Maxim – bourgeois companionship now seems mere paternalism on his part, doglike devotion on hers. Rebecca becomes the figure which reveals the girl's unfulfilled desires. She is what is missing from the marriage; she is body to the girl's endless cerebration, the absent centre around which the narrative and its definitions of femininity turn. But even as the girl finds herself lacking, the older-woman narrator begins to hint darkly at Rebecca's 'real nature' and to signal to the reader that the distance between Rebecca and the girl is in fact proof-positive of the girl's superior femininity and true worth. *Rebecca* thus offers the reader the chance to have her cake and eat it, to slide like the girl between possible sexual identities, but unlike the girl to be in the know all along. The reader can have the pleasure of finding Rebecca desirable *and* of condemning her in advance. I want to argue this position is an androcentric one and fraught with difficulty for the woman reader. It is difficult because it offers a control of the discourses that define femininity, which women, since they themselves remain subject to those discourses, can never wholly enjoy. The reader, like the girl, wants to be like Rebecca, but dare not. And yet once that process of identification with Rebecca has been set in motion its effects can never be fully contained nor its disruptive potential fully retrieved. This narrative of wishful projection and identification, displacement and repulsion is then the story of all women, of what we go through in the constructing and maintaining of our femininity.

In fact the hints at Rebecca's deviancy become so obvious that the girl's social and sexual purity is only, just about believable. When Ben, the local 'idiot', says, for example, 'You're not like the other one.... She gave you the feeling of a snake' (162). One wonders how the girl is still able to ignore the negative connotations of Rebecca's phallic sexuality. The point of this 'innocence' *is*, however, that it is almost wilful. The girls's inability to see Rebecca as deviant slowly becomes a *refusal* to do so, so caught up is she in the development of her own fantasy of powerfully sexual and autonomous female subjectivity.

Of course it is Mrs. Danvers, Rebecca's devoted housekeeper, who acts as catalyst and midwife here. She actively feeds the girl's sense of herself as 'a second-rate person' (80) until the fantasy of that other self takes over and actually begins to direct the girl's behaviour. In an extraordinary scene in the West wing Mrs. Danvers acts out Rebecca's seduction of the girl, inviting her to touch Rebecca's lingerie, put her hands inside her slippers, to imagine her waiting in bed. Importantly, though, the girl has already performed these actions, if timidly: Mrs. Danvers merely ratifies her desires. Shortly afterwards the girl day-dreams an incident between Maxim and Rebecca, with herself cast as Rebecca. Maxim who has watched her silent reverie comments that she looked 'older suddenly, deceitful' (210).

This desire of the girl to be like Rebecca reaches its full expression when, misled by Mrs. Danvers, she unknowingly copies a fancy dress costume identical to one worn by Rebecca. This is the moment of her most complete social and sexual confidence as mistress of Manderley and as Mrs. de Winter:

> Everybody looked at me and smiled. I felt pleased and flushed and rather happy. People were being nice...It was suddenly fun, the thought of the dance, and that I was to be the hostess. (218)

'Being Rebecca' leads of course to her social and sexual disgrace, to the novel's crisis when it seems that the girl's marriage is all but destroyed. The girl wrongly interprets Maxim's horror at her appearance as evidence of her inadequacy, believing that her difference is her tragedy. Significantly alone in bed (Maxim fails to join her after the ball incident) she submits to Rebecca's triumph:

> There was nothing quite so shaming, so degrading as a marriage that had failed...Rebecca was still mistress of Manderley. Rebecca was still Mrs de Winter.... I should never be rid of Rebecca. Perhaps I haunted her as she haunted me. (242–244)

The boundaries which shored up the girl's identity have now been dissolved. The projection of her desire which the imaginary Rebecca represents now threatens to undermine not just the basis of her marriage but also to jeopardize the girl's only known route into acceptable middle-class womanhood and into being a person, a self.

This is when the girl decides to return to the West wing and when she hears the truth about Rebecca from Mrs. Danvers. Tellingly du Maurier's description of Rebecca's childhood cruelty and ostensible hearlessness is shot through with envy and admiration. It is unmistakeably appealing:

> She was never one to stand mute and still and be wronged. 'I'll see them in hell, Danny', she'd say. . . . She had all the courage and spirit of a boy. . . . She ought to have been a boy. . . . She did what she liked, she lived as she liked. She had the strength of a little lion. . . . She cared for nothing and for no one. (253–5)

The key moment in Mrs. Danvers's account of Rebecca's unnaturalness, of her refusal to be a good girl and a proper wife, comes when she describes Rebecca's relation to sexual pleasure – 'It was like a game to her. Like a game.' This is the giveaway, the telltale sign of Rebecca's criminality for which she was punished with death. The girl, however, is so immersed in her fantasies of Rebecca as a *positive* alternative to her own imagined failure as wife and woman that she refuses to listen. Her need to endorse other approved versions of sexuality leads her to contemplate suicide. Either she or Rebecca must survive – the two sexualities cannot co-exist.

This is the book's crisis. Now every attempt must be made to separate Rebecca out from the girl's and the reader's identification with her. Rebecca must be externalized, taken out of the realm of imaginary projections of subjectivity and put back into the world. This means that in terms of the text, she must be forcibly reinscribed within that range of social discourses which will condemn *her* difference and so legitimate the girl's. At this climax the girl is saved from suicide by the ships' hooters sounding a shipwreck. They also signal the return of Rebecca in person, as it were. Her body is about to be found in her sabotaged boat – 'Je Reviens' – and her coming back leads to Maxim's confession of murder. From now on the text runs all downhill in its rewriting of who Rebecca was. Maxim's final testimony needs only to be compared with that of Mrs. Danvers, quoted above, to gauge the disproportionate force with which the text reasserts its allegiance to a bourgeois morality, whereby women's pursuit of sexual pleasure outside of marriage must be brutally tabooed.

> She was vicious, damnable, rotten through and through. We never loved each other, never had one moment of happiness together. Rebecca was incapable of love, of tenderness, of decency. She was not even normal. (283)

But this diatribe is a measure too of Rebecca's disruptive force: of what is at stake, fictionally and socially, that she needs to be so profoundly denigrated. This devaluation suggests too that for the girl and the reader once to have fallen for Rebecca is never to be free of the possibilities she offers. Perhaps after all Rebecca will have the last word.

REBECCA'S MURDER

What then is the significance of Rebecca's murder? To know this we have to know her crime. Rebecca refused to obey the law whereby women exchange their bodies for social place. Moreover, by treating sex as a game, she exposed the ways in which femininity is powerfully over-determined – definitions of female sexuality are not just saturated with class meanings, but produce them and ensure their continuation. Rebecca's sins have therefore been against the whole fabric of the social order – against family (her lover, Jack Favell, was her cousin), against class (she even made overtures to the workmen), against property (turning Manderley into a 'filthy den' (287)), and most importantly against her husband. Rebecca's most heinous crime, which drove Maxim to shoot her, was, of course, to taunt him with a future heir of Manderley who might not be his. What is at stake in her murder is the continuance of male authority and of masculinity itself, as it is defined through ownership and the power of hierarchy. The sexual and the social underpin each other.

Maxim's only attempt to mitigate or excuse his actions is via an appeal to a kind of aristocratic patriotism which offers itself as a moral discourse transcending the considerations of gender and class, even though the language of his sentiments is obviously steeped in them:

> I thought about Manderley too much...Christ said nothing about stones, and bricks, and wall, the love that a man can bear for his plot of earth, his soil, his little kingdom. (286)

Manderley here is Little England as well as Little Eden. Both are lost through the love of a woman. It is a measure of the social support du Maurier must have felt she could rely on that this crime of Maxim's can not only be forgiven but actually celebrated. Emphatically, the confession chapter ends:

> If it had to come all over again I should not do anything different. I'm glad I killed Rebecca. I shall never have any remorse for that, never, never. (313)

Importantly, Maxim's revelations are recorded by the girl not in a mood of sober consideration (for after all, what kind of man remarries six months after murdering his first, and as he believed, pregnant wife?) but of heady joy. For a vital sleight of hand is taking place which will shift our attention from the crime back to the questions of romance, and in so doing establish the girl once and for all as model wife and woman.

Maxim's confession has a revealing sequence. It is not enough for him to admit to murder, he must also stress that he never loved Rebecca, that the crime was one of hatred not of passionate jealousy. Thus the girl's relief at Maxim's emotional 'freedom' can replace the problem of his guilt. Maxim's crime becomes a statement of his love for the girl and can then be recast as a test of her love for him. Now it seems she has the chance to be happily married after all, if she will agree to be complicit in the murder.

> I had listened to his story, and part of me went with him like a shadow in his tracks. I too had killed Rebecca, I too had sunk the boat there in the bay.... All this I had suffered with him...but the rest of me sat there on the carpet...caring for one thing only, repeating a phrase over and over again, 'He did not love Rebecca...'Now at the ringing of the telephone, these two

> selves merged and became one again. I was the self that I had always been. I was not changed. But something new had come upon me that had not been before. (297)

The girl, in becoming narrator of the crime, transfers her identification from Rebecca to Maxim, and invites the reader to do the same. Her own identity solidifies and secures itself around this endorsement of murder. She is no longer torn in loyalties between Maxim and Rebecca, between different femininities. The murdering of Rebecca is the price the girl must pay to guarantee the success of her marriage and to take on the status of good middle-class woman. She is rewarded with the identity of Mrs. de Winter, the security of belonging to the male, but only at the cost of underwriting his definitions of what femininity should be. In order to become a social subject – to think of herself *as* a self – she learns to accept the regulation of female heterosexuality through class differences which themselves necessitate sexual competition between women.[4]

Yet for the girl to learn about Rebecca is in some measure to repeat Rebecca's fall, to lose her own sexual innocence. Maxim's cry of no regrets is immediately followed by his mourning of the girl's entry into womanhood. She no longer has that 'young lost look'; she has finally got hold of that 'knowledge', which Maxim warned her earlier, must 'be kept under lock and key' (211) by fathers and husbands. If Rebecca's crime was to be too 'natural', too much of a woman, how then can the girl be both sexual and different from her? The text's confusion at this point is worth noting. Up until now Maxim's and the girl's sexual relations have either been played down or literally written out of the text – their honeymoon takes place between chapters. Now that the girl has lost her symbolic virginity they are able to become real lovers: 'He had not kissed me like this before' (279). At the same time, their new happiness must not be misconstrued as *simply* sexual – 'there was', we are assured 'nothing feverish or urgent about this'. Nevertheless du Maurier must still add that their lovemaking 'was not like stroking Jasper, Maxim's dog, anymore'! This coy ambivalence points to the fact that, having discovered the joys of sex, the second Mrs de Winter must take pains to see that she does not end up murdered too. If Maxim found his first wife dispensable because of her sexuality, what is to stop him from finding his second equally flawed? Hence the remorseless logic of a Bluebeard. Women are all the potential victims of a femininity which is not just endlessly defining us in terms of sexual status – we are wives, mothers, virgins, whores – but which marks us as representing 'the sexual' itself. Where women's sexual desirability is competitively organized around male approval and social reward, there will always be a Rebecca who is both an idealized alternative to our elusive subjectivity and a radical undermining of it.

What saves the girl is her middle-classness. This is also what commits her to a cycle of repression and denial. Those other possibilities for female sexuality which exist outside the perimeters of middle-class femininity, and which had, in the figure of Rebecca, all but seduced her, she must now firmly repress:

> something...that I wanted to bury for ever more deep in the shadows of my mind with old forgotten terrors of childhood. (263)

And yet it is clear that Rebecca can never be forgotten since she is the condition for the girl knowing 'who she is'. As the girl's femininity is defined against Rebecca's, Rebecca becomes more, not less, important. It is their difference from each other that gives each meaning. The girl and Rebecca need each other in order to *mean* at all. In imagining the drama of romance as a murder, the novel shows successful heterosexuality to be a construct, not a natural given. Correct femininity has to be learnt, and whilst Rebecca's murder recalls all the discourses which condemn her, it cannot do so without revealing their social and therefore arbitrary order. Within such a system of differences the girl is equally a deviant Rebecca and this for the reader could be a potentially revolutionary reversal.

For the girl in *Rebecca* the impulse from which the story-telling originates is the desire, not to forget, but to remember. Her act of repression can be seen as one of definition and expression – the unconscious literally making sense of the conscious in a dynamic, not a static relation. As older-woman narrator she looks back and relives the trauma of her marriage, within a narrative whose structure is circular. For she must constantly refabricate the illusion of her coherent social and sexual identity. As the ambiguity of the opening sentence suggests, she has dreamt of a return to Manderley and this dream keeps on coming back:

Last night I dreamt I went to Manderley again. She becomes a kind of Ancient Mariner of her story of middle-class femininity, as much the victim as the producer of its fictionality. The more she tries to control her life, tell her own story, the more she is brought back to Rebecca who has disrupted and defined both. It is Rebecca who is the named subject of the novel, she who dictates its movement, pushes epilogue to prologue, and structures the impossibility of its ending.

It was Rebecca, of course, who originally drew me to write. It seemed to me that there was a whole alternative narrative to be written from her point of view. Bold, independent, cooped up with her stuffed shirt of a middle-aged playboy husband, in the middle of nowhere, in a house surrounded by grasslands and sea, Rebecca is the wife who refuses to go mad. The force for my identification came through from du Maurier's own, from the image of a confidently sexual woman which she herself could not resist.

> Rebecca seizing life with her two hands; Rebecca, triumphant, leaning down from the minstrel's gallery with a smile on her lips. (284)

Rebecca's fictional come-uppance underlines all the more her dangerous appeal. She has to be more than murdered. Not only does Maxim escape freely and get a new adoring wife into the bargain, he is finally vindicated. The dénouement reveals that far from growing a baby inside her, Rebecca was growing a cancer. She would have died of her sins anyway, so there was no harm in making sure. And then the final, brutally gratuitous touch: the doctor's X-rays, we are told, indicated a malformed uterus:

> which meant she could never have had a child; but that was quite apart, it had nothing to do with the disease. (383)

Don't the forces of social and fictional retribution seem just a mite excessive? Even with all this overkill Rebecca refuses to stay dead. There *is* to be no going back, but not in the sense intended by the new Mrs de Winter. There can be no undoing of the crime she commits against herself in order to find a name. Her middle-class femininity is to be her punishment as well as her salvation.

For middle-class readers in the 1930s Rebecca's murder appears to offer an ideal fictive solution to those all too seductive deviant femininities. It is less than simple, however. Rebecca is no longer 'out there', the wife in the attic of the Gothic text, but *inside* the female subject, the condition of its existence. The process of identification which the novel depends upon is, in more ways than one, fatal. For Rebecca does, after all, get what she wants. She lures Maxim into killing her and thereby alters forever the balance of his authority and power. Ultimately, she robs him of his place. For we know from the very first page that something goes wrong with Maximilian de Winter's *second* marriage. That initial and final mystery has still to be solved – the mystery of Maxim and his child-bride finding themselves homeless, countryless, and childless.

HAPPY EVER AFTER?

I want to stress that it is the ways in which class intersects with gender priorities that determine the dénouement and leave it finally unresolved. The 'psychic' cannot therefore be seen as somehow existing outside history or the 'social' but is in fact its material. Class and gender differences do not simply speak to each other, they cannot speak *without* each other. What is at stake in *Rebecca* is for the girl to become both wife of Maxim and mistress of Manderley, and it is the latter which she must forego. For if Manderley cannot be ruled or even haunted by Rebecca then it is inconceivable, within the imaginative model of social relations in the text, for the girl to take Rebecca's place. The problem of their sexual identification has to be dealt with equally forcibly in the arena of class differences. Notably, the girl's first action as a newly confident Mrs de Winter is to bully the housemaid and dismiss Mrs Danvers's stale menu. Both acts make her the mistress. Her new-found sexual status and her superior class position differentiate and strengthen each other.

The problem is of course that the girl's actions are here too Rebecca-like for comfort. On arrival at Manderley she had in fact deplored the wastefulness of its aristocratic kitchens – though typically the text dwells lingeringly on the breakfast spread before condemning it. Now she is throwing bourgeois thrift to the winds. The girl cannot stay within this ambiguous class position and yet it is equally impossible to imagine a happy ending for the de Winters within that original bourgeois romanticization of marriage.

One cannot see Maximilian de Winter settling down to a cosy middle-class existence, the model for which is provided by the cameo sketch of Dr Baker near the end of the novel and whose domesticity is felt to be both appealing and trite. The proto-type for Maximilian was in fact called 'Henry' (du Maurier, 1981); like Brontë's Rochester, he ended up physically crippled and maimed. Daphne du Maurier decided after all not to call her hero 'Henry' and in so doing made it impossible for him to find true happiness pottering about the herbaceous borders with a wife busy sewing on the boys' nametapes – a fate suitable for many of the adorably dull husbands in the novels of the war-years to come.

Thus Maxim's loss of place, of Manderley itself, is a social, psychic and fictional necessity within the terms set up by the girl's assumption of Rebecca's position. It is interesting to see just how over-determined their self-imposed exile is. For it is certainly not 'realistically' necessary. After all, once Rebecca's cancer has been discovered and the verdict of her suicide accredited, what is to stop the couple, if not re-building Manderley, then finding another mansion house in the West country, or at least in the parklands of Surrey? Why do they have to leave England altogether? The point of asking these questions, which are of the 'how-many-children-had-lady-Macbeth?' variety, is to see how certain possibilities are not imaginable within the text. Maxim and the girl must be left without a place. All kinds of necessities are met by their exile. Firstly, the text can invoke a compensatory moral discourse which equates Maxim's economic loss with a psychological crippling, and can therefore atone for his crime. Losing your stately home is a fair cop for murdering your wife. Secondly, the couple can be placed literally outside of the English class system and the problem of whose class position is to be endorsed, is neatly avoided. And this can then be the price that the new Mrs de Winter has to pay. Reading *Country Life* and listening to the World Service can thus be shown to be both a far sadder and a greater thing than to be mistress of Manderley. Notably, Mrs de Winter lacks those sons who would so obviously need a Home (see pp. 74–5 for details), so again the problem of class inheritance and of competing notions of the family are sidestepped. The couple's exile is also used to appeal to a 'universal' Englishness and their position made poignant by relying on a mildly jingoistic patriotism with its dislike of 'abroad' and of foreigners, which had all the more force in 1938, with the Empire on the wane. The logic of Maxim's crime is, of course blurred and it seems that Rebecca is responsible for his loss of home, authority and even for the sunset of the Empire. Through her fall, the couple are exiled from their little Eden, leaving the garden of England to become overgrown by social and racial anarchy.

This epilogue is placed though, as I have said, at the beginning of the novel. By the end of *Rebecca* the reader may well have forgotten these details and their relation to the plot. The text actually closes with the burning of Manderley, apparently instigated by Mrs Danvers (though we do not know this for sure; the conflagration is also a kind of spontaneous combustion). This is a far more ambivalent ending since it is impossible to mourn the loss of Manderley without mourning too the loss of Rebecca who made it what it was – 'the beauty of Manderley...it's all due to her, to Rebecca' (287). The death of Manderley is in a way brought home as the real tragedy, as a place untouched by the demands of capital, a site of feudal freedom, which like Rebecca herself could at least operate outside of an encroaching bourgeois hegemony of social and sexual value.

Manderley has to burn to keep the whole range of readers happy, to leave Maxim and his new wife finally unplaced, free-floating outside of the allegiances of class and family. This is both the end and the beginning of the girl's story – where in fact we came in. Interestingly, unlike Jane Eyre, the girl does not find family and social place at the end of her story. She ends as she began, abroad, a paid companion. But the last page of the novel also ends with a dream, a dream of discovery which again has murderous consequences:

> Back again into the moving unquiet depths. I was writing letters in the morning-room.... But when I looked down to see what I had written it was not my...handwriting.... I got up and went to the looking-glass. A face stared back at me that was not my own.... The face in the glass stared back at me and laughed. And then I saw that she was sitting on a chair...and Maxim was brushing her hair.... It twisted like a snake, and he took hold of it with both hands and smiled at Rebecca and put it round his neck. (396)

The dream points exactly to the act of writing as the moment of danger. For the girl in *Rebecca*, the narrating is both a making safe and opening up of subjectivity, a volatile disclosure which puts her 'self' at risk. Rebecca acts out in this dream what the girl also desires. Perhaps, then, the de Winters *do* need to go abroad to save Maxim's skin – not from the scaffold, but from his wife. Perhaps the whole of the narrative should be seen as a kind of displaced revenge, a revenge which the ordinary middle-class girl dare not acknowledge as her own, and which only feminism would allow her to speak.

REBECCA'S STORY – TO BE CONTINUED

The ending of *Rebecca* resists a simple resolution in favour of the middle-class reader. If the ordinary girl triumphs, that triumph involves a deep sense of loss. Du Maurier, herself a displaced aristocrat, was perhaps drawn to query that shifting of values which historically was taking place. The texts of the 1930s are full of these dying houses. *Rebecca* is unique, however, in using its aristocratic class mythology to interrogate bourgeois definitions of femininity. There is no straight-forward model for social mobility in the novel because what is central to it is the question of female sexual pleasure. However much Rebecca is finally condemned as a deviant woman, the text still does foreground the problem for women of desiring an autonomous sexuality. No doubt the novel is a snobbish farewell to Manderley but looking into the 1940s it also registers, I think a collective gritting of the teeth by those women who suspected that to be a 'Mrs Miniver' would be a lesser thing than to be a Rebecca de Winter.[5] In the war years that followed, romance began to move into a more conservative terrain, one which tabooed the erotic and minimized the conflict between the demands of middle-class marriage and femininity, and the desire for sexual excitement and pleasure (Harper, 1982; Anderson, 1974).

Rebecca marks an outpost in the late 1930s, a transitional moment historically and fictionally, when the demands of middle-class femininity could be discussed and even dismantled with a public and popular form like romance. It demarcates a feminine subjectivity which is hopelessly split within bourgeois gendered relations. The girl's autobiography of gendered experience dramatizes the contradictory pressures which middle-class sexual ideologies were to place upon women, pressures which were in some measure to be responsible for their politicization some thirty years later.

Much of the popular fiction of the 1940s and 1950s can therefore be seen as a space where women as writers and readers seek to resolve and secure a gendered and desirous subjectivity by celebrating a staunch British middle-classness, with differing degrees of inevitable failure. Like Freud's hysteric 'suffering from reminiscences' their writing continually makes visible the tensions within the social construction of femininity whose definitions are never sufficient and are always reminders of what is missing, what could be.

The continuation of Rebecca's disruptive story can be glimpsed and sometimes openly followed in the novels which in the 1950s began to centre on the pressures and contradictory demands of middle-class femininity. The bleak and abrupt closures of the early novels of Elizabeth Taylor, the comic refusal of Barbara Pym to write novels about 'a full life', describing instead the lives of elderly or single women, the silences and madnesses of writers like Antonia White, Jean Rhys and Pym herself, have to be understood also as responses to the decade's regulation of acceptable femininity through its public discourses on marriage, motherhood and home (Weeks, 1981; Wilson, 1977 and 1980, Birmingham Feminist History Group, 1979). It is not until the 1960s, with its renewed emphasis on sexual pleasure and with the happy housewives themselves breaking into print, that personal and marital collapse become openly the subject of many literary narratives. The shift from the Gothic 'Other' of female sexuality to its resiting within the individualized trauma of the gendered subject can no longer be contained. Jean Rhys rewrites both *Jane Eyre* and *Rebecca* in her own dramatic comeback. *Wide Sargasso Sea* (1966). This time the revenant mad wife tries to tell her own story and finishes it by coming down from the attic to set fire to the house. It would be wrong, however, to characterize this moment as one of social rebellion pure and simple. For within literary discourse, 'the return of the repressed' (Wilson 1980) is imagined by white, middle-class writers as actually maddening. Anna, in Doris Lessing's *Golden Notebook* (1961), finds a personal artistic freedom which is also a private hell, as much a place of individualized confinement as of sexual protest. Perhaps then it is not too fanciful to suggest that it is only from inside the collectivity of a feminist politics that Rebecca's story could ever be imagined without fear of social psychic or fictive retribution.

POSTSCRIPT: THE FICTION OF ROMANCE

How then does *Rebecca* say anything at all about the formulaic fiction in which frail flower meets bronzed god? I would like to see *Rebecca* as the absent subtext of much romance fiction, the crime behind the scenes of Mills and Boon. For it seems to me that perhaps what romance tries to offer us is a 'triumph' over the unconscious, over the 'resistance to identity which lies at the very heart of psychic life' (Rose, 1983:9). *Rebecca* acts out the process of repression which these other texts avoid by assuming a fully-achievable, uncomplicated gendered subject whose sexual desire is not in question, not produced in struggle, but given. Above all, romance fiction makes heterosexuality easy, by suspending history in its formulae (whether costume, hospital or Caribbean drama) and by offering women readers a resolution in which submission and repression are not just managed without pain or humiliation but managed at all.

Thus although women are undoubtedly represented as sexual objects, there might be a sense in which women are also offered unique opportunities for reader-power, for an imaginary control of the uncontrollable in the fiction of romance. Within that scenario of extreme heterosexism can be derived the pleasure of reconstructing any heterosexuality which is not 'difficult'. Romance offers us relations impossibly harmonized; it uses unequal heterosexuality as a dream of equality and gives women uncomplicated access to a subjectivity which is unified and coherent *and* still operating within the field of pleasure.

Perhaps then the enormous readership of romance fiction, the fact that so many women find it deeply pleasurable, can be registered in terms other than those of moralizing shock. Romance is read by over 50 per cent of all women, but it is no coincidence that the two largest audiences are those of young women in their teens and 'middle-aged housewives'. (See Anderson, 1974, for discussion of readership patterns and responses and Euromonitor for more recent data.) I would suggest that these are both moments when the *impossibility* of being successfully feminine is felt, whether as a 'failure' ever to be feminine enough – like the girl's in *Rebecca* – or whether in terms of the gap between fulfilling social expectations (as wife and mother) and what those roles mean in reality. That women read romance fiction is, I think, as much a measure of their deep dissatisfaction with heterosexual options as of any desire to be fully identified with the submissive versions of femininity the texts endorse. Romance imagines peace, security and ease precisely because there is dissension, insecurity and difficulty. In the context of women's lives, romance reading might appear less a reactionary reflex or an indication of their victimization by the capitalist market, and more a sign of discontent and technique for survival. All the more so because inside a boring or alienating marriage, or at the age of fifteen, romance may be the only popular discourse which speaks to the question of women's sexual pleasure. Women's magazines, for example, do at least prioritize women and their lives in a culture where they are usually absent or given second place.

Patterns of romance reading are also revealing. Readers often collect hundreds, which are shared and recycled amongst friends. Reading romance fiction means participating in a kind of subculture, one which underlines a collective identity as women around the issue of women's pleasure and which can be found outside a political movement. As Janet Batsleer has pointed out, romances are not valued because like 'Great Art' they purport to be unrepeatable stories of unique characters, they are valued precisely as ritual and as repetition. It is difficult then to assume that these narratives are read in terms of a linear identification – it is not real and rounded individuals who are being presented and the endings are known by *readers* to be a foregone conclusion. Romance offers instead of closure a postponement of fulfilment. They are addictive because the control they gesture toward is always illusory, always modified and contained by the heterosexuality which they seek to harmonize. In a sense the activity of reading repeats the compulsion of desire and testifies to the limiting regulation of female sexuality. Romances may pretend that the path to marriage is effortless (obstacles are there to be removed) but they have to cry off when the action really starts – after marriage. The reader is left in a permanent state of foreplay, but I would guess that for many women this is the best heterosexual sex they ever get.

I want to suggest then that we develop ways of analysing romances and their reception as 'symptomatic' rather than simply reflective. Romance reading then becomes less a political sin or moral betrayal than a kind of 'literary anorexia' which functions as a protest against, as well as a restatement of, oppression. Their compulsive reading makes visible an insistent search on the part of readers for more than what is on offer. This is not, of course, any kind of argument for romance fictions being somehow progressive. Within the realities of women's lives however, they may well be *transgressive*. Consumerist, yes; a hopeless rebellion, yes; but still, in our society, a forbidden pleasure – like cream cakes. Romance does write heterosexuality in capital letters but in so doing it is an embarrassment to the literary establishment since its writers are always asking to be taken seriously. Their activity highlights of course the heterosexism of much orthodox and important Literature. For, leaving aside the representation of femininity, what other models are available *anywhere* for alternative constructs of masculinity? Romance is not being wilfully different in its descriptions of virility as constituted around poisitions of authority, hierarchy and aggression. Male, left-wing critics might do well to address themselves to projects which set out to deconstruct 'normal' male heterosexuality – a phenomenon which does after all exist outside war-stories and cowboy books.

To say, as I have, that subjectivity is at stake in the practices of reading and writing is not to retreat into 'subjectivism'. It is to recognize that any feminist literary critical enterprise is asking questions about social and historical formations, not just as they operate 'out there', but as they inform and structure the material 'in there' – the identities through which we live, and which may allow us to become the agents of political change. Fiction is pleasurable at least in part because it plays with, displaces and resites these other fictions, and we need a language as critics of 'popular culture' which can politicize without abandoning the categories of entertainment. To say that everyone's art is somebody's escapism is not to underestimate the effects of literary discourse, but to try to situate these effects across the vast spectrum of the production of meaning, of which literary texts are part. It would suggest too that it is not so much the abolition of certain literary forms which feminism necessitates as the changing of the conditions which produce them. I for one think that there will still be romance after the revolution.

If I have a soft spot for romance fiction then it is because nothing else speaks to me in the same way. It is up to us as feminists to develop a rigorous and compassionate understanding of how these fictions work in women's lives, keeping open the spaces for cultural and psychic pleasure whilst rechanneling the dissatisfactions upon which they depend. That then would seem to me to be the point of returning to Manderley.

NOTES

Alison Light would like to thank Cora Kaplan for helping to clarify many of her thoughts and sentences.

1 I am referring here very briefly to the enormous body of theoretical arguments which have emerged largely from the work of the French Marxist Louis Althusser. For extended discussion of this work, and the different directions it has taken since the late 1960s see, for example, Coward and Ellis (1977), Barrett (1980). For an analysis of the historical and political relations between Marxism, feminism and psychoanalysis, see Rose 1983.

2 Barrett (1982) takes up some of these points but see also Coward (1982) and Rose (1983) for the importance of psychoanalysis as offering ways into the questions of subjectivity, representation and sexual politics.

3 In her original notebook for the novel, du Maurier put a lengthy epilogue in its proper place (du Maurier, 1981). All references to *Rebecca* are to the Pan 1975 edition.

4 *Rebecca* might also be seen – like all romances – as being about adolescence and as such a re-enactment of the choices and traumas of Oedipalization: Maxim replaces the girl's lost father (who gave her such a 'very lovely and unusual name' (27)), but is only able to become her lover once the girl has moved from identification with Rebecca's clitoral (phallic) sexuality. Mrs Danvers is important here as Rebecca's lover in an almost lesbian relationship. The girl moves to a passive 'vaginal femininity, organized and defined by Maxim. I would argue that *Rebecca* also recognizes that moment of becoming a gendered subject as always involving a psychic division within the subject which continually resists the assumption of a coherent social and sexual identity.

5 *Mrs Miniver,* by Jan Anstruther, began as a series for *The Times* based on her own 'typically middleclass' family life. Published as a novel in 1939, it was a huge bestseller; the wartime film of the book is supposed to have helped bring the Americans into the war.

REFERENCES

Anderson, Rachel (1974) *The Purple Heart Throbs: The Sub-Literature of Love* London: Hodder and Stoughton.
Barrett, Michèle (1980) *Women's Oppression Today* London: Verso and NLB.
Barrett, Michèle (1982) 'Feminism and the Definition of Cultural Politics' in Brunt and Rowan (1982).
Batsleer, Janet (1981) 'Pulp in the Pink' *Spare Rib*, no. 109.
Beauman, Nicola (1983) *A Very Great Profession: The Woman's Novel 1914–39* London: Virago.
Birmingham Feminist History Group (1979) 'Feminism as Femininity in the Nineteen-fifties?' *Feminist Review* no. 3.
Brunt, Rosalind and Rowan, Caroline, eds (1982) *Feminism, Culture and Politics* London: Lawrence and Wishart.
Coward, Rosalind and Ellis, John (1977) *Language and Materialism* London: Routledge and Kegan Paul.
Coward, Rosalind (1982) 'Sexual Politics and Psychoanalysis: Some Notes on their Relation' in Brunt and Rowan (1982).
Du Maurier, Daphne (1938) *Rebecca* London: Victor Gollancz; (1975) London: Pan.
Du Maurier, Daphne (1981) *The Rebecca Notebook and Other Memories* London: Victor Gollancz.
Euromonitor Readership Surveys
Harper, Sue (1982) 'History with Frills: Costume Fiction in World War II' *Red Letters* no. 14.
Lessing, Doris (1962) *The Golden Notebook* London: Panther.
Margolies, David (1982) 'Mills and Boon – Guilt without Sex' *Red Letters* no. 14.
Rhys, Jean (1966) *Wide Sargasso Sea* Harmondsworth, Penguin.
Rose, Jacqueline (1983) 'Femininity and its Discontents' *Feminist Review* no. 14.
Weeks, Jeffrey (1981) *Sex, Politics and Society* Harlow: Longman.
Wilson, Elizabeth (1977) *Women and the Welfare State* London: Tavistock.
Wilson, Elizabeth (1980) *Only Halfway to Paradise: Women in Postwar Britain 1945–1968* London: Tavistock.

21

Cora Kaplan

Pandora's Box: Subjectivity, Class and Sexuality in Socialist-Feminist Criticism

> Feminist criticism, as its name implies, is criticism with a Cause, engaged criticism. But the critical model presented to us so far is merely engaged to be married. It is about to contract what can only be a *mésalliance* with bourgeois modes of thought and the critical categories they inform. To be effective, feminist criticism cannot become simply bourgeois criticism in drag. It must be ideological and moral criticism; it must be revolutionary.
>
> *Lillian Robinson, 'Dwelling in Decencies'*

> The 'Marriage' of marxism and feminism has been like the marriage of husband and wife depicted in English common law: marxism and feminism are one, and that is marxism...we need a healthier marriage or we need a divorce.
>
> *Heidi Hartmann, 'The Unhappy Marriage of Marxism and Feminism'*

In spite of the attraction of matrimonial metaphor, reports of feminist nuptials with either mild-mannered bourgeois criticism or macho mustachioed Marxism have been greatly exaggerated. Neither liberal feminist criticism decorously draped in traditional humanism, nor her red-ragged rebellious sister, socialist-feminist criticism, has yet found a place within androcentric literary criticism, which wishes to embrace feminism through a legitimate public alliance. Nor can feminist criticism today be plausibly evoked as a young deb looking for protection or, even more problematically, as a male 'mole' in transvestite masquerade. Feminist criticism now marks out a broad area of literary studies, eclectic, original and provocative. Independent still, through a combination of choice and default, it has come of age without giving up its name. Yet Lillian Robinson's astute pessimistic prediction is worth remembering. With maturity, the most visible, well-defined and extensive tendency within feminist criticism has undoubtedly bought into the white, middle-class, heterosexist values of traditional literary criticism, and threatens to settle down on her own in its cultural suburbs. For, as I see it, the present danger is not that feminist criticism will enter an unequal dependent alliance with any of the varieties of male-centred criticism. It does not need to, for it has produced an all too persuasive autonomous analysis which is in many ways radical in its discussion of gender, but implicitly conservative in its assumptions about social hierarchy and female subjectivity, the Pandora's box for all feminist theory.

This reactionary effect must be interrogated and resisted from within feminism and in relation to the wider socialist-feminist project. For, without the class and race perspectives which socialist-feminist critics bring to the analysis both of the literary texts and of their conditions of production, liberal feminist criticism, with its emphasis on the unified female subject, will unintentionally reproduce the ideological values of mass-market romance. In that fictional landscape the other structuring relations of society fade and disappear, leaving us with the naked drama of sexual difference as the only scenario that matters. Mass-market romance tends to represent sexual difference as natural and fixed – a constant, transhistorical femininity in libidinized struggle with an equally 'given' universal masculinity. Even where class difference divides lovers, it is there as narrative backdrop or minor stumbling-block to the inevitable heterosexual resolution. Without overstraining the comparison, a feminist literary criticism which privileges gender in isolation from other forms of social determination offers us a similarly partial reading of the role played by sexual difference in literary discourse, a reading bled dry of its most troubling and contradictory meanings.

The appropriation of modern critical theory – semiotic with an emphasis on the psychoanalytic – can be of great use in arguing against concepts of natural, essential and unified identity: against a static femininity and masculinity. But these theories about the production of meaning in culture must engage fully with the effects of other systems of difference than the sexual, or they too will produce no more than an anti-humanist avant-garde version of romance. Masculinity and femininity do not appear in cultural discourse, any more than they do in mental life, as pure binary forms at play. They are always, already, ordered and broken up through other social and cultural terms, other categories of difference. Our fantasies of sexual transgression as much as our obedience to sexual regulation are expressed through these structuring hierarchies. Class and race ideologies are, conversely, steeped in and spoken through the language of sexual differentiation. Class and race meanings are not metaphors for the sexual, or vice versa. It is better, though not exact, to see them as reciprocally constituting each other through a kind of narrative invocation, a set of associative terms in a chain of meaning. To understand how gender and class – to take two categories only – are articulated together transforms our analysis of each of them.

The literary text too often figures in feminist criticism as a gripping spectacle in which sexual difference appears somewhat abstracted from the muddy social world in which it is elsewhere embedded. Yet novels, poetry and drama are, on the contrary, peculiarly rich discourses in which the fused languages of class, race and gender are both produced and re-represented through the incorporation of other discourses. The focus of feminist analysis ought to be on that heterogeneity within the literary, on the intimate relation there expressed between all the categories that order social and psychic meaning. This does not imply an attention to content only or primarily, but also entails a consideration of the linguistic processes of the text as they construct and position subjectivity within these terms.

For without doubt literary texts do centre the individual as object and subject of their discourse. Literature has been a traditional space for the exploration of gender relations and sexual difference, and one in which women themselves have been formidably present. The problem for socialist feminists is not the focus on the individual that is special to the literary, but rather the romantic theory of the subject so firmly entrenched within the discourse. Humanist feminist criticism does not object to the idea of an immanent, transcendent subject but only to the exclusion of women from these definitions which it takes as an accurate account of subjectivity rather than as a historically constructed ideology. The repair and reconstitution of female subjectivity through a rereading of literature becomes, therefore, a major part, often unacknowledged, of its critical project. Psychoanalytic and semiotically oriented feminist criticism has argued well against this aspect of feminish humanism, emphasizing the important structural relation between writing and sexuality in the construction of the subject. But both tendencies have been correctly criticized from a socialist-feminist position for the neglect of class and race as factors in their analysis. If feminist criticism is to make a central contribution to the understanding of sexual difference, instead of serving as a conservative refuge from its more disturbing social and psychic implications, the inclusion of class and race must transform its terms and objectives.

The critique of feminist humanism needs more historical explication than it has so far received. Its sources are complex, and are rooted in that moment almost 200 years ago when modern feminism and Romantic cultural theory emerged as separate but linked responses to the transforming events of the French Revolution. In the heat and light of the revolutionary decade 1790–1800, social, political and aesthetic ideas already maturing underwent a kind of forced ripening. As the progressive British intelligentsia contemplated the immediate possibility of social change, their thoughts turned urgently to the present capacity of subjects to exercise republican freedoms – to rule themselves as well as each other if the corrupt structures of aristocratic privilege were to be suddenly razed. Both feminism as set out in its most influential text, Mary Wollstonecraft's *A Vindication of the Rights of Woman* (1972), and Romanticism as argued most forcefully in Wordsworth's introduction to *Lyrical Ballads* (1800) stood in intimate, dynamic and contradictory relationship to democratic politics. In all three discourses the social and psychic character of the individual was centred and elaborated. The public and private implications of sexual difference as well as of the imagination and its products were both strongly linked to the optimistic, speculative construction of a virtuous citizen subject for a brave new egalitarian world. Theories of reading and writing – Wollstonecraft's and Jane Austen's as well as those of male Romantic authors – were explicitly related to contemporary politics as expressed in debate by such figures as Tom Paine, Edmund Burke and William Godwin.

The new categories of independent subjectivity, however, were marked from the beginning by exclusions of gender, race and class. Jean-Jacques Rousseau, writing in the 1750s, specifically exempted women from his definition; Thomas Jefferson, some twenty years later, excluded blacks. Far from being invisible ideological aspects of the new subject, these exclusions occasioned debate and polemic on both sides of the Atlantic. The autonomy of inner life, the dynamic psyche whose moral triumph was to be the foundation of republican government, was considered absolutely essential as an element of progressive political thought.

However, as the concept of the inner self and the moral psyche was used to denigrate whole classes, races and genders, late nineteenth-century socialism began to de-emphasize the political importance of the psychic self, and redefine political morality and the adequate citizen subject in primarily social terms. Because of this shift in emphasis, a collective moralism has developed in socialist thought which, instead of criticizing the reactionary interpretation of psychic life, stigmatizes sensibility itself, interpreting the excess of feeling as regressive, bourgeois and non-political.

Needless to say, this strand of socialist thought poses a problem for feminism, which has favoured three main strategies to deal with it. In the first, women's psychic life is seen as being essentially identical to men's, but distorted through vicious and systematic patriarchal inscription. In this view, which is effectively Wollstonecraft's, social reform would prevent women from becoming regressively obsessed with sexuality and feeling. The second strategy wholly vindicates women's psyche, but sees it as quite separate from men's, often in direct opposition. This is frequently the terrain on which radical feminism defends female sexuality as independent and virtuous between women, but degrading in a heterosexual context. It is certainly a radical reworking of essentialist sexual ideology, shifting the ground from glib assertions of gender complementarity to the logic of separatism. The third strategy has been to refuse the issue's relevance altogether – to see any focus on psychic difference as itself an ideological one.

Instead of choosing any one of these options, socialist-feminist criticism must come to grips with the relationship between female subjectivity and class identity. This project, even in its present early stages, poses major problems for the tendency. While socialist feminists have been deeply concerned with the social construction of femininity and sexual difference, they have been uneasy about integrating social and political determinations with an analysis of the psychic ordering of gender. Within socialist feminism, a fierce and unresolved debate continues about the value of using psychoanalytic theory, because of the supposedly ahistorical character of its paradigms. For those who are hostile to psychoanalysis, the meaning of mental life, fantasy and desire – those obsessive themes of the novel and poetry for the last two centuries – seems particularly intractable to interpretation. They are reluctant to grant much autonomy to the psychic level, and often most attentive to feeling expressed in the work of non-bourgeois writers, which can more easily be read as political statement. Socialist feminism still finds unlocated, unsocialized psychic expression in women's writing hard to discuss in non-moralizing terms.

On the other hand, for liberal humanism, feminist versions included, the possibility of a unified self and an integrated consciousness that can transcend material circumstance is represented as the fulfilment of desire, the happy closure at the end of the story. The psychic fragmentation expressed through female characters in women's writing is seen as the most important sign of their sexual subordination, more interesting and ultimately more meaningful than their social oppression. As a result, the struggle for an integrated female subjectivity in nineteenth-century texts is never interrogated as ideology or fantasy, but seen as a demand that can actually be met, if not in 1848, then later.

In contrast, socialist-feminist criticism tends to foreground the social and economic elements of the narrative and socialize what it can of its psychic portions. Women's anger and anguish, it is assumed, should be amenable to repair through social change. A positive emphasis on the psychic level is viewed as a valorization of the anarchic and regressive, a way of returning women to their subordinate ideological place within the dominant culture, as unreasoning social beings. Psychoanalytic theory, which is by and large morally neutral about the desires expressed by the psyche, is criticized as a confirmation and justification of them.

Thus semiotic or psychoanalytic perspectives have yet to be integrated with social, economic and political analysis. Critics tend to privilege one element or the other, even when they acknowledge the importance of both and the need to relate them. A comparison of two admirable recent essays on Charlotte Brontë's *Villette*, one by Mary Jacobus and the other by Judith Lowder Newton, both informed by socialist-feminist concerns, can illustrate this difficulty.

Jacobus uses the psychoanalytic and linguistic theory of Jacques Lacan to explore the split representations of subjectivity that haunt *Villette*, and calls attention to its anti-realist gothic elements. She relates Brontë's feminized defence of the imagination, and the novel's unreliable narrator-heroine, to the tension between femininity and feminism that reaches back to the eighteenth-century debates of Rousseau and Wollstonecraft. Reading the ruptures and gaps of the text as a psychic narrative, she also places it historically in relationship to nineteenth-century social and political ideas. Yet the social meanings of *Villette* fade and all but disappear before 'the powerful presence of fantasy', which 'energizes *Villette* and satisfies that part of the reader which also desires constantly to reject reality for the sake of an obedient, controllable, narcissistically pleasurable image of self and its relation to the world' (Jacobus 1979, p. 51). In Jacobus's interpretation, the psyche, desire and fantasy stand for repressed, largely positive elements of a forgotten feminism, while the social stands for a daytime world of Victorian social regulation. These social meanings are referred to rather than explored in the essay, a strategy which renders them both static and unproblematically unified. It is as if, in order to examine how *Villette* represents psychic reality, the dynamism of social discourses of gender and identity must be repressed, forming the text's new 'unconscious'.

Judith Lowder Newton's chapter on *Villette* in her impressive study of nineteenth-century British fiction, *Women, Power, and Subversion* (1981), is also concerned with conflicts between the novel's feminism and its evocation of female desire. Her interpretation privileges the social meanings of the novel, its search for a possible *détente* between the dominant ideologies of bourgeois femininity and progressive definitions of female autonomy. For Newton, 'the internalized ideology of women's sphere' includes sexual and romantic longings – which for Jacobus are potentially radical and disruptive of mid-Victorian gender ideologies. The psychic level as Newton describes it is mainly the repository for the worst and most regressive elements of female subjectivity: longing for love, dependency, the material and emotional comfort of fixed class identity. These desires which have 'got inside' are predictably in conflict with the rebellious, autonomy-seeking feminist impulses, whose source is a rational understanding of class and gender subordination. Her reading centres on the realist text, locating meaning in its critique of class society and the constraints of bourgeois femininity.

The quotations and narrative elements cited and explored by Jacobus and Newton are so different that even a reader familiar with *Villette* may find it hard to believe that each critic is reading the same text. The psychic level exists in Newton's interpretation, to be sure, but as a negative discourse, the dead weight of ideology on the mind. For her, the words 'hidden', 'private' and 'longing' are stigmatized, just as they are celebrated by Jacobus. For both critics, female subjectivity is the site where the opposing forces of femininity and feminism clash by night, but they locate these elements in different parts of the text's divided selves. Neither Newton nor Jacobus argues for the utopian possibility of a unified subjectivity. But the *longing* to close the splits that characterize femininity – splits between reason and desire, autonomy and dependent security, psychic and social identity – is evident in the way each critic denies the opposing element.

My comments on the difficulties of reading *Villette* from a materialist feminist stance are meant to suggest that there is more at issue in the polarization of social and psychic explanation than the problem of articulating two different forms of explanation. Moral and political questions specific to feminism are at stake as well. In order to understand why female subjectivity is so fraught with *Angst* and difficulty for feminism, we must go back to the first full discussion of the psychological expression of femininity, in Mary Wollstonecraft's *A Vindication of the Rights of Woman*. The briefest look will show that an interest in the psychic life of women as a crucial element in their subordination and liberation is not a modern, post-Freudian preoccupation. On the contrary, its long and fascinating history in 'left' feminist writing starts with Wollstonecraft, who set the terms for a debate that is still in progress. Her writing is central for socialist feminism today, because she based her interest in the emancipation of women as individuals in revolutionary politics.

Like so many eighteenth-century revolutionaries, she saw her own class, the rising bourgeoise, as the vanguard of the revolution, and it was to the women of her own class that she directed her arguments. Her explicit focus on the middle class, and her concentration on the nature of female subjectivity, speaks directly to the source of anxiety within socialist feminism today. For it is at the point when women are released from profound social and economic oppression into greater autonomy and potential political choice that their social and psychic expression becomes an issue, and their literary texts become sites of ambivalence. In their pages, for the last 200 years and more, women characters seemingly more confined by social regulation than women readers today speak as desiring subjects. These texts express the politically 'retrogade' desires for comfort, dependence and love as well as more acceptable demands for autonomy and independence.

It is Mary Wollstonecraft who first offered women this fateful choice between the opposed and moralized bastions of reason and feeling, which continues to determine much feminist thinking. The structures through which she developed her ideas, however, were set for her by her mentor Jean-Jacques Rousseau, whose writing influenced the political and social perspectives of many eighteenth-century English radicals. His ideas were fundamental to her thinking about gender as well as about revolutionary politics. In 1792, that highly charged moment of romantic political optimism between the fall of the Bastille and the Terror when *A Vindication* was written, it must have seemed crucial that Rousseau's crippling judgement of female nature be refuted. How else could women freely and equally participate in the new world being made across the Channel? Rousseau's ideas about subjectivity were already immanent in Wollstonecraft's earlier book *Mary: A Fiction* (1788). Now she set out to challenge directly his offensive description of sexual difference which would leave women in post-revolutionary society: exactly where they were in unreformed Britain, 'immured in their families, groping in the dark' (Wollstonecraft 1975a, p. 5).

Rousseau had set the terms of the debate in his *Emile* (1762), which describes the growth and education of the new man, progressive and bourgeois, who would be capable of exercising the republican freedoms of a reformed society. In Book V, Rousseau invents 'Sophie' as a mate for his eponymous hero, and here he outlines his theory of sexual asymmetry as it occurs in nature. In all human beings passion was natural and necessary, but in women it was not controlled by reason, an attribute of the male sex only. Women therefore,

> must be subject all their lives, to the most constant and severe restraint, which is that of decorum; it is therefore necessary to accustom them early to such confinement that it may not afterwards cost them too dear.... we should teach them above all things to lay a due restraint on themselves. (Rousseau 1974, p. 332)

To justify this restraint, Rousseau allowed enormous symbolic power to the supposed anarchic, destructive force of untrammelled female desire. As objects of desire Rousseau made women alone responsible for male 'suffering'. If they were free agents of desire, there would be no end to the 'evils' they could cause. Therefore the family, and women's maternal role within it, were, he said, basic to the structure of the new society. Betrayal of the family was thus as subversive as betrayal of the state; adultery in *Emile* is literally equated with treason. Furthermore, in Rousseau's regime of regulation and restraint for bourgeois women, their 'decorum' – the social expression of modesty – would act as an additional safeguard against unbridled, excessive male lust, should its natural guardian, reason, fail. In proscribing the free exercise of female desire, Rousseau disarms a supposed serious threat to the new political as well as social order. To read the fate of a class through the sexual behaviour of its women was not a new political strategy. What is modern in Rousseau's formulation is the harnessing of these sexual ideologies to the fate of a new progressive bourgeoisie, whose individual male members were endowed with radical, autonomous identity.

In many ways, Mary Wollstonecraft, writing thirty years after *Emile*, shared with many others the political vision of her master. Her immediate contemporary Thomas Paine thought Rousseau's work expressed 'a loveliness of sentiment in favour of liberty', and it is in the spirit of Rousseau's celebration of liberty that Wollstonecraft wrote A *Vindication*. Her strategy was to accept Rousseau's description of adult women as suffused in sensuality, but to ascribe this unhappy state of things to culture rather than nature. It was, she thought, the vicious and damaging result of Rousseau's punitive theories of sexual difference and female education when put into practice. Excessive sensuality was for Wollstonecraft, in 1792 at least, as dangerous if not more so than Rousseau had suggested, but she saw the damage and danger first of all to women themselves, whose potential and independence were initially stifled and broken by an apprenticeship to pleasure, which induced psychic and social dependency. Because Wollstonecraft saw prepubescent children in their natural state as mentally and emotionally unsexed as well as untainted by corrupting desire, she bitterly refuted Rousseau's description of innate infantile female sexuality. Rather, the debased femininity she describes is constructed through a set of social practices which by constant reinforcement become internalized parts of the self. Her description of this process is acute:

> Every thing they see or hear serves to fix impressions, call forth emotions, and associate ideas, that give a sexual character to the mind.... This cruel association of ideas, which every thing conspires to twist into all their habits of thinking, or, to speak with more precision of feeling, receives new force when they begin to act a little for themselves. (Wollstonecraft 1975a, p. 177)

For Wollstonecraft, female desire was a contagion caught from the projection of male lust, an ensnaring and enslaving infection that made women into dependent and degenerate creatures, who nevertheless had the illusion that they acted independently. An education which changed women from potentially rational autonomous beings into 'insignificant objects of desire' was, moreover, rarely reversible. Once a corrupt subjectivity was constructed, only a most extraordinary individual could transform it, for 'so ductile is the understanding and yet so stubborn, that the association which depends on adventitious circumstances, during the period that the body takes to arrive at maturity, can seldom be disentangled by reason' (p. 116).

What is disturbingly peculiar to *A Vindication* is the undifferentiated and central place that sexuality as passion plays in the corruption and degradation of the female self. The overlapping Enlightenment and Romantic discourses on psychic economy all posed a major division between the rational and the irrational, between sense and sensibility. But they hold sensibility *in men* to be only in part an antisocial sexual drive. Lust for power and the propensity to physical violence were also, for men, negative components of all that lay on the other side of reason. Thus sensibility in men included a strong positive element too, for the power of the imagination depended on it, and in the 1790s the Romantic aesthetic and the political imagination were closely allied. Sexual passion controlled and mediated by reason, Wordsworth's 'emotion recollected in tranquillity', could also be put to productive use in art – by men. The appropriate egalitarian subjects of Wordsworth's art were 'moral sentiments and animal sensations' as they appeared in everyday life (Wordsworth and Coleridge 1971, p. 261). No woman of the time could offer such an artistic manifesto. In women the irrational, the sensible, even the imaginative are all drenched in an overpowering and subordinating sexuality. And in Wollstonecraft's writing, especially in her last, unfinished novel *Maria, or the Wrongs of Woman* (1798), which is considerably less punitive about women's sexuality in general than *A Vindication,* only maternal feeling survives as a positively realized element of the passionate side of the psyche. By defending women against Rousseau' denial of their reason, Wollstonecraft unwittingly assents to his negative, eroticized sketch of their emotional lives. At various points in *A Vindication* she interjects a wish that 'after some future revolution in time' women might be able to live out a less narcissistic and harmful sexuality. Until then they must demand an education whose central task is to cultivate their neglected 'understanding'.

It is interesting and somewhat tragic that Wollstonecraft's paradigm of women's psychic economy still profoundly shapes modern feminist consciousness. How often are the maternal, romantic-sexual and intellectual capacity of women presented by feminism as in competition for a fixed psychic space. Men seem to have a roomier and more accomodating psychic home, one which can, as Wordsworth and other Romantics insisted, situate all the varieties of passion and reason in creative tension. This gendered eighteenth-century psychic economy has been out of date for a long time, but its ideological inscription still shadows feminist attitudes towards the mental life of women.

The implications of eighteenth-century theories of subjectivity were important for early feminist ideas about women as readers and writers. In the final pages of *A Vindication,* decrying female sentimentality as one more effect of women's psychic degradation, Wollstonecraft criticizes the sentimental fictions increasingly written by and for women, which were often their only education. 'Novels' encouraged in their mainly young, mainly female audience 'a romantic twist of the mind'. Readers would 'only be taught to look for happiness in love, refine on sensual feelings and adopt metaphysical notions respecting that passion'. At their very worst the 'stale tales' and 'meretricious scenes' would by degrees induce more than passive fantasy. The captive, addicted reader might, while the balance of her mind was disturbed by these erotic evocations, turn fiction into fact and 'plump into actual vice' (p. 183). A reciprocal relationship between the patriarchal socialization of women and the literature that supports and incites them to become 'rakes at heart' is developed in this passage. While Wollstonecraft adds that she would rather women read novels than nothing at all, she sets up a peculiarly gendered and sexualized interaction between women and the narrative imaginative text, one in which women become the ultimately receptive reader easily moved into amoral activity by the fictional representation of sexual intrigue.

The political resonance of these questions about reader response was, at the time, highly charged. An enormous expansion of literacy in general, and of the middle-class reading public in particular, swelled by literate women, made the act of reading in the last quarter of the eighteenth century an important practice through which the common sense and innate virtue of a society of autonomous subject-citizens could be reached and moulded. An uncensored press, cheap and available reading matter and a reading public free to engage with the flood of popular literature, from political broadsheets to sensational fiction, was part of the agenda and strategy of British republicanism. 'It is dangerous', Tom Paine warned the government in the mid-1790s after his own writing had been politically censored, 'to tell a whole peole that they shall not read.' Reading was a civil right that supported and illustrated the radical vision of personal independence. Political and sexual conservatives, Jane Austen and Hannah More, as well as the republican and feminist left, saw reading as an active, not a passive function of the self, a critical link between the psychic play of reason and passion and its social expression. New social categories of readers, women of all classes, skilled and unskilled working-class males, are described in this period by contemporaries. Depending on their political sympathies, observers saw these actively literate groups as an optimistic symptom of social and intellectual progress or a dire warning of imminent social decay and threatened rebellion.

Wollstonecraft saw sentiment and the sensual as reinforcing an already dominant, approved and enslaving sexual norm, which led women to choose a subordinate social and subjective place in culture. The damage done by 'vice' and 'adultery', to which sentimental fiction was an incitement, was a blow to women first and to society second. Slavish legitimate sexuality was almost as bad for women in Wollstonecraft's view as unlicensed behaviour. A more liberal regime for women was both the goal and the cure of sentimental and erotic malaise. In *A Vindication* women's subjection is repeatedly compared to all illegitimate hierarchies of power, but especially to existing aristocratic hegemony. At every possible point in her text, Wollstonecraft links the liberation of women from the sensual into the rational literally and symbolically to the egalitarian transformation of the whole society.

'Passionlessness', as Nancy Cott has suggested (Cott 1978), was a strategy adopted both by feminists and by social conservatives. Through the assertion that women were not innately or excessively sexual, that on the contrary their 'feelings' were largely filial and maternal, the imputation of a degraded subjectivity could be resisted. This alternative psychic organization was represented as both strength and weakness in nineteenth-century debates about sexual difference. In these debates, which were conducted across a wide range of public discourses, the absence of an independent, self-generating female sexuality is used by some men and women to argue for women's right to participate equally in an undifferentiated public sphere. It is used by others to argue for the power and value of the separate sphere allotted to women. And it is used more nakedly to support cruder justifications of patriarchal right. The idea of passionlessness as either a natural or a cultural effect acquires no simple ascendancy in Victorial sexual ideology, even as applied to the ruling bourgeoisie.

As either conservative or radical sexual ideology, asexual femininity was a fragile, unstable concept. It was constructed through a permanently threatened transgression, which fictional narrative obsessively documented and punished. It is a gross historical error to infer from the regulatory sexual discourses in the novel the actual 'fate' of Victorian adulteresses, for novels operated through a set of highly punitive conventions in relation to female sexuality that almost certainly did not correspond to lived social relations. However, novels do call attention to the difficulty of fixing such a sexual ideology, precisely because they construct a world in which there is no alternative to it.

One of the central weaknesses of humanist criticism is that it accepts the idea advanced by classical realism that the function of literature is mimetic or realistic representation. The humanist critic identifies with the author's claim that the text represents reality, and acts as a sympathetic reader who will test the authenticity of the claim through the evidence of the text. The Marxist critic, on the other hand, assumes that author and text speak from a position within ideology – that claims about fictional truth and authenticity are, in themselves, to be understood in relation to a particular historical view of culture and art which evolved in the Romantic period. Semiotic and psychoanalytic theories of representation go even further in rejecting the possibility of authentic mimetic art. They see the literary text as a system of signs that constructs meaning rather than reflecting it, inscribing simultaneously the subjectivity of speaker and reader. Fiction by bourgeois women writers is spoken from the position of a class-specific femininity. It constructs us as readers in relation to that subjectivity through the linguistic strategies and processes of the text. It also takes us on a tour, so to speak, of a waxworks of other subjects-in-process – the characters of the text. These fictional characters are there as figures in a dream, as constituent structures of the narrative of the dreamer, not as correct reflections of the socially real.

It is hard for feminism to accept the implications of this virtual refusal of textual realism, if only because literature was one of the few public discourses in which women were allowed to speak themselves, where they were not the imaginary representations of men. None the less, the subjectivity of women of other classes and races and with different sexual orientations can never be 'objectively' or 'authentically' represented in literary texts by the white, heterosexual, middle-class woman writer, however sympathetically she invents or describes such women in her narrative. The nature of fiction and the eccentric relation of female subjectivity itself both to culture and to psychic identity, as understood from a psychoanalytic perspective, defeats that aim. We can, however, learn a great deal from women's writing about the cultural meanings produced from the splitting of women's subjectivity, especially her sexuality, into class and race categories. But before we say more about this way of reading women's writing we need a more precise working definition of 'class'.

Unlike subjectivity, 'class' has been a central category for socialist-feminist criticism, but remains somewhat inert within it, if not within socialist-feminist theory as a whole. Socialist critics hesitate to identify their own object of study, the literary text, as a central productive site of class meaning, because it seems too far away from 'real' economic and political determinations. The same worry, conversely, can induce a compensatory claim that *all* the material relations of class can be discovered within the discourse; indeed, that they are most fully represented there, because language is itself material. These positions, which I confess I have parodied a little, remain unresolved in current debate, although efforts at *détente* have been made. They indicate the uneasy relationship between the political and the literary in the Marxist critical project, an unease shared by socialist feminists too.

Among socialist historians in the last few years the understanding of the history of class has undergone vigorous reappraisal in response to debates about the changing composition and politics of the working class in modern capitalist societies. In a recent collection of essays, *The Languages of Class*, the British historian of the nineteenth century, Gareth Stedman Jones, proposes some radical approaches to that history which have an immediate relevance for the analysis of representation. First of all, Stedman Jones asks for a more informed and theoretical attention by historians to the linguistic construction of class. '"Class" is a word embedded in language and should be analysed in terms of its linguistic content', he states. In the second place, 'class' as a concept needs to be unpacked, and its differential construction in discourse recognized and given a certain autonomy:

> because there are different languages of class, one should not proceed upon the assumption that 'class' as an elementary counter of official social description, 'class' as effect of theoretical discourse about distribution or productive relations, 'class' as the summary of a cluster of culturally signifying practices

> or 'class' as a species of political or ideological self-definition, share a single reference point in anterior social reality. (Stedman Jones 1983, pp. 7–8)

While 'anterior social reality' hangs slightly loose in this formulation, the oppressively unitary character of class as a concept is usefully broken down. Class can be seen as defined in different terms at different levels of analysis, as well as being 'made' and 'lived' through a variety of languages at any given point in history.

How can this pulling apart of the languages of class help socialist-feminist critics to put class and gender, social and psychic together in a non-reductive way? First of all, these distinctions put a useful space between the economic overview of class – the Marxist or socialist analysis – and the actual rhetoric of class as it appears in a novel. The class language of a nineteenth-century novel is not only or even primarily characterized by reference to the material circumstances of the protagonists, though that may be part of its representation there. The language of class in the novel foregrounds the language of the self, the inner discourse of the subject *as* class language, framing that discourse through the dissonant chorus of class voices that it appropriates and invents. In the novel, class discourse *is* gendered discourse; the positions of 'Emile' and 'Sophie' are given dramatic form. Class is embodied in fiction in a way that it never is either in bourgeois economic discourse or in Marxist economic analysis. In those discourses of class, gender is mystified, presented in ideological form. In fiction, though difference may be presented through sexual ideologies, its immanent, crucial presence in the social relations of class, as well as its psychic effects, is strongly asserted. Fiction refuses the notion of a genderless class subjectivity, and resists any simple reduction of class meaning and class identity to productive forces. This refusal and resistance cannot be written off, or reduced to the humanist ideologies of transcendence which those fictions may also enunciate, for the presence of gendered subjectivity in nineteenth-century fiction is always 'in struggle' with the Romantic ideologies of unified identity.

Within socialist-feminist cultural analysis it has been easier to describe the visual or linguistic fusion of class and gender meanings in representation than it has been to assess the role such fusion plays in the construction of either category. Let us assume that in these signifying practices class is powerfully defined through sexual difference, and vice versa, and that these representations are constitutive of certain class meanings, not merely a distorted or mendacious reflection of other languages. 'Class' needs to be read through an ensemble of these languages, often contradictory, as well as in terms of an economic overview. The overpowering presence of gender in some languages of class and its virtual absence in others needs to be related not to a single anterior definition of class reality, but to the heterogeneous and contradictory nature of that reality.

Literature is itself a heterogeneous discourse, which appropriates, contextualizes and comments on other 'languages' of class and gender. This process of intertextuality – the dialogic, as the Russian critic Bakhtin called it (Bakhtin 1981) – undermines the aspirations of the text towards a unifying definition. The language of class in the nineteenth-century novel obsessively inscribes a class system whose divisions and boundaries are at once absolute and impregnable and in constant danger of dissolution. Often in these narratives it is a woman whose class identity is at risk or problematic; the woman and her sexuality are a condensed and displaced representation of the dangerous instabilities of class and gender identity for both sexes. The loss and recuperation of female identity within the story – a favourite lost-and-found theme from *Mansfield Park* to *Tess* – provides an imaginary though temporary solution to the crisis of both femininity and class. Neither category – class or gender – was ever as stable as the ideologies that support them must continually insist. The many-layered, compacted representations of class and gender found in imaginative literature are not generic metaphors, peculiar to fiction, drama and poetry, though in them they are given great scope. They occur in many other nineteenth-century discourses – metonymic, associative tropes which are linked by incomparable similarities, through a threat to identity and status that inheres to both sets of hierarchies, both structures of difference.

The class subjectivity of women and their sexual identity thus became welded together in nineteenth-century discourses and took on new and sinister dimensions of meaning. Ruling groups had traditionally used the sexual and domestic virtue of their women as a way of valorizing their moral authority. By focusing on the issue and image of female sexual conduct, questions about the economic and political integrity of dominant groups could be displaced. When the citizen subject became the crucial integer of political discourse and practice, this type of symbolization, which was always 'about' sexual difference as well as 'about' the political, took on new substantive, material meaning. The moral autonomy of individuals and the moral behaviour of social groups now converged in a political practice and theory –liberal, constitutional and legitimated through an expanding franchise – in which the individual voter was the common denominator of the political. Women, as we have seen, were explicitly excluded from these political practices, but, as we have also seen, attempts to naturalize that exclusion were never wholly successful. Feminism inserted itself into the debate just at the point where theories of innate difference attempted to deny women access to a full political identity. The debate about women's mental life signalled, as I have suggested, a more general anxiety about non-rational, unsocial behaviour. Female subjectivity, or its synecdotal reference, female sexuality, became the displaced and condensed site for the general anxiety about individual behaviour which republican and liberal political philosophy stirred up. It is not too surprising that the morality of the class as a whole was better represented by those who exercised the least political power within it, or that the punishment for female sexual transgression was fictionally represented as the *immediate* loss of social status.

The ways in which class is lived by men and women, like the ways in which sexual difference is lived, are only partly open to voluntary, self-conscious political negotiation. The unconscious processes that construct subjective identity are also the structures through which class is lived and understood, through which political subjection and rebellion are organized. Arguing for the usefulness of psychoanalysis in historical analysis, Sally Alexander emphasizes that its theories do not imply a universal human nature. Rather,

> Subjectivity in this account is neither universal nor ahistorical. First structured through relations of absence and loss, pleasure and unpleasure, difference and division, these are simultaneous with the social naming and placing among kin, community, school, class which are always historically specific. (Alexander 1984, p. 134)

Literary texts give these simultaneous inscriptions narrative form, pointing towards and opening up the fragmentary nature of social and psychic identity, drawing out the ways in which social meaning is psychically represented. It is this symbolic shaping of class that we should examine in fiction. Literary texts tell us more about the intersection of class and gender than we can learn from duly noting the material circumstances and social constraints of characters and authors.

However mimetic or realistic the aspirations of fictions, it always tells us less about the purely social rituals of a class society organized around the sexual division of labour than about the powerful symbolic force of class and gender in ordering our social and political imagination. The doubled inscription of sexual and social difference is the most common, characteristic trope of nineteenth-century fictions. In these texts, the difference between women is at least as important an element as the difference between the sexes, as a way of representing both class and gender. This salient fact often goes unnoticed in the emphasis of bourgeois criticism on male/female division and opposition. In turn, this emphasis on heterosexual antagonisms and resolutions effaces the punitive construction of alternative femininities in women's writing. If texts by women reveal a 'hidden' sympathy between women, as radical feminist critics often assert, they equally express positive femininity through hostile and denigrating representations of women. Imperilled bourgeois femininity takes meaning in relation to other female identities, and to the feminized identities of other social groups which the novel constructs and dialogizes. The unfavourable symbiosis of reason and passion ascribed to women is also used to characterize both men and women in the labouring classes and in other races and cultures. The line between the primitive and the degraded feminine is a thin one, habitually elided in dominant discourse and practically used to limit the civil and political rights of all three subordinated categories: blacks, women and the working class.

Through that chain of colonial associations, whole cultures became 'feminized', 'blackened' and 'impoverished' – each denigrating construction implying and invoking the others. 'True womanhood' had to be protected from this threatened linguistic contamination, not only from the debased subjectivity and dangerous sexuality of the lower-class prostitute, but from all other similarly inscribed subordinate subjectivities. The difference between men and women in the ruling class had to be written so that a slippage into categories reserved for lesser humanities could be averted.

These fragmented definitions of female subjectivity were not only a mode through which the moral virtue of the ruling class was represented in the sexual character of its women; they also shaped, and were shaped by, the ways in which women of the middle and upper classes understood and represented their own being. It led them towards projecting and displacing on to women of lower social standing and women of colour, as well as on to the 'traditionally' corrupt aristocracy, all that was deemed vicious and regressive in women as a sex.

It is deeply troubling to find these projected and displaced representations in the writing of sexual and social radicals, and in the work of feminists from Wollstonecraft to Woolf, as well as in conservative sexual and social discourses. They are especially marked in those texts and writers who accept in whole or in part the description of mental life and libidinal economy of the Enlightenment and the moral value attached to it. In *A Vindication,* working-class women are quite unselfconsciously constructed as prostitutes and dirty-minded servants corrupting bourgeois innocence. Turn the page over and you will also find them positioned in a more radical sense as the most brutalized victims of aristocratic and patriarchal despotism. Note the bestial descriptions of the female poor in Elizabeth Barrett Browning's *Aurora Leigh.* Remember the unhappy, ambivalent and contradictory relationship to black subjectivity, male and female, of many mid-nineteenth-century American feminists and abolitionists. Most distressing of all, because nearer to us in time, think about the contrast between Woolf's public polemical support of working-class women and the contempt with which the feelings and interests of her female servants are treated in her diaries, where they exist as lesser beings. These representations are neither natural nor inevitable. They are the historic effects of determinate social divisions and ideologies worked through psychic structures, worked into sexual and social identity. If they are understood they can be changed.

In Ann Radcliffe's *Mysteries of Udolpho,* one of the most popular of theEnlightenment gothic novels of the 1790s, the heroine, Emily, flees from the sinister importunities of her titled foreign host. The scene is rural Italy, as far away as possible from genteel British society. Emily's flight from the castle is precipitous, and in her terror and haste she forgets her hat. Within the world of the text, Emily's bare head threatens her identity as pure woman, as surely as do the violent, lascivious attentions of her pursuer. Both the narrative and her flight are interrupted while Emily restores her identity by purchasing 'a little straw hat' from a peasant girl. A woman without a hat was, in specular terms, a whore; the contemporary readership understood the necessary pause in the story. They understood too that the hat, passed from peasant to lady, securing the class and sexual status of the latter, was not only a fragment of domestic realism set against gothic fantasy. Hat and flight are part of a perfectly coherent psychic narrative in which aristocratic seducer, innocent bourgeois victim, peasant girl and straw hat play out the linked meanings of class and sexuality.

Stories of seduction and betrayal, of orphaned, impoverished heroines of uncertain class origin, provided a narrative structure through which the instabilities of class and gender categories were both stabilized and undermined. Across the body and mind of 'woman' as sign, through her multiple representations bourgeois anxiety about identity is traced and retraced. A favourite plot, of which *Jane Eyre* is now the best-known example, sets the genteel heroine at sexual risk as semi-servant in a grand patriarchal household. This narrative theme allowed the crisis of middle-class femininity to be mapped on to the structural sexual vulnerability of all working-class servants in bourgeois employment. Such dramas were full of condensed meanings in excess of the representation of sexuality and sexual difference. A doubled scenario, in which the ideological and material difference between working-class and bourgeois women is blurred through condensation, it was popular as a plot for melodrama with both 'genteel' and 'vulgar' audiences.

We do not know very much so far about how that fictional narrative of threatened femininity was understood by working-class women, although it appeared in the cheap fiction written for servant girls as well as in popular theatre. Nineteenth-century bourgeois novels like *Jane Eyre* tell us almost nothing about the self-defined subjectivity of the poor, male or female. For, although they are both rich sources for the construction of dominant definitions *of* the inner lives of the working classes, they cannot tell us anything about how even these ideological inscriptions were lived *by* them. For an analysis of the subjectivity of working-class women we need to turn to non-literary sources, to the discourses in which they themselves spoke. That analysis lies outside the project of this paper but is, of course, related to it.

I want to end this chapter with an example of the kind of interpretative integration that I have been demanding of feminist critics. No text has proved more productive of meaning from the critic's point of view than Charlotte Brontë's *Jane Eyre*. I have referred to the condensation of class meanings through the characterization and narrative of its heroine, but now I want to turn to that disturbing didactic moment in volume I, chapter 12, which immediately precedes the entry of Rochester into the text. It is a passage marked out by Virginia Woolf in *A Room of One's Own,* where it is used to illustrate the negative effect of anger and inequality on the female literary imagination. Prefaced defensively – 'Anybody may blame me who likes' – it is a passage about need, demand and desire that exceed social possibility and challenge social prejudice. In Jane's soliloquy, inspired by a view reached through raising the 'trap-door of the attic', the Romantic aesthetic is reasserted for women, together with a passionate refusal of the terms of feminine difference. Moved by a 'restlessness' in her 'nature' that 'agitated me to pain sometimes', Jane paces the top floor of Thornfield and allows her 'mind's eye to dwell on whatever bright visions rose before it':

> to let my heart be heaved by the exultant movement which, while it swelled it in trouble, expanded it with life; and, best of all, to open my inward ear to a tale that was never ended – a tale my imagination created, and narrated continuously; quickened with all of incident, life, fire, feeling, that I desired and had not in my actual existence (Brontë 1976, p. 110)

This reverie is only partly quoted by Woolf, who omits the 'visionary' section, moving straight from 'pain...' to the paragraph most familiar to us through her citation of it:

> It is in vain to say that human beings ought to be satisfied with tranquillity; they must have action; and they will make it if they cannot find it. Millions are condemned to a stiller doom than mine, and millions are in silent revolt against their lot. Nobody knows how many rebellions besides political rebellions ferment in the masses of life which people earth. Women are supposed to be very calm generally: but women feel just as men feel; they need exercise for their faculties, and a field for their efforts as much as their brothers do; they suffer from too rigid a restraint, too absolute a stagnation, precisely as men would suffer; and it is narrow-minded in their more privileged fellow-creatures to say that they ought to confine themselves to making puddings and knitting stockings, to playing on the piano and embroidering bags. It is thoughtless to condemn them, or laugh at them, if they seek to do more or learn more than custom has pronounced necessary for their sex.
>
> When thus alone I not unfrequently heard Grace Poole's laugh...

This shift from feminist polemic to the laugh of Grace Poole is the 'jerk', the 'awkward break' of 'continuity' that Woolf criticizes. The writer of such a flawed passage

> will never get her genius expressed whole and entire. Her books will be deformed and twisted. She will write in a rage where she should write calmly. She will write foolishly where she should write wisely. She will write of herself when she should write of her characters. She is at war with her lot. How could she help but die young, cramped and thwarted? (Woolf 1973. p. 70)

It is a devastating, controlled, yet somehow uncontrolled indictment. What elements in this digression, hardly a formal innovation in nineteenth-century fiction, can have prompted Woolf to such excess? Elaine Showalter analyses this passage and others as part of Woolf's 'flight into androgyny', that aesthetic chamber where masculine and feminine minds meet and marry. Showalter's analysis focuses on Woolf's aesthetic as an effect of her inability to come to terms with her sexuality, with sexual difference itself. Showalter's analysis is persuasive in individual terms, but it does not deal with all of the questions thrown up by Brontë's challenge and Woolf's violent response to it. In the sentences that Woolf omits in her own citation, Brontë insists that even the confined and restless state could produce 'many and glowing' visions. Art, the passage maintains, can be produced through the endless narration of the self, through the mixed incoherence of subjectivity spoken from subordinate and rebellious positions within culture. It was this aesthetic that Woolf as critic explicitly rejected.

However, the passage deals with more than sexual difference. In the references to 'human beings' and to unspecified 'millions', Brontë deliberately and defiantly associates political and sexual rebellion even as she distinguishes between them. In the passage the generic status of 'men' is made truly trans-class and transcultural when linked to 'masses', 'millions' and 'human beings', those larger inclusive terms. In 1847, on the eve of the second great wave of modern revolution, it was a dangerous rhetoric to use.

Its meaningful associations were quickly recognized by contemporary reviewers, who deplored the contiguous relationship between revolution and feminism. Lady Eastlake's comments in the *Quarterly Review* of 1849 are those most often quoted:

> We do not hesitate to say, that the tone of mind and thought which has overthrown authority and violated every code human and divine abroad, and fostered chartism and rebellion at home is the same which has also written *Jane Eyre.*

Yet Charlotte Brontë was no political radical. She is pulled towards the positive linking of class rebellion and women's revolt in this passage through her anger at the misrepresentation and suppression of women's identity, not via an already held sympathy with the other masses and millions. It is a tentative, partial movement in spite of its defiant rhetoric, and it is checked in a moment by the mad, mocking female laughter, and turned from its course a few pages later by the introduction of Rochester into the narrative. For Woolf, Jane's soliloquy spoils the continuity of the narrative with its 'anger and rebellion'. Woolf turns away, refuses to comprehend the logical sequence of the narration at the symbolic level of the novel.

Jane's revolutionary manifesto of the subject, which has its own slightly manic register, invokes that sliding negative signification of women that we have described. At this point in the story the 'low, slow ha'ha!' and the 'eccentric murmurs' which 'thrilled' Jane are ascribed to Grace Poole, the hard-featured servant. But Grace is only the laugh's minder, and the laugh later becomes 'correctly' ascribed to Rochester's insane wife, Bertha Mason. The uncertain source of the laughter, the narrator's inability to predict its recurrence – 'There were days when she was quite silent; but there were others when I could not account for the sounds she made – both mark out the 'sounds' as the dark side of Romantic female subjectivity

Retroactively, in the narratives the laughter becomes a threat to all that Jane had desired and demanded in her roof-top reverie. Mad servant, mad mistress, foreigner, nymphomaniac, syphilitic, half-breed, aristocrat, Bertha turns violently on keeper, brother, husband and, finally, rival. She and her noises become the condensed and displaced site of unreason and anarchy as it is metonymically figured through dangerous femininity in all its class, race and cultural projections. Bertha must be killed off, narratively speaking, so that a moral, Protestant femininity, licensed sexuality and a qualified, socialized feminism may survive. Yet the text cannot close off or recuperate that moment of radical association between political rebellion and gender rebellion, cannot shut down the possibility of a positive alliance between reason, passion and feminism. Nor can it disperse the terror that speaking those connections immediately stirs up – for Woolf in any case.

Woolf was at her most vehement and most contradictory about these issues, which brought together for her, as for many other feminists before and after, a number of deeply connected anxieties about subjectivity, class, sexuality and culture. Over and over again in her critical writing, Woolf tries to find ways of placing the questions inside an aesthetic that disallows anger, unreason and passion as productive emotions. Like Wollstonecraft before her, she cannot quite shake off the moral and libidinal economies of the Enlightenment. In 'Women and Fiction' (1929) she frames the question another way:

> In *Middlemarch* and in *Jane Eyre* we are conscious not merely of the writer's character, as we are conscious of the character of Charles Dickens, but we are conscious of a woman's presence – of someone resenting the treatment of her sex and pleading for its rights. This brings into women's writing an element which is entirely absent from a man's, unless, indeed, he happens to be a working man, a Negro, or one who for some other reason is conscious of disability. It introduces a distortion and is frequently the cause of weakness. The desire to plead some personal cause or to make a character the mouthpiece of personal discontent or grievance always has a distressing effect, as if the spot at which the reader's attention is directed were suddenly two-fold instead of single. (Woolf 1979, p. 47)

Note how the plea for a sex, a class, a race becomes reduced to individual, personal grievance, how subordinate position in a group becomes immediately pathologized as private disability, weakness. Note too how 'man' in this passage loses its universal connotation, so that it only refers normatively to men of the ruling class. In this passage, as in *Jane Eyre,* the metonymic evocation of degraded subjectivities is expressed as an effect of subordination, not its rationale nor its cause. But the result is still a negative one. For the power to resist through fictional language, the language of sociality and self; the power to move and enlighten, rather than blur and distress through the double focus, is denied. Instead, Woolf announces the death of the feminist text, by proclaiming, somewhat prematurely, the triumph of feminism.

> The woman writer is no longer bitter. She is no longer angry. She is no longer pleading and protesting as she writes. . . . She will be able to concentrate upon her vision without distraction from outside. (Woolf 1979, p. 48)

This too is a cry from the roof-tops of a desire still unmet by social and psychic experience.

Although the meanings attached to race, class and sexuality have undergone fundamental shifts from Wollstonecrafts's (and Woolf's) time to our own, we do not live in a post-class society any more than a post-feminist one. Our identities are still constructed through social hierarchy and cultural differentiation, as well as through those processes of division and fragmentation described in psychoanalytic theory. The identities arrived at through these structures will always be precarious and unstable, though *how* they will be so in the future we do not know. For the moment, women still have a problematic place in both social and psychic representation. The problem for women of woman-as-sign has made the self-definition of women a resonant issue within feminism. It has also determined the restless inability of feminism to settle for humanist definitions of the subject, or for materialism's relegation of the problem to determinations of class only. I have emphasized in this chapter some of the more negative ways in which the Enlightenment and Romantic paradigms of subjectivity gave hostage to the making of subordinate identities, of which femininity is the structuring instance. Although psychoanalytic theories of the construction of gendered subjectivity stress difficulty, antagonism and contradiction as necessary parts of the production of identity, the concept of the unconscious and the psychoanalytic view of sexuality dissolve in great part the binary divide between reason and passion that dominates earlier concepts of subjectivity. They break down as well the moralism attached to those libidinal and psychic economies. Seen from this perspective, 'individualism' has a different and more contentious history within feminism than it does in androcentric debates.

It is that history which we must uncover and consider, in both its positive and its negative effects, so that we can argue convincingly for a feminist rehabilitation of the female psyche in non-moralized terms. Perhaps we can come to see it as neither sexual outlaw, social bigot nor dark hiding-place for treasonable regressive femininity waiting to stab progressive feminism in the back. We must redefine the psyche as a structure, not as a content. To do so is not to move away from a feminist politics which takes race and class into account, but to move towards a fuller understanding of how these social divisions and the inscription of gender are mutually secured and given meaning. Through that analysis we can work towards change.

REFERENCES

Alexander, Sally (1984) 'Women, Class and Sexual Difference', *History Workshop*, 17, pp. 125–49.

Bakhtin, M. M. (1981) *The Dialogic Imagination: Four Essays*, ed. Michael Holquist, Austin, Texas: University of Texas Press.

Brontë, Charlotte (1976) *Jane Eyre* (1847) ed. Margaret Smith. London: Oxford University Press.

Cott, Nancy F. (1978) 'Passionlessness: An Interpretation of Victorian Sexual Ideology, 1790–1850', *Signs*, 2, 2, pp. 219–33.

Hartmann, Heidi (1981) 'The Unhappy Marriage of Marxism and Feminism: Towards a More Progressive Union'. In Lydia Sargent ed., *The Unhappy Marriage of Marxism and Feminism: A Debate on Class and Patriarchy*, pp. 1–42 London: Pluto Press.

Jacobus, Mary (1979) 'The Buried Letter: Feminism and Romanticism in *Villette*'. In Mary Jacobus ed., *Woman Writing and Writing about Women*, pp. 42–60. London: Croom Helm.

Marxist-Feminist Literature Collective (1978) 'Women's Writing: *Jane Eyre, Shirley, Villette, Aurora Leigh*'. In 1848: *The Sociology of Literature*, proceedings of the Essex conference on the Sociology of Literature (July 1977), pp. 185–206.

Newton, Judith Lowder (1981) *Women, Power, and Subversion: Social Strategies in British Fiction 1778–1860*. Athens, Ga.: University of Georgia Press.

Radcliffe, Ann (1966) *The Mysteries of Udolpho* (1794). London: Oxford University Press.

Robinson, Lillian S. (1978) 'Dwelling in Decencies: Radical Criticism and the Feminist Perspective'. In *Sex, Class and Culture*, pp. 3–21. Bloomington Ind.: Indiana University Press.

Rousseau, Jean-Jacques (1974) *Emile* (1762). London: Dent.

Said, Edward W. (1978) *Orientalism.* London: Routledge and Kegan Paul.

Stedman Jones, Gareth (1983) *Languages of Class: Studies in English Working Class History* 1832–1982. Cambridge: Cambridge University Press.

Wollstonecraft, Mary (1975a) *A Vindication of the Rights of Woman* (1972). New York: Norton.

Wollstonecraft, Mary (1975b) *Maria, or The Wrongs of Woman* (1798). New York: Norton.

Woolf, Virginia (1973) *A Room of One's Own* (1929). Harmondsworth: Penguin.

Woolf, Virginia (1979) 'Women and Fiction'. In Michèle Barrett ed., *Women and Writing*, 44–52. London: Women's Press.

Wordsworth, William, and Coleridge, Samuel Taylor (1979) *Lyrical Ballads* (1798, 1800), ed. R.L. Brett and A.R. Jones. London: Methuen.

22

Toril Moi

Feminism and Postmodernism: Recent Feminist Criticism in the United States

In the United States, my book *Sexual/Textual Politics*[1] has been criticized on two major accounts. First, it has been accused of simply identifying with 'French' positions in order to hammer traditional American feminist criticism. In my opinion such criticisms tend to overlook my own materialist feminist position, influenced by the British 'New Left' tradition, which structures my critique of *both* camps. But I have also been taken to task for simply leaving out French-inspired American feminism. Now I can at least make up for this omission by criticizing that too.

More seriously: in this paper I want to discuss some of the problems raised by recent French-inspired American feminist theory and criticism. Given the stringent limitations of space imposed on me, I have chosen to organize my arguments around one single pioneering text which explores the uneasy relationship between postmodernism and feminism, Alice Jardine's *Gynesis: Configurations of Woman and Modernity.*[2]

Before turning to this text, however, I would like to make the position from which I speak somewhat more explicit. I do not simply speak from a 'European' or 'British,' as opposed to an 'American', position; I also speak out of a current of socialist feminism which in Europe, or at least in Britain and Scandinavia where I live and work, is much *more* mainstream than in the USA. I think it is correct to say that since the 1960s, socialist feminism in its various forms has been the *dominant* trend in British and Scandinavian feminism, both inside and outside academic institutions. When addressing a US audience, then, I see my attempt to assess recent trends in US feminist theory as the most valuable contribution I can make towards the development of a feminist dialogue across narrow national preoccupations. Drawing on recognizably 'British' readings of recent French theories in order to question current 'American' readings of the very same material will further help to illuminate and enact the differences between us.[3] This is not, of course, to advocate some kind of comfortable cultural relativism or to reduce my own views to an unsurprising reflection of my own cultural background: I firmly believe that some positions are not only preferable but simply more rational than others. In general, I would characterize my project, both here and in *Sexual/Textual Politics,* as an effort to argue for a *politicized* understanding of feminism, as opposed to a *depoliticized* one. My aim then, is not first and foremost to demonstrate my difference, but to convince.

At first glance, feminism and postmodernism would seem to be strange bedfellows indeed. If postmodernism, at least in Lyotard's sense of the term,[4] sees all metanarratives, including feminism, as repressive enactments of metaphysical authority, what then can it mean to declare oneself a feminist postmodernist or, perhaps more accurately, a postmodern feminist? Does it mean anything at all? I once saw a large piece of graffiti in the ladies' room in my Oxford library. It simply read, 'Catholic feminists.' A few days later a different hand had added, 'sure have problems.' Is 'postmodern feminism' simply another oxymoron a new quagmire of contradictions for feminists to sink in? Or is it a uniquely enabling theoretical development which will permit us finally to escape the patriarchal paradigms of Western thought? Or do we – in an ironically liberal gesture – have to declare that the truth probably lies somewhere in between? In this paper I will use the term 'postfeminism' to cover the different configurations of feminism and postmodernism around today.

THE IMPOSSIBILITY OF FEMINISM

Before I turn to the problems of postfeminism, I want briefly to outline my own position on feminism. I now hold that feminism is strictly speaking an impossible position. I'll expand on this point. Like Alison Jaggar in her excellent book *Feminist Politics and Human Nature,*[5] I start from an agonistic definition of feminism, which I see as the struggle against all forms of patriarchal and sexist oppression. Such an oppositional definition posits feminism as the necessary *resistance* to patriarchal power. Logically, then, the aim of feminism, like that of any emancipatory theory, is to abolish itself along with its opponent. In a non-sexist, non-patriarchal society, feminism will no longer exist.

I would now like to argue that feminism as defined above is an impossible undertaking. First, feminism is committed to the struggle for equality for women, a struggle which has often been seen simply as the effort to make women become *like* men. But the struggle for equal rights historically and politically commits feminists to emphasize the *value* of women *as they are* (i.e, *before* equal rights have been won). For the very case for equal rights rests precisely on the argument that women are *already* as valuable as men. But given women's *lack* of equal rights, this value must be located as *difference*, not as equality: women are of equal human value *in their own way*. This logic, which avoids taking the male as the norm, has been evident in Western Feminism since its inception. My point is that under patriarchy even equal rights feminism *has* to assert the value of women *as* women, since it is the only way efficiently to *counter* the systematic devaluation of women and women's work under patriarchy. Equality and difference are not *in this sense* antitheses. But a discourse of female difference, even so, is not readily compatible with one of female equality. Articulated in isolation, the emphasis on female difference comes disturbingly to echo the very patriarchal prejudices against which the champions of women's equality are struggling. And in fact, when it comes to taking sides in specific political struggles, these two feminisms often seem to be poles apart. This is indeed how Julia Kristeva describes them in 'Women's Time'[6] – as two different and opposing stages of the feminist movement. But such a straightforward *division* of these two feminisms will not do, since the one (that of difference) is a necessary effect of the discourse of the other. There is crucially both a potential contradiction and a productive dialetical tension between them.

Given this logic, a feminist cannot settle for either equality or difference. Both struggles must be *aporetically* fought out. but we also know that both approaches are caught in the end in a constraining logic of *sameness* and *difference.* Julia Kristeva therefore suggests that feminism from now on must operate in a third space: that which deconstructs all identity, all binary oppositions, all phallogocentric logic. I agree that it is urgently necessary for feminists to deconstruct sexualized binary thought. But in deconstructing patriarchal metaphysics, we also risk deconstructing the very logic that sustains the two forms of feminism outlined above. These three 'spaces' of feminism, in other words, are logically and often strategically incompatible.

Unlike Kristeva, however, I believe that feminists today have to hold all three positions simultaneously. Simply to take up Kristeva's 'third position' of deconstructed identities, as she herself advocates, is clearly impossible. For, if we still live in metaphysical space, our necessary utopian wish to deconstruct sexual identities always runs up against the fact that patriarchy itself persists in oppressing women *as women.* We must, then, at once live out the contradictions of all three feminisms *and* agonistically take sides: simply sitting on the fence will never demolish patriarchy. As feminists we will have to make hard and often unpalatable political choices in the full knowledge of what we are giving up. Since every choice is an act of exclusion, to take up a political position means accepting the pain of loss, sacrifice, and closure, *even* if our choice entails following the free-wheeling paths of Derridean deconstruction.

A final point: I am not, of course suggesting that we are entirely free to choose our own political positions – or our own style. With Freud and Lacan I believe that what we say is never quite what we think we say. Drawing on the same logic, Derrida has shown that every discourse engenders its own blind spots and contradictions. And, like Marx, I believe that our specific material position in society and history crucially limits the range of ideological and political options available to us. This is, nevertheless, not to say that we have no choice at all: my discourse of political strategies and choice places itself *within* the constraints outlined by these sobering reminders of the limits of analytical self-reflection.

ATLANTIC POSTFEMINISM

So far, postfeminism remains a relatively parochial concern, the offspring of a purely Franco-American affair. Alice Jardine's *Gynesis,* for instance, makes much play of its own transatlantic position, deliberately hovering between Paris and New York, only truly at home in a space Jardine discreetly alludes to as 'that in-between state' (13). But there is, perhaps, in her text also a feeling of unease about this lofty location – for is she not in danger of drowning in the Atlantic? This at least is how I read her sudden need to affirm that she is 'neither "above it all" nor somewhere in the middle of the Atlantic' (18). Literal-minded readers will conclude that she must be in Iceland. For, in spite of the odd reference to 'Anglo-American' feminism, Britain remains firmly excluded from her discourse: there is, unfortunately, no trace at all in *Gynesis* of the rich and varied socialist-feminist work carried out by British women over the past two decades.

'England' does make a few puzzling appearances in Jardine's text, as for instance, towards the end of her introduction, where she emphasizes the need for 'feminist theoreticians in France, England, the United States, and (especially) elsewhere' (26) to rethink feminism in the light of postmodernism. 'England' is listed here on a par with France and the Unitd States. But this is not to say that there is an equal exchange of ideas in this triangle: Jardine's impressive bibliography lists only one item of contemporary British theory and that is Stephen Heath's famous 1977 essay on difference according to the French.[7] *Gynesis* is the staging of an intimate Franco-American *pas-de-deux,* not a rehearsal of the narrative plots of triangulated desire. Occupying centre-stage, this couple neatly block out British materialist feminism. And what are we to make of the half-repressed, parenthetical '(especially) elsewhere'? Are Scandinavian, German, or Welsh feminists in particularly dire straits at the moment? Or is the uneasy parenthetical reference aimed at Third World women? Perhaps this passage is simply another attempt to claim global relevance for postmodern strategies? However that may be, it is the repression of the British and not of the Third World which returns to disrupt and unsettle Jardine's text. For how else am I to read her reference to that famous *English* modernist, James Joyce? (91).

POSTFEMINIST FEMINISM

As might be expected, postmodern feminists are reluctant to espouse labels or definitions of any kind. Alice Jardine, for one, rejects them out of hand. The word 'feminism' is particularly troublesome to her:

> Who and what, then do we mean by 'feminist'? That word. . .poses some serious problems. Not that we would want to end up by demanding a definition of what feminism is, and therefore, of what one must do, say, and be, if one is to acquire that epithet; dictionary meanings are suffocating, to say the least. (20)

I take this to be a defeatist position for feminists. Definitions may well be constraining: they are also enabling. Why else would women struggle for so long for their right to name the world? To name is to exercise power. The notion that closure, or conceptually rigorous definitions, is *merely* constraining is a fashionable dogma of poststructuralism: such a simplistic view is not only utterly undialectical, but also a travesty of the thought of Jacques Derrida himself.

In the end Jardine nevertheless ventures a definition of feminism. '"Feminism,"' she writes, 'is generally understood as a "movement from the point of view of, by, and for women"' (15). Her copious use of quotes makes it exceptionally difficult to tell whether she actually *agrees* with this 'general understanding'. Jardine may not be saying this, but neither, apparently, is anybody else. I will, nevertheless, take the risk of attributing this reluctant definition to Jardine herself. Stressing as she does the necessity of locating feminist *criticism* within 'very precise political struggles and practices' (15), Jardine does try to provide some specificity to this general position. But given the absence of any effort to outline a specific political or social context for these 'precise struggles', they remain paradoxically abstract and *general,* an observation which also holds true for *Gynesis* as a whole. On the whole, though, feminism is presented as a movement by women which takes on very different and very specific forms in different contexts. To my mind this understanding of feminism smacks of the French 'Psych et Po' group's emphasis on 'moving women' (*des femmes en mouvements*), characteristic of much Parisian feminism in the 1970s.

But this is surely not a sufficient understanding of feminism. Is any political struggle involving a movement of women working for their own good automatically feminist? The British Tory Women's Conference, for example? Jardine's definition empties feminism of any agonistic content, suppressing its resistance to patriarchal power. My general agonistic definition won't, of course, allow us to *prescribe* a universally correct feminist practice, but it has the merit of implying that feminists have to take sides. Sometimes, of course, we will be *wrong* in our political decisions: some postfeminism seems to me not even specific enough to be that, and consequently, in its endless self-qualifying openness, it comes to display its own kind of closure.

Traditionally, the deconstruction of theory has always been the practice which it generates. But there is a sense in which Jardine's postmodernism pushes her into a kind of theoreticism: no specific practice is ever allowed to deconstruct her theory. In fact, it would be inaccurate even to claim that she *has* a theory. Instead, she tries to deconstruct theory from the *other,* postmodernist side, as it were, denouncing it as yet another reactionary Enlightenment narrative. The effect of these discursive moves is to leave her in a kind of untheorizable theoreticism prone precisely to the idealist abstraction and generalization she is eager to avoid.

Lacking any conflictive element, Jardine's infinitely flexible concept of feminism as a ceaselessly gyrating movement of women makes her reluctant to criticize even plainly anti-feminist theory formations. On the one hand, she argues, the French theories with which she is concerned have 'posited themselves as profoundly, that is to say conceptually and in *praxis*, anti- and/or post-feminist' (20). But she is not about to take issue with this alarming trend: 'In this study', she continues, 'one of the things I have tried to accomplish is to clarify the "anti- and/or post-feminism" of contemporary French thinking as exemplary of modernity, without getting overly caught up in explicit value judgements or polemics' (21).

But can feminist intellectuals in fact avoid polemics and value judgments without ending up, more or less unwittingly, on the wrong side? And if Jardine is simply saying that she wants to give a 'scholarly' and 'objective' account of the 'anti- and/or post-feminism' of recent French theory, the implication is that objective research somehow precludes political commitment.

To me, Jardine's steadfast refusal of what Elaine Showalter has called 'feminist critique'[8] represents a symbolic rejection of what I take to be a recognisably *French* caricature of American feminism, perceived as strident, loud, unsubtle, and unsophisticated. Instead, Jardine prefers the suave choreography of her transatlantic *pas-de-duex* with French theory. But to me, as to a whole tradition of American feminism, a feminist intellectual is one who seeks to stress her own politics, not one who seeks to replace it with geography.

POSTFEMINIST GYNESIS

I want now to turn to Jardine's central neologism: *gynesis*. There is, incidentally, an interesting contradiction between Jardine's rejection of labels and definitions and her obvious – and understandable – pleasure in being able to *name* her own textual discovery. *Gynesis,* then, is the name for a *textual process,* which she describes as follows:

> the putting into discourse of 'woman' as that *process* diagnosed in France as intrinsic to the condition of modernity; indeed, the valorization of the feminine, woman, and her obligatory, that is historical connotations, as somehow intrinsic to new and necessary modes of thinking, writing, speaking. (25)

Focusing on the necessary blind spot, the repressed contradictions and paradoxical self-deconstruction of every discourse, Jardine labels this the 'master-narratives' own "nonknowledge"' (25). 'This other-than-themselves', she continues, 'is almost always a "space" of some kind (over which the narrative has lost control), and this space has been coded as *feminine*, as *woman*' (25). *Gynesis,* then, is the process of putting woman or the feminine into discourse as the unknown other of every text. This has traditionally been represented as a *negative* process, a process of patriarchal repression of the feminine. But Jardine is not offering us simply another version of Irigaray's *Speculum.*[9] Instead, in a brave and original move, she focuses on what one might call *positive gynesis,* the deliberate *valorization* of repressed femininity. This, she argues, can be found first and foremost in French postmodernist theory produced by men, and this is why she chooses to focus on the process whereby theorists such as Lacan ('la femme'), Derrida ('double chiasmic invagination', 'hymen', etc.), and Deleuze ('becoming woman') become 'participants in the process of gynesis in France' (27).

The process of *gynesis* as theorized by Jardine gives rise to a series of questions. Is *gynesis* possible within an explicitly *feminist* discourse? Or should we rather look for the silent exclusion or explicit circulation of the masculine in such texts? and is there not a danger that the process of gynesis, however positively valorized, might simply repeat the patriarchal exclusion of woman?

Here I want particularly to focus on the crucial point about *gynesis* – and, *par extension* – of postmodern feminism: the easy move in which the 'Other' and its fashionable quasi-synonyms (unreadability, undecidability, the semiotic processes, the unconscious, and so on) is simply *equated* with 'woman', 'women' or, even more frequently, 'the feminine'. The next, equally unargued move is to assume that any discourse which speaks of this 'femininity' is a *feminist* discourse. But just as any 'Other' is not a woman, simply to speak of femininity has never been sufficient to turn patriarchal ideology into feminism. The naming of woman, or the textualization of femininity, can only produce emancipatory effects if they are placed in an anti-patriarchal context. If they are not, they will simply coincide with traditional sexism. Since Jardine chooses not to discuss the political and theoretical *limits* and *limitations* of her own neologism, it remains a disappointingly nebulous, abstract concept, apparently striving for global validity.

But simply to equate woman with otherness deprives the feminist struggle of any kind of specificity. What is repressed is not *otherness,* but specific, historically constructed agents. Women under patriarchy are oppressed because they are *women,* not because they are irredeemable Other. Anti-semitism is directed against Jews, and South-African racism against blacks, not simply against abstract Otherness. The promotion and valorization of Otherness will never liberate the oppressed. It is, of course, hopelessly idealist to assume that Otherness somehow *causes* oppression. The fact that the oppressors tend to equate the oppressed group with ontological Otherness, perceived as a threatening, disruptive, alien force, is precisely an ideological manoeuvre designed to mask the concrete material grounds for oppression and exploitation. Only a materialist analysis can provide a credible explanation of *why* the burden of Otherness has been placed on this or that particular group in a given society at a given time.

This tendency always and everywhere to 'put into discourse' general Otherness reveals the profoundly abstract and universalizing effects of postfeminist discourse. But if postfeminism sees feminism as an endless choreography of women, or rather, of ontological Otherness, such feminism firmly places itself *outside time.* In this sense, post-feminism can never *be* postfeminist. Feminism defined as an agonistic struggle, on the other hand sees postfeminism as the meaningful *end* of its efforts: if true postfeminism presupposes postpatriarchy, only a feminist can be a postfeminist.

. . .

POSTFEMINISM AND ENLIGHTENMENT THOUGHT

Present-day feminism is a historically specific movement, rooted in French Enlightenment thought (Mary Wollstonecraft) and in British liberalism (John Stuart Mill), and consequently wedded, in deeply critical style, to notions of truth, justice, freedom, and equality. The Enlightenment we seek to dismantle in the name of our political values is precisely a major source of such values. On this point, at least, I am happy to register the support of that staunch defender of Enlightenment thought, Jacques Derrida. Speaking at the ICA in London in May 1985, he summarizes his own position as follows:

> We. . .have to deconstruct, to take the time to deconstruct Enlightenment. But when I say we have to deconstruct a thing, I do not say we are *against* it, or that in any situation I will fight it, be on the other side. I think we should be on the side of Enlightenment without being too naive, and on some occasions be able to question its philosophy.[10]

But if Derrida is prepared to declare himself 'on the side of Enlightenment', he will not do as much for feminism. In the same interview he dclares: 'I am not against feminism, but I am not simply for feminism.'[11] But who says that it is a matter of being 'simply for feminism'? What I am objecting to here is the easy reduction of feminism to simplistic dogmatism: I don't know of a single feminist who, in a touching display of blind faith, is content with being 'simply for feminism'. This is neither deconstruction, nor postmodernism, but simply an enactment of traditional liberalism which unfailingly presents recognizable political positions as simplistic ideological dogmatisms, quite unable to face the complexities of the real, empirical world. Unlike Derrida here, as feminists we need to *situate* our deconstructive gestures in specific political contexts. And this means deliberately imposing certain kinds of closure on our own texts. After Derrida we know that no text is without some form of closure. Our texts will not therefore be *more* metaphysical than others. On the contrary, the need to *work through* our material in order to increase our awareness of our own limitations and the necessity of defining certain limits for our discourse recalls a properly *analytical* (as in psychoanalytical) stance, not simply a reenactment of metaphysical authoriy. If I am here alluding to a certain reading of Freudian psychoanalysis, it is precisely because such psychoanalysis to me represents an attempt at producing an emancipatory discourse which at once enacts and disrupts the conventional rules of Enlightenment rationality.

Alice Jardine's radical rejection of Enlightenment thought makes her look for a feminism which will allow us to 'give up the quest for truth' (63). For the truth that women are oppressed? Or is truth here merely the old metaphysical bugbear, which all of us now, happily, agree to disclaim? And if this is so, what exactly does such a position achieve? as I have argued above, to take up a position – to claim the truth of one's own analysis – means deliberately running the risk of being *wrong:* that is to say, we make ourselves *more* – not *less* – vulnerable by revealing our own hand in this way. The choice here is not primarily between open-ended deconstructive or Lacanian discourses presenting themselves as feminine, unaggressive, and non-authoritative, on the one hand, and arrogant metaphysical truth enacting masculinist assumptions of power and submission, on the other, but rather between a sophisticated, but self-protective narcissism, on the one hand, and a some times blunt, but also more exposed and vulnerable discourse, on the other.

My critique of postfeminism, then, is primarily that it avoids taking sides, and moreover, that given its abstract, ontological feminization or Otherness, it cannot do otherwise. In this way, postfeminism represents a particular development of *one* of the three conflicting discourses of feminism. In its eagerness to please the high priests of poststructuralism and postmodernism, postfeminism takes little or no account of other forms of feminism, and thus unwittingly enacts as scenario of exclusion and delimitation as rigorous as any Enlightenment taxonomy. My own view is that it is only by attempting the impossible wager of constructing a materialist feminist theory that *includes* the three feminisms outlined in this paper that we will manage to push feminist criticism and theory past the political *impasse* of postfeminism. It sould be obvious by now that such a project cannot succeed if it simply rejects postfeminism altogether.

NOTES

1 Toril Moi, *Sexual/Textual Politics: Feminist Literary Theory* (London: Methuen, 1985).

2 Alice Jardine, *Gynesis: Configurations of Women and Modernity* (Ithaca: Cornell University Press, 1985). Subsequent references will appear in the text.

3 Some of my main sources of inspiration are, for example, Michèle Barrett, ed. *Virginia Woolf: Women and Writing* (London: The Women's Press, 1979); Catherine Belsey, *Critical Practice* (London: Methuen, 1980); Rosalind Coward, *Patriarchal Precedents: Sexuality and Social Relations* (London: Routledge, 1983), *Female Desire: Women's Sexuality Today* (London: Paladin, 1984), and with John Ellis, *Language and Materialism* (London: Routledge, 1977); Cora Kaplan, *Sea Changes: Culture and Feminism* (London: Verso, 1986; Terry Lovell, *Consuming Fiction* (London: Verso, 1987); Juliet Mitchell, *Psychoanalysis and Feminism* (London: Allen Lane, 1974); and Jacqueline Rose,

Sexuality in the Field of Vision (London; Verso, 1986), and edited with Juliet Mitchell, *Feminine Sexuality: Jacques Lacan and the Ecole Freudienne* (London: Macmillan, 1982).

4 Jean-François Lyotard, *La condition postmoderne* (Paris: Minuit, 1979). Translated by Geoff Bennington and Brian Massumi as *The Postmodern Condition: A Report on Knowledge*, foreword by Fredric Jameson (Manchester: Manchester University Press, 1984).

5 Alison M. Jaggar, *Feminist Politics and Human Nature* (Totowa, NJ: Rowman and Allanheld, 1983).

6 In 'Women's Time' (trans. Alice Jardine and Harry Blake, *The Kristeva* Reader, ed. Toril Moi (Oxford: Blackwell, 1986), 187–213), Kristeva sees the feminism of difference as a simple *reaction* against that of equality. Her third space, essentially deconstructive, however, is one in which the three 'generations' or 'spaces' exist together: Kristeva writes about the '*parallel* existence of all three in the same historical time, or even that they be interwoven one with the other' (209). Although I am obviously deeply indebted to Kristeva's vision of the three 'spaces' or 'generations' of feminism, there are some differences between her positions and mine: I see the feminism of difference as the necessary implication of that equality, not simply as its opposing mirror-image; I see the third space as a painfully *contradictory* yet necessary one, not as one where the three 'generations' unproblematically 'interweave' with each other in what sounds a little like a cosy version of Lacan's imaginary; and finally, I stress the social and material conditions which oblige us always to cut through and open up what I take to be the impossible space of the third generation if we are to take up recognizably political positions (Kristeva does not, presumably, because her essay was written in 1979, at a time when she had long since decided to relinquish her active interest in politics).

7 Stephen Heath, 'Difference', *Screen* 19, no. 3 (Autumn 1978): 51–112.

8 Elaine Showalter, 'Towards a Feminist Politics', *Women Writing and Writing about Women*, ed. Mary Jacobus (London: Croom Helm, 1979), 22–41.

9 Luce Irigaray, *Speculum de l'autre femme* (Paris: Minuit, 1974).

10 Jacques Derrida, in conversation with Geoff Bennington, 'On Colleges and Philosophy', in *ICA Documents* 4 and 5, ed. Lisa Appignanesi (London: ICA, 1985), 69.

11 Ibid., 71.

Notes on the Authors

Parveen Adams is a lecturer in the Department of Human Science at Brunel University. She founded and co-edited the feminist journal *m/f* from 1978 to 1986, and is editor of *Language in Thinking* (1972), and co-editor of an *m/f* reader due for publication in 1990 by MIT.

Sally Alexander lectures in cultural studies at the Polytechnic of East London and has written on feminism and women's work in the nineteenth century. She is at present working on a social history of women in the 1920s and 1930s.

Floya Anthias teaches sociology at Thames Polytechnic, London. She is co-editor of *Women, Nation, State* (with N. Yuval-Davis), and is presently preparing three volumes for publication on racism, ethnicity, class, and the modern state.

Michèle Barrett is the author of *Women's Oppression Today* (1989), and co-author with Mary McIntosh of *The Anti-Social Family* (1982). She is a Professor of Sociology at City University, London.

Johanna Brenner teaches sociology at Portland State University.

Cynthia Cockburn is a researcher based at The City University, London. Her books include *Brothers: Male Dominance and Technological Change* (1983), *Machinery of Dominance: Women, Men and Technological Know-How* (1985) and *Two-Track Training: Sex Inequalities in the Youth Training Scheme* (1987).

Rosalind Coward has written on female sexuality and feminism. Her books include *Patriarchal Precedents* (1983), *Female Desire* (1984) and *The Whole Truth: The Myth of Alternative Health* (1989).

Germaine Greer's books include *The Female Eunuch* (1980), *The Obstacle Race: The Fortunes of Women Painters and their Work* (1979), *Sex and Destiny* (1984) and *Daddy, We Hardly Knew You* (1989).

Catherine Hall is a senior lecturer in cultural studies at The Polytechnic of East London. She is co-author (with Leonore Davidoff) of *Family Fortunes* (1987). She is currently working on gender and ethnicity.

Cora Kaplan lectured in the School of English and American Studies at the University of Sussex from 1969 until 1988. She is now Professor of English at Rutgers University. Her most recent book is *Sea Changes: Culture and Feminism* (1986).

Alison Light lectures in English in the Humanities Department, Brighton Polytechnic. She has written a study, 'British Women's Writings and the Conservative Imagination', in *The Feminine Nation* (Routledge, forthcoming).

Christina Loughran completed her Ph.D. in Sociology on feminism in Northern Ireland in 1987. She teaches history and political studies in a Belfast grammar school.

Mary McIntosh co-authored *The Anti-Social Family* (with Michèle Barrett), (1982). She has written on women and welfare, sexuality and prostitution. She teaches sociology at the University of Essex.

Juliet Mitchell, the author of *Psychoanalysis and Feminism* (1974) and *Women: the Longest Revolution* (1984), is a practising psychoanalyst in London. She writes and lectures on literature, women and psychoanalysis.

Toril Moi is the author of *Sexual/Textual Politics* (1985). She is the editor of *French Feminist Thought* (1987), and *The Kristeva Reader* (1986). She is at present working on a study of Simone de Beauvoir.

Ann Oakley is Deputy Director of the Thomas Coram Research Institute, University of London. Her books include *Housewife* (1974), *The Sociology of Housework* (1974), *From Here to Maternity* (1981), *The Captured Womb* (1984), *Taking it Like a Woman* (1984) and a novel, *The Men's Room.*

Ann Phoenix is a research officer at the Thomas Coram Research Unit, Institute of Education, University of London and has recently finished working on a longitudinal study of 16–19 year old first-time mothers. She is currently working on a study of 'Social Identity in Adolescence'.

Maria Ramas is a graduate student in History at UCLA. She is the author of 'Freud's Dora, Dora's Hysteria' in *Sex and Class in Women's History*, eds, J. Newton, M. Ryan and J. Walkowitz (1983).

Jacqueline Rose is the author of *Sexuality in the Field of Vision* (1986) and *The Case of Peter Pan: The Impossibility of Children's Fiction.* She is co-editor and translator of *Feminine Sexuality: Jacques Lacan and the École Freudienne* (1982). She teaches at the University of Sussex.

Joanna Ryan has worked in the field of psychology and mental health. She has co-authored (with Frank Thomas) *The Politics of Mental Handicap,* (1980) and has edited (with Sue Cartledge) the collection *Sex and Love* (1983).

Felly Nkweto Simmonds is from Zambia, and has worked as a teacher in Zambia, Tanzania, and Sierra Leone, and as a development education worker in Britain.

Carolyn Steedman's books include *The Tidy House* (1984), *Policing the Victorian Community* (1984), *Landscape For a Good Woman* (1986) and *The Radical Soldier's Tale* (1988). She is a senior lecturer in Arts Education at the University of Warwick.

Jenny Bourne Taylor teaches cultural studies at the University of Sussex. She is the author of *Notebooks, Memoirs, Archives,* 1982 and *In the Secret Theatre of the Home,* 1988, studies of, respectively, Doris Lessing and the nineteenth-century sensation novel.

Elizabeth Wilson teaches at the Polytechnic of North London. Her books include *Women and the Welfare State* (1977), *Only Halfway to Paradise: Women in Britain, 1945–68* (1980), *Mirror Writing* (1982), *Adorned in Dreams* (1985), *Prisons of Glass*, a novel (1986) and *Hallucinations* (1988).

Nira Yuval-Davis is a Senior Lecturer at Thames Polytechnic, London. She has co-edited (with Uri Davis and Andrew Mack) *Israel and the Palestinians, Power and the State* and (with F. Anthias) *Women–Nation–State.* She is currently preparing three books on racism, on race in Australia and on women and fundamentalism.

Index